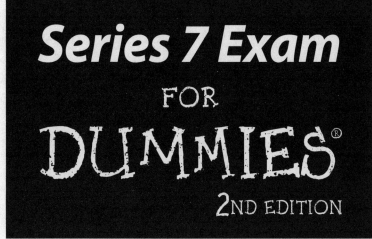

Series 7 Exam FOR DUMMIES®

2ND EDITION

by Steven M. Rice

John Wiley & Sons, Inc.

Series 7 Exam For Dummies®, 2nd Edition

Published by
John Wiley & Sons, Inc.
111 River St.
Hoboken, NJ 07030-5774
www.wiley.com

Published by John Wiley & Sons, Inc., Hoboken, New Jersey

Published simultaneously in Canada

For general information on our other products and services, please contact our Customer Care Department within the U.S. at 877-762-2974, outside the U.S. at 317-572-3993, or fax 317-572-4002.

For technical support, please visit www.wiley.com/techsupport.

Wiley publishes in a variety of print and electronic formats and by print-on-demand. Some material included with standard print versions of this book may not be included in e-books or in print-on-demand. If this book refers to media such as a CD or DVD that is not included in the version you purchased, you may download this material at http://booksupport.wiley.com. For more information about Wiley products, visit www.wiley.com.

Library of Congress Control Number: 2012935794

ISBN: 978-1-118-20986-8 (pbk); ISBN 978-1-118-22871-5 (ebk); ISBN 978-1-118-23126-5 (ebk); ISBN 978-1-118-26608-3 (ebk)

Manufactured in the United States of America

10 9 8 7 6 5

About the Author

After earning a high score on the Series 7 exam in the mid '90s, **Steve Rice** began his career as a stockbroker for a broker dealership with offices in Nassau County, Long Island, and in New York City. In addition to his duties as a registered representative, he also gained invaluable experience about securities registration rules and regulations when he worked in the firm's compliance office. But only after Steve began tutoring others in the firm to help them pass the Series 7 did he find his true calling as an instructor. Shortly thereafter, Steve became a founding partner and educator in Empire Stockbroker Training Institute (`http://www.empirestockbroker.com/`) which has grown into one of the largest and most successful securities training schools in the country.

In addition to writing the *Series 7 Exam For Dummies,* Steve developed and designed the Empire Stockbroker Training Institute online (*Series 7, Series 6, Series 63, Series 66,* and more) exams. Steve has also co-authored a complete library of securities training manuals for classroom use and for home study, including the *Series 4, Series 6, Series 7, Series 11, Series 24, Series 63, Series 65,* and *Series 66.* Steve's popular and highly acclaimed classes, online courses, and training manuals have helped tens of thousands of people achieve their goals and begin their lucrative new careers in the securities industry.

Steve lives on Long Island, NY, with his wife, Melissa Kollen-Rice, a real estate attorney, author of the book *Buying Real Estate Foreclosures,* and owner/instructor of LI Real Estate Training School.

Dedication

I dedicate this book to my beautiful wife, Melissa. Melissa is the love of my life, my inspiration, and my best friend.

Author's Acknowledgments

A fantastic team over at John Wiley & Sons, Inc. made this book possible. I'd like to start by thanking my acquisitions editor, Michael Lewis, for seeing something in me that told him that I was the right man for the job. I believe that he may be one of the few people in this world who sleeps as little as my wife and I. Michael's rapid responses to my e-mails during the days, evenings, and weekends were quite comforting as I was beginning this journey.

Many thanks also go to my project editor, Linda Brandon, for her weekly, friendly little e-mails that helped keep me on track when I was wearing thin. Linda's guidance and critiques were truly invaluable in the writing of this book. She was always there when I needed her and is a professional all the way.

I would also like to thank my copy editor, Christy Pingleton, for helping me to become a better writer. Christy's suggestions on how to make the book more *Dummies* style ultimately made this book much more fun to read.

Next, I'd like to thank the technical editors, Christopher Rohn and William Addiss, for their attention to detail and thoughtful contributions. Viewing the final product, I can tell you one thing: They are the best.

During this project, I wasn't able to put in my normal 60-hour week at my school. I'd like to thank my partner, Rueben Martinez, my office manager (and sister) Sharlene Wegner, and the rest of the staff at Empire Stockbroker Training Institute for picking up the slack so perfectly while I was out.

This book would have been much more difficult to write without my dad, Tom Rice. He has always been my role model, inspiring me as to how I want to live the rest of my life. I have the best dad a person could ask for, and I'm extremely blessed to have him, his wife Maggie, and my other sister Sharlet in my corner.

Finally, I want to thank my wonderful wife, Melissa. There's no way I could have finished this book if not for her. As a lawyer and real estate school owner, she's the busiest person I know. As busy as she is, she always makes me her top priority. Melissa was with me every day, every step of the way. She not only read every page of this book several times but also pre-edited and made great suggestions. Her undying love and support helped me through the toughest times. I am eternally grateful, and I love her forever.

Publisher's Acknowledgments

We're proud of this book; please send us your comments at `http://dummies.custhelp.com`. For other comments, please contact our Customer Care Department within the U.S. at 877-762-2974, outside the U.S. at 317-572-3993, or fax 317-572-4002.

Some of the people who helped bring this book to market include the following:

Acquisitions, Editorial, and Vertical Websites

Project Editor: Linda Brandon

(Previous Edition: Alissa Schwipps)

Acquisitions Editor: Michael Lewis

Copy Editor: Christine Pingleton

Assistant Editor: David Lutton

Editorial Program Coordinator: Joe Niesen

Technical Editor: Christopher Rohn, Financial Adviser; William Addiss, New York Institute of Finance Instructor

Editorial Manager: Jennifer Ehrlich; Carmen Krikorian

Editorial Assistant: Rachelle Amick

Art Coordinator: Alicia B. South

Cover Photos: © iStockphoto.com/alengo; © iStockphoto.com/kraska

Cartoons: Rich Tennant (`www.the5thwave.com`)

Composition Services

Project Coordinator: Sheree Montgomery

Layout and Graphics: Carl Byers, Carrie A. Cesavice, Sennett Vaughan Johnson, Mark Pinto, Erin Zeltner

Proofreaders: Jacqui Brownstein, John Greenough

Indexer: Claudia Bourbeau

Special Help

Rachelle Amick

Publishing and Editorial for Consumer Dummies

Kathleen Nebenhaus, Vice President and Executive Publisher

David Palmer, Associate Publisher

Kristin Ferguson-Wagstaffe, Product Development Director

Publishing for Technology Dummies

Andy Cummings, Vice President and Publisher

Composition Services

Debbie Stailey, Director of Composition Services

Contents at a Glance

Table of Contents

Introduction

So you want to be a stockbroker? The good news is that a career in the securities field can be extremely lucrative and rewarding. The not-so-good news is that anyone who plans to become a stockbroker and sell securities in any of the 50 states must first pass the Series 7 exam, a monster of a test. And to accomplish this, you have to commit time and effort.

I passed the Series 7 exam the first time with a very high score, but it required weeks of study and sacrifice. Those who aren't totally prepared on exam day are in for an unpleasant wake-up call. I always get a few students in every class who've enrolled after they already failed the exam the first (or second) time they took it. Most of them initially expected the same easy ride that they'd experienced in high school or college. Not only were they wrong, but they also had to pay hundreds of dollars to reregister for the exam and wait another 30 days (a mandatory FINRA rule) before they could retake the exam.

Back to the good news again. You're obviously interested in doing well, so you probably won't be one of those people. This book can help you pass the Series 7 and achieve your goal.

About This Book

This book is not a comprehensive content review. That's what textbooks are for. Rather, *Series 7 Exam For Dummies* is designed to be a supplement, a handy guide as you figure out how to think not only like a financial adviser but also like the test designers do (and no, I don't mean to tap into your potential as an evil mastermind).

I cover the topics that always appear on the test, offer formulas, provide definitions, and go over the foundational information you need to know. I also include lots of tips and memory tricks. But the real benefit of this book is finding out how to study and think through problems as well as you possibly can. That's why I help you choose a study program, explain how to handle specific question types, warn you about common mistakes, connect concepts, and show you how to pull questions apart and get to the bottom of what's being asked. You then get to apply this knowledge in a two-part full-length practice test so you get a taste of the Series 7 experience.

This is a reference book, and most sections are self-contained. In other words, you can read a section and understand it without looking over the text that comes before it. When some background information is helpful, I give cross-references to related topics. Therefore, you can pretty much jump in and out whenever you find topics you like (and when you find those you don't). And like all good tour guides, I also point you to some other sites of interest — topics you can explore further on your own.

Conventions Used in This Book

I use the following conventions throughout the text to make things consistent and easy to understand:

- All web addresses appear in `monofont`.

  When this book was printed, some web addresses may have needed to break across two lines of text. In those instances, you can rest assured that no extra characters (such as hyphens) have been added to indicate the break. Just type in exactly what you see in this book, pretending the break doesn't exist.
- New terms appear in *italics* and are closely followed by easy-to-understand definitions. Italics may also indicate emphasis.
- Key words in bulleted and numbered lists are **bold** to highlight the most important info.
- The use of gender-related pronouns alternates throughout the book (no preferential treatment is intended).

I've scattered sample questions throughout this book so you can test your understanding of new info and get a feel for Series 7 questions. And of course, for those sections that don't include questions, remember that the practice tests that come with this book deal with all kinds of subjects.

I also use the language and lingo of the FINRA. That means you see official names (like the Federal Reserve Board), nicknames (the Fed), and acronyms galore (like the FRB). That way, during the test, understanding the POPs, YTMs, TEYs, NAVs, EPSs, ADRs, LMVs, DRs, and so on shouldn't be too much of a hassle.

What You're Not to Read

You don't have to read the index straight through or dally over the Library of Congress number and other publisher information, but most of the information here is important — the basic, need-to-know ideas. You can skim through the topics you know well and spend more time on those you don't, but I do suggest looking everything over.

If you're short on time (as you probably are) and aren't ready for a break just yet, you can skip the sidebars, those little gray boxes that contain interesting but nonessential information.

Foolish Assumptions

While writing this book, I made a few assumptions about you and why you picked up this book. For starters, I assume that you're looking for a no-nonsense study guide to supplement your textbook or prep course — one that provides a ton of example questions and some sample exams. Look no further! Whether you're preparing to take the test for the first time, retaking the test after a less-than-stellar performance, or looking for a refresher before you recertify, this is the book for you!

How This Book Is Organized

This book is organized into six parts and 22 chapters. Each part explains the test itself or covers a major area of study on the Series 7 exam. A glance at the Table of Contents can give you the specifics, but here's a quick overview of what's in each part.

Part I: Gearing Up for the Series 7 Exam

In this part, Chapter 1 gives you an overview of the Series 7 exam format and the registration process for taking the exam. Chapter 2 introduces you to exam prep courses and the types of study materials available. It also helps you develop and stick to a study plan. Chapter 3 runs down the kinds of questions on the Series 7 exam and explains how to handle them, and Chapter 4 tells you what to expect on exam day.

Part II: Mastering Basic Security Investments

This part covers the securities (stocks and bonds) that form the foundation of an investor's portfolio. Chapter 5 covers the security registration process. Chapter 6 introduces you to stocks (common and preferred). Chapters 7 and 8 acquaint you with bonds (corporate, U.S., and municipal).

Part III: Delving Deeper: Security Investments with a Twist

Part III covers additional strategies for buying and selling securities. Chapter 9 describes the process by which investors borrow money to purchase securities by opening margin accounts. Chapter 10 covers the role of investment companies in helping investors diversify their portfolios. Chapter 11 reviews direct participation programs (DPPs), more commonly known as limited partnerships; it mentions their formation, function, structure, tax advantages, and tax disadvantages. Chapter 12 introduces options, another type of investment vehicle that savvy investors use.

Part IV: Playing Nicely: Serving Your Customers and Following the Rules

This part covers the stockbroker's role in scrutinizing a customer's account, monitoring market conditions that can affect the account, and making appropriate recommendations that meet each customer's individual investment goals.

Chapter 13 helps you identify market conditions that can affect a customer's investment objectives. Chapter 14 covers how new securities are brought to the market and how existing securities are traded on the market. Chapter 15 goes into taxes; it distinguishes between long-term and short-term capital gains and losses for income tax purposes, explains the effect of retirement plans on an individual's income taxes, and gives retirement plan contribution limits. Chapter 16 looks at rules and regulations; it reviews the stockbroker's responsibilities for opening, closing, transferring, and handling a customer's account.

Part V: Putting Your Knowledge to Good Use: A Practice Exam

Jackpot! In this part you can find a two-part practice exam (Chapters 17 and 19) with 125 questions each — enough questions to simulate both three-hour parts of the actual Series 7 (without those pesky experimental questions that don't count toward your score). To make the tests really useful, you also get the correct answers and explanations (Chapters 18 and 20). Completing and evaluating practice tests is one of the best ways to prepare for the Series 7 and to gauge your readiness for the real deal.

Part VI: The Part of Tens

This part is standard in all *For Dummies* books, and this book is no exception. In Chapter 21, I reveal ten Series 7 exam traps to avoid, and in Chapter 22, I give you ten ways to make money as a stockbroker.

Icons Used in This Book

To make this book easier to read and use, I include some icons to help you find and fathom key ideas and information.

This icon highlights example Series 7 test questions (which I follow with helpful answer explanations).

This icon is attached to shortcuts and insider advice for studying for and passing the Series 7 exam.

This icon points to information that's especially important to remember in order to do well on the test.

This icon warns you away from actions that can harm your work and drop your score.

Where to Go from Here

Although you can read this book from start to finish, you can certainly work your way through in more creative ways. Where you start is up to you, though please, please don't start with the tests! Give yourself a good grounding in the content here, and then use the tests to evaluate your understanding and show you where to focus your studies. You can flip to the topics you think you understand fairly well to boost your confidence or skip directly to whatever's giving you trouble — let the index and the table of contents be your guides. If you have a good understanding of how to take the Series 7 exam, from how it's structured to how to tackle questions, then you can go directly to the chapters in Parts II or III, which address types of securities. If you're feeling shaky on the legal aspects, check out the FINRA rules and regulations in Part IV. Everyone, however, can probably benefit from Part I's test-taking basics and info on study plans. Wherever you go, feel free to take detours to your text-books, flash cards, FINRA websites, and any other resources for more information. Just remember to come back so you don't miss anything here!

Part I

Gearing Up for the Series 7 Exam

"I always get a good night's sleep the day before a test so I'm relaxed and alert the next morning. Then I grab my pen, eat a banana, and I'm on my way."

In this part . . .

Are you looking for a job that can lead to wealth and success? Do you find satisfaction in helping people? Are you comfortable with mathematical calculations? If so, a career as a stockbroker is likely to be very rewarding for you.

By now, I'm sure you're aware of the hurdle that stands between you and your riches: the Series 7 exam. So in this part, I review the computerized exam format and the procedures for registering to take the exam, and I uncover the topics tested on the Series 7. I help you select the right study course and materials to prepare yourself for exam day, and I explain how to organize your study time efficiently and effectively — even when your time is limited. I also give you test-taking tips to maximize your chances of selecting the correct answer choices. Finally, I let you know what to expect on test day (because the only surprises that day should involve the triumphant return of your social life).

Chapter 1

So You Want to Sell Securities: Introducing the Series 7 Exam

In This Chapter

- Introducing the Series 7
- Taking a look at companion tests
- Getting a sponsor and registering to take the exam
- Uncovering topics tested on the Series 7
- Mastering the computerized exam format

Congratulations on your interest in becoming a stockbroker! But before you can lose yourself in the energy of the office, the eager voices of your clients, and the warm glow of success, you have to face the Series 7. In this chapter, I give you an overview of the Series 7 exam, including its purpose, structure, format, scoring, and some helpful tips to guide you through the registration procedure.

What Is the Series 7 Exam, Anyway?

The Series 7 exam qualifies you to hold the title General Securities Registered Representative (stockbroker), to sell many different types of securities, and to hopefully make stacks of money for your clients (and a bit for yourself). Individuals who earn their license by passing the Series 7 exam are qualified to solicit, purchase, and/or sell securities products, including

- Corporate stocks and bonds
- Municipal bonds
- U.S. government bonds
- Options
- Direct participation programs (limited partnerships)
- Investment-company securities
- Variable contracts

The exam's purpose is to protect the investing public by ensuring that the registered reps who sell securities have mastered the skills and general knowledge that competent practicing stockbrokers need to have.

The Series 7 itself is a computer-based exam given at Prometric and Pearson VUE (Virtual University Enterprises) test centers throughout the United States. The 250-question exam, administered by the Financial Industry Regulatory Authority (FINRA), is six long, arduous hours in duration. A score of 72 percent or better gets candidates a passing grade and puts big smiles on their faces.

The sections later in this chapter explain the setup of the Series 7 and give a rundown of how to register for the exam. If you have other questions, contact the FINRA Call Center at 301-590-6500 or visit `www.finra.org/Industry/Compliance/Registration/QualificationsExams/RegisteredReps/Brochure/P009865`.

Profiling the Series 7 Exam-Taker

The Series 7 exam is for people who want to

- Enter the securities industry
- Become registered representatives
- Work for a securities broker-dealer

Although some less-prestigious exams (for example, the Series 6 and 62) can qualify you to sell some securities, most broker-dealers want their rising stars (that's you) to have the Series 7 license. That way, you can work with almost the whole kit and caboodle — corporate stocks and bonds, municipal and U.S. government bonds, options, direct participation programs, investment companies, variable contracts, and so on.

People who have a long and sordid history of embezzlement, forgery, and fraud are generally disqualified and precluded from taking the exam. Candidates must disclose any prior criminal records, and the FINRA reviews each application on a case-by-case basis.

One's Not Enough: Tackling the Series 63 or Series 66

You don't have to pass any prerequisite exams before you can take the Series 7; however, you do need to pass the Series 63 or Series 66 to be able to work in the securities industry because these exams and the Series 7 are corequisites in most states. You can take the Series 63 or 66 either before or after you take the Series 7, but most people start studying for the Series 63 or 66 and register to take it right after passing the Series 7.

Note: Even if you live in a state that doesn't require either of these licenses, you still need to obtain one if you want to sell securities to someone who lives in a state that does require it. Just figure that your firm will require you to obtain the 63 or 66 to sell securities — your firm should tell you which one to take. The following sections explain what the two state-licensing exams cover.

Series 63: Uniform Securities Agent State Law Exam

The Series 63 is a 65-question test that the North American Securities Administrator Association (NASAA) developed, and it's designed to qualify candidates as securities agents. The Series 63 exam covers state securities regulation rules as well as rules prohibiting unethical and dishonest business practices (not that you'd do anything like that). The Series 63 used to be the most common test taken along with the Series 7. Judging by class sizes, however, I would say that around twice as many Series 7 students are now taking the Series 66 as compared to the Series 63.

Series 66: Uniform Combined State Law Exam

The Series 66 is a 100-question NASAA exam that combines the Series 63 and the Series 65 (Uniform Investment Adviser). The Series 66 is designed to qualify candidates as both securities agents and investment adviser representatives (IARs). The Series 65 portion of the Series 66 allows you to collect a fee for just giving investment advice. This license was implemented several years ago, and it'll most likely be required if you work for one of the bigger broker-dealers. More and more firms are requiring the Series 66 because it gives their registered reps an additional service to provide for their clients and an additional way for you (and your firm) to make money.

Securing Sponsorship and Signing Up

All candidates (that's you) must have a sponsoring broker in order to register for the Series 7 exam. After passing the exam, your license will be in your own name; however, you have to be working for a firm in order for your license to be active. Generally, a firm hires you and then acts as your sponsor.

The following sections explain the basic exam requirements and help you navigate your way through the exam registration process.

Filling out an application to enroll

For you to obtain admission to the Series 7, your sponsoring firm has to file an application form (called a *U-4*) and pay the required processing fees with the Central Registration Depository (CRD). The U-4 is an annoying little form with about a gazillion pages that requires you to remember where you were ten years ago. You're also required to submit your fingerprints, and you have to complete this step through an approved facility. Your firm will likely recommend the place they use — often the local police precinct. (Be advised that your sponsoring firm will probably frown upon your fingerprints if they're attached to your mug shot.)

If you want to see a preview of the U-4 registration form that you're responsible for filling out and that your firm has to submit, visit the FINRA website (`www.finra.org`) and search for U-4.

It's a date! Scheduling your exam

After your firm files the application with the Central Registration Depository and receives your enrollment notification, you can schedule an appointment to take the exam by contacting the Prometric or Pearson VUE Testing Center. Locate the test center nearest you by calling either the Prometric center (800-578-6273) or the Pearson VUE center (866-396-6273) during business hours. Or you can visit `www.pearsonvue.com/finra` or `www.prometric.com/FINRA/default.htm` to schedule online.

Your Series 7 exam enrollment is valid for 120 days — you have to take the exam within this time frame. When scheduling your exam appointment, be ready to provide the exam administrators with

- Your name and Social Security number
- The name of your firm
- A telephone contact to reach you and your employer
- The name of the securities exam you're registering to take
- Your desired test date

Getting an appointment usually takes about one to two weeks, depending on the time of year (you may wait longer in the summer than around Christmastime). Prometric and Pearson VUE will confirm your appointment on the phone or via e-mail.

I suggest putting pressure on yourself and scheduling the exam a little sooner than you think you may be ready to take it; you can always move the test date back. You know yourself best, but I think most students study better when they have a target test date.

You have a choice of locations to take the exam. If you're a travelin' man (or woman), you may want to schedule your exam at a location far away (maybe even in a different state) to get the test date that you want.

After you have your test date set, you may find that you're ready sooner or will be ready later than your scheduled appointment. The exam center administrators are usually pretty accommodating about changing appointments and/or locations as long as you call before noon at least two business days before your test date.

You can get an extension from the 120-day enrollment only if you call within ten days of your enrollment expiration and if no earlier test dates are available.

Planning ahead for special accommodations

If you require special accommodations when taking your Series 7 exam, you can't schedule your exam online. You have to contact the FINRA Special Conditions Team at 800-999-6647. Read on for info on what the test administrators can do if you have a disability or if English isn't your first language.

Asking about test center luxuries

Series 7 test centers are required to comply with FINRA site guidelines; however, some of the older centers may not have the amenities that the newer ones do (such as lockers and earplugs). To protect yourself from a whole variety of unpleasant, unexpected site surprises on exam day, the FINRA website (`www.finra.org`) offers general information, including test center security guidelines (including candidate ID requirements, personal items allowed, and provided aids), test center rules of conduct, and so on. For more site-specific questions, like whether a cafeteria, vending machines, or lockers are on site, ask the center's administrator when you schedule your test date.

Depending on your testing center, the FINRA may have to authorize you to bring medical devices and supplies — such as insulin pumps, eyedrops, and inhalers — into the testing room. If you need authorization, call FINRA Field Support Services (FSS) at 800-999-6647 after scheduling the exam. For a list of personal items that may need approval, visit `www.finra.org/Industry/Compliance/Registration/QualificationsExams/RegisteredReps/Qualifications/p010830`.

Americans with Disabilities Act (ADA) candidates

If you're disabled or learning impaired, the FINRA provides testing modifications and aids in compliance with the provisions of the Americans with Disabilities Act (ADA). To qualify for ADA provisions, your disabilities have to permanently limit a major life activity, such as learning, speech, hearing, or vision.

To apply for special accommodations, you need to submit documentation from your physician or licensed healthcare professional to the FINRA, along with a letter from your sponsoring firm requesting the special arrangements. Additionally, you have to submit the FINRA Special Accommodations Eligibility Questionnaire and Special Accommodations Verification Request Form for all special arrangement requests (you can find links to the forms at `www.finra.org/Industry/Compliance/Registration/QualificationsExams/RegisteredReps/Qualifications/p010830`.

You may request the accommodations you want approved; possible aids include

- Extra time
- A written exam (pencil and paper)
- A reader, writer, or recorder
- A sign language interpreter
- A large-print exam booklet
- Wheelchair-accessible locations

The FINRA reserves the right to make all final decisions about accommodations on a case-by-case basis.

English as a second language (ESL) candidates

If English is your second language, you can request additional time to take the exam when you schedule your Series 7 test date. If the FINRA approves, you receive an extra 30 minutes to complete each part (one hour total) of the Series 7 exam.

To qualify for this extra time, you have to provide the test center administrator with a letter from your firm, written in English on company letterhead, signed by your supervisor or manager, with your name and Social Security number. The letter should indicate that English is your second language. The supervisor's original signature has to be on the letter; a photocopy without the original signature won't be accepted.

Just in case: Cancelling as an option

If something comes up or if you feel you're just not ready, you can cancel your appointment to take the Series 7 exam without penalty if you do so at least 10 business days before the exam date. If a holiday falls within the cancellation period, you have to cancel an additional business day earlier. For example, if you're scheduled to take the exam on a Wednesday, you have to cancel on Tuesday two weeks before your exam date. If a holiday falls in-between those dates, you have to cancel on Monday two weeks before your exam date. For more information, you can visit www.finra.org/Industry/Compliance/Registration/QualificationsExams/RegisteredReps/Qualifications/P120071.

If you cancel after the proscribed deadline, if you don't show up to take the exam, or if you show up too late to take the exam, FINRA will charge your firm a cancellation fee equal to the Series 7 exam fee paid by your firm. Don't try the old "I forgot" excuse, because not only is it ineffective, but I'm somewhat sure that it's illegal in all 50 states, Canada, and the U.S. territories.

Taking a Peek at the Tested Topics

As a practical exam, the Series 7 requires you to master vocabulary, handle customer accounts, understand the rules and regulations that govern the securities industry, and yes, work with some math formulas. For ease of use (and because humans have a limited life span), this book focuses on the most commonly tested topics on the Series 7 exam. Here's an overview of what to expect:

- The underwriting process (how new securities come to market) (Chapter 5)
- Common and preferred stock (Chapter 6)
- Corporate bonds and U.S. government securities (Chapter 7)
- Securities issued by local governments (municipal bonds) (Chapter 8)
- Margin accounts (using money borrowed from broker-dealers to purchase securities) (Chapter 9)
- Investment companies (including mutual and closed-end funds) (Chapter 10)
- Direct participation programs (limited partnerships) (Chapter 11)
- Options (Chapter 12)
- Analyzing the benefits and risks associated with investments; making appropriate recommendations to customers (Chapter 13)
- Following how new securities are brought to the market and how existing securities are traded in the market (Chapter 14)
- Risk considerations and income-tax implications that stock market investors face (Chapter 15)
- Rules and regulations governing the purchase and sale of securities and the registered representative's responsibility for maintaining accurate recordkeeping (Chapter 16)

The FINRA has released a listing of the distribution of questions on the Series 7 exam. See Table 1-1 for the number of questions devoted to each activity that a registered rep performs.

Table 1-1 Distribution of Series 7 Exam Questions

Activity Performed by a Registered Rep	*Number of Questions*	*Percent of Exam*
Provides customers with information on investments and makes suitable recommendations	70	28%
Seeks business for the broker-dealer through customers and potential customers	68	27%
Obtains and verifies customers' purchase and sales instructions, enters orders, and follows up	58	23%

Activity Performed by a Registered Rep	Number of Questions	Percent of Exam
Evaluates customers' other security holdings, financial situation and needs, financial status, tax status, and investment objectives	27	11%
Opens accounts, transfers assets, and maintains appropriate account records	27	11%
Total	**250**	**100%**

Each of these activities falls under multiple areas of study. For example, to correctly answer questions that address the topic of handling customer accounts, you have to know enough about different types of stocks, bonds, and so on to be able to guide your customers, including which investments are more beneficial to retirees and which work better for investors who are just entering the workforce.

Although Table 1-1 shows the outline of the exam, I (and most other study material providers) break the chapters down by similar content to keep you from having to jump back and forth through your study material.

Understanding the Exam Format and Other Exam Details

To make sure you don't walk into the testing center, take one look at the computer screen, go into shock, and start drooling on the keyboard, I use the next few sections to cover some of the testing details for the Series 7 exam.

Reviewing the exam basics

The Series 7 exam is a computerized, closed book (in other words, no book), six-hour exam. The exam consists of 260 multiple-choice questions (although only 250 of them count toward your score — see the next section), and it's divided into two three-hour sessions. You take a mandatory 30–60 minute break between sessions.

You can take bathroom breaks at any time, but the clock continues to tick away, so you may want to reconsider drinking a mega-jumbo iced latte in the morning before you arrive at the exam center.

For information on the types of questions to expect, see Chapter 3. Flip to Chapter 4 for an overview of how your exam day may progress.

Practicing on ten additional trial questions

To ensure that new questions to be introduced in future exams meet acceptable standards prior to inclusion, you answer ten additional, unidentified questions that don't count toward your score. In other words, you get 260 questions to answer (130 in each half), but only 250 are scored.

Note: If you see a question on the Series 7 that doesn't seem even remotely similar to anything that you've studied (or even heard about), it may very likely be an experimental question.

Mastering the computerized format and features

Although you don't need any previous computer experience to do well on the exam, you don't want your first encounter with a computerized exam to be on the date of the Series 7. Being familiar with the way the questions and answer choices will appear on the screen is essential. Figure 1-1 can help you prepare for exam day.

A friendly exam-center employee will give you an introductory lesson to familiarize you with how to operate the computer before the exam session begins. Although the computer randomly selects the specific questions from each category, the operating system tracks the difficulty of each question and controls the selection criteria to ensure that your exam isn't ridiculously easier or harder than anyone else's.

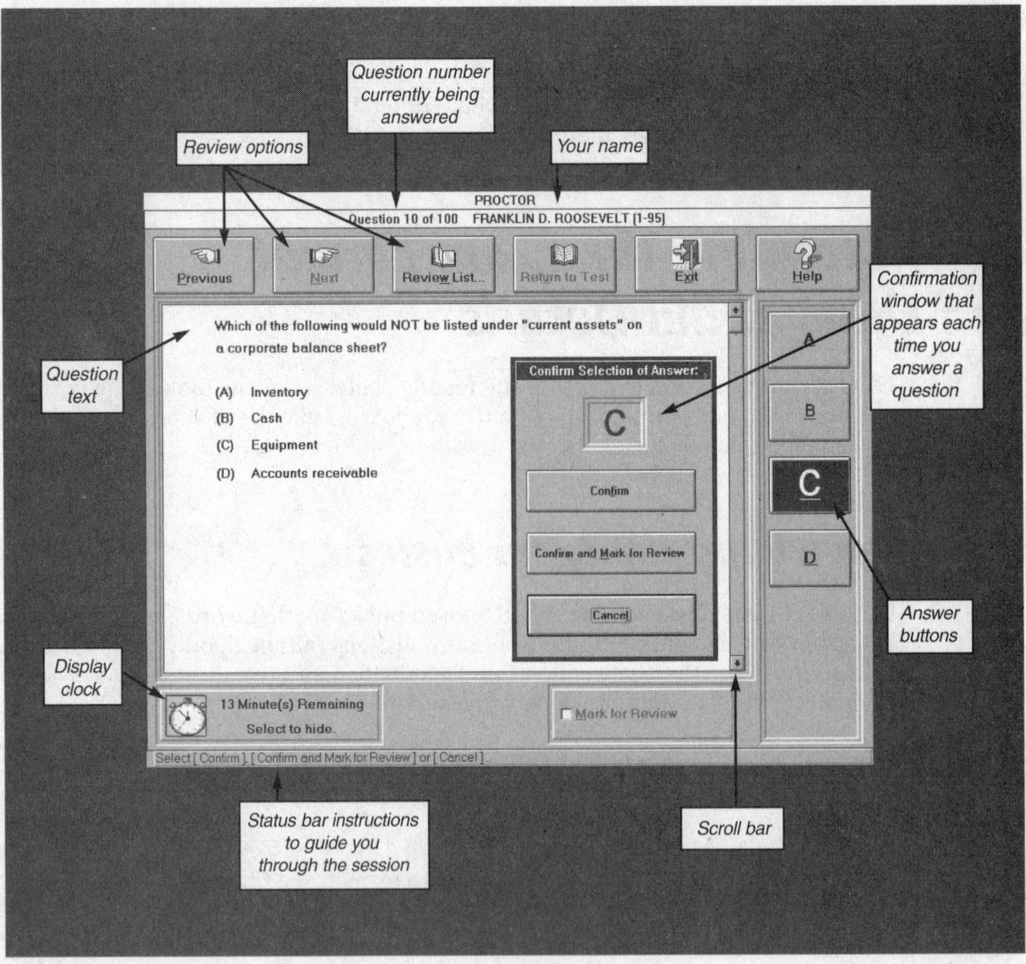

Figure 1-1: The PROCTOR computer system lets you select answers and mark them for review.

The following list describes some important computer exam features:

- Scroll bars for moving the questions on the screen
- A clock to help you track how much time you have left during each part (if the clock is driving you batty, you can hide it with a click of the mouse)
- A confirmation box that requires you to approve your answer choice before the computer proceeds to the next question

- An indication of which question you're currently on
- A choice of answering the questions by
  - Typing in the letter for the correct answer on the keyboard
  - Using the mouse to point and click on the correct answer
  - At some test centers, using a computer with a touch screen that lets you select the answer by pressing lightly against the monitor with your fingertip
- The capability of changing your answers or marking questions that you're unsure of for later review, which allows you to go back and answer them at any time during that particular part

You can mark answers for review or change responses only for the part of the test you're currently taking. In other words, after you begin the second part, you can't go back and change answers from the first part.

Although you can review and change all your answers at the end of each half, don't. Your brain is going to feel like it went through a blender by the time you get there. Review only your *marked* questions and change the answers only if you're 100 percent sure that you made a mistake. As an instructor, I know that people change a right answer to a wrong one five times more often than they change a wrong one to a right one.

Instant gratification: Receiving and evaluating your score

Remember having to wait weeks for a standardized test score, hovering somewhere between eagerness and dread? Those days are gone. At the end of the Series 7, the system calculates your score and displays a grade result on the computer screen. Although the wait for your grade to pop up may feel like an eternity, it really takes only 30–45 seconds to see your grade. When you sign out, the test center administer will tackle you (well, approach you) and give you a printed exam report with your grade and the diagnostic score results with your performance in the specific topics tested on your exam.

A little testing info from the FINRA

The FINRA website (`www.finra.org`) is certainly worth checking out. It contains all the nitty-gritty details about the Series 7 and related exams. Use this website for the following:

- **FINRA Current Uniform Registration Forms for Electronic Filing In WEB CRD:** This page includes the U-4 Series 7 registration forms and a link to the Uniform Forms Reference Guide, with contact numbers and other explanatory information for filers.
- **FINRA Test Center Rules of Conduct:** Just in case you're unable to distinguish the Series 7 test center from that third-period algebra class you had back in high school, the FINRA gives you the rules and regulations for taking the Series 7 (do not hide a list of equations under the brim of your baseball cap, do not roam the halls during your restroom break, and do not pass notes, no matter how bored you are).
- **FINRA Registration and Exam Requirements:** This section gives a comprehensive list of the categories of securities representatives and the exam requirements.
- **FINRA Appointments and Enrollment:** Here you find FINRA tips for scheduling appointments to take the Series 7 exam, info about obtaining extensions, and the exam cancellation policy.
- **FINRA Registration Exam Fee Schedule:** Check out this page to see the fees for registering for the Series 7 Exam.

Each question on the Series 7 exam is worth 0.4 point, and candidates need a score of 72 or better to achieve a passing grade. This percentage translates to 180 questions out of 250 that you have to answer correctly. The scores are rounded down, so a grade of 71.6 is scored as 71 on the Series 7. When I took the exam, back when the passing grade was 70, one of the other students from my class got a 69.6 (which was rounded down to a 69), and he had the NASD (now called the FINRA) review his exam to try and get him the extra point. Needless to say, they ruled against him and he had to take the exam again.

You passed! Now what?

After you pass the Series 7, Series 63, and/or Series 66 exam, the FINRA will send your firm confirmation that you passed. At that point, you can buy and sell securities for your customers in accordance with your firm's customary procedures.

To continue working as a registered rep, you'll need to fulfill the FINRA's continuing education requirements. Within 120 days after your second anniversary as a registered rep, and every three years thereafter, you have to take a computer-based exam covering regulatory elements such as compliance, regulatory, ethical and sales practice standards. at either the Pearson VUE or Prometric exam center. In addition, there is a requirement (called a brokerage firm element) which requires broker dealers to keep their registered representatives updated on job and product-related topics.

So you need a do-over: Retaking the exam

Sorry to end this chapter on a negative note, but the Series 7 is a difficult exam, and certainly a lot of people need a do-over.

If you fail the Series 7, your firm has to request a new test date and pay for you to retake the test. Your sponsors can send in one page of the U-4 requesting a new exam, or they can apply online through the Central Registration Depository (CRD) system. You should reapply immediately, though you have to schedule the new test date for at least 30 days after the day you failed (that's 30 days of prime studying time!). If you fail the exam three times, you're required to wait six months before you can retake the exam.

Use the time between exams to understand what went wrong and fix it. Here are some of the reasons people fail the Series 7 exam and some of the steps you can take to be successful:

- **Lack of preparation:** You have to follow, and stick to, a well-constructed plan of study. You have your diagnostic printout after you take the exam, and you can use that to focus on the areas of study where you fell short.

  Prep courses can help you identify and focus on the most commonly tested topics and provide valuable tips for mastering difficult math problems. Also consider tutoring sessions tailored to accommodate your busy schedule and pinpoint the areas of study where you need the most help.

- **Nerves won out:** Some people are just very nervous test-takers, and they need to go through the process to get comfortable in unfamiliar situations. Next time around, they know what to expect and pass with flying colors.

  The people who are the most nervous about taking the exam tend to be the ones who haven't prepared properly. Make sure that you're passing practice exams on a consistent basis with grades in at least the high 70s before you attempt to take the real exam.

- **Insufficient practice exams:** You need to take enough practice exams before you take the real test. I think getting used to the question formats and figuring out how to work through them is as important as learning the material to begin with.

Check out Chapter 2 for info on setting up a study schedule and making the most of your practice exams.

Chapter 2

Preparing for the Series 7 Exam

In This Chapter

- Investing in a prep course versus studying on your own
- Finding time to study and using study strategies
- Staying focused and building test-taking skills
- Evaluating your readiness

When you're preparing for the Series 7 exam, a good cup of java and an all-nighter just aren't gonna cut it. Neither will a frantic two-week study session like the ones that used to work miracles when you were taking college finals. The Series 7 is a mini-marathon of the test world, and as with all endurance events, you need to train for it both mentally and physically.

In this chapter, I discuss your options for studying to take the Series 7 exam. If you plan to enroll in a Series 7 exam prep course, I cover what to look for when selecting a course. I also help you organize your study time efficiently and effectively — even when your preparation time is limited.

Courses and Training Materials: Determining the Best Way to Study

When deciding how to go about studying for the Series 7 exam, your first mission is to identify the training mode that best suits your needs. If you're likely to benefit from a structured environment, you may be better off in a classroom setting. A prep course can also give you emotional guidance and support from your instructors and others in your class who are forging through this stressful ordeal with you. On the other hand, if you're the type of person who can initiate and follow a committed study schedule on your own every day, you may be able to pass the Series 7 exam without a prep course, and you can save the money you would have spent for classes. The following sections help you evaluate these options in more detail.

Back to school: Attending a prep course

People who learn best by listening to an instructor and interacting with other students benefit from attending prep courses. Unfortunately, not all Series 7 exam prep courses and training materials are created equally. Unlike high school or college courses, the content of Series 7 prep courses and the qualifications of the instructors who teach them aren't regulated by your state's Department of Education, the Securities and Exchange Commission (SEC), the Financial Industry Regulatory Authority (FINRA), or any other government agency. Do some research to locate the Series 7 training course that works best for you.

The following sections explain some things to consider and questions to ask before enrolling. Take a look at the info you gather and trust your gut. Is the primary function of the prep course to train students to be successful on the Series 7 exam, as it should be? Or do you suspect it's the brainchild of a broker-dealer who's looking for extra revenue to supplement her failing stockbroker business? (Run away!)

Training school background

To find information about a program you're considering, browse the training school's website or contact the school's offices. Find out how many years the training school has been in business and check with the Better Business Bureau or the Department of Consumer Affairs to see whether anyone has filed any complaints. Look for a school that has stayed in business at least five years. This staying power is generally a sign that the school is getting referral business from students who took the course and passed the Series 7.

Try to get recommendations from others who took the course. Word of mouth is an essential source of referrals for most businesses, and stockbroker training schools are no different. The stockbroker firm you're affiliated with (or will be affiliated with) should be able to recommend training schools.

Courses offered through a local high school's continuing education program can be just as effective as those offered through an accredited university or a company that focuses solely on test prep, as long as the right instructors are teaching them. Read on.

Qualifications of the course instructor(s)

The instructor's qualifications and teaching style are even more important than the history of the company running the course (see the preceding section). An instructor should be not only knowledgeable but also energetic and entertaining enough to keep you awake during the not-so-exciting (all right, *boring*) parts.

When looking for a course, find out whether the teacher has taken — and passed — the Series 7 exam. If so, the instructor probably knows the kinds of questions you'll be asked and can help you focus on the relevant exam material. The instructor is also likely to have developed good test-taking skills that she can share with her students.

Whether the instructor is a part-timer or full-timer may be important. For example, a full-time instructor who teaches 30 classes a year probably has a better grasp on the material than a part-time instructor who teaches four classes a year. By the same token, an instructor who owns the school that offers the course probably has greater interest in the success of the students than someone who's paid to teach the class by the hour. Use your best judgment.

Before you register, ask whether you can monitor a class for an hour or so with the instructor who would be training you. If the company says no, I suggest finding another course because that course provider may have something to hide. While you're at it, make sure the classroom is comfortable, clean, and conducive to learning.

Texts, course content, and extra help

To really benefit from a course, you need good resources — in terms of not only the actual training material but also the people in the classroom. These elements affect how the class shapes up and what you actually learn:

- **Training material:** Will you have a textbook to study from or just some handouts? The instructor should provide you with textbooks that include sample exams, and a prep course should be loaded with in-class questions for you to work on. The course should also provide you with chapter exams that you can work on at night before the next session (yes, homework is a good thing). Remember, the more questions you see and answer, the better.

- **In-class practice tests:** You want a prep course that includes test sessions where the instructor grades your exams, identifies incorrect answers, and reviews the correct answers.
- **Instructor availability:** Ask whether the course instructors will be available to answer your questions after the class is over — not only at the end of the day but also during the weeks after you've completed the course and are preparing for the Series 7.

The practical details

The perfect course can't do you any good if you never show up for class. Here are some issues to consider about the course offering:

- **Days and times:** Make sure the class fits your schedule. If getting there on time is too stressful or you can't attend often enough to justify the expense, you won't benefit from registering to take the course.
- **Class size:** If more than 30 to 35 people are in the class, the instructor may not be able to give you the individual attention you need.
- **Cost:** Obviously, cost is a major concern, but it definitely shouldn't be your only consideration. Choosing a course because it's the least expensive one you can find may be a costly mistake if the course doesn't properly prepare you. You end up wasting your time and spending more money to retake the exam. You can expect to pay anywhere from $400 to $800 for a standard Series 7 prep course, including training materials (textbooks and final exams).

Quite a few people don't pass the first time around, so find out whether the school charges a fee for retaking the prep course if you don't pass the Series 7 exam or even if you feel that you're not quite ready to take the test.

Selecting prep material to study on your own

If you're the type of person who can follow a committed study schedule on your own every day, you may be able to pass the Series 7 exam without a prep course. Many different types of study aids are available to help you prepare.

No matter what your learning style is, I'm a firm believer in using a textbook as a primary training aid. You can use online courses, online testing programs, CDs, apps, and flash cards as supplements to your textbook, but give your textbook the starring role. By virtue of its portability and ease of use (you don't have to turn it on, plug it in, or have access to the Internet, and it can never, ever run out of batteries), the textbook is simply the most efficient and effective choice.

Taking a course online

Remember that not all classes take place in brick-and-mortar buildings. For people who want to take a course but have scheduling constraints or lack a vehicle for commuting, instructor-led virtual classrooms may be an option. Students interact through online chats, e-mail, message boards, and/or phone conferences. Classes may be scheduled at specific times, or you may work on your own time at your own pace. Before purchasing an online course, find out whether you can monitor one for an hour or so to see whether it meets your needs.

Note: Some so-called "online courses" may consist solely of a packet of study materials without any outside instruction. Make sure the course you sign up for has the features you want.

My personal favorites are the Empire Stockbroker Training Institute's *Series 7 Coursebook* and its companion, *Series 7 Final Exams* (www.empirestockbroker.com). The textbook focuses on the relevant exam topics, is easy to read and understand, and includes plenty of practice questions and detailed explanations. Securities Training Corporation (www.stcusa.com) and Kaplan Financial (www.kaplanfinancial.com) also publish quality Series 7 books. A lot of the better Series 7 course textbooks are available online rather than in book stores..

In addition to *Series 7 Exam For Dummies,* 2nd Edition, and a textbook, consider investing in one or more of the following popular study aids:

- **Online testing:** I'm all for online testing. Certainly, the more exams you take, the better. If the practice exam simulates the real test, it's even more valuable. With this study aid, you have access 24 hours a day, 7 days a week, and can pace yourself to take the exams at your leisure. Select a program (for example, www.empirestockbroker.com always has the most current, updated simulated exams) with a couple thousand questions or more, along with answers and explanations.
- **CD-ROMs:** For the student who prefers interactive learning materials, CD-ROMs may offer everything from practice exams and tutorials to customizable study calendars. Computer programs vary, so shop around.
- **Audio CDs:** You may be able to find audio CDs to help you prepare for the Series 7. This form of training can be beneficial as a review for people who already have a decent understanding of the course material. You can listen to taped material while on the go or in your home.

  Personally, I think recording your own notes — especially on topics you're having trouble with — is a better use of your time. Putting the info in your own words, saying ideas out loud, and listening to the recordings can really help reinforce the concepts.
- **Flash cards:** For those who already have a grasp on the subject matter, flash cards are good because you can tuck 'em in your pocket and look at 'em anytime you want. Commercial cards may be confusing and long-winded. You're better off making cards that focus on the areas that are most problematic for you.

Managing Your Study Time Wisely

Unless you're a direct descendent of Albert Einstein, you probably need to allow yourself as much time as possible to prepare for the Series 7 exam.

Get your affairs in order. Go to the dentist and get that sore tooth filled, pay your bills, get your flu shot, visit your friends and relatives, finish any critical home improvement projects — basically, clear the decks as best you can so you can concentrate on your studies. The following sections can help you establish a study plan.

Blocking out some time to study

You have to use your time efficiently, and to accomplish this, you need to grab every spare moment and channel it into study time. If you're attending a Series 7 prep course, your instructors should help you (and your classmates) set up a study schedule for before, during, and after you complete the course.

If you're in charge of carving out your study time, then plan your study regime as if it were a full-time, 40-hour-per-week job and allot approximately 200–250 hours over a four- to six-week period for studying. If you don't have a job (other than studying), I suggest that you put in at least five or six hours a day. (For advice on how to study well, please look at "Exploring Study Strategies"; the following section discusses setting up an actual schedule.)

Especially for those of you who continue to work at your full-time job, now may be the time to have a heart-to-heart with your boss to negotiate some extra study time. After all, you need to work this out only for the next six weeks. Can you take vacation time? Will your boss allow you flex time (where you agree to work two hours later each day for four days and have the fifth day off)? Can you arrange a quiet place at work to study during breaks and lunch time?

Set aside a consistent time to study on a daily basis. If possible, schedule your study time around your internal clock. For example, if you're the type who needs a brass band to wake you up and get your mind functioning first thing in the morning but you're wide awake and ready to go at midnight, you may be better off with a study schedule that begins later in the day and lasts into the night. By contrast, if you're leaping out of bed like a jack-in-the-box at the crack of dawn but are dead on your feet by 10 p.m., a morning study schedule would be more favorable.

You never know when extra time to study will present itself, so carry your textbooks or some flash cards with you whenever you leave home. You can read or drill yourself whenever you find some spare time — on the train, waiting in line, and yes, even during your trips to the restroom.

It's a plan: Getting into a study routine

Establishing and sticking to a study routine is essential. Many people find the Series 7 exam to be difficult because they have to absorb so much material in a relatively short time span. Furthermore, most of the information on the test is easy to forget because it's not info you use every day. Therefore, you have to reinforce your knowledge on a daily basis by constantly reviewing and revisiting the old information while learning new material. You'll continue to follow this routine over and over and over again.

Setting up shop: Finding an ideal place to study

When you're first learning new material, set yourself up in a place where you have as few distractions as possible — the local library, a separate room, even the bathtub. One of my students used to retreat to his car in the driveway after dinner while his wife put their young kids to bed.

The exam room, with its small cubicles, places you in proximity with other people who are taking the exam at the same time. If clicks of the mouse, taps on the keyboard, the scratch of pencil on paper, and the frustrated sighs of less-prepared test-takers are likely to distract you, you may want to use earplugs, which are available at most exam centers. If, however, you don't want to use earplugs, you can prepare for the worst by subjecting yourself to a somewhat noisy study environment somewhere along the line. (When I was taking my exam before earplugs were permitted, construction crews were working in the next room. Luckily, I'd studied in noisy settings; otherwise, the sound of screw guns and workmen talking would have driven me to distraction!) Go to a coffee shop (or any populated establishment) during lunch hour, or turn on a fan or a radio to familiarize yourself with background noise while you're taking your practice exams.

Organizing yourself to cover all the topics you'll be tested on is crucial. If you're taking a prep course or home study course, a huge benefit is that during the course, the time necessary to learn and review all the subject matter will be allotted for you.

If you're trying to study on your own, get yourself a course textbook and divide the pages by the number of days you have available for studying. Be sure to allow yourself an extra week or two for practice exams. Review each chapter and complete each chapter exam until you have a firm grasp on a majority of the information. Take notes, highlight, and review the material you're having problems with until you feel comfortable with the concepts. Initially, you'll spend a majority of your time on new material; after that, you'll spend your time reviewing and taking chapter quizzes.

During the last one to two weeks leading up to the exam, take as many practice exams as possible. Remember to review each exam thoroughly before moving onto the next one. For more helpful tips, check out the section "Exploring Study Strategies" later in this chapter.

Give it a rest: Taking short breaks

If you find yourself reading the same words over and over and wondering what the heck you just read, it's probably time to take a break. Taking short (5- to 10-minute) breaks can help you process and absorb information without confusing new ideas with the old.

When you reach your saturation point and really start zoning out, you can practice a bit of productive procrastination — walk the dog, shower, do some sit-ups and/or push-ups, grab a meal or a snack, or do anything else that lets you move around or take care of the little things that have to get done. A little human contact can go a long way too, provided you have the discipline to hit the books again.

Sometimes, taking a break from one study method can be as good as taking a break from studying altogether. Use multiple types of study material (textbooks, class notes, flash cards, and so on). If, for example, you get sick of looking at a textbook, try reviewing your notes, flipping through or creating some flash cards, or taking some online practice exams.

Staying focused from day to day

Passing the Series 7 exam is a rite of passage. It's your ticket to wealth, fame, and fortune (or at least a decent job). If you put the time and effort into studying for the Series 7, you'll be rewarded. If not, you'll have to relive the nightmare over and over again until you reach your objective. To reap your reward as quickly as possible, make a resolution: Until you pass the Series 7, commit to limiting your social life, and devoting most of your waking hours to one purpose — studying for the exam. Repeat after me: "This is my life for now."

If you find that you really need to take a mental health day off at some point, make sure that you don't separate yourself from your textbooks for more than one day — jump right back into the Series 7 fire the next day.

Under no circumstances (except in the case of a family emergency) should you stop studying for more than one day within a two-week period. I've had students who were doing quite well come back to take another prep class because their test dates were too far off and they'd put the books down for a while. The next thing they knew, they'd forgotten half of what they'd learned. Fortunately, the information comes back faster the second time around.

To keep focused on your studies without permanently forgetting about otherwise important life activities, prepare a file folder labeled "To do after I pass the Series 7." If anything comes up while you're studying, instead of interrupting your study time or stressing about things that need to be done, write down the task or event on a piece of paper, place it in your to-do file, and put it out of your mind.

Devoting time to practice tests

Certainly, when you're first going over new material, you should spend most of your time learning the information and taking chapter quizzes. After you feel like you have a good handle on the material, you should start taking full practice exams to see where you stand. (This book includes questions throughout Parts II–IV, followed by two 125-question practice exams with answers and explanations in Part V.) The last week or two before the exam should be almost entirely devoted to taking practice exams and reviewing them.

After you move into the practice-test phase, continue to use your textbook not only to reference material you don't understand, but also to ensure you don't forget what you've learned. Too many people rely solely on the tests and forget to read their textbook now and then. Figure on rereading one to two chapters per day. After taking a practice exam, always completely review it before you move on to the next one. And don't listen to the people who say you have to take three or four practice exams a day; you're better off taking one exam per day and spending twice as long reviewing it as you spent taking it. This method helps ensure that you know the subject matter and that you won't make the same mistakes twice.

Practice exams can help you gauge whether you're ready for the real Series 7. See "Knowing When You're Ready" at the end of this chapter for details.

If you run out of exams to take, it's better to purchase more or see whether someone else in your firm has a different book with tests you can borrow than to take the same exams over and over again.

Avoiding study groups

Unless your study group includes your instructor, I recommend that you avoid a study group like the plague. The problem with study groups is that everyone wants to study the information that she's having problems with, and chances are not everyone is struggling with the same thing. And if everyone *is* having the same problem, who can help you? I strongly feel that your time is better spent studying on your own.

If you really feel you'd benefit from studying with someone else, try to arrange a tutoring session with a Series 7 instructor.

Staying in shape

Ignoring the importance of physical fitness when you prepare to take the Series 7 exam is a big mistake. The exam itself (and the prep time you put into your study schedule) is not only mentally exhausting but physically demanding as well. You have to be able to stay alert and concentrate on difficult questions for two three-hour sessions. In the weeks leading up to the test, any exercise you can do to keep yourself physically fit — including cardiovascular exercise such as jogging or bike riding — can help out. A workout also gives you a great reason to take a study break.

Exploring Study Strategies

The more ways you work with a piece of information, the better able you'll be to recall it. Here are some study strategies to supplement your routine of reading your textbook and taking practice exams:

- **Aim to understand concepts and relationships, not just formulas and definitions.** Having a good grasp of how ideas are related can provide a safety net for when rote memory fails; you may be able to make educated guesses, re-create formulas, or come up with something to jog your memory. When you see an equation, try to figure out where the numbers come from and what the formula really tells you.
- **Create an outline of your notes or write flash cards.** Using your own words, try to put the more difficult areas of study into an outline or on flash cards. The whole process of condensing large mountains of information into your own abbreviated outline helps you process and absorb difficult concepts.
- **Mark up your textbook.** You don't have to return your textbook to the library, so use the margins to rephrase ideas, draw diagrams, repeat formulas or equations, and highlight unfamiliar words.
- **Tape yourself reading your notes and then play back the tape at night while you're falling sleep or when you're driving.** Although the play-it-at-night technique has been known to give some people nightmares, this temporary condition usually clears up after the exam. I've also heard some people proclaim the nighttime playback is "as soothing as Sominex." (If it prevents you from falling asleep, turn off the tape and opt for getting some rest.)

  Note: While you're sleeping, the brain may process ideas you learned during your waking hours; however, you generally have to be paying attention to remember something new. The main benefit comes from making the initial recording and letting study material be the last thing you hear before you fall asleep.
- **Use sticky notes to flag difficult topics or concepts.** As you study, put a sticky note on a section or page in the book where you need more work. After you've filled your book(s) with stickies, concentrate your study on those difficult areas (where the stickies are). After you feel that you have a good grasp on this information, remove the note from the book. As you learn more and more, you'll whittle down the number of pages with stickies until you've removed them all from the textbook.

Developing Solid Test-Taking Skills

To be successful on the Series 7, developing your test-taking skills is just as important as mastering the concepts that form the basis of the questions. The best way to develop test-taking skills is to take practice tests, such as the ones in this book. Following are some tips that can also help you polish up your skills.

Read the question carefully

Don't be fooled. Exam creators love to trip you up by making you jump ahead and answer the question — incorrectly — before you read the entire problem. Often one of the last words in the call (specific inquiry) of the question is worded in the negative, like "all of the following are true *except,*" or "which of the following is the *least* likely to," and so on. When reviewing the answers to a practice test, these questions cause some students to groan or slap themselves in the head when they realize their mistake. Don't worry — this common reaction usually goes away after you start getting better at taking exams.

Look for phrases that lead to the topic tested

Try to identify the specific category that the question is testing you on. If you study for the number of hours that I recommend (see "Blocking out some time to study"), you'll most likely cover the material the question references at some point, and you'll be able to identify the topic that the question applies to. After you know the topic, your brain can retrieve the information you need from its mental file cabinet, making it easier for you to focus on the applicable rule, equation, or concept so you can answer the question correctly.

Work with what you have

If possible, work with the facts — and only the facts — in the question. Too often, students add their own interpretation to the question and turn a straightforward problem into a mess. Use the facts that are given, dump the garbage information that isn't necessary to answer the question, and don't make the question more difficult or assume that there's more to the question than what appears.

Adding irrelevant information into a question seems to be a very common practice for students (for example, they ask, "Yeah, but what if she were married?"). My standard answer is, "Did it say that in the question?" to which the response is *no.* Don't make your life more difficult by adding your own speculations into the question; just answer the question that's given to you.

Don't obsess; mark for review

If you experience brain freeze while taking the exam, don't panic or waste valuable time on one question. Eliminate any answer(s) you know must be wrong (if any), take your best guess, and *mark the question for review* so you can easily return to it later. The question may even resolve itself. For example, another question may trigger your memory as you continue to take the exam, and the correct answer to the earlier question may become clear.

Keep track of time

Time yourself so you're always aware of how much time you have left to complete the exam. One way to do so is to figure out which question you need to be up to at the end of each half-hour; use that as a benchmark to keep track of your progress. In each of your two sessions, you have three hours to complete the exam. You have to answer 130 questions in each session (5 don't count toward your score). This gives you 1.38 minutes (or 1 minute and 22.8 seconds) to answer each question.

Translating these numbers to half-hour benchmarks gets you the results shown in the following table.

Time	*Number of Questions Completed*
30 minutes	22
1 hour	44
1.5 hours	66
2 hours	88
2.5 hours	110
3 hours	130

Memorize these benchmarks, write them on your scrap paper (or dry erase board) as soon as the exam administrators allow you to begin, and keep referring to your watch or the clock on the computer screen to track your progress in relation to the benchmark. If you find yourself falling behind, pick up your pace. If you're really falling behind, mark the lengthier, more difficult questions for review and spend your time answering the easier questions. Why waste two minutes on one long question for 0.4 of a point when you could answer two shorter questions in that time and earn twice as many points?

Most students don't have a problem finishing the Series 7 exam on time. If you easily and consistently finish 125-question Series 7 practice exams in less than three hours, you should be okay on the real Series 7.

When you are taking the Series 7 exam at the test center, if you find yourself obsessing over the clock on the computer to the point that you can't concentrate on the question in front of you, hide it by clicking on the lower left-hand corner of the computer screen. (Check out Figure 1-1 in Chapter 1.)

Master the process of elimination

The Series 7 exam is a standardized exam. This format makes it similar to other practical exams of this type: The best way to find the correct answer may be to eliminate the incorrect answers one at a time. I help you develop this crucial skill as you tackle the topic-specific questions throughout this book.

Maintain your concentration

To maintain your concentration, read the *stem* of the question (the last question before the answer choices) first to keep yourself focused on what the question is asking. Next, read through the entire problem (including the stem) to get a grip on the facts you have to consider to select the correct answer. You can then anticipate the correct answer and read all of the answer choices to see whether your anticipated answer is there. If you don't see your answer and none of the other choices seem to fit, reread the stem to see whether you missed an important fact. Check out Chapter 3 for more detailed test-taking tips.

You can also take care to keep yourself physically alert. The last hour or so of each session is usually the most difficult. I recommend eating a small protein bar prior to starting the test to help keep your levels of energy and concentration high. Forget high-sugar/high-carb foods; leave them for after the exam. These foods boost your sugar level temporarily, but when the level drops, your energy and concentration levels sink like a lead balloon.

Low energy levels can lead to sloppy mistakes. If you feel yourself fading, do whatever it takes to stay alert and focused: Get up and get a drink of water, splash some water on your face, stretch, or dig your fingernails into the palms of your hands.

Think carefully before changing your answers

In general, if you select an answer and you can't really explain why, maybe it was just a *gut* answer. You're five times more likely to change to a wrong answer than to the right one, so change your answer only if

- You didn't read the question correctly the first time and missed a major point that changes the answer choice (for example, you didn't see the word *except* at the end of the question).
- You're absolutely sure you made a mistake.

Use the scrap paper wisely

In the testing room, you receive six pieces of letter-sized scrap paper (or a dry erase board), all of which will be collected — so restrain yourself from writing any obscenities about the exam or its creators. Here are some more productive ways to use this valuable resource:

- **Mark dubious questions for review.** You have to answer each question before you can go to the next, so if you're not sure of the correct answer, eliminate the wrong answers, take your best guess, and mark the question for review later. On your scrap paper, write down the numbers of any questions you want to check before the end of the session.
- **Eliminate wrong answers.** You can't write on the computer screen, so for each question, you may find it helpful to write *A, B, C,* and *D* on your scrap paper (in a column) as they appear on the screen and eliminate answers directly on your paper.
- **Do a brain dump.** After the exam begins and before your brain gets cluttered with Series 7 exam questions, use your scrap paper or dry erase board to jot down the formulas you've memorized or topic matters that tend to give you problems so that you can refresh your memory during the exam. Your scrap paper or dry erase board will be collected at the end of the first session, so repeat the brain dump process after you begin the afternoon session.

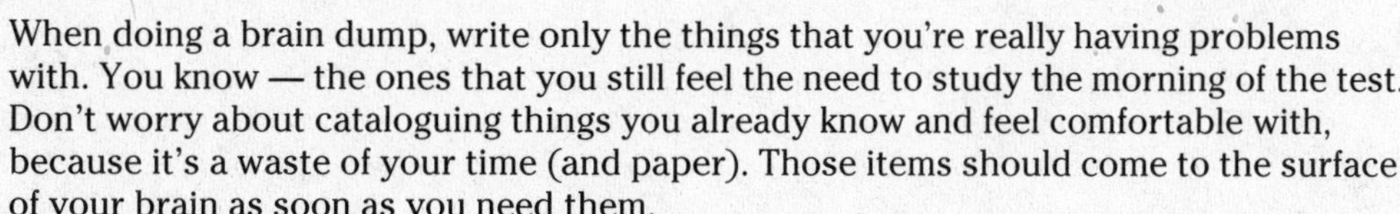

When doing a brain dump, write only the things that you're really having problems with. You know — the ones that you still feel the need to study the morning of the test. Don't worry about cataloguing things you already know and feel comfortable with, because it's a waste of your time (and paper). Those items should come to the surface of your brain as soon as you need them.

- **Time yourself.** Write down your half hour benchmarks (prepared for you in the "Keeping track of time" section earlier in this chapter) on your scrap paper and check periodically to make sure you stay on track.
- **Perform calculations and draw diagrams.** Use the scrap paper to work out math problems, create seesaws, or make any other diagrams that help you rack up points.

Knowing When You're Ready

Your goal is to consistently score 80 to 85 percent on the sample tests that you take to ensure that you're ready for the real exam.

To determine your readiness, consider your scores on the practice exams the *first time* you take them. In other words, don't convince yourself that you're ready if you score 85 percent on an exam that you've already taken three times. If you take a practice exam more than once, you may just be remembering the answers. I'm not against taking the same exams more than once, but don't use exams you've taken before to gauge how prepared you are.

My company and some other companies sell an exam as a final benchmark to test a student's readiness to take the Series 7 exam. We call ours The Annihilator — a 250-question exam designed to be four to six points harder than the real exam. Students who pass with a 72 or better are most likely ready to take the Series 7.

Chapter 3

Examining and Mastering Question Types

In This Chapter

- Exploring the composition of Series 7 exam questions
- Analyzing the purpose and intent of a question
- Identifying the correct answer
- Mastering the process of elimination

Yes, I know, I know: "Why can't they just ask regular questions?" This problem has perplexed Series 7 test takers throughout the ages (all right, maybe not, but it *does* bug me). The test designers have riddled the old pick-the-best-answer questions with all kinds of pitfalls. The people in charge want you to choose combinations of correct answers and pick out exceptions; they expect you to pull numbers from balance sheets and apply complex formulas; and, as if you don't have enough to worry about, they even give you extraneous information to try to trip you up. Sheesh!

In this chapter, I introduce you to the types of questions to expect on the Series 7 exam, and I show you how to analyze the facts in the questions and identify what the examiners are *really* testing you on. I also show you how to use the process of elimination to find the right answer and, if all else fails, how to logically guess the best answer.

Familiarizing Yourself with Question Formats

The Series 7 exam is a beast of a test that poses questions in many different ways. You have to deal with multitiered Roman numeral nightmares, open- and closed-ended sentences, and killers like *except* and *not.* In this section, I show you how the examiners phrase the questions and how they can trip you up if you aren't careful.

Working with the straight shooters: The straightforward types

Straightforward question types include a group of sentences with the facts followed by a question or incomplete sentence; you then get four answer choices, one of which correctly answers the question or completes the idea.

Closed-stem questions

You'll find more closed-stem questions than any other question type on the Series 7 exam, so you'd better get a handle on answering these babies, for sure. Thankfully, closed-stem questions are fairly run-of-the mill. They begin with one or more sentences containing information and end with a question (and, appropriately enough, a question mark). The question mark is what makes closed-stem questions different from open-stem questions, which I discuss in the next section. Your answer choices, lettered (A) through (D), may be complete or incomplete sentences. Here's a basic closed-stem question.

Mr. Bearishnikoff is a conservative investor. Which of the following investments would you recommend to him?

(A) Buying put options

(B) Buying long-term income adjustment bonds

(C) Buying common stock of an aggressive growth company

(D) Buying Treasury notes

The right answer is Choice (D). The first sentence tells you that Mr. Bearishnikoff is a conservative investor. This detail is all the information you need to answer the question correctly, because you know that conservative investors aren't looking to take a lot of investment risks and that U.S. government securities such as Treasury notes (T-notes) are considered the safest of all securities — they're backed by the fact that the government can always print more money to pay off the securities that it issues.

Of course, sometimes the phrasing of the answer choices can help you immediately cut down the number of feasible answer choices. For instance, Mr. Bearishnikoff would probably balk at investing in an *aggressive growth* company, which certainly doesn't sound stable or safe. Check out the section titled "Picking up clues when you're virtually clueless: The process of elimination" for details on raising your odds of answering questions correctly.

By the way, the *you* in the question refers to you on your good days, when you're considerate and rational and have had a sufficient amount of sleep. Mr. Bearishnikoff probably wouldn't appreciate any rogue-elephant investing, even if you think he should be more daring. The question also assumes normal market conditions, so don't recommend a different investment because you think the government is going to collapse and T-notes are going to take a dive. Just accept the conditions the problem presents to you.

Be careful to focus only on the information you need to answer the question. The Series 7 exam creators have an annoying tendency to include extra details in the question (such as the maturity date, coupon rate, investor's age, and so on) that you may not need. See "Focusing on key information," later in this chapter, for some tips on zeroing in on the necessary info.

Open-stem questions

An open-stem question poses the problem as an incomplete sentence, and your mission, should you choose to accept it, is to complete the sentence with the correct answer. The following example shows how you can skillfully finish other people's thoughts.

The initial maturity on a standard option is

(A) three months

(B) six months

(C) nine months

(D) one year

The answer you want is Choice (C). *Options* give the purchaser the right to buy or sell securities at a fixed price (see Chapter 12). Options are considered *derivatives* (securities that derive their value from another security) because they're linked to an underlying security. Standard options have an initial maturity of nine months. On the other hand, Long-Term Equity AnticiPation Securities (LEAPS) may have initial maturities of one, two, or three years. But this example question asks about a standard option; therefore, you don't assume that it's a LEAP.

The preceding example is quite easy. Anyone who has been studying for the Series 7 exam should know the answer. However, what makes the Series 7 so difficult is that the exam is loaded with so many date-oriented details. Not only do you have to memorize the initial maturities of all the different securities, but unfortunately (and believe me, I feel your pain), you also have to remember a truckload of time frames (for example, accounts are frozen for 90 days, new securities can't be purchased on margin for 30 days, an options account agreement must be returned within 15 days after the account is approved, and so on).

Date-oriented details are excellent material to include in your flash cards. See Chapter 2 for more study suggestions.

Encountering quirky questions with qualifiers

To answer questions with qualifiers, you have to find the 'best answer' to the question. The qualifier keeps all answer choices from being correct because only one answer rises above the rest.

Working with extremes: Most, least, best

Recognizing the qualifier in the question stem and carefully reading every single answer choice are very important. Check out the following example.

Which of the following companies would be MOST affected by interest rate fluctuations?

(A) SKNK Perfume Corp.

(B) Bulb Utility Co.

(C) Crapco Vitamin Supplements, Inc.

(D) LQD Water Bottling Co.

The answer is Choice (B). Although all companies may be somewhat affected by interest rate fluctuations, the question uses the word *most.* If interest rates increase, companies have to issue bonds with higher coupon (interest) rates. This higher rate, in turn, greatly affects the companies' bottom lines. Therefore, you're looking for a company that issues a lot of bonds. Utility companies are most affected by interest rate fluctuations because they're *highly leveraged* (issue a lot of bonds).

Making exceptions: Except or not

When a question includes the word *except* or *not,* you're looking for the answer that's *the exception* to the rule stated in the stem of the question. In other words, the correct answer is always the *false* answer. The question can be open (as it is in the next example) or closed.

Right off the bat, look for an *except* or *not* in the stem of every question on the Series 7. Many students who really know their material accidentally pick the wrong answer on a few questions because they carelessly miss the *except* or *not.*

Take a look at the following exception problem.

A stockholder owns 800 shares of WHY common stock. WHY stockholders were given cumulative voting rights. If there are three vacancies on the board of directors, stockholders can cast any of the following votes EXCEPT

(A) 800 for one candidate

(B) 800 for each candidate

(C) 2,400 for one candidate

(D) 900 for each candidate

The answer you're looking for is Choice (D). Cumulative voting rights give smaller stockholders (not height-wise, but in terms of the number of shares they own) an easier chance to gain representation on the board of directors because a stockholder may combine his total voting rights and vote the cumulative total in any way he wants. Here, the stockholder has a total of 2,400 votes to cast (800 shares × 3 vacancies = 2,400 votes).

In this example, you may be tempted to select Choices (A), (B), or (C), any of which would be correct if you were asked for the number of votes this stockholder *could* cast. For example, the stockholder can use 800 shares to vote for only one candidate (Choice A) — he doesn't have to use all 2,400 votes. Choice (B) is another possible voting arrangement because nobody said the stockholder has to use all his votes for one candidate. Choice (C) is an option because the stockholder has a total of 2,400 votes to cast. In this question, however, you're looking for the number of votes the stockholder *can't* cast because the word *except* in the question stem requires you to find a false answer. Therefore, Choice (D) is the correct answer because in order to cast 900 votes for each candidate, the stockholder would need a total of 2,700 votes (900 × 3).

If you're one of the unlucky people who get an "all of the following are false except" question, you have to find the *true* answer. Don't forget, two negatives in a sentence make a positive statement. You may want to try rephrasing the question so you know whether you're looking for a true or false answer.

Roman hell: Complex multiple choice

Yes, the Series 7 exam creators even sneak complex (two-tiered) Roman numeral questions in on you. They can pose the question by asking you to put something in order, or they can ask you to find the best combination in a series of answer choices. To make things even more enjoyable, sometimes they even add *except* and *not* to the question (see the preceding section).

Imposing order: Ranking questions

To answer a ranking question, you have to choose the answer that places the information in the correct order — for example, first to last, last to first, highest to lowest, lowest to highest, and so on. Check out the following example.

In which order, from first to last, are the following actions taken when opening a new options account?

I. Send the customer an ODD.

II. Have the ROP approve the account.

III. Execute the transaction.

IV. Have the customer send in an OAA.

(A) I, II, III, IV

(B) II, I, IV, III

(C) III, I, II, IV

(D) I, III, II, IV

The correct answer is Choice (A). Wasn't it nice of me to arrange all the answers in order for you? Because option transactions are so risky, the customer has to receive an options risk disclosure document (ODD) prior to opening the account. Statement I has to come first, so you can immediately eliminate Choices (B) and (C), giving you a 50 percent chance of answering correctly. After the client receives the ODD, the registered options principal (ROP) needs to approve the account before any transactions can be executed; II has to come before III, so you can finish the problem here — the answer is Choice (A). Last but not least, the customer signs and returns an options account agreement (OAA) within 15 days after the account is approved by the ROP.

Taking two at a time

The Roman numeral format also appears on the Series 7 with questions that offer two answer choices as the correct response. In these types of questions, you choose the responses that best answer the question.

Which TWO of the following are the minimum requirements for an investor to be considered accredited?

I. An individual with a net worth of $500,000

II. An individual with a net worth of $1,000,000

III. An individual who earned $200,000 per year in the most recent two years and has a reasonable expectation of reaching that same level in the current year

IV. An individual who earned $300,000 per year in the most recent 3 years and has a reasonable expectation of reaching that same level in the current year

(A) I and III

(B) I and IV

(C) II and III

(D) II and IV

The correct answer is Choice (C). Statements I and II both deal with net worth; III and IV deal with earnings. Therefore, you're dealing with two questions in one; to be accredited, the answer to at least one of these two questions must be satisfactory:

- What is the individual's minimum net worth?
- What is the individual's minimum income?

To be considered an accredited (sophisticated) investor, the minimum requirement is a net worth of $1,000,000 and/or a yearly income of $200,000 in the most recent two years, with a reasonable expectation of reaching that same level in the current year. If the word *minimum* were not used in the question, answer IV would also be correct.

A little mystery: Dealing with an unknown number of correct statements

In the preceding section, the question states that only two responses can be correct. The following question may have one, three, or four correct answers. You can recognize this type of question simply by glancing at your answer choices. To make the problem more difficult (don't hate me, now), I add an *except* because I'm feeling really good about you, and I just know you're up to it.

All of the following are considered violations EXCEPT

I. rehypothecation

II. commingling

III. odd lot transactions

IV. forward pricing

(A) I only

(B) II only

(C) I, III, and IV only

(D) I, II, III, and IV

The correct answer is Choice (C). The only violation among the choices listed is commingling. *Commingling* occurs when a broker-dealer combines a customer's account with his own or combines a customer's fully paid securities with margined securities. (Chapter 16 fills you in on rules and regulations.)

You're looking for the choices that are *not* violations, so you want to identify the actions that are allowed. If you eliminate commingling, Roman numeral II, your choices are A (I only) or C (I, III, and IV only). You know that I is correct because it's in both answer choices, so you need to evaluate only III and IV. (You have to check only one of these because you know that if III is correct, IV must be as well; if III is false, so is IV.) Odd lot transactions (III) are ones for fewer than 100 shares (a round lot) and are okay. Forward pricing (IV) is what mutual funds do with orders placed by investors, allowing them to purchase or sell at the next price (usually at the end of the day), which is also okay. Choice (C) is correct because it's the only one that lists all three correct choices (I, III, and IV).

Looking at exhibits: Series 7 diagram questions

The Series 7 exam also gives some exhibit questions, which may include newspaper clippings, option prices, bond prices, trading patterns, a specialist's book, income statements, balance sheets, and so on. Out of the exhibit questions you get, some of them just require you to find the correct information; others require a little calculating. I wouldn't be too concerned about them if I were you, because most of them are quite easy.

Take a look at the following problem.

GHI Corporation Balance Sheet at 12-31-XX
(In Thousands)

Assets		**Liabilities**	
Cash and cash equivalents	$8,000	Accounts payable	$1,000
Receivables (net)	$1,000	Wages payable	$800
Inventory	+$3,000	Taxes payable	$700
Total current assets	**$12,000**	Interest payable	+ $500
		Total current liabilities	$3,000
Notes receivable due after one year	$1,000	Long-term debt 8%	+$4,000
		Total liabilities	**$7,000**
Property, plant, and equipment (net)	$4,000		
Goodwill	+$1,000	**Stockholder's Equity**	
Total long-term assets	**$6,000**	Preferred stock $100 par 9%	$2,000
		Common stock $1 par	$2,000
		Paid-in capital	$4,000
Total assets	**$18,000**	Retained earnings	+$3,000
		Total stockholder's equity	**$11,000**
		Total liabilities and stockholder's equity	**$18,000**

What is the working capital of GHI Corp.?

(A) $7,000

(B) $7,000,000

(C) $9,000

(D) $9,000,000

The answer you're looking for is Choice (D). This example accurately portrays the difficulty level of most of the exhibit questions on the Series 7 exam. After you remember the formula for working capital (see Chapter 13), you simply have to find the information you need — the current assets and current liabilities — on the balance sheet so you can answer the question:

working capital = current assets – current liabilities

= $12,000,000 – $3,000,000

= $9,000,000

You may wonder why the answer is in millions instead of thousands. Notice that the top of the balance sheet says "in thousands," which tells you that you have to multiply the numbers in the balance sheet by 1,000.

When you answer exhibit questions, take care not to miss labels like "in thousands" in headings or scales on a graph that would change your answer. Almost nothing is worse than missing a question that you know how to figure out because you carelessly overlook something right in front of you.

The following question has you locate information on call options.

Option			Calls		Puts	
CDE	Strike Price	Expiration	Vol	Last	Vol	Last
68.50	65	Aug	10	3.75	90	0.10
68.50	65	Sep	40	4.50	120	0.80
68.50	65	Nov	20	6.75	4	1.80
68.50	65	Feb	21	7.00	—	—
68.50	70	Aug	140	0.40	5	2.00
68.50	70	Sep	155	1.70	1	3.00
68.50	70	Nov	28	3.00	30	4.35
68.50	75	Feb	40	2.60	—	—
68.50	80	Nov	70	0.65	—	—

What is the time value of a CDE Nov 65 call?

(A) 4.00

(B) 3.25

(C) 3.00

(D) 2.40

The right answer is Choice (B). This question involves options (see Chapter 12 for calculations and more information). The first step is to find the premium for the CDE Nov 65 call in the exhibit. To accomplish this, line up the 65 strike price with the Nov expiration month; you find it in the third row of data. Follow that row over to the fifth column to get the premium for the Nov 65 call. In this case, it's 6.75. Next, use the following formula: P = I + T, where P = premium, I = intrinsic value (the in-the-money amount), and T = time value (how long an investor has to use the option).

First, enter the premium into the equation. Next, you have to determine the intrinsic value (how much the option is in-the-money). Call options go in-the-money when the price of the stock is above the strike price. The stock price is 68.50 (left column) and the strike price is 65, so the option is 3.50 in-the-money (68.50 – 65 = 3.50). After placing those two numbers (6.75 and 3.50) in the equation, you see that the time value has to be 3.25:

$$P = I + T$$

$$6.75 = 3.50 + T$$

$$T = 3.25$$

Shredding the Questions: Tips and Tricks

In Chapter 2, I give you general exam proficiency tips. In this section, I show you how to improve your analysis of topic-specific Series 7 questions. I also provide you with more sample exam questions to further demonstrate the art of choosing the correct answers.

Focusing on key information

The Series 7 exam questions can be particularly difficult if you rush through the exam and miss details that change the meaning of the question.

When you first start taking practice exams, read through the question to determine what's being asked; then go back to the beginning of the problem to identify the key facts and underline and/or highlight them. Marking the questions may seem time-consuming when you first begin to study, but if you get into the habit of picking out key words in each question, zoning in on the important information should be second nature by the time you take the test. Of course, you can't underline items on the computer screen at the testing center (the test center administrators may get upset if you write on the computer screen). So instead, if you find yourself getting distracted by useless information, use the scrap paper or dry erase board to write down the information you do need.

This example zeroes in on the essential information.

A 55-year-old investor purchases a <u>6 percent</u> DEF convertible mortgage bond at 90 with 10 years until maturity. If the bond is currently trading at <u>97</u>, what is the <u>current yield</u>?

(A) 5.72%

(B) 6.00%

(C) 6.19%

(D) 6.67%

The correct answer is Choice (C). When determining the current yield of a bond, all you need is the market price of the bond and the coupon (interest) rate (see Chapter 7). The fact that the investor is 55 years old or that the bond is a convertible mortgage bond that was purchased at $900 (90 percent of $1,000 par) with 10 years until maturity means nothing in terms of determining the answer. Underline or highlight what you do need (6 percent, 97, current yield) so you don't get distracted.

To determine the current yield, divide the annual interest by the market price. The annual interest is $60 (6 percent of $1,000 par) and the market price is $970 (97 percent of $1,000 par):

$$\text{current yield} = \frac{\text{annual interest}}{\text{market price}} = \frac{\$60}{\$970} = 6.19\%$$

To avoid confusion when faced with a math problem, read the stem of the question to determine what's being asked; before you consider the rest of the question, jot down the formula you need to calculate your answer.

Answer me this: Picking the correct answer

The Series 7 exam is a practical, multiple-choice exam. The correct answer has to be one of the choices. This setup means you don't have to *provide* the correct answer; you just have to *recognize* it when you see it.

Picking up clues when you're virtually clueless: The process of elimination

When you don't straight-out know an answer, your approach can definitely make the difference between passing and failing the exam. Your best strategy may be eliminating the wrong answers. In theory, you should be able to eliminate, one by one, three incorrect answers for each question.

Even if you can't eliminate three incorrect answers, you'll certainly be able to eliminate one or two answers that are definitely wrong. Don't try to guess the right answer until you've axed as many wrong answers as you can. Obviously, if you can get the choices down to two potential answers, you have a 50-50 chance of answering correctly.

For an answer choice to be correct, every aspect has to be correct, and the selection has to specifically answer the question that's asked. As a rule of thumb on the Series 7 exam, a more-precise answer is correct more often than a less-precise answer, and a longer answer usually (but not always) prevails over a short answer.

If a response is potentially correct, write *T* for *true* next to the answer in your practice exam, and if a response is wrong, eliminate it by writing *F* for *false* next to the answer. If you do this step correctly, you should end up with three Fs and one T, with T indicating the correct answer. Or, if the question is looking for a false answer, you should end up with three Ts and one F (see the earlier section "Making exceptions: Except or not" for more info on this scenario). On the actual test, you can write the letters A through D on your scrap paper or dry erase board and mark the answer choices appropriately.

Always look to eliminate any wrong answers that you can. Pay attention to the wording, and get rid of choices that simply sound wrong or make statements that are too broad or absolute. If you're still undecided, use your scrap paper or dry erase board to write down the question number and the answer choices that remain. Take your best guess and mark the answer for review. When you review, look at your scrap paper or dry erase board to help you zone in on your potential answers. Change your answer only if you're sure you made a mistake.

Stop opposing me: Dealing with opposite answers

If you see two opposing answer choices, only one can be right. Traditionally, in practical exams like the Series 7, when you see two answer choices that are complete opposites, the exam creators are trying to test your knowledge of the correct rule, procedure, or law, so one of those opposing choices is most likely the correct answer. Take a look at the following example.

Which of the following is TRUE of UGMA accounts?

(A) There can be only one minor and one custodian per account.

(B) There can be more than one minor and one custodian per account.

(C) Securities can only be purchased on margin.

(D) They must be set up for children who have reached the age of majority.

Getting down with numbers: Eliminating some math

The process of elimination can get you out of some messy calculations. When dealing with math, look at the answer choices before you begin working out the problem. You may be able to get the answer without doing any calculations at all. For instance, if you have a forward stock split, you know that the number of shares has to increase and that the price of the stock has to decrease (see Chapter 6). If three of the answers fail to meet these conditions, you have your answer right off the bat.

The answer you want is Choice (A). Notice that Choices (A) and (B) oppose each other. If you have two opposing answers, in almost all cases, one of them is the right answer. Therefore, you can ignore Choices (C) and (D), which gives you a 50-percent chance of getting the answer right. Uniform Gifts to Minors Act (UGMA) accounts are set up for minors who are too young to have their own accounts. Each account is limited to one minor and one custodian. (See Chapter 16 for details on custodial accounts.)

Facing Roman numerals: Not as hard as you think

Complex (two-tiered) multiple-choice questions, with both Roman numerals and letters, can be really frustrating because they usually signal the test taker (you) that you need more than one correct answer. Well, today's your lucky day, because I show you a shortcut that can help you blow these questions right out of the water.

Traditionally, the first tier of these types of questions gives you several statements preceded by Roman numerals; the second tier (preceded by letters) provides you with choices about which of those statements are correct. Fifteen different combinations of I, II, III, and IV are possible (16 if you count "none of the above," which is almost never correct), but each problem can list only four of them in the answer choices. Because of the limited answer choices, you may not have to evaluate every statement — certain combinations of Roman numerals may be logically impossible.

Read the question carefully, and then mark *T* for *true* or *F* for *false* next to the Roman numerals to indicate whether they're correct answers to the question. If a Roman-numeral statement is correct, circle that number in the choices that follow the letters in the second tier. If the Roman-numeral statement is false, all the letter answers that include that numeral must also be false, and you can cross them out. If you're really lucky, three of the Roman numerals can be eliminated right away, leaving you with one answer choice.

Look over this Roman numeral question.

Which of the following is TRUE of the 5% Markup Policy?

I. It covers commissions charged to customers when executing trades on an agency basis.

II. It covers markups on stock sold to customers from inventory.

III. It covers markdowns on stock purchased from customers for inventory.

IV. Riskless and simultaneous transactions are covered.

(A) I and IV only

(B) IV only

(C) II and III only

(D) I, II, III, and IV

The correct answer is Choice (D). The 5% Markup Policy applies to nonexempt securities sold to or purchased from customers. This situation is one where you should look at the Roman-numeral statements and pick out those that you know answer the question. For example, if you know statement I is right (which it is), put a T (for true) next to it. Next, look at Choices (A), (B), (C), and (D) and eliminate Choices (B) and (C), because neither one includes the Roman numeral I. Because both answers that remain, (A) and (D), include the Roman numerals I and IV, you don't even have to bother reading statement IV — it's in both remaining answers, so you know it has to be true. Write T next to the Roman numeral IV. If you know that either statement II or III is correct (which they both are), the answer has to be Choice (D) because it's the only one that lists all the correct choices.

Don't make the same mistake twice

When studying for the Series 7 exam, the practice exams can help you pinpoint your weaker areas of knowledge. The questions you answer incorrectly can be your best learning tools if you thoroughly review the explanations for each wrong answer. You may be tempted to jump from one practice exam to the next without taking adequate time to review your wrong answers. Don't do it! If you put the effort into finding out why your choices are wrong when you're practicing, you're less likely to repeat the same mistake on the Series 7 exam, when it really counts.

Chapter 4

Surviving Test Day

In This Chapter

- Getting ready the day before
- Arriving at the test center and checking in
- Experiencing the exam
- Viewing your exam results

You've done your homework, taken practice exams, and completed your prep course, and now the day of reckoning is upon you. You're ready to exchange the gazillion hours of study and hard work for your Series 7 license. The last hurdle awaits you at the test center.

In this chapter, I give you a snapshot of the Series 7 exam experience so you know the procedure before, during, and after you take the exam and can hit the ground running.

Composing Yourself the Day Before

On the day before the exam, review the information that you're still having problems with until noon; then call it a day. Get away from the books, go out to dinner (maybe skip the spicy foods and alcohol), go to a movie. Rest your mind. If you've put the required time and effort into studying up to now, you'll benefit more from a good night's rest than anything you can learn in the final hours the night before your exam. Taking the evening off can help prevent brain fatigue and make zoning into exam mode easier tomorrow, when it counts most.

Before you go to sleep, gather the items you need to take with you to the exam. If you prepare yourself the night before, you'll be more relaxed on exam day. Here are some activities to complete the night before the exam to finalize your preparations for the big day:

- Make sure you have the proper government-issued ID bearing your name, signature, and a recent photo. The name on your ID must identically match the name on the Web CRD registration form. An expired ID won't be accepted. Official (primary) identification can be in the form of a valid passport, a driver's license, or a military ID card. A current (unexpired) State ID is acceptable in lieu of a driver's license, as long as it includes the person's full name as it appears on the Web CRD registration form, an expiration date, the student's signature, and a current photograph.

  If you use a military ID that doesn't have a signature, you need to bring a secondary form of ID with a signature. Secondary ID can be a valid credit card, a bank automatic-teller machine (ATM) card, a library card, a U.S. Social Security card, an employee ID/work badge, or a school ID.

- Pack earplugs (if allowed — ask when you schedule your exam).
- Put your lunch and/or a snack with the rest of your stuff.

Doing test runs in the final weeks

Getting too little sleep (you'll be a nervous wreck) or too much sleep (you'll be in a stupor) the night before the exam can be a disaster. For the week before the exam (if possible), follow the routine you'll be following on the day of your exam. Set your alarm at the same time you'll wake up on exam day, take your practice exams for two three-hour intervals at the same time as you'll be taking the real exam, and so on.

Also, the day of the exam is not the time to find out that a big construction project is underway on the exact route you're taking to get to the test center, the traffic is backed up for miles, and you'll be at least an hour late. The last thing you need to worry about on exam day is getting to the test center late and having to reschedule your exam.

To help avoid this disaster, do a test run sometime before the test date. Travel the route you'll take at the same time (and, if possible, on the same day of the week) as your exam date to get a preview of what you can expect. You may even be able to check your local newspaper for details on upcoming construction or repairs that may affect roadways and public transportation. Having an alternate route established in advance is also a good idea in case your route of choice isn't the best option on exam day.

- Bring study materials — including the topics and/or math formulas you're having trouble with — for a final review before you enter the test center.
- Have your watch ready to make sure you're on time, that you don't take too long between the first and second halves of the exam, and that you complete both sessions before your time is up.
- Lay out your clothes (dress in layers in case the test center feels like either your refrigerator or your oven).
- Review the directions to the exam site. Make sure you have a charged cellphone and the test center number in case you get lost.

Additionally, you have to bring at least one finger with you, preferably yours, so that the exam administrators can take a fingerprint (though you probably have that packed already).

You can't bring study material, textbooks, briefcases, purses, electronic devices, cellphones, notes of any kind, or your really smart friend with you into the testing room. Calculators, pencils, and scrap paper or a dry erase board will be provided for you at the exam center, and the exam administrators will collect the calculators, pencils, and all scrap paper (used and unused) or dry erase board at the end of each session.

Making the Most of the Morning

Now the big day is here. Certainly, you don't have to dress up for the pictures the Series 7 administrator takes, but you should at least do what you need to do to feel awake and alive and good about yourself (do some push-ups, take a shower, shave, whatever).

Be sure to eat at least a light breakfast. You may feel like you're too nervous to eat, but if you're hungry when you take the exam, you won't be able to concentrate. And if you overeat, you'll be wasting valuable energy (and blood flow!) digesting the meal — energy your brain needs to sustain you. To avoid an energy crash, I suggest a protein bar, fruit, and/or veggies rather than sugar or carbs.

Grab everything you packed up the night before (see the preceding section) and head out the door.

Leave your home in time to arrive at the test center at least 30 minutes before your scheduled exam so you have time to check in. I recommend that you arrive at the test center 1½ hours before the exam so you have 1 hour to review the topics and/or math formulas that give you the most trouble and a half-hour to check in.

Arriving on the Scene

The Series 7 exams are administered by Thompson Prometric and Pearson VUE, and you can contact either company for additional information. In this section, I cover the steps to take upon your arrival at the exam center.

In Chapter 1, I discuss the availability of special accommodations if you're disabled or learning impaired or if English is your second language. If you require special accommodations, contact the FINRA Special Conditions Team at (800) 999-6647 for information about registration and for instructions about arriving at the exam center.

Taking advantage of one last chance to cram

The information you review just before the exam will be on the surface of your mind. When you arrive at the exam center (or even during your commute if you take public transportation), do some last-minute cramming. Review the topics and/or math formulas you're having trouble with.

Each Series 7 exam center is set up differently; you may find areas in the building where you can study, or you may have to study outside in your car, on a bench, or at a nearby coffee shop. When you're ready to enter the exam center (30 minutes before the exam) you can leave your books in your vehicle if the exam center doesn't have lockers (see the section "Getting seated").

Signing in

To enter the Series 7 exam center, you have to provide the administrators with valid ID. (See "Composing Yourself the Day Before" for what constitutes "valid.") After you're inside the test center, you have to sign in and get photographed and fingerprinted. In addition, before you begin the exam, you have to read a form called the Rules of Conduct and agree to the terms. A preview of the Rules of Conduct is available on the FINRA website (`http://www.finra.org/Industry/Compliance/Registration/QualificationsExams/p016189`).

Getting seated

Basically, the only things you may bring into the testing room are your own sweet self and possibly a set of earplugs. You can store all other personal property in a locker at the exam center. (All new testing sites are supposed to have lockers, but some older sites may have been grandfathered without them. You can ask when you make your appointment.) For a list of the (mostly) medical items you can bring into the exam room, including which ones need inspection or preauthorization, please call your testing center.

Some exam centers have cafeterias and/or vending machines with snacks and drinks, but you can't even bring chewing gum into the exam room. I don't know why — maybe because of the noise, or maybe so the exam staff doesn't have to scrape gum wads off computer screens.

The exam administrators escort you to the exam room. In the testing room, you receive six 8½-x-11-inch pieces of scrap paper (or a dry erase board), a pencil, and a basic calculator. You'll have to return the paper, pencil, and calculator to the exam center administrators at the end of the session (yes, even the unused scrap paper). You can't bring anything else into the cubicle where you take the exam.

Taking the Exam

Take a deep breath, crack your knuckles, and get ready to make things count — this Series 7 exam is the genuine article. The exam is six long hours in duration, and you're graded on a total of 250 questions. The test designers have even prepared a bonus for you: To ensure that new questions to be introduced in future exams meet acceptable standards, you also answer 10 additional, unidentified questions that don't count toward your score. Lucky you! This means that you answer 260 questions, but only 250 really count.

You get three hours to answer 130 questions in the first half of the exam and three hours to answer 130 questions in the second half. In between the two sessions, you have a much-needed 30- to 60-minute break to grab a bite to eat.

Most test centers offer the inspirational creature comforts of the office: You take your Series 7 in a cubicle (approximately 4 feet wide) with a computer and a small desk area. You may leave your cubicle for restroom breaks at any time, if necessary. The clock continues to run, however, so try to limit your intake of fluids before each session.

Tackling the first half

Just before you begin your first session, a member of the test center staff will walk you through the steps of how to use the computerized system. Don't worry — you don't need any previous computer experience to understand the way the computer operates (it's that easy). If you do have any tech problems during the test, you can use the help button or summon the exam administrators. A picture of how a question appears on the computer screen is in Chapter 1.

As the test begins, you're ready to put all those test-taking skills to use (check out Chapter 2 for a rundown of what those skills are). Write down everything you think you're likely to forget, right off the bat. Keep track of time. Mark questions for review. Concentrate on the facts in question, and look for key words that can give you clues. Use your amazing powers of elimination to identify wrong answer choices. Work your magic with specific question types (see Chapter 3). You've done your homework, so be confident.

You can't return to the first-session questions after finishing the session and signing out of your computer, so before the first session ends, double-check the answers you marked for review. Don't change any answers unless you're certain your initial answer is wrong.

If you're one of those speed demons (and I hope you're not) who finishes each half of the test in an hour and are tempted to review all your answers, don't do it. Go over only the questions you marked for review. If you try to review all the questions, not only will you drive yourself bonkers, but you'll also do more harm than good by second-guessing your right answers.

After completing the first session, you get to leave your cubicle and take a short break.

Staying relaxed, focused, and conscious

Here are some ways to keep stress at bay and make sure you're giving the test the attention it deserves:

- If you feel tense, take a few slow, deep breaths and give yourself a mini-massage.
- If you find yourself growing tired, stretch, sit up straight, or go to the restroom just for a chance to walk around.
- Give your eyes a rest from the computer screen by looking away from the computer every so often.

  Avoid looking at someone else's computer screen — it's not only frowned upon, it will get you ejected.
- If you have trouble focusing, write down significant details from the question. If you're stuck on a multipart question, break down the question into segments. Try drawing diagrams. If you're still having trouble, choose a tentative answer and mark the question for review.
- Don't lose track of your mission here — now is not the time to let up. Visualize success and hang in there!

Taking a break: At long last, lunch

After the first session, you get a minimum of 30 minutes and a maximum of 60 minutes for a lunch break before you begin the second session. You may have an upset stomach by this point, but you'll definitely benefit from eating something — first, to keep up your energy level and second, to keep yourself from being distracted by the sounds your empty stomach would otherwise serenade you with during the second half of the exam.

Many test centers have vending machines on-site; others have a full cafeteria. Select protein bars, water, fruit, and other food that'll increase your stamina and provide you with longer lasting energy. Remember, you can also bring your own food and keep it in your locker to eat after the first half.

After sitting at the computer for three hours, it may be a good idea to force yourself to walk around a bit, stand up, and fraternize with fellow test-takers to work off some nervous energy (or at least try to wake yourself up).

The test center Rules of Conduct say that during the break (and after the exam is completed), candidates may not discuss the exam with others, even those who are taking a different exam. Enjoy other topics of conversation.

Heading down the home stretch: Completing the second half

You follow the same procedure for taking the second half of the exam that you did in the first half. You get on the computer and answer another 130 questions in three hours.

You may find your endurance tested during the last hour or so. If your energy level and concentration start slipping and time allows, you may want to take a bathroom break and splash some water on your face to wake yourself up. If nothing else, the walk should at least get your blood flowing.

After you complete the second half of the exam, look over the questions you marked for review. As with the first half, change answers only if you're absolutely, 100-percent sure you made a mistake. Everyone is on her own time schedule, so as soon as you're done with your review, you're ready for the moment of truth.

Getting the Results: Drum Roll Please . . .

You've completed many hours of studying. You've deprived yourself of weekend parties and long afternoons of leisure. Your social life has been almost nonexistent, and if you're the type who becomes unpleasant when in a stressful state of being, you may have alienated the people who used to hang out with you.

After surviving six hours of mental abuse from taking the Series 7 exam, you're ready to push the button that reveals your score and can change your life.

The time may seem much longer, but in reality, you have to wait approximately 30 seconds before your score is revealed. Your grade and the word *passed* or *failed* appear on the computer screen. If your grade is 72 or better, you pass the exam. (Please remember that you're now a professional and refrain from doing a victory dance in the middle of the test center.) If your score is less than 72, you don't pass the exam. Don't call your friends and tell them you've decided to become an astronaut or firefighter instead. You can retake the test, so you may still have a future on Wall Street. See Chapter 1 for what to do next.

After you receive your exam score, you can leave your cubicle. Bring your scrap paper or dry erase board, pencil, and calculator with you, and turn them over to the exam center staff.

Regardless of whether you pass or fail the exam, you receive a printout of your grade and the breakdown of your performance on the Series 7 exam topics, which is unfortunately pretty vague. Employers receive a copy of the results in the mail, or, if tied into the FINRA computer system, they can get results online.

Part II
Mastering Basic Security Investments

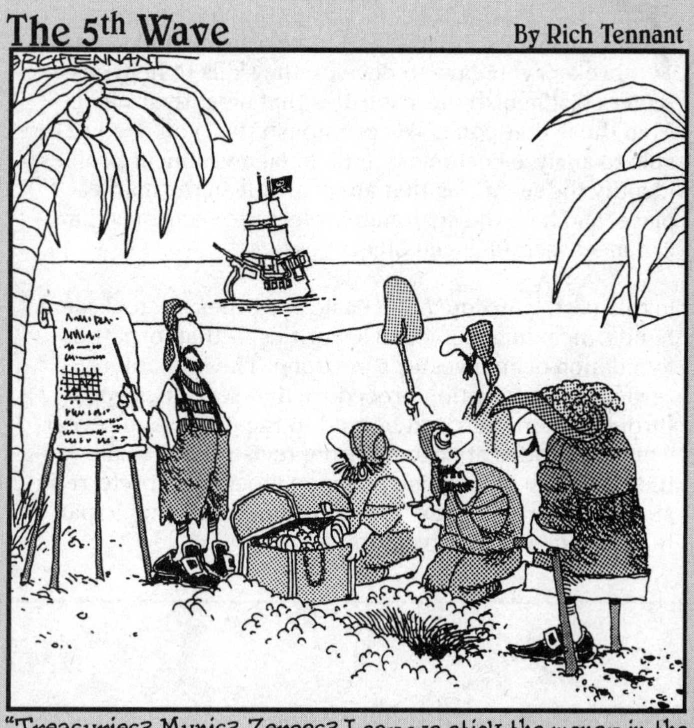

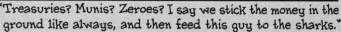

"Treasuries? Munis? Zeroes? I say we stick the money in the ground like always, and then feed this guy to the sharks."

In this part . . .

For the Series 7 exam (and to be a successful stockbroker) you have to develop the skills to help customers distinguish the securities that meet their needs from those that don't. To accomplish this, you need to be able to analyze customers' individual investment profiles, identify the securities that are available in the marketplace, and help the customers select the securities that can meet their financial objectives.

In this part, I introduce the basic securities — stocks and bonds, including municipal securities — that form the foundation of an investor's portfolio. These chapters review the registration procedure that securities go through before they can be sold to the public and reveal which securities are exempt from registration. Finally, they help you distinguish common stock from preferred stock, corporate bonds from U.S. bonds, and municipal bonds from general obligation bonds.

Chapter 5

Underwriting Securities

In This Chapter

- Understanding the specifics of registering securities
- Knowing the types of offerings
- Spotting exempt securities
- Reviewing additional topics tested

All issuers of securities need a starting point, just as all securities need a birth date (just not the kind that's celebrated with funny-looking hats and a cake). Most securities go through a registration procedure before the public can buy them. The Series 7 exam tests your ability to recognize the players and institutions involved in the registration process.

In this chapter, I cover topics related to bringing new issues (securities) to market. You find out about key players, types of security offerings, kinds of securities that don't need to be registered, and other details about the underwriting process. (Check out the "For Further Review" section at the end of this chapter for a list of related topics you should be well-versed on before taking the test.) This chapter also includes a few practice questions to help you measure how well you understand the topic.

Bringing New Issues to the Market

A lot of things need to happen before securities hit the market. Not only do the securities have to be registered, but the issuer has to find a broker-dealer (like your firm) to sell the securities to the public. The Series 7 exam tests your expertise in answering questions about this process.

Starting out: What the issuer does

For an entity to become a corporation, the founders must file a document called a *corporate charter* (bylaws) in the home state of their business. Included in the corporate charter are the names of the founders, the type of business, the place of business, the number of shares that can be issued, and so on. If a corporation wants to sell securities to the public, it has to register with states and the Securities and Exchange Commission (SEC). Read on for info on how the registration process works.

The securities acts

Registration helps ensure that securities issued to the public adhere to certain regulations (though antifraud rules also apply to exempt securities). The following acts are designed to protect investors from unscrupulous issuers, firms, and salespeople (see Chapter 16 for details on other rules and regulations).

The Securities Act of 1933: This act — also called the Truth in Securities Act, the Paper Act, the Full Disclosure Act, the Prospectus Act, and the New Issues Act — regulates new issues of corporate securities. An issuer of corporate securities must provide full and fair disclosure about itself and the offering. Included in this act are rules to prevent fraud and deception.

The Securities Exchange Act of 1934: The Act of 1934, which established the SEC, was enacted to protect investors by regulating the over-the-counter (OTC) market and exchanges, such as the New York Stock Exchange (NYSE). (Chapter 14 can tell you more about markets.) In addition, the Act of 1934 regulates

- The extension of credit in margin accounts (see Chapter 9)
- Transactions by insiders
- Customer accounts
- Trading activities

The Trust Indenture Act of 1939: This act prohibits bond issues valued at over $5 million from being offered to investors without an indenture. The trust indenture is a written agreement that protects investors by disclosing the particulars of the issue (coupon rate, maturity date, any collateral backing the bond, and so on). As part of the Trust Indenture Act of 1939, all companies must hire a trustee who's responsible for protecting the rights of bondholders.

Registering securities with the SEC

When a company wants to go public (sell stock to public investors), it has to file a registration statement and a prospectus with the SEC.

The *registration statement* includes

- The issuer's name and a description of its business
- The names and addresses of all of the company's control persons, such as officers, directors, and anyone owning more than 10 percent of the corporation's securities
- What the proceeds of the sale will be used for
- The company's capitalization
- Complete financial statements
- Any legal proceedings against the corporation that may have an impact on it

For details regarding the prospectus, see "Getting the skinny on the issue and issuer: The prospectus" later in this chapter.

Blue skies: Registering with the states

All *blue sky laws,* or state laws that apply to security offerings and sales, say that in order to sell a security to a customer, the broker-dealer (brokerage firm), the registered representative, and the security must be registered in the customer's home state. The issuer is responsible for registering the security not only with the U.S. Securities and Exchange Commission (the SEC) but also in each state in which the securities are to be sold.

Here are the methods of state security registration:

- **Notification (registration by filing):** Notification is the simplest form of registration for established companies. Companies who have previously sold securities in a state can renew their previous application.
- **Coordination:** This method involves registering with the SEC and states at the same time. The SEC helps companies meet the blue sky laws by notifying all states in which the securities are to be sold.
- **Qualification:** Companies use this registration method for securities that are exempt from registration with the SEC but require registration with the state.

Role call: Introducing the team players

The following list explains who's involved in the securities registration and selling process. Registered reps can work for any of these firms:

- **Investment banking firm:** An *investment banking firm* is an institution (a broker-dealer) that's in the business of helping issuers raise money. You can think of investment bankers as the brains of the operation, because they help the issuer decide what securities to issue, how much to issue, the selling price, and so on. Not only do investment bankers advise issuers, but they usually underwrite the issue and may also become the managing underwriter in the offering of new securities.
- **Underwriter:** The *underwriter* is a broker-dealer that helps the issuer bring new securities to the public. Underwriters purchase the securities from the issuer and sell them to the public for a nice profit (yippee!).
- **Syndicate:** When an issue is too large for one firm to handle, the syndicate manager (managing underwriter) forms a syndicate to help sell the securities and relieve some of the financial burden on the managing underwriter. Each syndicate member is responsible for selling a portion of the securities to the public (see the upcoming section titled "Agreeing to sell your share: Western versus Eastern accounts" for details).
- **Managing (lead) underwriter:** The managing underwriter (syndicate manager) is the head firm that's responsible for putting together a syndicate and dealing directly with the issuer. The managing underwriter receives financial compensation (buckets-o-bucks) for each and every share sold.
- **Selling group:** In the event that the syndicate members feel they need more help selling the securities, they can recruit selling group members. These members are brokerage firms that aren't part of the syndicate. Selling group members help distribute shares to the public but don't make a financial commitment (that is, they don't purchase shares from the issuer) and therefore receive less money per share when selling shares to the public.

Who gets what: Distributing the profits

When larger issues come to market, the lead underwriter often has to form a syndicate to help sell the securities. When selling the securities to the public, each entity (the lead underwriter, syndicate members, selling group members, and so on — see the preceding section) receives a different portion of the selling profits.

The *spread* is the difference between the amount the syndicate pays the issuer when purchasing new shares or bonds and the public offering price for each share or bond sold. For example, if the syndicate buys shares from the issuer at $8.00 per share and then turns around and sells them to the public for $9.00 per share, the spread is $1.00 ($9.00 – $8.00). Naturally, you get the following formula:

spread = public offering price – price paid to the issuer

So the spread is just the initial profit from selling the security; you still have to divvy it up among the salespeople. The syndicate splits the spread into the manager's fee and the takedown, so you get the following equation:

spread = syndicate manager's fee + takedown

Here's what you need to know about the manager's fee and the takedown:

- **Takedown:** The *takedown* is the profit that each syndicate member makes when selling shares or bonds to the public. Remember that the syndicate members are the ones taking the financial risk and therefore deserve the lion's share of the sale's proceeds. You can use the spread formula (spread = syndicate manager's fee + takedown) to calculate this value, rearranging the terms like this: takedown = spread – syndicate manager's fee. For example, if the spread is $1.00 and the manager's fee is $0.15, the takedown is $0.85 ($1.00 – $0.15). The takedown may be further broken down as follows:
    - **Concession:** The *concession* is the profit that the selling group makes when selling shares or bonds to the public. Selling group members don't step up to the plate financially and therefore don't receive as much of the sale's proceeds as syndicate members do. The concession is paid out of the takedown. The profit made by syndicate members on shares or bonds sold by the selling group is called the *additional takedown.* The formula looks like this:

      takedown = additional takedown + concession
    - **Reallowance:** The portion of the takedown that's available for firms that aren't part of the syndicate or selling group is the *reallowance.* For example, assume ABC Corporation is in the process of issuing new shares. You're a stockbroker, and one of your customers calls you up to let you know that she's interested in purchasing shares of ABC Corporation from you, but you're not one of the official distributors of the stock. No sweat. You contact the syndicate manager, who gives you a discount off the public offering price (POP). That discount is the reallowance.
- **Syndicate manager's fee:** This part of the spread is the profit the syndicate manager makes on shares or bonds sold by anyone. This fee is usually the smallest of all the listed fees.

The following question tests your knowledge of distribution of profits.

Nogo Auto Corp., which specializes in fuel-efficient cars, is in the process of selling new shares of their company to the public. Nogo contacts Thor Broker-Dealer Corp. to underwrite the securities. Thor realizes that the issue is too big to underwrite by itself, so it forms a syndicate. Nogo will receive $15.00 per share for each share issued and the public offering price will be $16.20. If the manager's fee is $0.25 per share and the concession is $0.40 per share, what is the additional takedown?

(A) $0.55

(B) $0.80

(C) $0.95

(D) $1.20

The correct answer is Choice (A). This question is a little tricky because you have to determine the takedown (the profit syndicate members make) before you can figure out the additional takedown. The additional takedown is the profit syndicate members make on shares sold by the selling group. The spread of $1.20 ($16.20 selling price – $15.00 to Nogo) is made up of the manager's fee of $0.25 and the takedown of $0.95 ($1.20 spread – $0.25 manager's fee). If the syndicate members had sold the shares by themselves, they would have received the takedown of $0.95 per share. However, the selling group sold the shares, receiving a concession of $0.40 per share. The concession is paid out of the takedown; thus, the additional takedown is $0.55 per share ($0.95 – $0.40).

Agreeing to sell your share: Western versus Eastern accounts

The *syndicate agreement,* also called the *agreement among underwriters,* is the contract among syndicate members. This agreement includes the fee structure (who gets what — see the preceding section). In addition to the bucks that each member of the syndicate gets when selling shares or bonds, the syndicate agreement lays out each syndicate member's amount of commitment (how many shares or bonds each party will sell). The syndicate manager can set up underwritings on a Western or Eastern account basis:

- **Western (divided) account:** In this securities underwriting, the syndicate agreement states that each syndicate member is responsible only for the shares or bonds originally allocated to it. If a syndicate member commits to selling 500,000 shares and sells them all, the syndicate member doesn't have to sell any more.

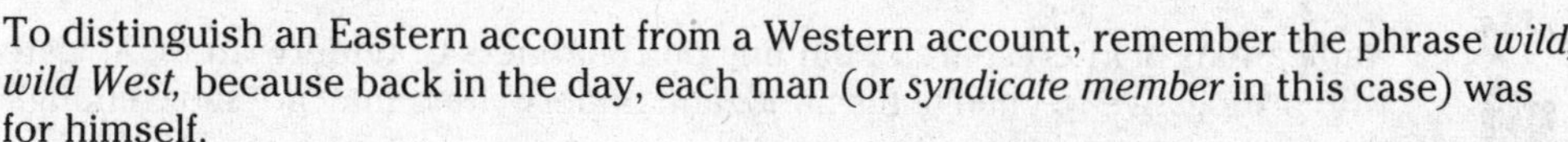

To distinguish an Eastern account from a Western account, remember the phrase *wild, wild West,* because back in the day, each man (or *syndicate member* in this case) was for himself.

- **Eastern (undivided) account:** In this securities underwriting, the syndicate agreement states that each syndicate member is responsible not only for the shares or bonds originally allocated to it but also for a portion of the shares or bonds left unsold by other (apparently less aggressive) members. A syndicate member that's originally responsible for 10 percent of the new issue is responsible for 10 percent of the shares or bonds left unsold by other members as well.

The following question tests your knowledge of Eastern and Western accounts.

A syndicate is underwriting $5,000,000 worth of municipal general obligation bonds. There are 10 syndicate members, each with an equal participation. Firm A, which is part of the syndicate, sells its entire allotment. However, $1,000,000 worth of bonds remain unsold by other members of the syndicate. If the syndicate agreement was set up on an Eastern account basis, what is Firm A's responsibility regarding the unsold bonds?

(A) No responsibility

(B) $100,000 worth of bonds

(C) $200,000 worth of bonds

(D) $1,000,000 worth of bonds

The right answer is Choice (B). Your key to this question is that the underwriting was done on an Eastern account basis. On an Eastern account basis, the underwriters (because they're so nice) have to help the slackers sell any shares of unsold bonds. Firm A sold all its bonds, so it has to help sell the remaining bonds that the other syndicate members didn't sell. Firm A's responsibility is in proportion to its original responsibility. Because it was responsible for 10 percent of the original issue (10 syndicate members with equal participation), it's responsible for selling 10 percent of the unsold bonds:

10% × $1,000,000 of unsold bonds = $100,000 worth of bonds

If the underwriting had been on a Western account basis, the correct answer would have been Choice (A).

Registering the securities

Unless the securities are exempt from registration (see "Exempt Securities" later in this chapter), the issuer has to go through a registration process with the SEC. The Series 7 tests you on the following items that relate to securities registration.

Cooling-off period

After the issuer files a registration statement (the filing date) with the SEC, a 20-day cooling-off period begins. During the 20-day (and often longer) cooling-off period, the good old SEC reviews the registration statement. At the end of the cooling-off period, the issue will (hopefully) be cleared for sale to the public (the effective date of registration).

During the cooling-off period, the underwriter (or underwriters) can obtain indications of interest from investors who may want to purchase the issue. Registered reps (like you in the not-too-distant future) scramble to get indications of interest from prospective purchasers of the securities.

Indications of interest aren't binding on customers or underwriters. A customer always has the prerogative to change his mind, and underwriters may not have enough shares available to meet everyone's needs.

A *tombstone ad* — a newspaper ad that's shaped like a, well, tombstone (it's rectangular with black borders) — is simply an announcement (but not an offer) of a new security for sale. It's the only advertisement allowed during the cooling-off period. These ads contain just a simple statement of facts about the new issue (for example, the issuer, type of security, amount of shares or bonds available, underwriter's name, and so on). In addition, tombstone ads often provide investors with information about how to obtain a prospectus. Tombstone ads are optional.

Underwriters and selling group members use the preliminary prospectus to obtain indications of interest from prospective customers. The preliminary prospectus must be made available to all customers who are interested in the new issue during the cooling-off period. I talk more about what that prospectus has to include in the section "Getting the skinny on the issue and issuer: The prospectus" a little later in this chapter.

Due diligence meeting

Toward the end of the cooling-off period, the underwriter holds a due diligence meeting. During this meeting, the underwriter provides information about the issue and what the issuer will use the proceeds of the sale for. This meeting is designed to provide such information to syndicate members, selling groups, brokers, analysts, institutions, and so on.

The last time syndicate members can back out of an underwriting agreement is toward the end of the cooling-off period (around the time of the due diligence meeting). You can assume that if syndicate members are backing out, it's most likely due to negative market conditions.

Getting the skinny on the issue and issuer: The prospectus

The issuer prepares a preliminary prospectus (sometimes with the help of the underwriter) that's sent in with the registration statement. The preliminary prospectus must be available for potential purchasers when the issue is in registration (during the cooling-off period) with the SEC. The preliminary prospectus is abbreviated, but it contains all the essential facts about the issuer and issue except for the final offering price (public offering price, or POP) and the *effective date* (the date that the issue will first be sold).

A preliminary prospectus is sometimes called a *red herring,* not because it smells fishy (or is totally misleading and irrelevant) but because a statement in red lettering on the cover of the preliminary prospectus declares that it's not the final version and that some items may change in the meantime.

The *final prospectus,* which is prepared toward the end of the cooling-off period, is a legal document that the issuer prepares; it contains material information about the issuer and new issue of securities. The final prospectus has to be available to all potential purchasers of the issue. It includes

- The final offering price
- The underwriter's spread (the profit the underwriters make per share)
- The delivery date (when the securities will be available)

Note: Because all mutual (open-end) funds constantly issue new securities, they must always have a prospectus available. In addition, many mutual funds also provide a *statement of additional information (SAI),* which provides more detailed information about the fund's operation that may be useful to some investors. A statement of additional information is also known as "Part B" of a fund's registration statement.

Counting the securities along the way

When a company issues securities and they're traded in the market, someone has to be responsible for keeping track of the owners of the securities, and someone has to make sure that the number of securities in the market isn't greater than it's supposed to be. These jobs are assigned to a registrar and a transfer agent:

- **Registrar:** The *registrar* is an independent entity that works along with a company's transfer agent to maintain a record of stock and bond owners. The main function of a registrar is to make sure that the outstanding shares don't exceed the amount of stock the issuer authorizes under its corporate *charter* (or *bylaws,* rules the company lives by).
- **Transfer agent:** The *transfer agent* maintains records of a corporation's stock and bond owners (much like a registrar) but also mails and cancels stock certificates as necessary.

An easy way to keep these folks straight is to remember that a registrar is responsible for counting things and a transfer agent is responsible for transferring or sending things.

Getting Up to Speed on the Types of Securities Offerings

Table 5-1 deals with the different types of offerings that you (as a mega-broker) should be familiar with. The offerings that follow usually require the services of an underwriter or underwriting syndicate to sell the securities to the public.

Table 5-1 Types of Securities Offerings

Type	*Description*	*Who Profits*
Initial public offering (IPO)	The first time an issuer sells stock to the public to raise capital; issuers usually hold back some stock for future primary offerings.	The bulk of the moolah raised goes to the issuer, and the rest goes to the underwriters.
Primary offering	An offering of new securities from an issuer that has previously issued securities; a company can have an initial public offering and several primary offerings if it wants to.	The proceeds of sale go to the issuer and underwriters.
Secondary offering	A sale of a large block of outstanding (stockholder-owned) securities or previously outstanding securities (treasury stock, or stock the issuer has repurchased); typically, one or more major stockholders of a corporation are the ones who make the secondary offerings; new investors are essentially buying used, so the number of shares outstanding doesn't change.	The sales proceeds don't go to the issuer (except with treasury stock); they go to the big shots selling the securities.
Split (combined) offering	A combination of a primary and secondary offering, with both new and outstanding securities.	A portion of the sales proceeds goes to the issuer, and a portion goes to the selling stockholders.

For initial public offerings (IPOs), a final prospectus needs to be available to all purchasers of the IPO for 90 days after the *effective date* (the first day the security starts trading).

With primary, secondary, or combined offerings, a final prospectus has to be available to all purchasers of the primary offering for 25 days after the effective date for all issuers whose securities are already listed on an exchange or NASDAQ. If an issuer has already issued securities but not on an exchange or NASDAQ, the final prospectus has to be available for 40 days after the effective date.

The following question tests your knowledge on the types of offerings, whether new or outstanding.

DEF Corp. is offering 2,000,000 shares of its common stock to the public; 1,500,000 shares are authorized but previously unissued, and insiders of the company are selling the other 500,000 shares. Which of the following are TRUE about this offering?

I. The EPS of DEF will increase.

II. The EPS of DEF will decrease.

III. The number of outstanding shares will increase by 500,000.

IV. The number of outstanding shares will increase by 1,500,000.

(A) I and III

(B) I and IV

(C) II and III

(D) II and IV

The answer you're looking for is Choice (D). This offering is a combined, or split, offering. The 1,500,000 shares that were previously unissued are a primary offering, and the 500,000 shares held by insiders are a secondary offering. Answering this question correctly requires a little bit of deduction on your part. You first have to note that unissued shares aren't considered part of the outstanding shares (because for stockholders, owning the shares before they're even offered would be a pretty impressive feat!). Because 1,500,000 shares were previously unissued (kept by the company for future use), the number of outstanding shares will increase by that amount. When considering whether the earnings per share (EPS) will increase or decrease, you can assume that the company earns the same amount of money. Now that same amount of money has to be divided among 1,500,000 more shares. Therefore, you deduce that the EPS will decrease, not increase.

Reviewing Exemptions

Certain securities are exempt from registration because of either the type of security or the type of transaction involved. You may find that securities that are exempt because of who's issuing them are a bit easier to recognize. You'll probably have to spend a little more time on the securities that are exempt from registration because of the type of transaction.

Exempt securities

Certain securities are exempt from the registration requirements under the Securities Act of 1933. Either these securities come from issuers that have a high level of creditworthiness, or another government regulatory agency has some sort of jurisdiction over the issuer of the securities. These types of securities include

- Securities issued by the U.S. government or federal agencies
- Municipal bonds (local government bonds)
- Securities issued by banks, savings institutions, and credit unions
- Public utility stocks or bonds
- Securities issued by religious, educational, or nonprofit organizations

- Notes, bills of exchange, bankers' acceptances, and commercial paper with an initial maturity of 270 days or less
- Insurance policies and fixed annuities

Fixed annuities are exempt from SEC registration because the issuing insurance company guarantees the payout. However, variable annuities require registration because the payout varies depending on the performance of the securities held in the separate account. For more info on annuities and other packaged securities, see Chapter 10.

Exempt transactions

Some securities that corporations offer may be exempt from the full registration requirements of the Securities Act of 1933 due to the nature of the sale. The following list shows you these exemptions:

- **Intrastate offerings (Section 3[a][11] and Rule 147):** An intrastate offering is, naturally, an offering of securities within one state. For such an offering to be exempt from SEC registration, the company must be incorporated in the state in which it's selling securities, 80 percent of its business has to be within the state, and it may sell securities only to residents of the state. The securities still require registration at the state level.

  Don't confuse *intra*state offerings (securities sold in one state) with *inter*state offerings (securities sold in many states). *Inter*state offerings do need SEC registration. To help you remember, think of an interstate roadway, which continues from one state to the next.
- **Regulation A (Reg A) offerings:** An offering of securities worth $5 million or less within a 12-month period is Regulation A. Although this company may seem large to you, it's relatively small in market terms. Regulation A offerings are exempt from the full registration requirements but the issuer still has to file a simplified registration or abbreviated registration statement.
- **Regulation D (Reg D) offerings:** Also known as a private placement, a Regulation D offering is an offering to no more than 35 unaccredited investors per year. Companies who issue securities through private placement are allowed to raise an unlimited amount of money but are limited in terms of the number of unaccredited investors. Sales of Reg D securities are subject to the sales limitations set forth under Rule 144.

  An *accredited investor* is one with a net worth of $1 million or more or an investor who has had a yearly income of at least $200,000 (for an individual investor) or $300,000 (for joint income with spouse) for the previous two years and is expected to earn at least that much in the current year.
- **Rule 144:** This rule covers the sale of restricted, unregistered, and control securities. According to Rule 144, sellers of these securities must wait anywhere from 6 months to a year, depending on whether the corporation that issued the securities is subject to the reporting requirements of the Securities Exchange Act of 1934 prior to selling the securities to the public. Additionally, the most an investor can sell at one time is 1 percent of the outstanding shares or the average weekly trading volume for the previous four weeks, whichever is greater.

The following example tests your ability to answer restricted-stock questions.

John Bullini is a control person who purchased shares of restricted stock and wants to sell under Rule 144. John has fully paid for the shares and has held them for over one year. There are 1,500,000 shares outstanding. Form 144 is filed on Monday, May 28, and the weekly trading volume for the restricted stock is as follows:

Week Ending	*Trading Volume*
May 25	16,000 shares
May 18	15,000 shares
May 11	17,000 shares
May 4	15,000 shares
April 27	18,000 shares

What is the maximum number of shares John can sell with this filing?

(A) 15,000

(B) 15,750

(C) 16,200

(D) 16,250

The right answer is Choice (B). The test writers often try to trick you on the Series 7 exam by giving you at least one week more than you need to answer the question. Because John has held his restricted stock for over a year, he can sell 1 percent of the outstanding shares or the averaged weekly trading volume for the previous four weeks, whichever is greater:

$$1\% \times 1{,}500{,}000 \text{ shares outstanding} = 15{,}000 \text{ shares}$$

$$\frac{16{,}000+15{,}000+17{,}000+15{,}000}{4 \text{ weeks}} = \frac{63{,}000}{4 \text{ weeks}} = 15{,}750 \text{ shares}$$

In this case, the previous four weeks are the top four in the list, but be careful; the examiners are just as likely to use the bottom four to give the table a different look.

Figure out 1 percent of the outstanding shares by multiplying the outstanding shares by 1 percent (easy, right?). In this case, you come up with an answer of 15,000 shares. That's one possible answer. The other possible answer is the average weekly trading volume for the previous four weeks. Add the trading volume for the previous four weeks (the top four in the chart) and divide by 4 to get an answer of 15,750 shares. Because you're looking for the greater number, the answer is Choice (B).

Even securities exempt from registration are subject to antifraud rules. All securities are subject to antifraud provisions of the Securities Act of 1933, which requires issuers to provide accurate information regarding any securities offered to the public.

For Further Review

To be properly prepared for the Series 7, you need to know the information in this chapter and have a good handle on the following terms and ideas related to underwriting securities:

- Negotiated versus competitive underwritings
- Firm commitment, all or none, mini-max, and best efforts underwritings
- Shelf offering Rule 415

- Deficiency letter
- Stabilizing price
- Penalty bid
- Pegging
- Market-out clause
- SEA Rule 144A
- Rule 145
- FINRA Rule 5130
- Regulation S
- Qualified institutional buyer (QIB)
- Chinese wall doctrine
- Seasoned issuer
- Allocation of orders
- Items in the registration form

Chapter 6

Corporate Ownership: Equity Securities

In This Chapter

- Understanding the types of equity securities
- Comparing common stock to preferred stock
- Calculating certain values for stock questions
- Reviewing related topics tested

Equity securities — such as common and preferred stock — represent ownership interest in the issuing company. All publicly held corporations issue equity securities to investors. Investors love these securities because they've historically outperformed most other investments, so an average (or above-average, in your case) stockbroker sells more of these types of securities than any other kind.

The Series 7 exam tests you on your ability to recognize the types of equity securities and on some other basic information. Although you may find that the Series 7 doesn't test you heavily on the info provided here, this chapter forms a strong foundation for many other chapters in the book. I think that you'll find it difficult (if not impossible) to understand what an option or mutual fund is if you don't know what a stock is. Needless to say, even though this chapter is small, don't ignore it or it may come back to bite you.

In this chapter, I cover the Series 7 exam topics that are the most tested and most difficult to understand relating to company ownership. (Check out the "For Further Review" section at the end of this chapter for a list of related topics not covered in this chapter that you should know before you take the test.) This chapter also gives you plenty of examples to familiarize you with the types of equities securities questions on the Series 7 exam.

Beginning with the Basics: Common Stock

Corporations issue common stock (as well as other securities) to raise business capital. As an equity security, common stock represents ownership of the issuing corporation. If a corporation issues 1 million shares of stock, each share represents one-millionth ownership of the issuing corporation. Read on for the ins and outs of common stock.

Understanding a stockholder's voting rights

One of the most basic rights that most common stockholders receive is voting rights — although rarely corporations issue *nonvoting common stock*. Nonvoting stock may be issued by corporations to protect their board of directors, but it's not as attractive to investors who like to have some control over who's running the company. Most preferred stock is nonvoting.

When investors have voting rights, every so often a corporation may have those investors vote to change members on the board of directors. Although investors may be able to vote on other issues (like stock splits —see "Splitting common stock" later in this chapter), the Series 7 focuses on voting to change board members.

Because having all stockholders actually attend the annual corporate meeting to vote would be difficult, stockholders usually vote by *proxy,* or absentee ballot.

Statutory (regular) voting

Statutory, or regular, voting is the most common type of voting that corporations offer to their shareholders. This type of voting is quite straightforward. Investors receive one vote for every share that they own multiplied by the number of positions to be filled on the board of directors (or issues to be decided). However, investors have to *split the votes evenly* for each item on the ballot.

For example, if an investor owns 500 shares and there are four positions to be filled on the board of directors, the investor has a total of 2,000 votes (500 shares × 4 candidates), which the investor must split evenly among all open positions (500 each). The investor votes yes or no for each candidate.

Cumulative voting

Cumulative voting is a little different from statutory voting (see the preceding section). Although the investor still gets the same number of overall votes as if the corporation were offering statutory voting, the stockholder can vote the shares in any way she sees fit. Cumulative voting gives smaller shareholders (in terms of shares) an easier chance to gain representation on the board of directors.

For example, if an investor owns 1,000 shares and three positions on the board of directors are open, the investor has a total of 3,000 votes (1,000 shares × 3 candidates), which the investor can use to vote for any candidate(s) in any way she sees fit.

Cumulative voting doesn't give an investor more voting power, just more voting flexibility. The only way to get more voting power is to buy more shares.

The following question tests your ability to answer a cumulative voting question.

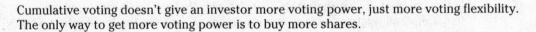

Bella Bearishnikoff owns 800 shares of CBA common stock. It is time for CBA to hold its annual shareholders' meeting, and there are four candidates for the board of directors. CBA offers its shareholders cumulative voting. Which of the following are acceptable votes from Bella?

I. 800 votes for each of the four candidates

II. 2,000 votes for one candidate and 400 votes for each of the other candidates

III. 3,200 votes for one candidate

IV. 3,200 votes for each of the candidates

(A) I only

(B) II and III

(C) I, II, and III

(D) I, III, and IV

The correct answer is Choice (C). Ms. Bearishnikoff has a total of 3,200 votes (800 shares × 4 candidates). Because CBA offers cumulative voting, she can vote the 3,200 votes in any way she likes. Statements I, II, and III are all correct because none of those choices require more than 3,200 votes. However, IV would require 12,800 votes. As a side note, if the question had asked about statutory voting, the answer would have been Choice (A).

Categorizing shares corporations can sell

All publicly held corporations have a certain quantity of shares that they can sell based on their corporate charter. These shares are broken down into a few categories depending on whether the issuer or investors hold the shares:

- **Authorized shares:** Authorized shares are the number of shares of stock that a corporation can issue. The issuer's bylaws or *corporate charter* (a document filed with the state that identifies the names of the founders of the corporation, the company's objectives, and so on) states the number of shares the company is authorized to sell. However, the issuer usually holds back a large percentage of the authorized stock (which it can sell later through a primary offering — see Chapter 5 for details on offerings).
- **Issued shares:** Issued shares are the portion of authorized shares that the issuer has sold to the public to raise money.
- **Outstanding shares:** Outstanding shares are the number of shares that are in investors' hands. This quantity may or may not be the same number as the issued shares. At times, an issuer may decide to repurchase its stock in the market to either help increase the demand (and the price) of the stock trading in the market or to avoid a *hostile takeover* (when another company is trying to gain control of the issuer). Stock that the issuer repurchases is called *treasury stock.*

  The standard formula for outstanding shares follows:

  $$\text{outstanding shares} = \text{issued shares} - \text{treasury stock}$$

The following question tests your understanding of outstanding shares.

ZZZ Bedding Corp. is authorized to issue 2,000,000 shares of common stock. However, ZZZ issues only 800,000 shares to the public. One year later, ZZZ repurchases 150,000 shares to increase the demand on the outstanding shares. How many shares does ZZZ have outstanding?

(A) 650,000

(B) 800,000

(C) 1,200,000

(D) 1,850,000

The right answer is Choice (A). You probably didn't have too much difficulty with this one. All the question is asking is how many shares are still outstanding in the market. Check out the following equation:

$$\text{outstanding} = \text{issued} - \text{treasury}$$
$$= 800{,}000 - 150{,}000$$
$$= 650{,}000$$

Because ZZZ issued only 800,000 shares of the 2,000,000 that it's authorized to issue, the most ZZZ ever had in the market was 800,000. However, a year after issuing those shares, ZZZ repurchased 150,000 shares, giving the company treasury stock. Therefore, the amount of outstanding shares is 650,000.

Considering the par value of common stock

Par value for common stock is not as important to investors as it is to bondholders and preferred stockholders (see the later section "Considering characteristics of preferred stock"). *Par value* for common stock is more or less a bookkeeping value for the issuer. Although issuers may set the par value at $1 (or $5, $10, or whatever), the selling price is usually much more. A stock's par value has no relation to the market price of the stock.

The amount over par value that an issuer receives for selling stock is called *paid-in capital, paid-in surplus,* or *capital surplus.*

The *stated par value* is printed on the stock certificate; it changes if the issuer splits its stock (see the next section). An issuer can also issue *no par value stock* (stock issued without a stated par value); in this case, the stock has a stated value that the corporation uses for bookkeeping purposes. A lack of par value doesn't affect investors.

Splitting common stock

You may ask yourself, "Why would a company split its stock?" The obvious answer is that the company wants to make the market price of the security more attractive. The normal unit of trading is 100 shares of stock (*a round lot*) and if the price of a security gets too high, the number of investors who can purchase it becomes limited. If Microsoft had never split its stock (which it has already done nine times), a round lot would cost investors about $750,000 at the time of this writing. Know a lot of investors who could afford that?

Companies may alternatively use a reverse split, consolidating shares so they can raise the price of the stock and perhaps boost investor confidence. The next couple of sections take you through splits so you know them forward and backward.

Stockholders can vote on stock splits (please see "Understanding a stockholder's voting rights" earlier in the chapter for info on types of voting). Be aware that after a stock split, investors may have more or fewer votes, but they still hold the same percentage of votes. When a company splits its stock, the number of authorized shares needs to be changed on the *corporate charter* (see the earlier section "Categorizing shares corporations can sell").

Forward splits

During a *forward stock split,* the number of shares increases and the price decreases without affecting the total market value of the outstanding shares. After a company forward splits its stock, investors receive additional shares, but the market price (and par value) per share drops. A forward split may be a 2-for-1, a 3-for-1, a 3-for-2, and so on, where A represents the first number and B represents the second number.

Use the following calculations to figure out an investor's position after an A-for-B split:

$$\text{shares after split} = \text{shares} \times \frac{A}{B}$$

$$\text{price after split} = \text{stock price} \times \frac{B}{A}$$

The following question tests your ability to answer a stock split question.

Bob Billingham owns 1,200 shares of DEF common stock at a current market price of $90 per share. If DEF splits its stock 3-for-1, what would Bob's position be after the split?

(A) 400 shares at $270 per share

(B) 400 shares at $90 per share

(C) 3,600 shares at $33.33 per share

(D) 3,600 shares at $30 per share

The answer you're looking for is Choice (D). A forward stock split, like a 3-for-1, increases the number of shares and decreases the price of the stock, so you can immediately cross off Choices (A) and (B). Now check your work:

$$1{,}200 \text{ shares} \times \frac{3}{1} = 3{,}600 \text{ shares}$$

$$\$90 \times \frac{1}{3} = \$30$$

A good way to double check your work is to make sure that the overall value of the investment doesn't change after the split. Using the example, Bob had $108,000 worth of DEF (1,200 shares × $90) before the split, and after the split he has $108,000 worth of DEF (3,600 shares × $30).

Reverse splits

A reverse stock split has the opposite effect on a security than a forward split does; with a reverse split, the market price of the security increases and the number of shares decreases. As with forward stock splits, the overall market value of the securities doesn't change. A company may reverse split its stock if the market price gets too low, whereby potential investors may think the company has a problem.

In the event of a reverse split, investors usually have to send in their old shares to the transfer agent to receive the new shares. If a company were executing a 1-for-3 reverse split, investors would receive one new share for every three they sent in.

You can use the same formula to determine an investor's position after a reverse split that you use for forward splits.

The following question tests your ability to answer a reverse stock split question.

Betty Billings owns 3,600 shares of GHI common stock at a current market price of $2 per share. If GHI reverse splits its stock 1-for-5, what would Betty's position be after the split?

(A) 600 shares at $10 per share

(B) 720 shares at $10 per share

(C) 18,000 shares at $0.40 per share

(D) 18,000 shares at $10 per share

The correct answer is Choice (B). With a reverse split, the number of shares has to decrease and the price has to increase, so you can immediately eliminate Choices (C) and (D). Check your work:

$$3{,}600 \text{ shares} \times \frac{1}{5} = 720 \text{ shares}$$

$$\$2 \times \frac{5}{1} = \$10$$

Sharing corporate profits through dividends

If a corporation is profitable (and the board of directors is in a good mood), the board of directors may decide to issue a dividend to investors. If and/or when the corporation declares a dividend, each shareholder is entitled to a *pro rata* share of dividends, meaning that every shareholder receives an equal proportion for each share that she owns. The Series 7 exam expects you to know the forms of dividends an investor can receive and how the dividends affect both the market price of the stock and an investor's position. Although the investor can receive dividends in cash, stock, or *property forms* (stock of a subsidiary company or sample products made by the issuer), I focus on cash and stock dividends because those scenarios are more likely.

Investors can't vote on dividends; instead, the board of directors decides dividend payouts. You can imagine that if this decision were left in the investor's hands, they'd vote for dividends weekly! For more info on voting, see "Understanding a stockholder's voting rights," earlier in this chapter.

Cash dividends

Cash dividends are a way for a corporation to share its profits with shareholders. When an investor receives cash dividends, it's a taxable event. Corporations aren't required to pay dividends; however, dividends provide a good incentive for investors to hold onto stock that isn't experiencing much growth. Although cash dividends are nice, the market price of the stock falls on the *ex-dividend date* (the first day the stock trades without a dividend) to reflect the dividend paid:

stock price – dividend = price on ex-dividend date

Try your hand at answering a cash dividend question.

ABC stock is trading for $49.50 on the day prior to the ex-dividend date. If ABC previously announced a $0.75 dividend, what will be the next day's opening price?

(A) $48.25

(B) $48.75

(C) $49.50

(D) $50.25

The correct answer is Choice (B). Check your work:

$49.50 – $0.75 = $48.75

The math's as simple as that. Because stocks are now trading in pennies instead of eighths like they used to, calculating the price on the ex-dividend date is a snap.

Stock dividends

Stock dividends are just like forward stock splits in that the investor receives more shares of stock (see the earlier section "Splitting common stock"), only the corporation gives a percentage dividend (5 percent, 10 percent, and so on) instead of splitting the stock 2-for-1, 3-for-1, or whatever. Unlike cash dividends, stock dividends aren't taxable to the stockholder because the investor's overall value of investment doesn't change.

The primary reason for a company to give investors a stock dividend is to make the market price more attractive to investors (if the market price gets too high, it limits the number of investors who can purchase the stock), thus adding *liquidity* (ease of trading) to the stock.

The following question tests your expertise in answering stock dividend questions.

Terry Trader owns 400 shares of OXX common stock at $33 per share. OXX previously declared a 10 percent stock dividend. Assuming no change in the market price of OXX prior to the dividend, what is Terry's position after the dividend?

(A) 400 shares at $30

(B) 440 shares at $33

(C) 400 shares at $36.30

(D) 440 shares at $30

The answer you want is Choice (D). In this case, you can find the answer without doing any math. Because the number of shares increases, the price of the stock has to decrease. Therefore, the only answer that works is Choice (D). I can't guarantee that you'll get a question where you don't have to do the math, but don't rule it out; scan the answer choices before pulling out your calculator.

Anyway, here's how the numbers work. You have to remember that the investor's overall value of investment doesn't change. Terry gets a 10 percent stock dividend, so she receives 10 percent more shares. Now Terry has 440 shares of OXX (400 shares + 40 shares [10 percent of 400]). Next, you need to determine her overall value of investment:

$$400 \text{ shares} \times \$33 = \$13{,}200$$

Because the overall value of investment doesn't change, Terry needs to have $13,200 worth of OXX after the dividend:

$$\frac{\$13{,}200}{440 \text{ shares}} = \$30 \text{ per share}$$

Terry's position after the split is 440 shares at $30 per share.

Getting Preferential Treatment: Preferred Stock

Equity securities represent shares of ownership in a company, and debt securities, well, represent debt (see Chapters 7 and 8 for info on debt securities). Although preferred stock has some characteristics of both equity and debt securities, preferred stock is an equity security because it represents ownership of the issuing corporation the same way that common stock does.

Considering characteristics of preferred stock

One advantage of purchasing preferred stock over common stock is that preferred shareholders receive money back (if there's any left) before common stockholders do if the issuer declares bankruptcy. However, the main difference between preferred stock and common stock has to do with dividends. Issuers of common stock pay a cash dividend only if the company's in a position to share corporate profits. By contrast, issuers of preferred stock are required to pay consistent cash dividends. Preferred stock generally has a par value of $100 per share and tends to trade in the market somewhere close to that par value.

Some of the drawbacks of investing in preferred stock over common stock are the lack of voting rights, the higher cost per share (usually), and limited growth. You can assume for

Series 7 exam purposes that preferred stockholders don't receive voting rights unless they fail to receive their expected dividends (a few other exceptions exist, but you don't need to worry about them now). Also, because the price of preferred stock remains relatively stable, preferred stockholders may miss out on potential gains that common stockholders may realize.

If the issuer can't make a payment because earnings are low, then in most cases, owners of preferred stock are still owed the missing dividend payment(s). The dividend (sharing of profits) that preferred stockholders receive is based on par value. Thus, although par value may be nothing more than a bookkeeping value when you're dealing with common stock, par value is definitely important to preferred stockholders.

To calculate the annual dividend, multiply the percentage of the dividend by the par value. For instance, if a customer owns a preferred stock that pays an 8 percent dividend and the par value is $100, you set up the following equation:

8% preferred stock × $100 par = $8 per year in dividends

If the issuer were to pay this dividend quarterly (once every three months), an investor would receive $2 every three months.

When working on a dividend question on preferred stock, you need to look for the par value in the problem. It's normally $100, but it could be $25, $50, and so on.

Getting familiar with types of preferred stock

You need to be aware of several types of preferred stock for the Series 7. This section gives you a brief explanation of the types and some of their characteristics. Some preferred stock may be a combination of the different types, as in cumulative convertible preferred stock. Here are the distinctions between noncumulative and cumulative preferred stock:

- **Noncumulative (straight) preferred:** This type of preferred stock is rare. The main feature of preferred stock is that investors receive a consistent cash dividend. In the event that the issuer doesn't pay the dividend, the company usually still owes it to investors. This isn't the case for noncumulative preferred stock. If the preferred stock is noncumulative and the issuer fails to pay a dividend, the issuer doesn't owe it to investors. An investor may choose noncumulative preferred stock over common stock because the company is still supposed to pay a consistent cash dividend.
- **Cumulative preferred:** Cumulative preferred stock is more common. If an investor owns cumulative preferred stock and doesn't receive an expected dividend, the issuer still owes that dividend. If the issuer declares a common dividend, the issuer first has to make up all delinquent payments to cumulative preferred stockholders.

The following question tests your understanding of cumulative preferred stock.

An investor owns ABC 8 percent cumulative preferred stock ($100 par). In the first year, ABC paid $6 in dividends. In the second year, it paid $4 in dividends. If a common dividend is declared the following year, how much must the preferred shareholders receive?

(A) $6

(B) $8

(C) $12

(D) $14

The right answer is Choice (D). Because ABC is cumulative preferred stock, issuers have to catch up preferred stockholders on all outstanding dividends before common shareholders receive a dividend. In this example, the investor is supposed to receive \$8 per year in dividends (8% × \$100 par). In the first year, the issuer shorted the investor \$2; in the second year, \$4. The investor hasn't yet received payment for the following year, so she is owed \$8. Add up these debts:

$$(\$8 - \$6) + (\$8 - \$4) + \$8 = \$2 + \$4 + \$8 = \$14$$

All preferred stock has to be either cumulative or noncumulative. Both types may have other features, including the ability to turn into other kinds of stock, offerings of extra dividends, and other VIP treatment. I run through some of these traits in the list that follows:

- **Convertible preferred:** Convertible preferred stock allows investors to trade their preferred stock for common stock of the same company at any time. Because the issuers are providing investors with another way to make money, investors usually receive a lower dividend payment than with regular preferred stock.

  The *conversion price* is the dollar price at which a convertible preferred stock par value can be exchanged into a share of common stock. When the convertible preferred stock is first issued, the conversion price is specified and is based on par value. The *conversion ratio* tells you the number of shares of common stock that an investor receives for converting one share of preferred stock.

  You can use the following conversion ratio formula for convertible preferred stock and also for convertible bonds (see Chapter 7 for info on convertible bonds):

  $$\text{conversion ratio} = \frac{\text{par value}}{\text{conversion price}}$$

  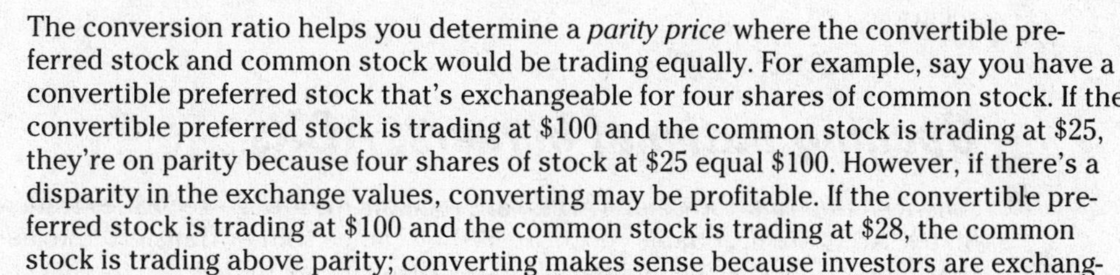

  The conversion ratio helps you determine a *parity price* where the convertible preferred stock and common stock would be trading equally. For example, say you have a convertible preferred stock that's exchangeable for four shares of common stock. If the convertible preferred stock is trading at \$100 and the common stock is trading at \$25, they're on parity because four shares of stock at \$25 equal \$100. However, if there's a disparity in the exchange values, converting may be profitable. If the convertible preferred stock is trading at \$100 and the common stock is trading at \$28, the common stock is trading above parity; converting makes sense because investors are exchanging \$100 worth of securities for \$112 worth of securities (\$28 × 4).

- **Callable preferred:** Callable preferred stock allows the issuer to buy back the preferred stock at any time at a price on the certificate. This stock is a little riskier for investors because they don't have control over how long they can hold the stock, so corporations usually pay a higher dividend on callable preferred stock than on regular preferred stock.

- **Participating preferred:** Although rarely issued, participating preferred stock allows the investors to receive common dividends in addition to the usual preferred dividends.

- **Prior (senior) preferred:** Preferred stockholders receive compensation before common stockholders in the event of corporate bankruptcy. In this case, senior preferred stockholders receive compensation even before other preferred stockholders. Because of the extra safety factor, senior preferred stock pays a slightly lower dividend than other preferred stock from the same issuer.

- **Adjustable (floating rate) preferred:** Holders of adjustable preferred stock receive a dividend that's reset every six months to match movements in the prevailing interest rates. Because the dividend adjusts to changing interest rates, the stock price remains more stable.

The following example gives you an idea of how to determine the conversion ratio.

If ABC preferred stock ($100 par) is convertible into common stock for $25, what is the conversion ratio?

(A) 1 share

(B) 4 shares

(C) 25 shares

(D) 100 shares

The answer you want is Choice (B). This equation is about as simple as the math gets on the Series 7 exam. Because the $100 par value preferred stock is convertible into common stock for $25, it's convertible into four shares:

$$\text{conversion ratio} = \frac{\text{par value}}{\text{conversion price}} = \frac{\$100}{\$25} = 4 \text{ shares}$$

If you'd like to have more fun (and I use that term loosely) with convertible securities, please visit the convertible bond section in Chapter 7.

Securities with a Twist

Some securities fall outside the boundaries of the more normal common and preferred stock, but I still include them in this equities chapter because they involve ownership in a company or the opportunity to get it. This section gives you an overview of those special securities.

Opening national borders: ADRs

American Depositary Receipts (ADRs) are receipts for foreign securities traded in the United States. ADRs are negotiable certificates (they can be sold or transferred to another party) that represent a specific number of shares (usually one to ten) of a foreign stock. ADR investors may or may not have voting privileges. U.S. banks issue them; therefore, investors receive dividends in U.S. dollars. The stock certificates are held in a foreign branch of a U.S. bank (the custodian bank) and, to exchange their ADRs for the actual shares, investors return the ADRs to the bank that's holding the shares. In addition to the risks associated with stock ownership in general, ADR owners are subject to currency risk (the risk that the value of the security may decline because the value of the currency of the issuing corporation may fall in relation to the U.S. dollar). For information on how the strength of the dollar affects the relative prices of goods in the international market, flip to Chapter 13.

Rights: The right to buy new shares at a discount

Corporations offer rights (subscription or preemptive rights) to their common stockholders. To maintain their proportionate ownership of the corporation, *rights* allow existing stockholders to purchase new shares of the corporation at a discount directly from the issuer, before the shares are offered to the public. Stockholders receive one right for each share owned. The rights are short-term (usually 30 to 45 days). The rights are marketable and may be sold by the stockholders to other investors. If existing stockholders don't purchase all the shares, the issuer offers any unsold shares to a standby underwriter. A *standby underwriter* is a broker-dealer that purchases any stock that wasn't sold in the rights offering and then resells the shares to other investors.

For the Series 7, you can assume that common stockholders automatically receive rights.

Because rights allow investors to purchase the shares at a discount, rights have a theoretical value. The board of directors determines that value when they decide how many rights investors need to purchase a share, as well as the discounted price offered to investors. To determine the value of a right, you can use one of two basic formulas: the cum rights formula or the ex-rights formula. Look closely at the question to determine which one you need. The following sections explore each.

Using the cum rights formula

You may have to find the value of a right while shares are still trading with rights attached. To find out how much of a discount each right provides, you can simply take the difference between the market price and the subscription price, divide that by the number of rights, and come up with a nice, round number. But not so fast! On the *ex-date* (the first day the stock trades without rights), the market price will drop by the value of the right. Before the ex-date, you can find the value of a right by using the cum (Latin for *with*) rights formula:

$$\text{value of a right}_{\text{cum rights}} = \frac{\text{M (market price)} - \text{S (subscription price)}}{\text{N (number of rights needed to purchase one share)} + 1}$$

The +1 in the denominator accounts for the later drop in the market price. Try out the following rights question.

DEF Corp. is issuing new shares through a rights offering. If a new share costs $16 plus four rights and the stock trades at $20, what is the theoretical value of a right prior to the ex-date?

(A) $0.20

(B) $0.80

(C) $1.00

(D) $1.20

The right answer is Choice (B). The stock is trading with (cum) rights (the words *prior to the ex-date* in the problem tip you off), so you need to use the cum rights formula to figure out the value of a right:

$$\frac{M-S}{N+1} = \frac{\$20-\$16}{4+1} = \frac{4}{5} = \$0.80$$

The theoretical value of a right is $0.80.

Using the ex-rights formula

When you calculate the value of a right on the *ex-date* (the first day the stock trades without rights), the market price has already fallen by the value of the right. You simply have to use the new market price and the subscription price to figure out the discount per right. If the stock is trading ex-rights, use the following formula to figure out the value of a right:

$$\text{value of a right}_{\text{ex-rights}} = \frac{\text{M (market price)} - \text{S (subscription price)}}{\text{N (number of rights needed to purchase one share)}}$$

The cum rights and ex-rights formulas are the same except for the +1 in the denominator. Because *ex* means *without,* remember that the ex formula is without the +1.

Warrants: The right to buy stock at a fixed price

Warrants are certificates that entitle the holder to buy a specific amount of stock at a fixed price; they're usually issued along with a new bond or stock offering. Warrant holders have no voting rights and receive no dividends. Bundled bonds and warrants or bundled stock and warrants are called *units.* They are long term and sometimes perpetual (without an expiration date). Warrants are *sweeteners* because they're something that the issuer throws into the new offering to make the deal more appealing; however, warrants can also be sold separately on the market. When warrants are originally issued, the warrant's exercise price is set well above the underlying stock's market price.

For example, suppose QRS warrants give investors the right to buy QRS common stock at $20 per share when QRS common stock is trading at $12. Certainly, exercising their warrants to purchase QRS stock at $20 wouldn't make sense for investors when they can buy QRS stock in the market at $12. However, if QRS rises above $20 per share, holders of warrants can exercise their warrants and purchase the stock from the issuer at $20 per share.

For Further Review

To be properly prepared to take the Series 7 exam, you need to know the information in this chapter and have a good handle on the following terms and ideas related to equity securities:

- Registrar and transfer agents
- Stockholders' rights
- Proxies
- Types of stock: Blue-chip, growth, emerging-growth, income, cyclical/counter-cyclical, defensive, speculative, special-situation
- Limited liability
- Sinking-fund provisions for preferred stock
- Preferred stock preference upon corporate dissolution
- Residual claim on assets
- Stock acquired through a consolidation or transfer
- Escrow receipt
- Anti-dilution agreement (as it applies to warrants)

Chapter 7

Debt Securities: Corporate and U.S. Government Loans

In This Chapter

- Understanding the specifics on bonds
- Examining securities issued by the U.S. government
- Looking at short-term bonds
- Reviewing additional topics tested

Instead of giving up a portion of their company (via stock certificates), corporations can borrow money from investors by selling bonds. Local governments (through municipal bonds) and the U.S. government also issue bonds. For Series 7 exam purposes, most bonds are considered safer than stocks.

Bondholders aren't owners of a company like stockholders are; they're creditors. Bondholders lend money to an institution for a fixed period of time and receive interest for doing so. This arrangement allows the institution to borrow money on its terms (with its chosen maturity date, scheduled interest payments, interest rate, and so on), which it can't do by borrowing from a lending institution.

The Series 7 exam tests you on your ability to understand the different types of bonds issued, terminology, and yes, some math. This chapter has you covered in topics relating to corporate and U.S. government debt securities. Check out the "For Further Review" section at the end of this chapter for a list of related topics, and pay attention to the example questions along the way.

Tackling Bond Terms, Types, and Traits

Before you delve deeper into bonds, make sure you have a good handle on the basics. Understanding the bond basics is a building block that can make all the rest of the bond stuff easier. In this section, I first review basic bond terminology and then move on to some bond characteristics.

Remembering bond terminology

The Series 7 exam designers expect you to know general bond terminology. (And I give it to you here — that's why I get paid the big bucks!) In this section, I help you reinforce the information you may have already learned from a prep course or study material (or are in the process of learning). This stuff is basic, but the Series 7 exam does test it:

- **Maturity date:** All issued bonds have a stated maturity date (for example, 20 years, 30 years, and so on). The maturity date is the year bondholders get paid back for the loans they made. At maturity, bondholders receive par value (see the next bullet).
- **Par value:** Par value is the face value of the bond. Although par value isn't significant to common stockholders (whose issuers use it solely for bookkeeping purposes), it's important to bondholders. For Series 7 exam purposes, you can assume that the par value for each bond is $1,000 unless otherwise stated in the question.

  Bond prices are quoted as a percentage of par value, often without the percent sign. A bond trading at 100 is trading at 100 percent of $1,000 par. Regardless of whether investors purchase a bond for $850 (85), $1,000 (100), or $1,050 (105), they'll receive par value at the maturity date of the bond, usually with interest payments along the way. Corporate bonds are usually quoted in increments of 1/8% (1/8% = 0.00125 or $1.25), so a corporate bond quoted at 99⅜ (99.375%) would be trading at $993.75.
- **Coupon rate:** Of course, investors aren't lending money to issuers for nothing; investors receive interest for providing loans to the issuer. The coupon rate on the bond tells the investors how much annual interest they'll receive.

  The coupon rate is expressed as a percentage of par value. For example, a bond with a coupon rate of 6 percent would pay annual interest of $60 (6% × $1,000 par value). You can assume that bonds pay interest semiannually unless otherwise stated. So in this example, the investor would receive $30 every six months.

  Bondholders receive *interest* (payment for the use of the money loaned), and stockholders receive *dividends* (see Chapter 6).
- **The bond indenture:** The *indenture* (also known as *deed of trust*) is the legal agreement between the issuer and the investor. It's printed on or attached to the bond certificate. All indentures contain basic terms:
  - The maturity date
  - The par value
  - The coupon rate (interest rate) and interest payment dates
  - Any collateral securing the bond (see "Comparing secured and unsecured bonds" later in this chapter)
  - Any callable or convertible features (check out "Contrasting callable and put bonds" and "Popping the top on convertible bonds" later in this chapter)

  The bond indenture also includes the name of a trustee. A *trustee* is an organization that administers a bond issue for an institution. It ensures that the bond issuer meets all the terms and conditions associated with the borrowing. Essentially, the trustee tries to make sure that the issuer does the right thing.

The following question tests your knowledge of bond interest.

Jane Q. Investor purchased 100 AA rated bonds issued by COW Corp. Jane purchased the bonds at 105 percent of par value, and they are currently trading in the market at 104. If the coupon rate is 7½ percent, how much annual interest does Jane receive?

(A) $37.50

(B) $75.00

(C) $3,750.00

(D) $7,500.00

The correct answer is Choice (D). This is a nice, easy question after you wade through the information that you don't need. You need only the number of bonds and the coupon rate to figure out the answer. Don't let yourself get distracted by the rating, purchase price, or market price. That information is there to confuse you.

Jane purchased 100 bonds at $1,000 par (remember you can assume $1,000 par) with a coupon rate of 7½ percent, so do the math:

100 bonds × $1,000 par × 7 1/2% = $7,500.00

Choice (C) would have been correct if the question had asked for the semiannual interest.

Identifying types of bond certificates

To make your life even more interesting, bond certificates can be delivered in different forms. Even though some types of bonds are no longer being issued, you'll still be tested on them when taking the Series 7 exam. Take a look:

- **Bearer bonds:** Bearer bonds are also known as *coupon bonds* because they have bearer coupons attached. This type of bond is not registered in a particular person's name. Instead, the holder submits coupons (representing interest payments) to the issuer once every six months to receive the stated interest amount. At maturity, the holder receives par value. Because of the inherent risk of bearer bonds (like cash, they can be lost or stolen), they're no longer issued. Why, you ask, do you have to study them if they're no longer issued? Many of them haven't yet matured and are still trading in the market.
- **Partially registered bonds:** Partially registered bonds are also called *registered coupon bonds* or *registered as to principal only*. This is a bond in which the principal (par value) — but not interest — is registered in the investor's name. Therefore, the bearer coupon payments can go to anyone, but only the person named on the bond can claim the principal payment at maturity. As with bearer bonds, this type of bond is no longer issued, but it's still traded in the market.
- **Fully registered bonds:** Fully registered bonds are currently the most common form of bond certificates. This type of bond is registered in an investor's name and doesn't have any bearer coupons attached. An investor doesn't have to submit coupons to receive the semiannual interest payments; the investor receives the interest automatically.
- **Book entry certificates:** Book entry certificates, or book entry securities, are recorded in electronic records called *book entries;* thus, the investor doesn't receive certificates or coupons. The U.S. government usually issues its securities in book entry form. Although a majority of the bonds trading in the market are bearer, fully registered, or partially registered, book entry certificates are becoming more popular.

On the Series 7 exam, all bearer and partially registered bonds that are in default should be delivered *with* any unpaid coupons attached. Bonds are considered in default when scheduled interest payments that are owed to the holder by the issuer have not been paid.

Now try your hand at a question about bond certificates.

Which of the following types of bond certificates require the investor to turn in coupons in order to receive interest payments?

I. Book entry bonds

II. Fully registered bonds

III. Bearer bonds

IV. Partially registered bonds

(A) I and III

(B) III and IV

(C) I, II, and IV

(D) I, III, and IV

The right answer is Choice (B). Here you see an example of a complex multiple-choice question. If you remember that book entry bonds don't require the investor to mail in anything, you know Statement I is wrong; therefore, you can immediately cross off Choices (A), (C), and (D). Both bearer bonds and partially registered bonds require the investor to turn in coupons to the issuer in order to receive interest payments. Book entry bondholders and fully registered bondholders receive interest from the issuer automatically without turning anything in.

Following bond issue and maturity schedules

Not only can bond certificates be in different forms, but they can also be scheduled with different types of maturities. Maturity schedules depend on the issuer's needs. The following list presents an explanation of the types of bond issues and maturity schedules:

- **Term bonds:** Term bonds are all issued at the same time and have the same maturity date. For example, if a company issues 20 million dollars' worth of term bonds, they may all mature in 20 years. Because of the large payment that's due at maturity, most corporations issuing this type of bond have a sinking fund. Most corporations issue term bonds because they lock in a coupon rate for a long period of time.

  A corporation creates a *sinking fund* when it sets aside money over time in order to retire its debt. Investors like to see that a sinking fund is in place because it lowers the likelihood of *default* (the risk that the issuer can't pay interest or par value back at maturity).
- **Series bonds:** These bonds are issued in successive years but have only one maturity date. Issuers of series bonds pay interest only on the bonds that they've issued so far. Construction companies that are building developments in several phases issue this type of bond.
- **Serial bonds:** In this type of bond issue, a portion of the outstanding bonds mature at regular intervals (for example, 10 percent of the entire issue matures yearly). Serial bonds are usually issued by corporations and municipalities to fund projects that provide regular income streams. Most municipal (local government) bonds are issued with serial maturity.

  A serial bond that has more bonds maturing on the final maturity date is called a *balloon issue.*

The Series 7 exam focuses mainly on term and serial bonds. A typical Series 7 exam question may ask, "Which of the following types of bonds is most likely to have a sinking fund?" Answer: Term bonds.

Comparing secured and unsecured bonds

The assets of the issuer may or may not back bonds. For test purposes, assume that bonds backed by *collateral* (assets that the issuer owns) are considered safer for the investor. *Secured bonds,* or bonds backed by collateral, involve a pledge from the issuer that a specific asset (for instance, property) will be sold to pay off the outstanding debt in the event of default. Obviously, with all else being equal, secured bonds normally have a lower yield than unsecured bonds.

The Series 7 tests your knowledge of several types of secured bonds:

- **Mortgage bonds:** These bonds are backed by property that the issuer owns. In the event of default or bankruptcy, the issuer must liquidate the property to pay off the outstanding bonds.

- **Equipment trusts:** This type of bond is mainly issued by transportation companies and is backed by equipment they own (for instance, airplanes or trucks). If the company defaults on its bonds, it sells the assets backing the bonds to satisfy the debt.
- **Collateral trusts:** These bonds are backed by financial assets (stocks and bonds) that the issuer owns. A *trustee* (a financial institution the issuer hires) holds the assets and sells them to pay off the bonds in the event of default.
- **Guaranteed bonds:** Guaranteed bonds are backed by a firm other than the original issuer, usually a parent company. If the issuer defaults, the parent company pays off the bonds.

Unsecured bonds are the opposite of secured bonds: These bonds are not backed by any assets whatsoever, only by the good faith and credit of the issuer. If a reputable company that has been around for a long time issues the bonds, the bonds aren't considered too risky. If they're issued by a relatively new company or one with a bad credit rating, hold onto your seat! Again, for Series 7 exam purposes, assume that unsecured bonds are riskier than secured bonds. Here's the lineup of unsecured bonds:

- **Debentures:** These bonds are backed only by the issuer's good word and written agreement (the indenture) stating that the issuer will pay the investor interest when due (usually semiannually) and par value at maturity.
- **Income bonds:** These bonds are the riskiest of all. The issuer promises to pay par value back at maturity and will make interest payments only if earnings are high enough. Companies in the process of reorganization usually issue these bonds at a deep discount (for example, the bonds sell for $500 and mature at par, or $1,000). For test purposes (and real-world purposes), you shouldn't recommend these bonds to investors who can't afford to take a lot of risk.

Because secured bonds are considered safer than unsecured bonds, secured bonds normally have lower coupon rates. You can assume that for the Series 7, the more risk an investor takes, the more reward he will receive. Remember the saying "more risk equals more reward." More reward may be in the form of a higher coupon rate or a lower purchase price. Either one — or both — lead to a higher yield for the investor.

Check out the following question for an example of how the Series 7 may test your knowledge of the types of bonds.

Jon Bearishnikoff is a 62-year-old investor who has 50 percent of his portfolio invested in common stock of up-and-coming companies. The other 50 percent of his portfolio is invested in a variety of stocks of more secure companies. Jon would like to start investing in bonds. Jon is concerned about the safety of his investment. Which of the following bonds would you LEAST likely recommend?

(A) Collateral trust bonds

(B) Mortgage bonds

(C) Equipment trust bonds

(D) Income bonds

The answer you're looking for is Choice (D). This problem includes a lot of garbage information that you don't need to answer the question. One of your jobs (should you decide to accept it) is to dance your way through the question and cherry-pick the information that you do need. The last sentence is usually the most important one when answering a question. Jon is looking for safety; therefore, you'd least likely recommend income bonds because they're usually issued by companies in the process of reorganizing. As a side note, if you become Jon's broker, he shouldn't have 100 percent of his investments in stock. At his age, Jon should have a decent amount of his portfolio invested in fixed-income securities.

Making Basic Bond Price and Yield Calculations

The Series 7 exam tests your knowledge of bond prices, bond yields, and how to calculate them. In this section, I review the relationship between bond prices and bond yields. I also show you how accrued interest can affect how much customers have to pay for the bond.

The relationship between outstanding bond prices and yields is an inverse one. You can assume for Series 7 exam purposes that if interest rates decrease, outstanding bond prices increase and vice versa. Say, for example, that a company issues bonds with a 7-percent coupon rate for $1,000. After the bonds are on the market, interest rates decrease. The company can now issue bonds with a 6-percent coupon rate. Investors with the 7-percent bonds are then in a very good position and can demand a premium for their bonds. Before I show you how the "seesaw" works, make sure you understand the different yields.

Finding bond yields

The following sections review the types of bond yields and how the Series 7 exam tests this topic.

Nominal yield (coupon rate)

The *nominal yield* (NY) is the easiest yield to understand because it's the coupon rate on the face of the bonds. For Series 7 exam purposes, you can assume that the coupon rate will remain fixed for the life of a bond. If you have a 7-percent bond, the bond will pay $70 per year interest (7% × $1,000 par value). When a problem states that a security is a 7-percent (or 6-percent or whatever) bond, it's giving the nominal yield.

Current yield

The *current yield* (CY) is the annual rate of return on a security. The CY of a bond changes when the market price changes; you can determine the CY by dividing the annual interest by the market price:

$$\text{Current yield (CY)} = \frac{\text{annual interest}}{\text{market price}}$$

The following question involves bond yields.

Monique Moneybags purchased one XYZ convertible mortgage bond at 105. Two years later, the bond is trading at 98. If the coupon rate of the bond is 6%, what is the current yield of the bond?

(A) 5.7%

(B) 6.0%

(C) 6.1%

(D) Cannot be determined

The correct answer is Choice (C). Yes, I'm giving you a question with a lot of unnecessary information. All I can tell you is that, unfortunately, you'll have to get used to it. The Series 7 exam creators are notorious for inserting useless (and sometimes misleading) information into the questions to daze and confuse you. In this case, you need only the annual interest and the market price to calculate the answer. Use the following formula to get your answer:

$$\text{CY} = \frac{\text{annual interest}}{\text{market price}} = \frac{\$60}{\$980} = 6.1\%$$

The annual interest is $60 (6% coupon rate × $1,000 par value), and the current market price is $980 (98% of $1,000 par). The facts that the bond is convertible (bondholders can trade it for common stock — see "Popping the top on convertible bonds" later in this chapter) or a mortgage bond (backed by the issuer's property) and that it was purchased at 105 ($1,050) are irrelevant.

"Cannot be determined," as tempting as it may be, is almost never the correct answer on the Series 7 exam.

Yield to maturity (basis)

The *yield to maturity* (YTM) is the yield an investor can expect if holding the bond until maturity. The YTM takes into account not only the market price but also par value, the coupon rate, and the amount of time until maturity. When someone yells to you, "Hey, what's that bond yielding?" (all right, maybe I run in a different circle of friends), he's asking for the YTM. The formula for YTM is as follows:

$$\text{YTM} = \frac{\text{annual interest} + \text{annual accretion or} - \text{annual amortization}}{(\text{market price} + \text{par value}) / 2}$$

$$\text{annual accretion} = \frac{\text{par value} - \text{market price}}{\text{years until maturity}}$$

$$\text{annual amortization} = \frac{\text{market price} - \text{par value}}{\text{years until maturity}}$$

This formula can be difficult to remember. If you have it down, kudos (whatever that means) to you. It's tested (although somewhat rarely) on the Series 7 exam, and you may be one of the unlucky blokes who need this formula. For more on accretion and amortization, please visit Chapter 15.

Yield to call

The *yield to call* (YTC) is the amount that the investor receives if the bond is called prior to maturity. The calculations are similar to those for the YTM (see the preceding section), but you substitute the call price for the par value. The chances of needing it on the Series 7 exam are even more remote than needing the YTM calculations.

Yield to worst

To determine the *yield to worst* (YTW), you have to calculate the yield to maturity and yield to call for all the call dates (if there's more than one) and choose the lowest. If you get a question on yield to worst, knowing the definition should be enough to get you by.

Using seesaw calculations for price and yields

In this section, I show you how to use a "seesaw" to help you better visualize the relationship between bond prices and yields. I know this method is a little goofy, but I'll do anything (well, *almost* anything) to help you pass the Series 7 exam.

Higher numbers make the seesaw rise, and lower numbers make it fall. Looking at the following diagram, you can see that if a bond is at par, the seesaw remains level. If the prices decrease, the yields increase, and if the prices increase, the yields decrease. The center support (*n*) represents the nominal yield (coupon rate) of the bond because it remains constant no matter what happens to the prices or other yields. (***Note:*** In the seesaw, NY stands for *nominal yield,* CY is *current yield,* YTM is *yield to maturity,* and YTC is *yield to call.*)

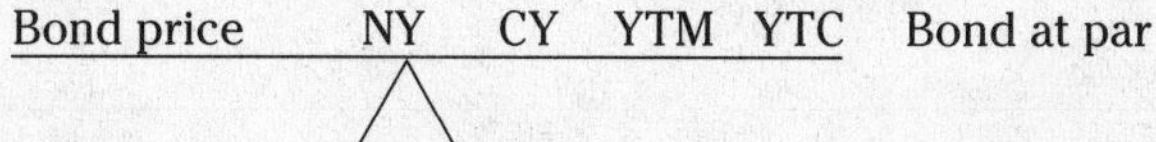

Check out the following problem and its explanation, which show you how to put the seesaw in motion.

Jonathan Bullinski purchased an 8-percent ABC bond yielding 9 percent. He purchased the bond at

(A) a discount

(B) par

(C) a premium

(D) a price that cannot be determined

The correct answer is Choice (A). The question states that the nominal yield is 8 percent and the bond is yielding 9 percent. The 9 percent is the yield to maturity:

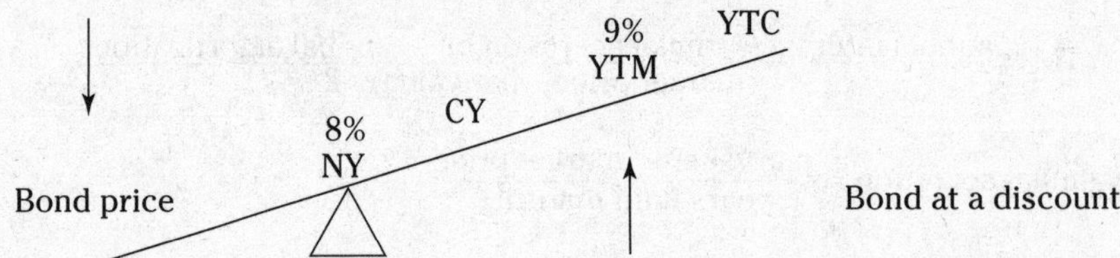

Because the YTM is greater than the NY, the right side of the seesaw goes up and the left side of the seesaw goes down. This means that the investor paid a price that was at a discount (below par). You can also determine that the current yield (CY) would have to be between 8 and 9 percent and the yield to call (YTC) would have to be greater than 9 percent.

If the YTM were lower than the NY, the seesaw would tip the opposite way, and the price would be at a premium rather than at a discount.

Calculating accrued interest

When investors purchase bonds in the market, they may have to pay an additional cost besides the market price (and, of course, your commission). The additional cost is called accrued interest. *Accrued interest,* which is due when bonds are purchased between coupon dates, is the portion of the interest still due to the seller. As you may remember, bonds pay interest once every six months. If an investor holds onto a bond for five months out of a six-month period, he is entitled to 5/6 of that next interest payment; that's accrued interest.

When taking the Series 7 exam, you need to be able to calculate the number of days of accrued interest that the buyer owes the seller. Although you can calculate the accrued interest with a few different methods, I'm here to make your life easier by showing you one of the simplest ways.

Accrued interest on corporate and municipal bonds is calculated on a 360-day year and assumes 30-day months. Accrued interest on U.S. government bonds is calculated using the actual days per year and the actual days per month.

The following sample question tests your ability to figure out this prorated amount.

Skippy Skippington III purchased a 6-percent corporate bond on Friday, October 21. The coupon dates are January 1 and July 1. How many days of accrued interest does Skippy owe?

(A) 115

(B) 117

(C) 120

(D) 122

The answer you want is Choice (A). You have to begin your calculations from the settlement date (the date that the issuer records the new owner's name). Corporate and municipal bonds settle in three business days. You're thrown a slight curveball in this question because you have to contend with a weekend.

Accrued interest is calculated from the previous coupon date up to, but not including, the settlement date.

Now you're probably asking yourself, "What the heck does that mean?" I can show you a nice, easy way to calculate the answer. Using the preceding example, assume that the settlement date is October 26. You would write it as 10/26 (tenth month and 26th day). The previous coupon date would be 7/1 (July 1). You can now set up a subtraction problem:

10/26

<u>–7/1</u>

3/25 (3 months × 30-day months) + 25 days = 115 days of accrued interest

First subtract the seventh month (July) from the tenth month (October). You end up with three months. Because corporate and municipal bonds calculate accrued interest using 30-day months, you have to multiply three months by 30 days to get an answer of 90 days. Subtract the previous coupon date (1) from the settlement date (26) to get an answer of 25 days. Add the 90 days and 25 days together, and you get 115 days as your answer.

Read carefully. To try to trip you up, the Series 7 exam writers may include the settlement date in the question. If this is the case, you don't need to add days to the trade date.

You can use the same formula to calculate accrued interest on U.S. government securities (for basic information, see "Exploring U.S. Government Securities" later in the chapter). However, U.S. government securities settle in one business day, not three. Additionally, U.S. government securities are calculated using actual days per month. The following example shows you how to calculate interest for a U.S. government securities question.

Skippy Skippington IV purchased a 5 percent T-bond on Monday, November 18. The coupon dates are January 1 and July 1. How many days of accrued interest does Skippy owe?

(A) 135

(B) 138

(C) 141

(D) 142

The right answer is Choice (C). Take a look at the following calculations:

11/19 The T-bond settled in one business day

<u>–7/1</u> The previous coupon date

4/18 (4 months × 30-day months) + 18 days = 138 days + 3 days for July, August, and October = 141 days of accrued interest

To get the settlement date, you have to add only one business day. Because the trade date is Monday, November 18, the settlement date is Tuesday, November 19 (11/19). Next, subtract the previous coupon date of July 1 (7/1), and you get an answer of 4 months/18 days. If you multiply the months by 30 as I do in the preceding example and add the days, you end up with 138 days. At this point, you add one day for each of the months that have 31 days (July, August, and October). Your answer is 141 days.

Your 31-day months are January, March, May, July, August, October, and December. All the rest of the months have 30 days, except for February, which has 28. For February, you subtract two days. I know what you're thinking: "What about leap year?" I haven't heard of anyone getting a leap-year question yet, but if you're that unlucky person, subtract only one day for February.

Determining the Best Investment: Comparing Bonds

As you grind your way through Series 7 exam questions, you may be asked to determine the best investment for a particular investor. You need to carefully look at the question for clues to help you choose the correct answer. (For instance, is the investor looking for safety? Is the investor close to retirement?) Consider several factors, including credit rating, callable and put features, and convertible features.

Considering bond credit ratings

The institutions that rate bonds are most interested in the likelihood of *default* (the likelihood that the interest and principal won't be paid when due). For the Series 7 exam, you can assume that the higher the credit rating, the safer the bond and, therefore, the lower the yield.

The two main bond credit rating companies are Moody's and Standard & Poor's (S&P). S&P ratings of BB and lower and Moody's ratings of Ba and lower are considered *junk bonds* or *high-yield bonds,* which have a high likelihood of default, as Table 7-1 explains. (Another credit rating service, called Fitch, uses the same rating symbols as Standard & Poor's.) ***Note:*** Different sources may show some slight variations in how S&P and Moody's ratings compare; however, the relationships here are the most common.

Table 7-1 Bond Credit Ratings (by Quality)

Quality	*S&P (Standard & Poor's)*	*Moody's*
Highest	AAA	Aaa
High	AA	Aa
Upper medium	A	A
Lower medium	BBB	Baa
Speculative (junk)	BB	Ba

Quality	S&P (Standard & Poor's)	Moody's
Speculative (junk): Interest or principal payments missed	B	B
Speculative (junk): No interest being paid	C	Caa
In default	D	D

As if these categories aren't enough, S&P can break down each category even further by adding either a plus (+) or minus (–) sign after the letter category. The plus sign represents the high end of the category, and the minus sign designates the lower end of the category. If you see no plus or minus sign, the bond is in the middle of the category. Moody's can further break down a category by adding a 1, 2, or 3. The number 1 is the highest ranking, 2 represents the middle, and 3 is the lowest. The top four ratings are considered *investment grade,* and the letters below that are considered *junk bonds* or *high-yield bonds.*

The rating company with the capital letters (S&P) uses all capital letters (AAA, AA, and so on). Additionally, S&P has an ampersand (&) between the "S" and the "P" in its name. Think of the ampersand as being like a plus sign to help you remember that S&P uses pluses and minuses within its categories.

Here's a typical bond-ratings question.

Place the following Standard & Poor's bond ratings in order from highest to lowest.

I. A+

II. AA

III. A–

IV. BBB+

(A) I, II, III, IV

(B) I, III, II, IV

(C) IV, I, II, III

(D) II, I, III, IV

The correct answer is Choice (D). When answering this type of question, always look at the letters first. The only time pluses or minuses come into play is when two answers have the same letters, as in Statements I and III. The highest choice is AA, followed by A+ because it's higher than A–, which is even higher than BBB+.

Contrasting callable and put bonds

As you may know, bonds can be issued in callable and put forms. Your mission for the Series 7 exam is to know which is better for investors and when bonds are likely to be called or put.

- **Callable bonds:** A *callable bond* is a bond that the issuer has the right to buy back from investors at the price stated on the indenture (deed of trust). Callable bonds are riskier for investors because investors can't control how long they can hold onto the bonds. To compensate for this risk, they're usually issued with a higher coupon rate (more risk = more reward).

  Most callable bonds are issued with call protection. *Call protection* is the amount of time (usually several years) that an issuer has to wait before calling its bonds. Some callable bonds also have a *call premium,* which is an amount over par value that an issuer has to pay if calling its bonds in the year or years immediately following the expiration of the call protection.

If there is a *make whole call provision*, it allows the issuer to call the bonds providing that the issuer makes a lump sum payment to investors that not only includes payment for the bond but also the present value of any future interest payments investors will miss because of the call.

Another type of bond that can be callable is a *step coupon bond*. Also known as stepped coupon bonds or step-up coupon securities, *step coupon bonds* typically start at a low coupon rate, but the coupon rate increases at predetermined intervals, such as every five years. The issuer typically has the right to call the bonds at par value at the time the coupon rate is due to increase.

- **Put bonds:** *Put bonds* are better for investors. Put bonds allow the investor to "put" the bonds back (redeem them) to the issuer at any time at the price stated on the indenture. Because the investors have the control, put bonds are (of course) rarely issued. Because these bonds provide more flexibility to investors (who have an interest in the bond and stock prices), put bonds usually have a lower coupon rate.

Remember, there's a direct correlation between interest rates and when bonds are called or put. Issuers call bonds when interest rates decrease; investors put bonds when interest rates increase. Check out the following question to see how this works.

Issuers would call their bonds when interest rates

(A) increase

(B) decrease

(C) stay the same

(D) are fluctuating

The correct answer is Choice (B). Being adaptable when taking the Series 7 exam can certainly help your cause. In this question, you have to look from the issuer's point of view, not the investor's. An issuer would call bonds when interest rates decrease because he could then redeem the bonds with the higher coupon payments and issue bonds with lower coupon payments to save money. Conversely, investors would put their bonds back to the issuer when interest rates increase so they could invest their money at a higher interest rate.

You can assume for Series 7 exam purposes that if interest rates increase, bond yields increase.

Popping the top on convertible bonds

Bonds that are convertible into common stock are called *convertible bonds*. Convertible bonds are attractive to investors because investors have an interest in the bond price as well as the price of the underlying stock. The Series 7 exam tests your expertise on whether converting a bond makes sense for an investor. This determination requires you to calculate the parity price of the bond or stock.

Parity occurs when a convertible bond and its underlying stock (the stock it's convertible into) are trading equally (that is, when a bond trading for $1,100 is convertible into $1,100 worth of stock).

When answering Series 7 exam questions relating to convertible bonds, you always need to get the *conversion ratio* (the number of shares that the bond is convertible into). Here's the formula for the conversion ratio:

$$\text{conversion ratio} = \frac{\text{par value}}{\text{conversion price}}$$

You can then use the conversion ratio to calculate the parity price:

parity price of the bond = market price of the stock × conversion ratio

Use the formula to answer the next example question.

Jane Q. Investor purchased a 6-percent DIM convertible bond. Her DIM bond is currently trading at 106, and the underlying stock is trading at 26. If the conversion price is 25, which of the following statements are TRUE?

I. The stock is trading above parity.

II. The stock is trading below parity.

III. Converting the bond would be profitable.

IV. Converting the bond would not be profitable.

(A) I and III

(B) I and IV

(C) II and III

(D) II and IV

The right answer is Choice (D). You can cross out two answers right away. If the stock is trading above parity, converting is always profitable. And if the stock is trading below parity, converting isn't profitable. Therefore, you can eliminate Choices (B) and (C) right away. You've just increased your odds of getting the question correct from 25 to 50 percent. To increase your odds from 50 to 100 percent, follow these equations:

$$\text{conversion ratio} = \frac{\text{par value}}{\text{conversion price}} = \frac{\$1,000}{\$25} = 40 \text{ shares}$$

parity price of the bond = market price of the stock × conversion ratio

parity price of the bond = \$26 × 40 shares = \$1,040

Currently, the bond is trading for \$1,060 (106 percent of \$1,000 par) and is convertible into stock valued at \$1,040 (the parity price of the bond). Because the value of the bond is greater than the converted value of the stock, the stock is trading below parity and converting wouldn't be profitable.

Here's another problem that involves parity price.

Victoria purchased a Spanko, Inc., convertible bond at 115 with a conversion ratio of 25. If the common stock for Spanko, Inc., is currently \$48 per share, when should Victoria convert her bond?

(A) Right away

(B) When the common stock falls below \$46 per share

(C) When the common stock increases to \$50 per share

(D) Never, because bonds are safer investments than stocks

The answer you want is Choice (A). Always assume for test purposes that if the stock is trading above parity, the investor should convert. You don't need to figure out the conversion ratio because it was already given in the question. Here's how to solve the problem:

parity price of the bond = market price of the stock × conversion ratio

parity price of the bond = \$48 × 25 shares = \$1,200

The bond is currently trading at $1,150 (115 percent of $1,000 par) and is convertible into $1,200 worth of stock. It certainly makes sense for the investor to convert at this point. Although you can try to make a point for Choice (C), it's not correct. On the Series 7 exam, if the stock is above parity, convert the bond. Convertible bonds and the underlying stock always seek parity. Even though $50 per share would be better than $48, the bond would also increase in price, and the conversion may not end up being as profitable.

Sometimes companies force a conversion (called a *forced* conversion) by calling bonds at a price that's less than parity. In this situation, converting is more advantageous for investors.

Exploring U.S. Government Securities

On the Series 7 exam, you need to know the basic types of U.S. government securities, their initial maturities, and certain characteristics.

As you may already know, the U.S. government also issues bonds. U.S. government bonds are considered the safest of all securities. Yes, you did read that correctly: the *safest of all securities.* I feel it's worth repeating. How can U.S. government securities be so safe when we're running such a large deficit? Guess what — I don't know, and you don't need to know, either. I can only assume that the U.S. government can always print more currency to make payments on their securities if needed. However, even U.S. government securities are subject to certain risks such as interest risk, reinvestment risk, purchasing power risk, and so forth (see Chapter 13).

U.S. government securities are now all issued and held in electronic (book-entry) form. However, because Treasury Bonds have maturities of up to 30 years, some are still out there in paper form.

Note: With government bonds, you use some of the same types of calculations you use for corporate bonds. The methods for determining accrued interest, for instance, are very similar. For more information, see "Calculating accrued interest," earlier in this chapter.

Understanding the types and characteristics of U.S. government securities

Table 7-2 gives you an overview of different types of U.S. government securities and their specifics. Memorize all the information in the following chart so you can ace U.S. government securities questions on the Series 7 exam.

Table 7-2 U.S. Government Securities and Time until Maturity

Security	*Initial Maturity*	*Characteristics*
T-bills (Treasury bills)	4, 13, 26, and 52 weeks	Issued at a discount and mature at par
T-notes (Treasury notes)	2, 3, 5, 7, and 10 years	Pay interest every 6 months
T-bonds (Treasury bonds)	10 to 30 years	Pay interest every 6 months
T-STRIPS (Separate Trading of Registered Interest and Principal of Securities)	6 months to 30 years	Issued at a discount and mature at par

Security	Initial Maturity	Characteristics
TIPS* (Treasury Inflation-Protected Securities)	5, 10, and 20 years	Pay interest every 6 months; par value and interest payments adjust according to inflation or deflation

** TIPS are tied to the Consumer Price Index (CPI), which measures inflation. The par value changes according to inflation. If inflation is high (prices of goods and services are increasing), the par value increases. If we're in a period of deflation (prices on goods and services are decreasing), the par value decreases. Because investors are getting a percentage of par value as their interest payments, the interest payments vary along with the par value.*

For the Series 7, remember that the interest received on U.S. government securities is exempt from state and local taxes. The interest received on municipal bonds is exempt from federal taxes (although I get into that a little more in the next chapter). Chapter 15 gives you the scoop on taxes.

The following question concerns various types of bonds and U.S. government securities.

One of your new customers calls to tell you that his wife just had a baby. He would like to start saving for the child's higher education. He has $30,000 to invest and seems genuinely concerned about the safety of his investment. Which of the following bonds would you MOST likely recommend to help him meet his goals?

(A) AA-rated corporate bonds with 18 years until maturity

(B) T-STRIPS with 18 years until maturity

(C) T-bonds with 18 years until maturity

(D) High-yielding corporate bonds

The right answer is Choice (B). The question gives you a couple clues. The investor is concerned about safety, so Choice (D) is definitely out. High-yielding corporate bonds are low-rated bonds and are a speculative (risky) investment. Out of the other three choices, (B) makes the most sense. If this customer were to invest $30,000 in the AA-rated corporate bonds or the T-bonds, he'd receive $30,000 at maturity, along with interest payments along the way. However, interest entails risk. T-STRIPS, on the other hand, don't pay interest, so investors can purchase them at a discount. Because the bonds mature in 18 years, perhaps this investor can purchase the T-STRIPS for around $400 each. He could buy 75 bonds with $1,000 par value, which would probably be worth $75,000 in 18 years.

When you see a question on the Series 7 exam about the best investment when planning for a future event (for instance, college), the right answer will most likely be either zero-coupon bonds or T-STRIPS.

In the tranches: Delving into packaged mortgages (CMOs)

Just when you thought you were going to get out of debt securities relatively unscathed, you have collateralized mortgage obligations (CMOs) thrown at you. *CMOs* are annoying little (or big) debt securities backed by pools of mortgages (GNMA/Ginnie Mae, FNMA/Fannie Mae, FHLMC/Freddie Mac). What makes matters worse is that you probably won't sell one in your entire career. However, CMOs are asset-backed securities covered on the Series 7 exam, and you need to know the basics in order to answer these questions correctly.

CMOs don't have a set maturity date and are subject to things called *extension risk* and *prepayment risk*. Take a look at these terms:

- **Average life:** The average amount of time until a mortgage is refinanced or paid off; for example, a 30-year mortgage may have an average life of 17 years
- **Prepayment risk:** The risk that a *tranche* (slice or portion) of the loan will be called sooner than expected due to decreasing interest rates; more people refinance when interest rates are low
- **Extension risk:** The risk that a tranche will be called later than expected due to a less-than-normal amount of refinancing; extension occurs when interest rates are high

CMOs are also broken down into tranches (slices) of varying maturity dates. The basic type of CMO has tranches that are paid in a specific sequence. All tranches receive regular interest payments, but only the tranche with the shortest maturity receives principal payments. After the shortest tranche is retired, the second-shortest receives principal payments until that tranche is retired, and then the principal is paid to the next tranche. This type of structure is known as a *plain vanilla* offering. The following list describes other types of CMO tranches:

- **Planned amortization class (PAC) tranches:** This type of CMO is the most common because it has the most certain prepayment date. The prepayment and extension risk can be somewhat negated by a companion tranche, which assumes a greater degree of the risk. Because of the relative safety of PAC tranches, they usually have the lowest yields.
- **Targeted amortization class (TAC) tranches:** This CMO is the second-safest. TAC tranche-holders have somewhat less-certain principal payments and are more subject to prepayment and extension risk. TAC tranches have yields that are low but not as low as those of PAC tranches.
- **Companion tranches (support bonds):** Companion tranches are included in every CMO that has PAC or TAC tranches. Companion tranches absorb prepayment risk associated with CMOs. The average life of a companion tranche varies greatly depending on interest rate fluctuations. Because more risk is associated with companion tranches, they have higher yields.
- **Z-tranches (accrual bonds):** Z-tranches are usually the last tranche (they have longest maturity) in a series of PAC or companion tranches. Z-tranches don't receive interest or principal until all the other tranches in the series have been retired. The market value of Z-tranches can fluctuate widely. Z-tranches are somewhat similar to a zero-coupon bond (which is bought at a discount and does not receive interest along the way).
- **Principal-only (PO) tranches:** Principal-only tranches are purchased at a price deeply discounted below face value. Investors receive face value through regularly scheduled mortgage payments and prepayments. The market value of a PO increases if interest rates drop and prepayments increase.
- **Interest-only (IO) tranches:** All CMOs with principal-only tranches also have interest-only tranches. IOs are sold at a deep discount below their expected value based on the principal amount used to calculate the amount of interest due. Contrary to PO tranches, the market value of an IO increases if interest rates increase and prepayments decrease.
- **Floating rate tranches:** These tranches appear with CMOs in which the interest rates are tied to an interest rate index (for instance, London Interbank Offered Rate/LIBOR). Investors can use these investments to hedge interest rate risk on other investments.

Although I discuss several types of tranches, the most important ones on the Series 7 exam are the PAC, TAC, companion, and Z-tranches.

The following question tests your understanding of tranches.

Companion tranches support

I. PO tranches

II. PAC tranches

III. TAC tranches

IV. IO tranches

(A) I only

(B) II only

(C) II and III only

(D) II, III, and IV

The answer you're looking for is Choice (C). Companion tranches absorb the prepayment risk associated with CMOs. All PAC and TAC tranches are supported by a companion tranche.

I know that this information is a lot to take in and may be a little confusing. Remembering the basics can help you get most of the questions correct: PAC tranches are the safest; TAC tranches are the second safest; companion tranches support PAC and TAC tranches; and Z-tranches have the longest maturity.

Backed by debt: Collateralized debt obligations (CDOs)

Now that you're a master of CMOs, I figure this is the point at which it makes the most sense to delve into collateralized debt securities (CDOs). The idea behind CDOs is quite similar to collateralized mortgage obligations because they're also broken down into tranches representing differing amounts of risk and/or maturities. Obviously, as with other investments, the more risk, the more reward (or potential reward). The difference with CDOs is that instead of being backed by mortgages, they're backed by a pool of bonds, loans, or other debt instruments. In the event of a shortfall of cash, holders of senior CDOs are paid first. I could break them down into classes for you, but fortunately, I think that would be more than you need to know for the Series 7 exam.

Playing It Safe: Short-Term Loans or Money Market Instruments

Every Series 7 exam includes a few questions on money market instruments. *Money market instruments* are relatively safe short-term loans that can be issued by corporations, banks, the U.S. government, and municipalities. Most have maturities of one year or less, and they're usually issued at a discount and mature at par value. The following list reviews some basic characteristics of money market instruments to help you earn an easy point or two on the Series 7 exam:

- **Repurchase agreements:** Repurchase agreements (Repos) are a contract between a buyer and a seller. The seller of the securities (usually T-bills) agrees to buy them back at a previously determined price and time. Repos are short-term loans.
- **Federal Funds:** Federal Funds are loans between banks to help meet reserve requirements. Federal Funds are usually overnight loans for which the rates change constantly depending on supply and demand.

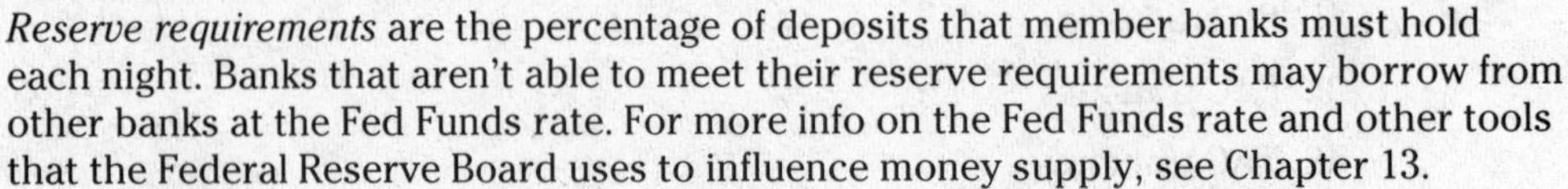

Reserve requirements are the percentage of deposits that member banks must hold each night. Banks that aren't able to meet their reserve requirements may borrow from other banks at the Fed Funds rate. For more info on the Fed Funds rate and other tools that the Federal Reserve Board uses to influence money supply, see Chapter 13.

- **Corporate commercial paper:** Commercial paper is unsecured corporate debt. Commercial paper is issued at a discount and matures at par value. Commercial paper is issued with an initial maturity of 270 days or less and is exempt from SEC registration.
- **Brokered (negotiable) certificates of deposit:** Brokered CDs are low-risk investments, which originate from a bank and are outsourced to broker-dealers to sell to investors. Unlike typical CDs, which are purchased directly from a bank, brokered CDs can be traded in the market. Negotiable certificates of deposit that require a minimum investment of $100,000 are often called *jumbo CDs.*
- **Eurodollars:** Eurodollars are American dollars held by a foreign bank outside the U.S. This situation is usually the result of payments made to overseas companies. Eurodollars are not to be confused with Eurodollar bonds (dollar-denominated bonds issued and held overseas).
- **Bankers' acceptances:** A bankers' acceptance (BA) is a time-draft (short-term credit investment) created by a company whose payment is guaranteed by a bank. Companies use BAs for the importing and exporting of goods.
- **T-bills:** The U.S. government issues T-bills at a discount, and they have initial maturities of 4, 13, 26, or 52 weeks. T-bills are somewhat unique in that they're sold and quoted on a discount-yield basis (YTM). U.S. government securities — and especially T-bills — are considered the safest of all securities.

Here's what a question on money market instruments may look like.

SNK Surfboard Company wants to import boogie boards from an Italian manufacturer in Sicily. SNK would use which of the following money market instruments to finance the importing of the boogie boards?

(A) T-bills

(B) Collateral trust bonds

(C) Repurchase agreements

(D) Banker's acceptances

The correct answer is Choice (D). You can eliminate Choice (B) right away because collateral trust bonds aren't money market instruments; they're secured long-term bonds. A banker's acceptance is like a post-dated check that's used specifically for importing and exporting goods.

Word association can help you here. If you see *importing, exporting,* or *time draft,* your answer is probably bankers' acceptance (BA).

For Further Review

I want you to be as prepared as possible to take the Series 7 exam, so I've compiled a list of items relating to this chapter that the Series 7 exam may test you on. Please look at the items one at a time and make sure you have a good handle on each of them:

- EE Bonds (U.S. Savings Bonds), HH bonds, and I bonds
- U.S. Government Agency Securities: Federal Farm Credit Consolidated Systemwide Bank, Federal Home Loan Bank, and Student Loan Marketing Association (Sallie Mae)
- Mortgage-backed securities: GNMAs (Ginnie Maes), FNMAs (Fannie Maes), and FHLMCs (Freddie Macs)
- Arbitrage
- Forced conversion
- Bond retirement (by redemption, refunding, or conversion)
- Good delivery for bonds
- Short and long coupons
- Comparative safety of different debt securities
- Sinking funds
- Trust Indenture Act of 1939
- Zero-coupon bonds
- Trustees
- Anti-dilution covenants
- Bonds trading flat
- Variable rate preferreds
- Auction rate securities
- Variable (adjustable) rate bonds
- Escrowed to maturity
- Sovereign debt

Chapter 8

Municipal Bonds: Local Government Securities

In This Chapter

- Understanding municipal bond basics
- Comparing general obligation bonds to revenue bonds
- Reviewing other types of municipal bonds
- Recognizing sources of municipal bond information
- Reviewing additional topics tested

Municipal bonds are securities that state governments, local governments, or U.S. territories issue. The municipality uses the money it borrows from investors to fund and support projects, such as roads, sewer systems, hospitals, and so on.

Even though you're most likely going to spend a majority of your time selling equity securities (stocks), for some unknown reason, the Series 7 tests heavily on municipal securities. As a matter of fact, municipal bonds are one of the most heavily tested areas on the entire exam. If you've flipped ahead, you may have noticed that this chapter isn't one of the biggest in the book. Why is that? Well, I cover a lot of the bond basics, such as par value, maturity, types of maturities (term, serial, and balloon), the seesaw, and so on, in Chapter 7. Also, you can find some of the underwriting information in Chapter 5.

In this chapter, I cover the Series 7 exam topics that are the most tested and most difficult to understand relating to municipal bonds. This chapter and the real exam focus mainly on the differences between GO (general obligation) bonds and revenue bonds. (Check out the "For Further Review" section for a list of related topics that you should have a firm grasp on before you take the test.) This chapter also gives you plenty of example questions for practice.

General Obligation Bonds: Backing Bonds with Taxes

Most Series 7 municipal test questions are on general obligation (GO) bonds. The following sections help you prepare.

General characteristics of GOs

When you're preparing to take the Series 7 exam, you need to recognize and remember a few items that are specific to GO bonds:

- **They fund nonrevenue producing facilities.** GO bonds are not self-supporting because municipalities issue them to build or support projects that don't bring in enough (or any) money to help pay off the bonds. GOs fund schools, libraries, police departments, fire stations, and so on.
- **They're backed by the full faith and credit (taxing power) of the municipality.** The taxes of the people living in the municipality back general obligation bonds.
- **They require voter approval.** Because the generous taxes of the people living in the municipality back the bonds, those same people have the right to vote on the project.

The following question tests your knowledge of GO bonds.

Which of the following projects are MORE likely to be financed by general obligation bonds than revenue bonds (discussed later in this chapter)?

I. New municipal hospital

II. Public sports arena

III. New junior high school

IV. New library

(A) I and II only

(B) III and IV only

(C) I and III only

(D) I, III, and IV only

The correct answer is Choice (B). Remember that GO bonds are issued to fund nonrevenue producing projects. A new municipal hospital and a public sports arena will produce income that can back revenue bonds. However, a new junior high school and a new library need the support of taxes to pay off the bonds and, therefore, are more likely to be financed by GO bonds.

Analyzing GO bonds

The Series 7 exam tests your ability to analyze different types of municipal securities and help a customer make a decision that best suits her needs. You should be able to analyze a GO bond like you'd analyze other investments; however, because they're backed by taxes rather than sales of goods and services (like most corporations are), GO bonds have different components to look at when analyzing the marketability and safety of the issue.

Ascertaining marketability

Many different items can affect the marketability of municipal bonds, including the characteristics of the issuer, factors affecting the issuer's ability to pay, and municipal debt ratios. You certainly want to steer investors away from municipal bonds that aren't very marketable, unless those investors are willing to take extra risk. Here's a list of some of the other items that can affect the bonds' marketability:

- **Quality (rating):** The higher the credit rating, the safer the bond, and therefore the more marketable it is.

- **Maturity:** The shorter the maturity, the more marketable the bond issue.
- **Call features:** Callable bonds are less marketable than noncallable bonds.
- **Interest (coupon) rate:** Everything else being somewhat equal, bonds with higher coupon (interest) rates are more marketable.
- **Block size:** The larger the block size, the more marketable the bond usually is.
- **Dollar price:** All else being equal, the lower the dollar price, the more marketable the bond is.
- **Issuer's name (local or national reputation):** Bonds are more marketable when the issuer has a good reputation for paying off its bonds on time.
- **Sinking fund:** If the issuer has put money aside to pay the bonds off at maturity, the bonds are more marketable because the default risk is lower.
- **Insurance:** If the bonds are insured against default, they're considered very safe and are much more marketable. Bond insurance is considered a *credit enhancement.*

Dealing with debt

One factor that influences the safety of a GO bond is the municipality's ability to deal with debt. After you consider the issuer's name, you can look at previous issues that the municipality had and find out whether it was able to pay off the debt in a timely manner.

In addition to the municipality's name (and credit history), you want to look at its current debt. *Net overall debt* includes the debt that the municipality owes directly plus the portion of the overlapping debt that the municipality is responsible for:

- **Net direct debt:** The debt that the municipality obtained on its own. Net direct debt comes from both GO bonds and short-term municipal notes (see the later section "Don't Forget Municipal Notes!"). Revenue bonds are not included in the net direct debt because they're self-supporting (see "Dealing with Revenue Bonds: Raising Money for Utilities and Such").
- **Overlapping debt:** Overlapping debt occurs when several authorities in a geographic area have the ability to tax the same residents. Take, for example, my wife's and my home-away-from-home, Las Vegas. Not only does Las Vegas have its own debt, but because it's part of Clark County, the Las Vegas residents are also responsible for part of Clark County's debt. In addition, because Las Vegas is in Nevada, the residents of Las Vegas are responsible for a portion of Nevada's debt.

To determine the debt *per capita* (per person), take the debt (overall, direct, or overlapping) and divide it by the number of people in the municipality. Obviously, for an investor, the lower this number is, the better.

Bringing in taxes, fees, and fines

Taxes — one of life's little certainties — are another factor that influence the safety of GO bonds. Property taxes (which local municipalities — not states — collect) and sales taxes are the driving force behind paying back investors. Aided and abetted by traffic fines and licensing fees, taxes put money in the municipal coffers and eventually in investors' hands. The following factors come into play:

- **Property values:** *Ad valorem* (property) taxes are the largest source of backing for GO bonds. Even though people living in a municipality want their property values to be low (at least for tax purposes), people investing in municipal bonds want the property values to be high. The higher the assessed value, the more taxes collected and the easier it is for the municipality to pay off its debt.

When you're dealing with Series 7 questions that ask you to calculate the ad valorem taxes for an individual, always go with the assessed value, not the market value. Ad valorem taxes are based on mills, or thousandths of a dollar (1 mill = $0.001). To help you remember that a mill equals 0.001, remember that *mills* has two *l*s, so you need to have two zeros after the decimal point.

- **Population:** Obviously, the more people who live in a municipality and pay taxes to back the bond issue, the better. Also, the population trend is important. Investors prefer to see more people moving into a municipality than moving out.
- **Tax base:** The tax base is comprised of the number of people living in the municipality, the assessed property values, and how much the average person makes. Larger tax bases are ideal.
- **Sales per capita:** Because sales taxes also support GO bonds, the amount of sales per capita (the amount of goods the average person buys) is also important.
- **Traffic fines and licensing fees:** You know that $100 speeding ticket that you got last month? The money that you paid in fines helped pay off some of the municipality's debt. I hope that makes you feel better.

Municipal GO bonds are backed by the huge taxing power of a municipality, so GO bonds usually have higher ratings and lower yields than revenue bonds. Because investors aren't taking as much risk, they don't get as much reward, or *yield.*

Try your hand at a question involving property taxes, an issue that affects the safety of GO bonds.

An individual has a house with a market value of $350,000 and an assessed value of $300,000. What is the ad valorem tax if the tax rate is 24 mills?

(A) $720

(B) $840

(C) $7,200

(D) $8,400

The answer you want is Choice (C). First make sure that you start with the assessed value; multiply it by the tax rate and then by 0.001 to get the answer:

$$\$300{,}000 \times 24 \times 0.001 = \$7{,}200$$

To keep yourself from making a careless mistake, multiply the three numbers separately; the tax rate may be single or double digits. Multiplying by 0.001 means moving a decimal point three places to the left, so 24 mills is $0.024, not $0.0024. In this case, if you multiplied $300,000 by 0.0024 (or 2.4 mills), you got a wrong answer, Choice (A).

Dealing with Revenue Bonds: Raising Money for Utilities and Such

Unlike the tax-backed GO bonds (see the preceding sections), *revenue bonds* are issued to fund municipal facilities that'll generate enough income to support the bonds. These bonds raise money for certain utilities, toll roads, airports, hospitals, student loans, and so on.

A municipality can also issue *industrial development revenue bonds* (IDRs) to finance the construction of a facility for a corporation that moves into that municipality. Remember that even though a municipality issues IDRs, they're actually backed by lease payments made by a corporation. Because the corporation is backing the bonds, the credit rating of the bonds is derived from the credit rating of the corporation.

Because IDRs are backed by a corporation rather than a municipality, IDRs are generally considered the riskiest municipal bonds. Additionally, because these bonds are issued for the benefit of a corporation and not the municipality, the interest income may not be federally tax-free to investors subject to the alternative minimum tax (AMT).

General characteristics of revenue bonds

Before taking the Series 7 exam, you need to recognize and remember a couple items that are specific to revenue bonds:

- **They don't need voter approval.** Because revenue bonds fund a revenue-producing facility and therefore aren't backed by taxes, they don't require voter approval. The revenues that the facility generates should be sufficient to pay off the debt.
- **They require a feasibility study.** Prior to issuing revenue bonds, the municipality hires consultants to prepare a feasibility study. The study basically answers the question, *Does this make sense?* The study includes estimates of revenues that the facility could generate, along with any economic, operating, or engineering aspects of the project that would be of interest to the municipality.

Analyzing revenue bonds

As with any investment, you need to check out the specifics of the security. For instance, when gauging the safety of a revenue bond, you want to see whether it has a credit enhancement (insurance), which provides a certain degree of safety. You also want to look at *call features* (whether the issuer has the right to force investors to redeem their bonds early). You can assume that if a bond is callable, it has a higher yield than a noncallable bond because the investor is taking more risk (the investor doesn't know how long she can hold onto the bond).

For Series 7 exam purposes (and if you ever sell one or more revenue bonds), you also need to be familiar with the revenue-bond-specific items in this section. For instance, municipal revenue bonds involve covenants, wonderful little promises that protect investors by holding the issuer legally accountable. Table 8-1 shows some of the promises that municipalities make on the municipal bond indenture.

Table 8-1 Revenue Bond Covenants

Type of Covenant	*Promises that the Municipality Will . . .*
Rate covenant	Charge sufficient fees to people using the facility to be able to pay expenses and the debt service (principal and interest on the bonds)
Maintenance covenant	Adequately take care of the facility and any equipment so the facility continues to earn revenue
Insurance covenant	Adequately insure the facility

If you see the word *covenant* on the Series 7 exam, immediately think of revenue bonds.

Other factors that provide investors with a certain degree of comfort are that municipalities must provide *financial reports* and are subject to *outside audits* for all of their revenue bond issues.

Obviously, municipalities don't want to default on their loans. That's why issuers use the *additional bonds test,* which says that if the municipality is going to issue more bonds backed by the same project, it must prove that the revenues will be sufficient to cover all the bonds. The indenture on the initial bonds may be open-ended or closed-ended. If it's open-ended, additional bonds will have equal claims to the assets. If it's closed-ended, any other bonds issued are subordinate to (in other words, rank lower than) the original issue.

A *catastrophe clause* states that if a facility is destroyed due to a catastrophic event such as a flood, hurricane, tornado, or the like, the municipality will use the insurance that it purchased to call the bonds and pay back bondholders.

The flow of funds relates only to revenue bonds. The *flow of funds* tells you what a municipality does with the money collected from the revenue-producing facility that's backing the bonds. Typically, the flow of funds is as follows:

1. **Operation and maintenance:** This item is normally the first that the municipality pays from revenues it receives. If the municipality doesn't adequately maintain the facility and pay its employees, it'll cease to run.
2. **Debt service:** Usually the next item paid after operation and maintenance is the *debt service* (principal and interest on the bonds).
3. **Debt service reserve:** After paying the first two items, the municipality puts aside money into the debt service reserve to pay one year's debt service.
4. **Reserve maintenance fund:** This fund helps supplement the general maintenance fund.
5. **Renewal and replacement fund:** This fund is for exactly what you'd expect — renewal projects (updating and modernizing) and replacement of equipment.
6. **Surplus fund:** Municipalities can use this fund for several purposes, such as redeeming bonds, paying for improvements, and so on.

Revenues are normally dispersed as I describe in the preceding list. This system is called a *net revenue pledge* because the *net revenues* (gross revenues minus operation and maintenance) are used to pay the debt service. However, if the municipality pays the debt service before paying the operation and maintenance, it's called a *gross revenue pledge.*

The *debt service coverage ratio* is an indication of the ability of a municipal issuer to meet the debt service payments on its bonds. The higher the debt service coverage ratio, the more likely the issuer is to be able to meet interest and principal payments on time.

The following question tests your debt service coverage ratio knowledge. Use the following formula to answer it.

$$\text{debt service coverage ratio} = \frac{\text{net } \textit{or} \text{ gross revenues}}{\text{principal} + \text{interest}}$$

A municipality generates $10,000,000 in revenues from a facility. It must pay off $6,000,000 in operating and maintenance expenses, $1,500,000 in principal, and $500,000 in interest. Under a net revenue pledge, what is the debt service coverage ratio?

(A) 1 to 1

(B) 1.5 to 1

(C) 2 to 1

(D) 4 to 1

The right answer is Choice (C). Because the question states that the municipality is using a net revenue pledge, you have to calculate the net revenue. First, using the earlier equation, figure the net revenue by subtracting the operation and maintenance expenses ($6,000,000) from the gross revenue ($10,000,000), which gives you $4,000,000. Next, take the $4,000,000 and divide it by the combined principal and interest. The principal is $1,500,000 and the interest is $500,000, which gives you a total of $2,000,000. After dividing the $4,000,000 by $2,000,000, you come up with a ratio of 2 to 1, which means that the municipality brought in two times the amount of money needed to pay the debt service (principal and interest). A debt service coverage ratio of 2 to 1 is considered adequate for a municipality to pay off its debt. A debt service coverage ratio of less than 2 to 1 may indicate that the municipality may have problems meeting its debt obligations.

Here's how your equation should look:

$$\text{debt service coverage ratio} = \frac{\text{net revenues}}{\text{principal} + \text{interest}}$$

$$\text{debt service coverage ratio} = \frac{\$10{,}000{,}000 - \$6{,}000{,}000}{\$1{,}500{,}000 + \$500{,}000} = \frac{\$4{,}000{,}000}{\$2{,}000{,}000} = 2 \text{ to } 1$$

If the question doesn't specifically ask for gross revenues or net revenues, you can assume net because that's the more common way that a municipality pays off its debt.

Examining Other Types of Municipal Bonds on the Test

Along with standard revenue and GO bonds (see the earlier sections on these topics), you're required to know the specifics of the following bonds:

- **Special tax bonds:** These bonds are secured by one or more taxes other than ad valorem (property) taxes. The bonds may be backed by sales taxes on fuel, tobacco, alcohol, and so on.
- **Special assessment (special district) bonds:** These bonds are issued to fund the construction of sidewalks, streets, sewers, and so on. Special assessment bonds are backed by taxes only on the properties that benefit from the improvements. In other words, if people who live a few blocks away from you get all new sidewalks, they'll be taxed for it, not you.
- **Double-barreled bonds:** These bonds are basically a combination of revenue and GO bonds. Municipalities issue these bonds to fund revenue-producing facilities (toll bridges, water and sewer facilities, and so forth), but if the revenues taken in aren't enough to pay off the debt, tax revenues make up the deficiency.
- **Limited-tax general obligation bonds (LTGO):** These bonds are types of general obligation bonds for which the taxes backing the bonds are limited. Limited-tax general obligation bonds are secured by all revenues of the municipality that aren't used to back other bonds. However, the amount of property taxes municipalities can levy to back these bonds is limited.
- **Public housing authority bonds (PHAs):** These bonds are also called new housing authority (NHA) bonds and are issued by local housing authorities to build and improve low-income housing. These bonds are backed by U.S. government subsidies, and if the issuer can't pay off the debt, the U.S. government makes up any shortfalls.

Because PHAs are backed by the issuer and the U.S. government, they're considered among the safest municipal bonds.

- **Moral obligation bonds:** These bonds are issued by a municipality but backed by a pledge from the state government to pay off the debt if the municipality can't. Given this additional backing of the state, they're considered safe. Moral obligation bonds need legislative approval to be issued.

Because they're called moral obligation bonds, the state has a *moral* responsibility — but not a legal obligation — to help pay off the debt if the municipality can't.

The following question tests your ability to answer questions about the safety of municipal bonds:

Rank the following municipal bonds in order from safest to riskiest.

I. Revenue bonds

II. Moral obligation bonds

III. Public housing authority bonds

IV. Industrial development revenue bonds

(A) I, II, III, IV

(B) III, II, I, IV

(C) II, III, IV, I

(D) II, IV, III, I

The correct answer is Choice (B). If you remember that public housing authority bonds are considered the safest of the municipal bonds because they're backed by U.S. government subsidies, this question's easy, because only one answer choice starts with III. Anyway, public housing authority bonds would be the safest; moral obligation bonds, which are also considered very safe because the state government has a moral obligation to help pay off the debt if needed, follow. Next come revenue bonds, which are backed by a revenue-producing facility. Remember that industrial development revenue bonds (IDRs) are considered the riskiest municipal bonds because although they're technically municipal bonds, they're backed only by lease payments made by a corporation.

Don't Forget Municipal Notes!

When municipalities need short-term (interim) financing, municipal notes come into play. These notes bring money into the municipality until other revenues are received. Municipal notes typically have maturities of one year or less (usually three to five months). Know the different types of municipal notes for the Series 7 exam:

- **Tax anticipation notes (TANs):** These notes provide financing for current operations in anticipation of future taxes that the municipality will collect.
- **Revenue anticipation notes (RANs):** These bonds provide financing for current operations in anticipation of future revenues that the municipality will collect.
- **Tax and revenue anticipation notes (TRANs):** These notes are a combination of TANs and RANs.
- **Grant anticipation notes (GANs):** These bonds provide interim financing for the municipality while it's waiting for a grant from the U.S. government. The notes are paid off from the grant funds once received.
- **Bond anticipation notes (BANs):** These bonds provide interim financing for the municipality while it's waiting for long-term bonds to be issued.

- **Construction loan notes (CLNs):** These notes provide interim financing for the construction of multifamily apartment buildings.
- **Project notes (PNs):** These bonds provide interim financing for the building of subsidized housing for low-income families.
- **Tax-exempt commercial paper:** These short-term bonds are usually issued by organizations such as universities with permission of the government. This debt obligation usually lasts only a few months to help the organization cover its short-term liabilities.

AON (all or none) is an order qualifier (fill an entire order at a specific price or not at all) or type of underwriting; it is not a municipal note, no matter how much it looks like one.

Municipal notes are not rated the same as municipal or corporate bonds (AAA, AA, A, and so on). Municipal notes have ratings as follows (from best to worst):

- **Moody's:** MIG 1, MIG 2, MIG 3, MIG 4
- **Standard & Poor's:** SP-1, SP-2, SP-3
- **Fitch:** F-1, F-2, F-3

The following question tests your knowledge of municipal notes.

Suffolk County, New York, would like to even out its cash flow. Which of the following municipal notes would Suffolk County MOST likely issue?

(A) RANs

(B) BANs

(C) CLNs

(D) TANs

The answer you want is Choice (D). You have to use a little common sense to answer this one. Because the question doesn't state that the municipality is constructing housing or issuing long-term bonds, you should cross out Choices (B) and (C). Likewise, you can't assume that the municipality will be collecting revenues from some project, so Choice (A) is out. However, municipalities collect property taxes at regular intervals, so (D) is the best choice.

Understanding the Taxes on Municipal Bonds

Municipal bonds typically have lower yields than most other bonds. You may think that because U.S. government securities (T-bills, T-notes, T-bonds, and so on) are the safest of all securities, they should have the lowest yields. Not so, because municipal bonds have a tax advantage that U.S. government bonds don't have: The interest received on municipal bonds is federally tax-free.

Comparing municipal and corporate bonds equally

The *taxable equivalent yield* (TEY) tells you what the interest rate of a municipal bond would be if it weren't federally tax-free. You need the following formula to compare municipal bonds and corporate bonds equally:

$$\text{taxable equivalent yield(TEY)} = \frac{\text{municipal yield}}{100\% - \text{investor's tax bracket}}$$

Because the investor's tax bracket comes into play with municipal bonds, municipal bonds are better suited for investors in higher tax brackets.

The following question tests your ability to answer a TEY question.

Mrs. Stevenson is an investor who is in the 30-percent tax bracket. Which of the following securities would provide Mrs. Stevenson with the BEST after-tax yield?

(A) 5-percent GO bond

(B) 6-percent T-bond

(C) 7-percent equipment trust bond

(D) 7-percent mortgage bond

The right answer is Choice (A). If you were to look at this question straight up without considering any tax advantages, the answer would be either (C) or (D). However, you have to remember that the investor has to pay federal taxes on the interest received from the T-bond, equipment trust bond, and mortgage bond but doesn't have to pay federal taxes on the interest received from the GO municipal bond. So you need to set up the TEY equation to be able to compare all the bonds equally:

$$\text{TEY} = \frac{\text{municipal yield}}{100\% - \text{investor's tax bracket}} = \frac{5\%}{100\% - 30\%} = \frac{5\%}{70\%} = 7.14\%$$

Looking into the Series 7 examiners' heads, you have to ask yourself, "Why would they be asking me this question?" Well, because they want to make sure that you know that the interest received on municipal bonds is federally tax-free. Therefore, if you somehow forget the formula, you're still likely to be right if you pick a municipal bond as the answer when you get a question like the preceding one.

Note: Although this situation is less likely, the Series 7 may ask you to determine the *municipal equivalent yield* (MEY), which is the yield on a taxable bond after paying taxes. Once you have that yield, you can compare it to a municipal bond to help determine the best investment for one of your customers. The formula for the municipal equivalent yield is as follows:

$$\text{MEY} = \text{municipal yield} \times (100\% - \text{investor's tax bracket})$$

Scot-free! Taking a look at triple tax-free municipal bonds

Bonds that U.S. territories (and federal districts) issue are triple tax-free (the interest is not taxed on the federal, state, or local level). These places include

- Puerto Rico
- Guam
- U.S. Virgin Islands
- American Samoa
- Washington, D.C.

Additionally, in most cases (there are a few exceptions), if you buy a municipal bond issued within your own state, the interest will be triple tax-free.

Unless you see the U.S. territories or Washington, D.C., in a municipal bond question, don't assume that the bonds are triple tax-free. Even if the question states that the investor buys a municipal bond issued within her own state, don't assume that it's triple tax-free unless the question specifically states that it is.

The tax advantage of municipal bonds applies only to interest received. If investors sell municipal bonds for more than their cost basis, the investors have to pay taxes on the capital gains.

Following Municipal Bond Rules

Yes, unfortunately, the Series 7 tests you on rules relating to municipal bonds. Rules are a part of life and a part of the Series 7 exam. This section covers just a few rules that are specific to municipal securities, but if you're itching for more regulations, don't worry — you can see plenty more rules in my favorite (and I use that term loosely) chapter: Chapter 16.

The 90-day apprenticeship period

The 90-day apprenticeship period rule says that new registered representatives can't engage in any municipal securities business with the public for their first 90 days in the industry. During this time, a registered rep may deal only with securities professionals such as dealers, and they may not receive commissions during this time.

The 90-day apprenticeship period applies only to municipal bonds. Fortunately, you can still receive commissions from selling other types of securities.

Confirmations

All confirmations of trades must be sent or given to customers at or before the completion of the transaction (settlement date). Municipal securities settle the regular way (three business days after the trade date). The following items are included on the confirmation:

- The broker-dealer's name, address, and phone number
- The capacity of the trade (whether the firm acted as a broker or dealer)
- The dollar amount of the commission (if the firm's acting as a broker)
- The customer's name
- Any bond particulars, such as the issuer's name, interest rate, maturity, call features (if any), and so on
- The trade date, time of execution, and the settlement date
- Committee on Uniform Securities Identification Procedures (CUSIP) identification number (if there is one)
- Bond yield and dollar price
- Any accrued interest
- The registration form (registered as to principal only, book entry, or fully registered)
- Whether the bonds have been called or pre-refunded
- Any unusual facts about the security

Advertising and record keeping

A brokerage firm has to keep all advertising for a minimum of three years, and these ads must be easily accessible (not in a bus storage locker) for at least two years.

The Municipal Securities Rulemaking Board (MSRB) requires a principal (manager) to approve all advertising material of the firm prior to its first use. The principal must ensure that the advertising is accurate and true.

Advertising includes any material designed for use in the public media. Advertising includes offering circulars, market and form letters, summaries of official statements, and so on. However, preliminary and final official statements are not considered advertising because they're prepared by the issuer; therefore, they don't require approval from a principal.

Gifts

According to MSRB rules, municipal securities dealers can't give gifts valued at more than $100 per year to customers. (The board kind of has this thing against bribery.) Business expenses are exempt from the rule.

If you get a question on the Series 7 exam relating to what qualifies as a gift, remember that business expenses are exempt. Business expenses can be airline tickets (for the customer to meet with you, not for the customer to vacation in the Bahamas), hotel expenses (for the customer's lodging while she's meeting with you), business meals, and so on.

Commissions

Although no particular guideline states what percentage broker-dealers can charge (as with the 5% markup policy — see Chapter 16), all commissions, markups, and markdowns must be fair and reasonable, and policies can't discriminate among customers. The items that firms should consider follow:

- The market value of the securities at the time of the trade.
- The total dollar amount of the transaction. Although you're going to charge more money for a larger transaction, the percentage charged is usually lower.
- The difficulty of the trade. If you had to jump through hoops to make sure the trade was completed, you're entitled to charge more.
- The fact that you and the firm that you work for are entitled to make a profit (which is, of course, the reason you got involved in the business to begin with).

You can't take race, ethnicity, religion, gender, sexual orientation, disability, age, funny accents, or how much you like (or dislike) the client into account.

Gathering Municipal Bond Info

As with other investments, you need to be able to locate information if you're going to sell municipal securities to investors. You may find that information about municipal bonds is not as readily available as it is for most other securities. Some municipal bonds are relatively *thin* issues (not many are sold or traded) or may be of interest only to investors in a particular geographic location. This section reviews some of the information that you have to know to ace the Series 7 exam.

The broker's broker

Yes, a *broker's broker* is exactly what you would expect: a broker for brokers. Broker's brokers specialize in trading municipal bonds with institutional customers (banks and municipal brokers) rather than with public customers. Broker's brokers help municipal dealers sell unsold portions of a municipal bond issue.

Additionally, broker's brokers maintain the anonymity of their clients.

By definition, brokers, including a broker's broker, have no inventory and do not make a market in securities (dealers do).

The bond resolution (indenture)

A *bond resolution* (indenture) provides investors with contract terms including the coupon rate, years until maturity, collateral backing the bond (if any), and so on. Although not required by law, almost every municipal bond comes with a bond indenture, which is printed on the face of most municipal bond certificates. It makes the bonds more marketable because the indenture serves as a contract between the municipality and a trustee who's appointed to protect the investors' rights. Included in the indenture are the flow of funds (see "Dealing with Revenue Bonds: Raising Money for Utilities," earlier in this chapter) and any assets that may be backing the issue.

Legal opinion

Printed on the face of municipal bond certificates, the legal opinion is prepared and signed by a *municipal bond counsel* (attorney). The purpose of the legal opinion is to verify that the issue is legally binding on the issuer and conforms to tax laws. Additionally, the legal opinion may state that interest received from the bonds is tax exempt.

If a bond is stamped *ex-legal,* it does not contain a legal opinion.

Here are the two types of legal opinions:

- **Qualified legal opinion:** The bond counsel has some reservations about the issue.
- **Unqualified legal opinion:** The bond counsel is issuing a legal opinion without reservations.

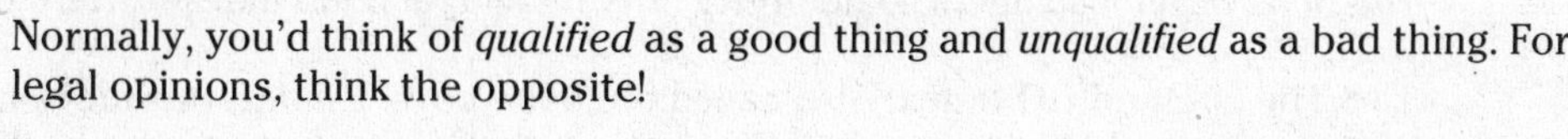

Normally, you'd think of *qualified* as a good thing and *unqualified* as a bad thing. For legal opinions, think the opposite!

Official statement

Municipal bonds don't have a prospectus; instead, municipalities provide an official statement. As with prospectuses, official statements come in *preliminary* and *final versions*. The preliminary version of the statement doesn't include an offering price or coupon rate. The *official statement* is the document that the issuer prepares; it states what the funds will be used for, provides information about the municipality, and details how the funds will be repaid. The official statement also includes

- The offering terms
- The underwriting spread (see Chapter 5)

- A description of the bonds
- A description of the issuer
- The offering price
- The coupon rate
- The feasibility statement
- The legal opinion

The Bond Buyer

The Bond Buyer, which is published Monday through Friday every week, is a newspaper that provides information about municipal issues, including new municipal bonds. (You can also find it online at `www.bondbuyer.com`.) Included in *The Bond Buyer* are the following statistics and information:

- **The visible supply:** The total dollar amount of municipal bonds expected to reach the market within the next 30 days
- **The placement ratio:** The percentage of new issues this week as compared to new issues offered for sale the previous week
- **Official notice of sale:** Municipalities looking to accept underwriting bids for new issues of municipal bonds publish the official notice of sale in *The Bond Buyer;* the official notice of sale includes
    - When and where bids can be submitted
    - The total amount of the sale
    - Amount of the good-faith deposit
    - The type of bond being offered (GO or revenue)
    - Methods for calculating cost (net interest cost or true interest cost)
    - The taxes backing the issue

Because GO bonds are backed by taxes paid by people living in the municipality, issuers are more likely to take bids by underwriters for GO bonds than for revenue bonds. The winning bid has the lowest net interest cost to the issuer (the lowest interest rate and/or the highest purchase price).

The Bond Buyer also offers some pretty nifty municipal bond indexes. Here they are:

- **The 20-Bond GO Index:** Also called the *Bond Buyer's Index,* this index measures the average yield of 20 municipal GO bonds with 20 years to maturity; all these bonds have a rating of A or better.

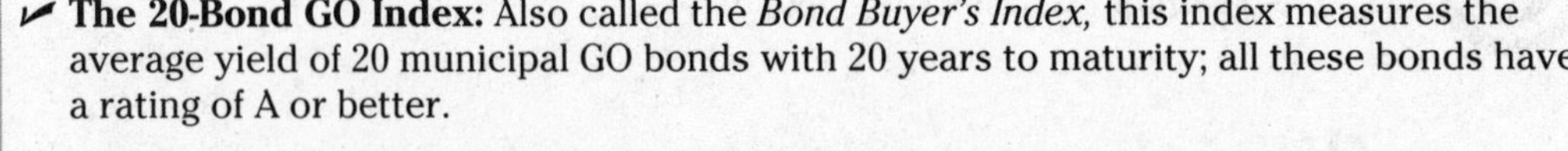

  To help you remember that *The Bond Buyer's* Index has 20 bonds with 20 years to maturity, remember that two *B*s equals two 20s.
- **The 11-Bond GO Index:** This index should be a nice, easy one for you to remember because it's the average yield of 11 bonds (of course) from the 20-bond index with a rating of AA or better.
- **The 25 Revenue Bond Index:** Also called the RevDex, this index is the average yield of 25 revenue bonds with 30 years to maturity, rated A or better.
- **The Municipal Bond Index:** Also called the 40-Bond Index, this index is the average dollar price of 40 highly traded GO and revenue bonds with an average maturity of 20 years and a rating of A or better.

Munifacts

Munifacts is a wire service provided by subscription to *The Bond Buyer;* it provides general information about proposed municipal securities, municipal securities prices, and general information relevant to the municipal bond market. Munifacts is of particular interest to municipal bond traders because it provides information about not only new municipal bonds but also municipal bonds in the secondary market.

Tracking down additional info

Along with Munifacts and *The Bond Buyer* (see the two preceding sections), investors and registered reps can also find additional information about municipal bonds in public newspapers, dealer offering sheets, and EMMA. EMMA (Electronic Municipal Market Access; `emma.msrb.org`) is a free comprehensive online source of information about municipal bonds and is designed specifically for the nonprofessional investor.

For Further Review

I'd love for you to be as prepared as possible to take the Series 7 exam, so I've compiled a list of Series 7 exam information related to this chapter that may show up on the test. Please take a look at the following items one at a time and make sure you know each of them well:

- Underwriting municipal bonds (see Chapter 5)
- Competitive underwritings versus negotiated underwritings
- Allocation of orders priority
- Characteristics of municipal bonds: auction rate, variable rate, lease revenue, Certificates of Participation, zero-coupon, original issue discount, taxable and advance (or pre-refunded)
- Political contributions
- Underwriters and conflicts of interest
- Control relationships
- Reoffering yields
- When-issued
- Good delivery
- Alternative minimum tax (AMT)
- Ratings for municipal bonds
- Additional Municipal Securities Rulemaking Board (MSRB) Rules
- The G Rules, specifically G-6, G-7, G-10, G-11, G-12, G-13, G-15, G-16, G-17, G-18, G-19, G-20, G-21, G-22, G-23, G-24, G-25, G-27, G-28, G-29, G-30, G-31, G-32, G-33, G-37, and G-39
- Enforcers of MSRB rules
- Reciprocal agreement
- Forms of ownership (bearer, registered as to principal only, fully registered, and book entry) (see Chapter 7)
- Zero-coupon municipal securities

- Municipal bond quotes (basis price, dollar price) (see Chapter 7)
- Original issue discount (OID)
- Diversification of municipal bonds: geographical, type, and rating
- Call or put features (see Chapter 7)
- Escrowed to maturity
- Accrued interest (see Chapter 7)
- Capital gains or losses
- Purchasing municipal securities on margin including bank-qualified issues
- Tax-exempt commercial paper
- Refunding methods: direct exchange, advance refunding, refunding at call dates, escrow to maturity, and crossover refunding
- Basis points
- Nature of the issuer's debt
- Factors that may affect the issuer's ability to pay
- Net debt to assessed valuation
- Yield calculations (see Chapter 7)
- Build America Bonds
- Real Time Reporting System (RTRS)
- ACATs

Part III

Delving Deeper: Security Investments with a Twist

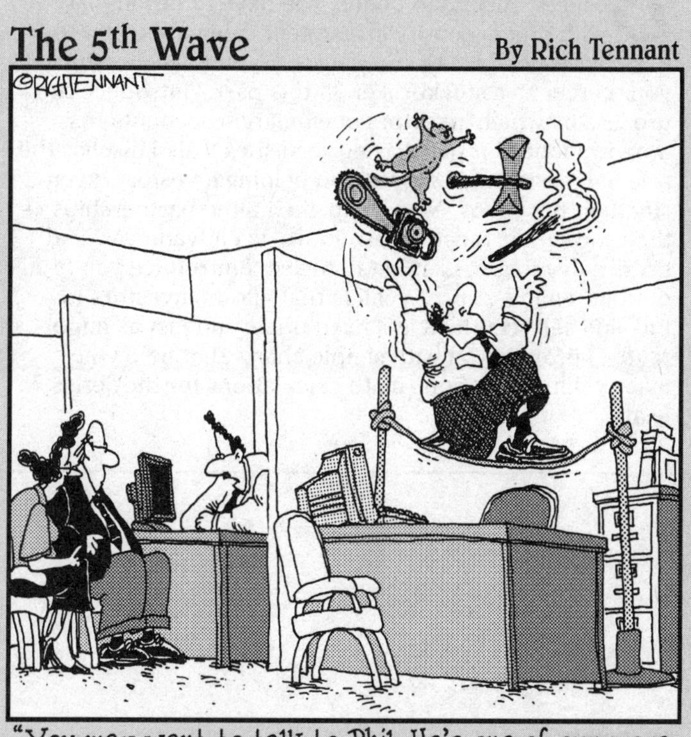

"You may want to talk to Phil. He's one of our more aggressive financial planners."

In this part . . .

Besides stocks and bonds, you have to be familiar with other security investment categories, first to pass the Series 7 exam and then to be more successful in your career as a stockbroker. In this part, I introduce the process by which investors open margin accounts to borrow money for purchasing securities. I also discuss the role of investment companies in helping investors diversify their portfolios. Next, I explain limited partnerships — their formation, function, structure, tax advantages, and tax disadvantages. Last but not least, I introduce you to options, an investment vehicle that allows investors to buy and sell securities at a fixed price; and just as importantly, I provide you with simple charts that help you master difficult options math calculations for the Series 7 exam.

Chapter 9

Borrowing Money and Securities: The Long and Short of Margin Accounts

In This Chapter

- Understanding the specifics of margin accounts
- Zoning in on the initial margin requirements
- Calculating with long margin accounts
- Summing up short margin accounts
- Reviewing additional topics tested

You don't necessarily need cold cash to buy securities. Thanks to the wonder of margin accounts, you can borrow money from a broker-dealer to purchase securities or borrow the securities themselves. Margin accounts allow customers to buy more securities from you (as a registered rep) than they otherwise would, thus leading to more money in your pocket (a greater commission). However, margin accounts are not without an additional degree of risk (which a lot of people found out back in 1929). Margin accounts are great if the securities held in the account are going in the right direction but horrible if they aren't.

In this chapter, I cover the Series 7 exam topics relating to short and long margin accounts and show you how to put those math skills to use. I also suggest related topics to study in the "For Further Review" section at the end of this chapter. And of course, I give you plenty of practice questions.

Practice a lot of these questions, because this stuff is tricky. The biggest mistake students make is mixing up the equations for long and short accounts. By doing the equations over and over again, you can avoid this pitfall. Additionally, the more questions you practice now, the easier the calculations will be for you to recall when you're taking the real exam.

Getting the Paperwork out of the Way

Because purchasing or selling short on margin involves extra risk, all customers must receive a risk disclosure document, which outlines those risks and some of the broker-dealer's rules. Besides receiving the margin risk disclosure document, the customer must sign a *margin agreement* before any securities can be purchased or sold short on margin. The margin agreement is broken down into three main sections:

- **The credit agreement:** Because the investors are borrowing money from the broker-dealer to purchase the securities, they're going to be charged interest on that money. The credit agreement discloses the terms for that borrowing, including the interest rate charged, the broker-dealer's method of computation, and situations under which the interest rate may change.

- **The hypothecation agreement:** This agreement states that all of the margined securities must be held in street name (in the name of the broker-dealer for the benefit of the customer). In addition, it allows the broker-dealer to use a portion of the customer's margined securities as collateral for a bank loan (*rehypothecation*). The hypothecation agreement also allows the broker-dealer to sell securities from the account in the event that equity falls below a certain level.
- **The loan consent form:** The loan consent form gives permission to the broker-dealer to loan a customer's margined securities to other investors or broker-dealers, typically for the short sale of securities.

Introducing Long and Short Margin Accounts

In margin accounts, investors either borrow some money to buy securities or borrow the securities themselves. As a result, margin accounts come in two varieties: long and short.

As you may remember, *long* means *to buy.* With a *long margin account,* the customer buys securities by coming up with a certain percentage of the purchase price of the securities and borrowing the balance from the broker-dealer. These optimistic investors are hoping for a bull market, because they want to sell the securities sometime later for a profit.

With a *short margin account,* an investor is borrowing securities to immediately sell in the market. The process sounds a bit backwards, but the investor is selling things he doesn't actually own. Hopefully, for this bearish customer, the price of the security will decrease so the investor can purchase the shares in the market at a lower price and then return them to the lender.

When a customer buys securities, he can purchase the securities in a cash or margin account, but when a customer sells short securities, the transaction must be executed in a margin account.

Playing by the Federal Reserve Board's Rules

The Securities Exchange Act of 1934 gives the Federal Reserve Board (FRB) the authority to regulate the extension of credit to customers in the securities industry. In addition to Regulation T (see the following section), the FRB decides which securities can be purchased on margin. (Chapter 13 can tell you more about the FRB and its role in influencing money supply.)

Regulation T

Regulation T is the Federal Reserve Board rule that covers the credit broker-dealers may extend to customers who are purchasing securities. Currently for margin accounts both long and short, Regulation T (Reg T) requires customers to deposit at least 50 percent of the current market value of the securities purchased on margin, and the balance is borrowed from the broker-dealer.

Regulation T is currently set at 50 percent; however, firms not willing to take as much risk may increase the house margin requirement to 55 percent, 60 percent, 65 percent, and so on. When you're taking the Series 7 exam, you should assume 50 percent unless the question states a different percentage.

Regulation T applies not only to margin accounts but also to cash accounts (see Chapter 16). When customers are purchasing securities in cash accounts, they have a certain number of business days to pay for the trade (one, three, or five). This delay is an extension of credit; therefore, it falls under Regulation T.

Reg T also identifies which securities can be purchased on margin and which ones can't. Securities that may be purchased on margin include

- Exchange-listed securities
- Most NASDAQ stocks
- Non-NASDAQ over-the-counter (OTC) securities approved by the Federal Reserve Board

Margin call

A *margin call* (also known as a *Fed call, federal call,* or *Reg T call*) is the broker-dealer's demand for a customer to deposit money in a margin account when purchasing or shorting (selling short) securities. If a customer is buying securities on margin, the customer may deposit fully paid securities in lieu of cash to meet the margin call.

For both long and short margin accounts, the margin call is the dollar amount of securities purchased (or shorted) multiplied by Regulation T (50 percent). So, for example, if an investor purchases $50,000 worth of securities on margin, the margin call would be $25,000. Here's how you figure that:

$$\text{margin call} = \text{the current market value of the securities} \times \text{Reg T}$$

$$\text{margin call} = \$50{,}000 \times 50\% = \$25{,}000$$

Opening a Margin Account: The Initial Requirements

The initial margin requirements for short and long accounts apply to the *first* transaction in a margin account only. After the account is established, the investor can purchase or short securities just by depositing Regulation T of the current market value of the securities purchased or shorted.

For an initial purchase in a margin account, customers must deposit a minimum of equity in their margin accounts. Currently, Regulation T calls for a minimum deposit of 50 percent of the current market value of the securities purchased or sold short. However, the Financial Industry Regulatory Authority (FINRA) and the New York Stock Exchange (NYSE) call for a minimum deposit of $2,000 or ask customers to pay for the securities in full (see the section "Starting long accounts" for more on how this works).

When you're taking the Series 7, pay attention to the wording of the question. Phrases like "opens a margin account," "in an initial transaction in a margin account," and so on indicate that the question is asking for the initial margin requirement rather than a margin call (see the preceding section for info on margin calls).

The following sections are based on the initial margin requirements for regular long and short margin accounts. If an investor wants to open a *day trading account*, the initial margin requirement is $25,000, and the investor must keep at least $25,000 in equity to continue trading. A day trading (pattern day trader) account is one in which the investor buys and sells the same security on the same day or sells short and buys the same security on the same day at least four times in five consecutive days.

Starting long accounts

To open a long margin account, the customer is required to deposit Regulation T or $2,000, whichever is greater. The exception to this rule occurs when a customer is purchasing less than $2,000 worth of securities on margin. In this case, the customer pays for the transaction in full. It certainly wouldn't make sense for a customer to purchase $1,000 of securities on margin and pay $2,000 when he could pay $1,000 if it were purchased in a cash account. Even if the customer pays in full, the account is still considered a margin account because the customer can make future purchases on margin as soon as he has over $2,000 in equity.

Table 9-1 shows you how Regulation T and the FINRA/NYSE requirements affect how much customers have to deposit when opening long margin accounts.

Table 9-1 Deposit Requirements for Long Margin Accounts

Dollar Amount of Purchase	*Regulation T Requirement*	*FINRA/NYSE Requirement*	*Amount Customer Must Deposit*
$6,000	$3,000	$2,000	$3,000
$3,000	$1,500	$2,000	$2,000
$1,000	$500	$1,000	$1,000

In short, here's how much an investor has to deposit:

Purchase Price	***Amount Owed***
Initial purchase < $2,000	Full purchase price
$2,000 ≤ initial purchase ≤ $4,000	$2,000
Initial purchase > $4,000	Reg T (50% of market value)

Opening short accounts

The minimum deposit for short accounts is fairly easy to remember. The $2,000 minimum required by the FINRA and NYSE applies to short margin accounts. Because of the additional risk investors take when selling short securities, the $2,000 minimum always applies, even if the customer is selling short only $300 worth of securities. In this case, the customer must deposit 50 percent of the current market value of the securities or $2,000, whichever is greater. Here's the breakdown:

Purchase Price	***Amount Owed***
Initial purchase ≤ $4,000	$2,000
Initial purchase > $4,000	Reg T (50% of market value)

Calculating Debit and Equity in Long Margin Accounts

The Series 7 asks you to calculate the numbers in a long margin account, which isn't too difficult if you take it one step at a time. The basic long margin account formula is as follows:

$$LMV - DR = EQ$$

In other words, *long market value minus debit balance equals equity.* The following sections describe the variables of this equation.

Long market value . . .

The *long market value* (LMV) is the current market value of the securities purchased in a margin account. The LMV does not remain fixed; it changes as the market value of the securities changes. Certainly, if an investor is long (owns) the securities, he wants the LMV to increase.

When a customer purchases securities on margin, the margin call (the amount the customer has to come up with) is based on the LMV of the securities. With Regulation T set at 50 percent, an investor has to deposit 50 percent of the value of the securities purchased on margin.

. . . Minus debit balance . . .

DR is the *debit balance* (also called the *debit record* or *debit register*); it's the amount of money that a customer owes a brokerage firm after purchasing securities on margin. The debit balance remains the same unless the customer pays back a portion of the amount borrowed by either selling securities in the account or by adding money to the account through dividends or payments.

Note: Although you aren't as likely to see a question about it on the Series 7 exam, the debit balance may be increased by interest charges imposed by the broker-dealer.

So, for example, if an investor purchases $20,000 worth of securities on margin, the debit balance would be $10,000. First you have to determine the margin call:

$$\text{margin call} = LMV \times \text{Reg T}$$

$$\text{margin call} = \$20{,}000 \times 50\% = \$10{,}000$$

Then use the margin call and the following formula to determine the debit balance:

$$DR = LMV - \text{margin call}$$

$$DR = \$20{,}000 - \$10{,}000 = \$10{,}000$$

. . . Equals equity

The *equity* (EQ) is the investor's portion of the account. When an investor initially opens a margin account, the equity is equal to the margin call. However, the equity changes as the market value of the securities in the account increases or decreases. When an investor has more equity than the Regulation T requirement, he has excess equity; if an investor has less equity than the Regulation T requirement, his account is restricted (see the later section "Checking out restricted accounts").

Note: When an investor has excess equity, he develops a line of credit known as a special memorandum account (SMA) (see "Let the Good Times Roll: Handling Excess Equity," later in the chapter). Remember that the SMA is built into the equity, not an addition to it. When a customer uses or removes the SMA, the equity decreases and the debit balance increases.

Putting it all together

The following question tests your ability to determine the debit balance in a long margin account.

Mr. Downey buys 1,000 shares of DEF common stock at $40 in a margin account. After Mr. Downey meets the margin call, what is the debit balance?

(A) $16,000

(B) $20,000

(C) $24,000

(D) $30,000

The correct answer is Choice (B). I know what you're thinking: "This is too easy." If the Series 7 gods are smiling down on you, you may actually get a question this straightforward. However, even if you don't, you still need a starting point, and this is a good one. First, set up the equation:

$$\text{LMV} - \text{DR} = \text{EQ}$$

Mr. Downey purchased $40,000 worth of stock (1,000 shares × $40 per share), so you need to enter $40,000 under the LMV (long market value). Next, figure out how much he needs to pay. Multiply the $40,000 × 50 percent (Regulation T), and you know that Mr. Downey has to come up with $20,000, which goes under the EQ (the investor's portion of the account). If the LMV is $40,000 and the EQ is $20,000, the DR (debit balance) has to be $20,000:

$$\$40{,}000 - \text{DR} = \$20{,}000$$

$$\text{DR} = \$20{,}000$$

Making Short Work of Calculations in Short Margin Accounts

On the Series 7 exam, you may be asked to calculate the numbers in a short margin account. You have to start by setting up the formula correctly. The basic short margin account formula is as follows:

$$\text{SMV} + \text{EQ} = \text{CR}$$

In other words, *short market value plus equity equals the credit balance.* The following sections describe the variables of this equation.

When a customer purchases securities, he has the choice of whether to pay in full or purchase on margin. When a customer is selling short (borrowed) securities, there is no option: The transactions must be executed in a margin account.

Short market value . . .

The *short market value* (SMV) is the current market value of the securities sold short in a margin account. Just as the LMV in a long account varies (see the earlier "Long market value . . ." section), so does the SMV. The SMV changes as the market value of the securities changes. If an investor is short the securities (selling borrowed securities), he wants the SMV to decrease so the investor can repurchase the securities at a lower price.

When a customer sells short securities on margin, the margin call (the amount the customer has to come up with) is based on the SMV of the securities. With Regulation T set at 50 percent, an investor has to deposit 50 percent of the value of the securities purchased on margin.

. . . Plus equity . . .

The *equity* (EQ) is the investor's part of the account. When an investor initially opens a short margin account, the equity is equal to $2,000 or Reg T (50 percent of the market value of the security), whichever is greater.

In a short margin account, the equity increases when the SMV of the securities decreases; when the SMV of the securities increases, the equity decreases.

When an investor has more equity than the Regulation T requirement, he has excess equity and develops an SMA (see the upcoming section titled "Let the Good Times Roll: Handling Excess Equity"); if an investor has less equity than the Reg T requirement, the account is restricted (see "Checking out restricted accounts," later in this chapter).

. . . Equals the credit balance

There's no debit balance (DR) in a short margin account because investors aren't borrowing money; they're borrowing securities. Instead, short margin accounts have a *credit balance* (also called a *credit record, credit register,* or *CR* for short). The credit balance is initially made up of the amount of money the investor received for selling the stock short (the *short market value*) and the amount that the investor had to deposit into the margin account to pay for the trade (the *equity*). The credit balance remains fixed unless the investor removes excess equity, more securities are shorted, or the investor covers some of his short positions.

For example, say that in an initial transaction in a margin account, an investor sells short $50,000 worth of securities with Reg T at 50 percent. First you determine the margin call:

$$\text{margin call} = \text{SMV} \times \text{Reg T } (50\%)$$

$$\text{margin call} = \$50{,}000 \times 50\% = \$25{,}000$$

Then you use the margin call and the following formula to determine the credit balance:

$$\text{CR} = \text{SMV} + \text{margin call}$$

$$\text{CR} = \$50{,}000 + \$25{,}000 = \$75{,}000$$

Putting the equation together

The following question tests your ability to determine the credit balance in a short margin account.

In an existing short margin account, Melissa Rice sold short 1,000 shares of HIJ common stock at $30. Prior to this transaction, the short market value of securities in the account was $52,000 and the equity was $25,000. What is Melissa's credit balance after the transaction?

(A) $15,000

(B) $45,000

(C) $77,000

(D) $122,000

The answer you want is Choice (D). This question is a little more difficult because the transaction happened in an existing margin account. Prior to this transaction, Melissa had a short market value (SMV) of $52,000 and an equity of $25,000, which means that the CR was $77,000:

$$SMV + EQ = CR$$

$$\$52{,}000 + \$25{,}000 = CR$$

$$CR = \$77{,}000$$

Because you know the existing CR, you only need to determine what happened to it as a result of the new transaction. Melissa shorted another $30,000 worth of stock (1,000 shares × $30 per share), so you need to enter $30,000 under the SMV (short market value). Next, figure out how much she needs to pay. Multiply the $30,000 ×.50 percent (Regulation T), and you know that Melissa has to come up with $15,000, which goes under the EQ (the investor's portion of the account). If the SMV increases by $30,000 and the EQ increases by $15,000, the CR (credit balance) has to increase by $45,000:

$$SMV + EQ = CR$$

$$\$30{,}000 + \$15{,}000 = CR$$

$$CR = \$45{,}000$$

Because the initial credit balance was $77,000 and it increased by $45,000, the credit balance after the transaction is $122,000.

Let the Good Times Roll: Handling Excess Equity

A special memorandum account (SMA) is a line of credit that a customer can borrow from his margin account or use to purchase more securities on margin. If all is right in the universe and the market goes in the right direction, the customer actually has more equity in the margin account than he needs, which generates an SMA. If a customer removes the SMA, he is borrowing money from the margin account; therefore,

- The equity is reduced for both long and short margin accounts.
- The debit balance (the amount owed to the brokerage firm) is increased for long margin accounts.
- The credit balance is decreased for short margin accounts.

After SMA is generated in a long or short account, it doesn't go away until a customer uses it, even if the account becomes restricted (see "Checking out restricted accounts," later in this chapter, for info on restriction). You can think of developing an SMA as establishing credit; after you establish credit (on a credit card, for example), it remains there until you use it.

SMAs for long margin accounts

When an investor purchases on margin, that customer has a leveraged position, so he has an interest in a larger amount of securities than he would've had if he had paid in full. When a customer has a long margin account, excess equity is created when the value of the securities in the account increases and the equity in the account increases above the margin requirement.

The following question tests your ability to answer a question on excess equity.

Mrs. Glorious purchased 1,000 shares of DUD Corp. on margin at $50 per share. If DUD is currently trading at $70 per share, what is Mrs. Glorious' excess equity?

(A) $5,000

(B) $7,500

(C) $10,000

(D) $20,000

The answer you're looking for is Choice (C). This question throws you a little curveball because you have to set up a new equation when the market price changes. You first need to find the debit balance. Mrs. Glorious purchased $50,000 worth of securities (1,000 shares × $50 per share), so enter $50,000 under the LMV (long market value). Then Mrs. Glorious had to deposit the Regulation T amount (50 percent) of the purchase, so enter $25,000 (50% × $50,000) under the EQ (the investor's portion of the account). This means she borrowed $25,000 (the DR) from the broker-dealer:

$$\text{LMV} - \text{DR} = \text{EQ}$$

$$\$50{,}000 - \text{DR} = \$25{,}000$$

$$\text{DR} = \$25{,}000$$

Now the curveball: The LMV changes to $70,000 ($70 × 1,000 shares). Because the DR (the amount borrowed from the broker-dealer) doesn't change, you bring the $25,000 to your new equation. You find that the EQ has increased to $45,000:

$$\text{LMV} - \text{DR} = \text{EQ}$$

$$\$70{,}000 - \$25{,}000 = \text{EQ}$$

$$\$45{,}000 = \text{EQ}$$

Now multiply the LMV by Regulation T to get the margin requirement, the amount that Mrs. Glorious should have in EQ to be at 50 percent. Take the $35,000 ($70,000 × 50%) and compare it to the EQ. Because Mrs. Glorious has $45,000 in equity, she has $10,000 in excess equity ($10,000 more than she needs):

$$\text{margin requirement} = \text{Reg T} \times \text{LMV}$$

$$\text{margin requirement} = 50\% \times \$70{,}000 = \$35{,}000$$

$$\text{SMA} = \text{EQ} - \text{margin requirement}$$

$$\text{SMA} = \$45{,}000 - \$35{,}000 = \$10{,}000$$

The *R* in *DR* should help you remember that the debit balance remains the same as the market price changes.

SMAs for short margin accounts

Unlike in a long account, an investor with a short margin account earns excess equity when the price of the securities in the margin account decreases. An SMA is a credit line that investors can withdraw as cash or use to help purchase or sell short more securities on margin.

Excess equity is the amount of equity that a customer has in a margin account that's above the Regulation T requirement.

The following question tests your knowledge on determining excess equity for a short account.

Mrs. Rice sold short 1,000 shares of HIJ Corp. on margin at $60 per share. If HIJ is currently trading at $50 per share, what is Mrs. Rice's excess equity?

(A) $5,000

(B) $7,500

(C) $10,000

(D) $15,000

The correct answer is Choice (D). This question has a twist because you have to use a new equation when the market price changes. Start by setting up the equation to find the credit balance. Mrs. Rice sold short $60,000 worth of securities (1,000 shares × $60 per share), so enter $60,000 under the SMV (short market value). Then Mrs. Rice had to deposit the Regulation T amount (50 percent) of the purchase, so enter $30,000 (50% × $60,000) under the EQ (the investor's portion of the account). The credit balance (CR) is $90,000:

$$\text{SMV} + \text{EQ} = \text{CR}$$

$$\$60{,}000 + \$30{,}000 = \text{CR}$$

$$\$90{,}000 = \text{CR}$$

Next, the SMV changes to $50,000 ($50 × 1,000 shares), so you need to calculate the investor's current equity. Put that value under the SMV. In a short account, the CR remains the same as the market price changes, so you need to bring the $90,000 straight down from the previous equation. This means that the EQ has increased to $40,000 (the difference between $50,000 and $90,000):

$$\text{SMV} + \text{EQ} = \text{CR}$$

$$\$50{,}000 + \text{EQ} = \$90{,}000$$

$$\text{EQ} = \$40{,}000$$

Now multiply the SMV by Regulation T to get the amount that Mrs. Rice should have in equity to be at 50 percent. Compare the margin requirement of $25,000 ($50,000 × 50%) to the current equity. Because Mrs. Rice has $40,000 in equity, she has $15,000 in excess equity ($15,000 more than she needs):

$$\text{margin requirement} = \text{Reg T} \times \text{SMV}$$

$$\text{margin requirement} = 50\% \times \$50{,}000 = \$25{,}000$$

$$\text{SMA} = \text{EQ} - \text{margin requirement}$$

$$\text{SMA} = \$40{,}000 - \$25{,}000 = \$15{,}000$$

The *R* in *CR* should help you remember that the credit balance remains the same as the market price changes.

Playing it SMA/RT: Using buying and shorting power for good

Buying power (for long accounts) and *shorting power* (for short accounts) are the dollar amounts of securities a customer can purchase on margin using his excess equity (SMA). You calculate both by dividing the SMA by Reg T:

$$\text{buying or shorting power} = \frac{\text{SMA}}{\text{Reg T}}$$

To help you calculate the buying or shorting power in a margin account, remember the phrase *People who are SMA/RT use their buying (or shorting) power.* This phrase can help you remember that to determine the buying or shorting power, you need to divide the SMA by Regulation T. As long as Regulation T is at 50 percent, you probably don't need this tip because the power will always be double the SMA (for example, $1,000 SMA can purchase $2,000 worth of securities on margin). However, if Regulation T (or house requirements) is anything other than 50 percent, this formula becomes very important.

Try your hand at the following question.

Mr. Smith has a long margin account with a market value of $20,000, a debit balance of $5,000, an equity of $15,000, and an SMA of $3,000. If Regulation T is set at 60 percent, what is the buying power?

(A) $3,000

(B) $5,000

(C) $6,000

(D) No buying power

The right answer is Choice (B). Because the question is nice enough to supply you with the SMA, you don't have to figure it on your own. The buying power of a margin account is how much in securities an investor can buy (or sell short) without depositing additional funds. All you need to do is divide the SMA by Regulation T:

$$\text{buying power} = \frac{\text{SMA}}{\text{Reg T}} = \frac{\$3{,}000}{60\%} = \$5{,}000$$

Looking at Limits When the Market Goes the Wrong Way

Often, securities don't go in the direction customers hope for. When this happens in a margin account, investors lose money at an accelerated rate. If the equity in a margin account drops below the Regulation T (or house) requirement, the account becomes restricted. However, if the equity in a long margin account drops below 25 percent (30 percent for a short account), the situation becomes much more serious. Read on for info on restricted accounts and minimum maintenance.

Checking out restricted accounts

In the previous sections, everything is coming up roses; but what if the market price of the securities held in a long margin account decreases instead of increases? What if the securities in a short margin account show wild success? If this happens, the account becomes restricted. *Restricted accounts* show up when the equity in the account is below the margin requirement. However, a restricted account doesn't mean that investors can't buy (or short) securities in the margin account; investors may still do so by coming up with the margin requirement of the new purchase.

Restricted long margin accounts

A restricted account is calculated the same way as the excess equity (see the earlier section "Let the Good Times Roll: Handling Excess Equity"), only the investor has less than 50 percent of the long market value (LMV) in equity instead of more than 50 percent. Check out the following example.

Macy Bullhorn purchased 500 shares of LMN common stock on margin when LMN was trading at $30 per share. If LMN is currently trading at $25 per share, by how much is Macy's margin account restricted?

(A) $1,250

(B) $2,500

(C) $5,000

(D) $6,250

The correct answer is Choice (A). You may notice the similarities between figuring out excess equity and determining whether an account is restricted. If an account is restricted, the account contains less equity than needed to be at 50 percent of the LMV. First, figure out Macy's debit balance. Macy purchased $15,000 worth of securities (500 shares × $30 per share), so enter $15,000 under the LMV (long market value). Then Macy had to deposit the Reg T amount (50 percent) of the purchase, so enter $7,500 (50% × $15,000) under the EQ (the investor's portion of the account). She borrowed $7,500 (the DR) from the broker-dealer:

LMV – DR = EQ

$15,000 – DR = $7,500

DR = $7,500

Next, find the investor's current equity. The LMV changes to $12,500 ($25 × 500 shares), so enter that under the LMV. Because the DR (the amount borrowed from the broker-dealer) doesn't change, bring the $7,500 straight down from the preceding equation. You find that the EQ has decreased to $5,000 ($12,500 – $7,500):

LMV – DR = EQ

$12,500 – $7,500 = EQ

$5,000 = EQ

Now multiply the LMV by Reg T to get the margin requirement, the amount Macy should have in equity to be at 50 percent. Take the $6,250 ($12,500 × 50%) and compare it to the current equity. Because Macy has only $5,000 in equity, her account is restricted by $1,250:

$$\text{margin requirement} = \text{Reg T} \times \text{LMV}$$

$$\text{margin requirement} = 50\% \times \$12{,}500 = \$6{,}250$$

$$\text{restriction} = \text{margin requirement} - \text{EQ}$$

$$\text{restriction} = \$6{,}250 - \$5{,}000 = \$1{,}250$$

You can calculate the excess equity (SMA) or determine whether an account is restricted in pretty much the same way. If the investor has more equity than needed, it's an SMA; if the investor has less than needed, the account is restricted.

Restricted short margin accounts

If the market price of the securities held in a short margin account increases instead of decreasing, the situation isn't so great. When this happens, the account becomes restricted. You can figure out whether the account is restricted the same way you figure out the excess equity, only the investor has less than 50 percent of the SMV in equity instead of more than 50 percent.

The following question tests your knowledge of restricted short accounts.

Mr. Willing sold short 400 shares of RST common stock on margin at $40 per share. If RST is currently trading at $44 per share, how much is the account restricted?

(A) $2,400

(B) $6,400

(C) $8,800

(D) $16,000

The answer you want is Choice (A). First, figure out the credit balance. Mr. Willing sold short $16,000 worth of securities (400 shares × $40 per share), so enter $16,000 under the SMV (short market value). Then Mr. Willing had to deposit the Reg T amount (50 percent) of the purchase, so enter $8,000 (50% × $16,000) under the EQ (the investor's portion of the account). You find that the credit balance (CR) is $24,000:

$$\text{SMV} + \text{EQ} = \text{CR}$$

$$\$16{,}000 + \$8{,}000 = \text{CR}$$

$$\$24{,}000 = \text{CR}$$

Next, find Mr. Willing's current equity. The SMV changes to $17,600 ($44 × 400 shares), so you need to put that under the SMV in a new equation. In a short account, the CR remains the same as the market price changes, so you need to bring the $24,000 straight down from the preceding equation. You can see that the EQ has decreased to $6,400 (the difference between $17,600 and $24,000):

$$\text{SMV} + \text{EQ} = \text{CR}$$

$$\$17{,}600 + \text{EQ} = \$24{,}000$$

$$\text{EQ} = \$6{,}400$$

Now multiply the SMV by Regulation T to get the amount Mr. Willing should have in equity to be at 50 percent. Take the \$8,800 (\$17,600 × 50%) and compare it to the EQ. Because Mr. Willing has only \$6,400 in equity (\$2,400 less than the Reg T requirement), his account is restricted by \$2,400:

$$\text{margin requirement} = \text{Reg T} \times \text{SMV}$$

$$\text{margin requirement} = 50\% \times \$17{,}600 = \$8{,}800$$

$$\text{restriction} = \text{margin requirement} - \text{EQ}$$

$$\text{restriction} = \$8{,}800 - \$6{,}400 = \$2{,}400$$

Keeping up with minimum maintenance

A margin account can be left restricted, but if a margin account falls below minimum maintenance, the situation is much more serious. Customers then have to deal with a *maintenance call* (or *maintenance margin call* or *Fed call*), which requires investors to deposit money into the margin account immediately.

Minimum maintenance on a long account

Minimum maintenance on a long margin account is 25 percent of the long market value. I'm sure that you'll be happy to know that the calculations are the same as for restricted accounts (see the preceding sections) until you get to the last step. Try the following question.

Mark Smithers III purchased 1,000 shares of UVW common stock on margin when UVW was trading at \$55 per share. If UVW is currently trading at \$35 per share, what is the maintenance call?

(A) \$1,250

(B) \$7,500

(C) \$8,750

(D) \$10,000

The right answer is Choice (A). You may notice that the equation looks almost exactly the same as the previous two examples except for the last step. An account may be left restricted, but if it falls below minimum maintenance, the customer must come up with enough money (or fully paid securities) to bring the account above minimum maintenance right away.

First, use the market value at the time of purchase to determine the debit balance. Mark purchased \$55,000 worth of securities (1,000 shares × \$55 per share), so enter \$55,000 under the LMV (long market value). Then Mark had to deposit the Reg T amount (50 percent) of the purchase, so enter \$27,500 (50% × \$55,000) under the EQ (the customer's portion of the account). You find that he borrowed \$27,500 (the DR) from the broker-dealer:

$$\text{LMV} - \text{DR} = \text{EQ}$$

$$\$55{,}000 - \text{DR} = \$27{,}500$$

$$\text{DR} = \$27{,}500$$

Then find Mark's current equity. The LMV changed to \$35,000 (\$35 × 1,000 shares), so you need to put that value under the LMV. Because the DR (the amount borrowed from the broker-dealer) doesn't change, you bring the \$27,500 straight down. Therefore, the EQ has decreased to \$7,500:

$$LMV - DR = EQ$$
$$\$35,000 - \$27,500 = EQ$$
$$\$7,500 = EQ$$

Now multiply the LMV by the 25 percent minimum maintenance requirement to get the amount Mark should have in equity to be at minimum maintenance. Take the $8,750 ($35,000 × 25%) and compare it to the current equity. Because Mike has only $7,500 in equity, he'll receive a maintenance call of $1,250:

$$\text{maintenance EQ} = \text{minimum maintenance \%} \times LMV$$
$$\text{maintenance EQ} = 25\% \times \$35,000 = \$8,750$$
$$\text{maintenance call} = \$8,750 - \$7,500 = \$1,250$$

Minimum maintenance on a short account

As with long margin accounts, short margin accounts can be left restricted, but if a margin account falls below minimum maintenance, the customer gets hit with a maintenance call. Minimum maintenance on a short margin account is 30 percent of the current market value. The rest of the calculations are similar to figuring out the SMA or how much the account is restricted (see "Checking out restricted accounts," earlier in this chapter) until you get to the last step.

Minimum maintenance for a long account is 25 percent of the current market value, and minimum maintenance on a short account is 30 percent of the current market value.

The following question tests your knowledge in determining the maintenance call for short accounts.

Mrs. Martinez sold short 1,000 shares of XYZ common stock on margin at $50 per share. If XYZ is currently trading at $60 per share, what is the maintenance call?

(A) $0

(B) $2,000

(C) $3,000

(D) $8,000

The correct answer is Choice (C). First, find Mrs. Martinez's credit balance. Mrs. Martinez sold short $50,000 worth of securities (1,000 shares × $50 per share), so enter $50,000 under the SMV (short market value). Then Mrs. Martinez had to deposit the Reg T amount (50 percent) of the purchase, so enter $25,000 (50% × $50,000) under the EQ (the investor's portion of the account). The credit balance (CR) is $75,000:

$$SMV + EQ = CR$$
$$\$50,000 + \$25,000 = CR$$
$$\$75,000 = CR$$

Next, find Mrs. Martinez's current equity. The SMV changed to $60,000 ($60 × 1,000 shares), so you need to put that value under the SMV. In a short account, the CR remains the same as the market price changes, so the CR is $75,000. Therefore, the equity has decreased to $15,000:

$$SMV + EQ = CR$$
$$\$60,000 + EQ = \$75,000$$
$$EQ = \$15,000$$

Now multiply the SMV by 30 percent to get the amount Mrs. Martinez should have in equity to be at minimum maintenance. Take the $18,000 ($60,000 × 30%) and compare it to the equity. Because Mrs. Martinez has only $15,000 in equity, she'll receive a maintenance call of $3,000:

$$\text{maintenance EQ} = \text{minimum maintenance \%} \times \text{SMV}$$

$$\text{maintenance EQ} = 30\% \times \$60{,}000 = \$18{,}000$$

$$\text{maintenance call} = \text{maintenance EQ} - \text{EQ}$$

$$\text{maintenance call} = \$18{,}000 - \$15{,}000 = \$3{,}000$$

For Further Review

I want you to be as prepared as possible to answer any possible margin question that can come your way on the Series 7 exam. Although I cover the main topics related to margin accounts and hopefully have given you more confidence when answering margin math questions, you also need to have a good understanding of the items that follow to be truly prepared to ace the margin questions on the exam:

- The margin requirement for U.S. government securities and municipal bonds
- The waiting period for buying new securities on margin
- Which securities can be purchased on margin and which ones can't
- The effect of dividends or cash deposits on a margin account
- The effect of interest charges on long margin accounts
- Calculating combined long and short margin accounts
- The loan value
- The rehypothecation percentage
- Buying and selling simultaneously
- Where the money goes when securities are sold
- The dollar value of securities that must be deposited or liquidated to meet a margin/maintenance call
- The margin requirement when selling short low-priced securities
- LEAPS (long-term options) purchased on margin
- The portfolio margin
- Ineligible accounts

Chapter 10

Delivering Diversification with Packaged Securities

In This Chapter

- Taking advantage of management investment companies
- Understanding face-amount certificate companies and UITs
- Reviewing REITs
- Looking at annuities
- Reviewing additional topics tested

Diversification is key when you're helping customers set up a portfolio of securities, and it's fairly easy when your customer has a good deal of money to invest. But what if an investor has limited resources? Certainly, such investors can't afford to buy several different securities, and you don't want to limit your customer to only one (heaven forbid it should go belly up). Packaged securities to the rescue! These securities, such as open-end funds, closed-end funds, face-amount certificate companies, UITs, real estate investment trusts (REITs), and annuities, offer variety within one security by investing a customer's money in a diversified pool of securities . . . for a cost, of course. A bit of profit-driven teamwork can ensure your customers' investments are much safer than, say, the blackjack tables in Vegas.

In this chapter, I cover topics relating to investment companies, REITs, and annuities. Open-end (mutual) funds and closed investment funds are only the beginning. I also discuss face-amount certificate companies and trusts like unit investment trusts (UITs). The "For Further Review" section at the end of this chapter can help you round out your studies, and the practice questions in this chapter may put you in that question-answering mood.

Diversifying through Management Investment Companies

The Investment Company Act of 1940 divides investment companies into three main types: management investment companies, face-amount certificate companies, and unit investment trusts. This section focuses on management investment companies, which the Series 7 tests more than the other types. I cover the other types in the aptly named "Considering Other Investment Company Options" section later on.

Management companies are, by far, the most familiar type of investment company. The securities held by the management companies are actively managed by portfolio managers.

Comparing open- and closed-end funds

Management companies have to be either open-end or closed-end funds. Make sure you know the difference between the two.

Open-end (mutual) funds

An open-end fund is more commonly known as a mutual fund. As with closed-end funds, *mutual funds* invest in many different securities to provide diversification for investors. The key difference is that mutual funds are constantly issuing and redeeming shares, which provides liquidity for investors. Because open-end fund shares are continuous offerings of new shares, a mutual fund prospectus must always be available. You need to understand the makings of the net asset value and the public offering price when taking the Series 7 exam:

- **Net asset value (NAV):** Fortunately, the net asset value or net asset value per share is determined the same way for both open and closed-end funds — by dividing the value of the securities held by the fund by the number of shares outstanding; however, with open-end funds, the NAV is the bid price. When investors redeem shares of a mutual fund, they receive the NAV. Mutual funds can't ever trade below the NAV.
- **Public offering price (POP):** For mutual funds, the public offering price (the ask price) is the NAV plus a sales charge.

  If a mutual fund doesn't charge a sales charge, it's called a *no-load fund.*

Closed-end funds

Unlike open-end funds, closed-end funds have a fixed number of shares outstanding (hence the word *closed*). Closed-end funds act more like stock than open-end funds because they issue new shares to the public, and after that, the shares are bought and sold in the market. Because they trade in the market, they're often called *publicly traded funds*. Although the net asset value of closed-end and open-end funds is figured the same, the public offering price is determined a little differently:

- **Net asset value (NAV):** The net asset value or net asset value per share is the parity price where the fund should be trading. You determine it by dividing the value of the securities held by the fund by the number of shares outstanding. Only closed-end funds may trade below the NAV (at a discount).
- **Public offering price (POP):** For closed-end funds, the public offering price (the ask price) depends more on supply and demand than the NAV. Investors of closed-end funds pay the POP (current market price) plus a broker's commission.

Note: Although closed-end funds are not purchased from and redeemed with the issuer, they do offer a high degree of liquidity. After the initial offering, they can be purchased or sold either on an exchange or over-the-counter (OTC).

Open and closed: Focusing on their differences

You can expect at least a few of the Series 7 questions relating to investment companies to test you on the differences between open-end and closed-end funds. Table 10-1 should help you zone in on the major distinctions.

Table 10-1 Comparing Open-End and Closed-End Funds

Category	*Closed-End*	*Open-End*
Capitalization	One-time offering of securities (fixed number of shares outstanding)	Continuous offering of new shares (no fixed number of shares outstanding)
Pricing the fund	Investors purchase at the current market value (public offering price, or POP) plus a commission	Investors purchase at the net asset value (NAV) plus a sales charge
Issues	Common stock, preferred stock, and debt securities	Common stock only
Shares purchased	Shares can be purchased in full only	Shares can be purchased in full or fractions (up to three decimal places)
Purchased and sold	Initial public offerings go through underwriters; after that, investors purchase and sell shares either over-the-counter or on an exchange (no redemption)	Shares are sold and redeemed by the fund only

The key difference between open-end and closed-end funds is the method of capitalization. An open-end (mutual) fund is a continuous offering of new securities, whereas a closed-end fund is a one-time offering of new securities.

Keeping your customer's investment objectives in mind

Unlike investors in face-amount certificate companies and unit investment trusts (see "Considering Other Investment Company Options," still to come), investors of open-end and closed-end funds have many choices available. Investors may be looking for safety, growth, a combination, and so on. This section gives you a glimpse into those investment choices.

The single most important consideration for customers who invest in packaged securities is the fund's investment objectives. This feature surpasses even the sales charge or management fees. As a registered rep, one of your primary jobs will be to help investors decide which type of fund would be best for them. The test-designers want to know you can handle that job. Comparing like-type funds is secondary. So without further ado, here are the major types (although variables within each fund can make a fund riskier or safer, I've placed the list in the normal order from safest to riskiest):

- **Money market fund:** This fund (as you've probably guessed) invests in money market instruments (short-term debt securities). You need to know the specifics of this fund more than other types of funds. Here are the key points:
  - It usually provides a check-writing feature (you're given a checkbook) as a way of redeeming shares.
  - It's always no-load (there's no sales charge).
  - It computes dividends daily and credits them monthly.
  - There's no penalty for early redemption.

- **Income fund:** The primary objective of an income fund is to provide current revenue (not growth) for investors. This type of fund invests most of its assets in a diversified portfolio of debt securities that pay interest and in preferred and common stock of companies that are known to pay consistent dividends in cash.

  Income funds are considered much safer (more conservative) investments than growth funds. You can assume for Series 7 exam (and real-life) purposes that income funds are better investment choices for retirees and investors who are looking for a steady cash flow without much risk.
- **Balanced fund:** A balanced fund is a combination of a growth fund and an income fund. Balanced funds invest in common stocks, preferred stocks, long-term bonds, and short-term bonds, aiming to provide both income and capital appreciation while minimizing risk. These funds don't get hammered too badly when the market is bearish but usually underperform when the market is bullish.
- **Growth fund:** This fund is exactly what you'd expect it to be; growth funds invest most of their assets in a diversified portfolio of the common stock of relatively new companies, looking for big increases in the stock prices. Growth funds offer a higher potential for growth but usually at a higher risk for the investor. This type of fund is ideal for an investor who's looking for long-term capital appreciation potential.

  Because of the inherent risk of investing in growth funds, they're better for younger investors who can take the risk because they have more time to recover their losses.
- **Specialized (sector) fund:** A specialized or sector fund is a type of fund that invests primarily in the securities of a single industry or geographical area. A specialized fund may invest only in financial services, healthcare, automotive stocks, Japanese securities, and so on. Because specialized funds are limited in their investments, you can assume that they're a little riskier (more volatile) than the average fund.
- **International or global fund:** An international fund invests in companies based anywhere outside of the investor's home country. A global fund invests in securities located anywhere in the world, including the investor's home country. Although international and global funds may be good to round out a portfolio, they aren't without their risks. Along with the risk that investors face by just investing in securities in general, holders of international and global funds also face currency risk, which is the risk that the currency exchange rate between the U.S. and foreign issuers will hurt investors. There's also the additional risk that politics in a particular country will harm the value of the fund.
- **Hedge fund:** This fund uses leverage (purchasing on margin — see Chapter 9), options (see Chapter 12), short sales, and other speculative investment strategies. Hedge funds usually perform better in a bearish market than the other funds do. This investment fund is considered the most speculative (riskiest).

Fund of a fund

Many funds are actually funds of funds, such as life-cycle funds. Life-cycle funds are also called *targeted* or *age-based* funds. The idea behind life-cycle funds is to automatically adjust the composition of the fund so that investors take less risk as they get older. Typically, younger investors can afford to take more financial risk and therefore invest a larger percentage of their portfolio in equity securities and a lesser percentage in fixed-income securities. As investors get older, the percentages should change so that a larger percentage of the portfolio is in fixed-income securities and a lesser percentage is in equity securities. Life-cycle funds are set up with targeted retirement dates. Investors choose the life-cycle fund that matches their retirement date, and the fund adjusts its fund holdings occasionally so that equity funds gradually decrease and funds that invest in fixed-income securities gradually increase.

Don't let the variety of funds distract you too much. So many different funds are out there that the choices could drive you crazy. I list the main types, but funds can invest by objective (as previously listed) or composition, such as with foreign stock funds (which invest in foreign securities), tax-exempt funds (which invest in municipal bonds), U.S. government funds, and so on. The composition of the fund should help you match it with your customer's objectives. For instance, a customer looking for safety and income may invest in a U.S. government bond fund.

Dealing with discounts and methods of investing

Investors who have the extra funds available may be able to receive a reduced sales charge for large dollar purchases. Breakpoints and the letter of intent are available to investors of open-end funds and unit investment trusts. Because closed-end funds, after the initial offering, are traded in the market, investors do not receive break points. Dollar cost averaging and fixed share averaging are most often used for open-end fund purchases but may apply to other investments as well.

Breakpoints

Funds have an investment adviser (portfolio manager) who gets paid a percentage of the value of the securities held in the fund. Therefore, one way to entice investors to spend more is to reduce the sales charge when they spend a certain minimum amount of money. That's where the breakpoint comes in.

Management investment companies divide purchase amounts into different tiers. Within a certain range, investors all pay the same sales charge percentage. But when investors spend enough to put them in the next tier (when they hit the *breakpoint*), they get a reduced sales charge. Breakpoints have no set schedule, so they vary from fund to fund.

Another discount, *rights of accumulation,* allows shareholders to receive a reduced sales charge when the amount of the funds held plus the amount purchased is enough to reach a breakpoint. There is no time limit for rights of accumulation.

Here are a few key points for you to remember for the Series 7 exam:

- Breakpoints must be disclosed in the prospectus.
- Breakpoints are not available to partnerships or *investment clubs* (several people pooling money together to receive reduced sales charges).
- Breakpoints are generally available to individual investors, joint accounts with family members, and corporations.

Letters of intent

A *letter of intent* (LOI) signed by an investor allows her to receive a breakpoint (quantity discount) right away with the initial purchase, even if the investor hasn't yet deposited enough money to achieve the breakpoint. This document states that as long as the investor deposits enough within a 13-month period, she will receive the discounted sales charge right away.

Here are a few specifics about the letter of intent that you need to know for the Series 7:

- The investor has *13 months* after the first deposit to live up to the terms of the letter of intent in order to maintain the reduced sales charge.
- The LOI may be *backdated for up to 90 days,* meaning that it may apply to a previous purchase. However, remember that if the LOI applies to a previous purchase, the 13-month period starts from the date of that previous transaction.

- While the investor is under the letter of intent, shares are held in escrow to pay for the difference in the sales charge. If the investor doesn't live up to the terms of the obligation, the fund sells the shares held in escrow.

Here's how a letter of intent may work. Suppose, for instance, that Mr. Smith purchased $2,000 worth of ABC Growth Fund two months ago and has another $7,000 to invest in the fund right now. Mr. Smith believes that he'll keep investing in ABC Growth Fund and would like to get a reduced sales charge for investments of $10,000 and up (see Table 10-2 for the breakpoints).

Table 10-2 Breakpoints for ABC Growth Fund

Purchase Amount	*Sales Charge*
\$1–\$9,999	7%
\$10,000–\$19,999	6%
\$20,000–\$39,999	4%
\$40,000 and up	2%

Mr. Smith signs a letter of intent and wants to apply it to his previous purchase. Because his previous purchase was two months ago, Mr. Smith has only another 11 months to invest the remaining $8,000 into ABC Growth Fund. Mr. Smith will receive the 6 percent sales charge on his $7,000 investment right now, which will be reduced by the overage he paid on the previous investment of $2,000. In other words, he'll pay only $400 sales charge on the current investment ($420 for this transaction minus the $20 overpaid from the previous investment) when he invests the $7,000. As long as Mr. Smith deposits the additional $1,000 by the end of the letter of intent's time frame, he'll pay the 6 percent sales charge. However, if Mr. Smith doesn't live up to the terms of the agreement, ABC Growth fund will sell the shares held in escrow to pay for the difference in the sales charge.

Investors may redeem their shares at any time, even if they're under a letter of intent.

Dollar cost averaging

If an investor is employing the *dollar-cost-averaging* formula, she is investing the same dollar amount into the same investment periodically. Although dollar cost averaging is primarily used for mutual funds, people can use it for other investments as well. Dollar cost averaging benefits the investor when the price of the security is fluctuating. The investor ends up buying more shares when the price is low and fewer shares when the price is high by depositing the same amount of money each time she makes a purchase.

Dollar cost averaging results in an *average cost per share* that is *lower than the average price per share* if the price of the fund fluctuates.

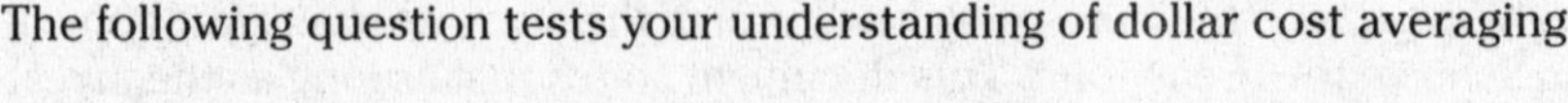

The following question tests your understanding of dollar cost averaging.

Mrs. Johnson deposits $1,000 into DEF growth fund in four separate months. The purchase prices of the fund are as follows:

Month 1: $40

Month 2: $50

Month 3: $50

Month 4: $40

What is the average cost per share for Mrs. Johnson?

(A) $40.00

(B) $44.44

(C) $45.00

(D) $48.35

The correct answer is Choice (B). On the surface, this question may look very easy to you and you may jump to Choice (C), but Choice (C) is the average price per share, not the average cost. Remember that because Mrs. Johnson is investing the same amount of money each month, she's able to buy more shares when the price is low and less when the price is high. In the first and fourth months, when the price was $40 per share, she was able to buy 25 shares each time. In the second and third months, she was able to buy only 20 shares each time:

$$\text{1st and 4th months} = \frac{\$1{,}000 \text{ invested}}{\$40 \text{ per share}} = 25 \text{ shares per month}$$

$$\text{2nd and 3rd months} = \frac{\$1{,}000 \text{ invested}}{\$50 \text{ per share}} = 20 \text{ shares per month}$$

Over the four months, Mrs. Johnson invested a total of $4,000 and purchased a total of 90 shares (25 + 20 + 20 + 25). The average cost per share is $44.44:

$$\text{average cost per share} = \frac{\text{total amount invested}}{\text{no. of shares purchased}} = \frac{\$4{,}000}{90 \text{ shares}} = \$44.44$$

If you use your sense of logic and watch for ways to eliminate answer choices, you may get away with doing very little math. Here, you can answer the question by finding the average price per share, which is *not* what the question is looking for. With dollar cost averaging, buying more when the price is low drives the average cost down; therefore, the average cost per share has to be between the minimum price per share ($40) and the average price per share ($45). The only number that fits these criteria is $44.44, or Choice (B).

You should be prepared to calculate the average cost per share, the average price per share ($45), and the amount saved per share ($0.56).

Fixed share averaging

Fixed share averaging is a nice, easy concept that doesn't require you to remember any more formulas. *Fixed share averaging* is just buying the same number of shares of a security (20 shares, 50 shares, 100 shares, and so forth) every so often (monthly, quarterly, and so on). Investors don't get any savings with this type of plan like they do with dollar cost averaging, but it does force investors to be disciplined and consistent with their investing.

Figuring the sales charge and public offering price of open-end funds

You need to know two basic formulas to determine the sales charge and public offering price of open-end funds. Yes, every chapter seems to have more formulas, but these formulas are pretty straightforward and shouldn't cause you too many sleepless nights.

Sales charge percent

The sales charge, which is set at a maximum of 8½ percent, is part of the public offering price (POP), or ask price, not something tacked on afterward like a sales tax. One of the tricks for calculating the sales charge for open-end funds is remembering that the POP equals 100 percent. Therefore, if the sales charge is 8 percent, the net asset value (NAV) is 92 percent of the POP. The formula for determining the sales charge percent is as follows:

$$\text{sales charge }\% = \frac{\text{ask} - \text{bid}}{\text{ask}} = \frac{\text{POP} - \text{NAV}}{\text{POP}}$$

The following question tests your expertise in calculating the sales charge of a mutual fund.

ABC Aggressive Growth Fund has a net asset value of $9.20 and a public offering price of $10.00. What is the sales charge percent?

(A) 6.8 percent

(B) 7.5 percent

(C) 8 percent

(D) 8.7 percent

The right answer is Choice (C). The first thing that you have to do is set up the equation. Start with the POP of $10.00 and subtract the NAV of $9.20 to get $0.80. Next, divide the $0.80 by the POP of $10.00 to get the sales charge of 8 percent:

$$\text{sales charge }\% = \frac{\text{POP} - \text{NAV}}{\text{POP}} = \frac{\$10.00 - \$9.20}{\$10.00} = \frac{\$0.80}{\$10.00} = 8\%$$

To help you remember that the ask (offer) price of a fund is the same as the POP, remember to ask your POP about it.

Public offering price (POP)

When taking the Series 7 exam, you may be asked to figure out the public offering price of a mutual fund when you're given only the sales charge percent and the NAV.

Remember, the sales charge is already a part of the POP, so the sales charge is *not* equal to the sales charge percent times the NAV. Use the following formula to figure out how much an investor has to pay to buy shares of the fund when you know only the NAV and the sales charge percent:

$$\text{public offering price} = \frac{\text{net asset value}}{100\% - \text{sales charge }\%}$$

The following question tests your ability to answer a POP question.

DEF Aggressive Growth Fund has a NAV of $9.12 and a POP of $9.91. If there is a 5 percent sales charge for investments of $30,000 and up, how many shares can an investor who is depositing $50,000 purchase?

(A) 5,045.409 shares

(B) 5,208.333 shares

(C) 5,219.207 shares

(D) 5,482.456 shares

The answer you want is Choice (B). Don't let the decimals throw you off; mutual funds can sell fractional shares. This investor isn't going to be paying the POP of $9.91 per share because she's receiving a breakpoint for a large dollar purchase (see "Breakpoints," earlier in this chapter). To figure out the POP for this investor, set up the formula:

$$\text{POP} = \frac{\text{NAV}}{100\% - \text{sales charge }\%} = \frac{\$9.12}{100\% - 5\%} = \frac{\$9.12}{95\%} = \$9.60 \text{ per share}$$

After working out the formula, you see that the investor is paying $9.60 per share instead of $9.91. Next, determine the number of shares the investor can purchase by dividing the amount of the investment by the cost per share:

$$\frac{\$50{,}000 \text{ invested}}{\$9.60 \text{ per share}} = 5{,}208.333 \text{ shares}$$

This investor is able to purchase 5,208.333 shares because of the breakpoint. Without the breakpoint, the investor would have been able to purchase only 5,045.409 shares.

Considering Other Investment Company Options

A couple of other types of investment companies — face-amount certificate companies and unit investment trusts (UITs) — aren't as popular as they used to be. Unfortunately, even though you may never sell any, you do need to know them for the Series 7 exam. You probably won't see more than a question or two on these topics. However, exchange-traded funds (ETFs) are becoming increasingly popular, and your chance of having a question on ETFs and/or inverse ETFs is around 100 percent.

Face-amount certificate companies

A *face-amount certificate* is a type of packaged security that's similar to a zero-coupon bond (see Chapter 7); investors make either a lump sum payment or periodic payments in return for a larger future payment. The issuer of a face-amount certificate guarantees payment of the face amount (a fixed sum) to the investor at a preset date. Very few face-amount certificate companies are around today.

Unit investment trusts (UITs)

A *unit investment trust* (UIT) is a registered investment company that purchases a fixed (unmanaged) portfolio of income-producing securities (typically bonds) and holds them in trust, which means that a UIT acts as a holding company for its investors. Then the company issues redeemable shares (units) that represent investors' interest in the trust. Unlike mutual funds, UITs are set up for a specific period of time and have a set termination date. Any capital gains, interest, and/or dividends are passed on to shareholders at regular intervals.

UITs have a finite number of shares outstanding and are distributed in the primary market at the initial public offering (IPO) price. Because a limited number of shares are outstanding and they must be redeemed with the issuer or sponsor, liquidity is very limited.

Like mutual (open-end) funds, UITs can be purchased by type, such as growth, income, balanced, international, and so forth.

Here are the two main categories of these trusts:

- **Fixed investment trusts:** These companies invest in a portfolio of debt securities, and the trust terminates when all the bonds in the portfolio mature.
- **Participating trusts:** These companies invest in shares of mutual funds. The mutual funds that the trust holds don't change, but the securities held by the underlying mutual funds do.

Because the portfolio of securities is fixed, UITs don't employ investment advisers and therefore have no investment adviser fees during the life of the trust. Nice break!

Exchange-Traded Funds (ETFs)

Exchange-traded funds, or ETFs, are closed-end index funds that are traded on an exchange. ETFs provide investors with diversification along with the ability to sell short and purchase shares on margin.

Inverse ETFs (also known as *Short ETFs* or *Bear ETFs*) are exchange-traded funds that are designed using many derivative products, such as options to attempt to profit from a decline in the value of the underlying securities (for example, the S&P 500). Inverse ETFs can be used to profit from a decline in a broad market index or in a specific sector, such as the energy or financial sectors.

Reducing Real Estate Risk with REITs

A *real-estate investment trust* (REIT) is a trust that invests in real-estate-related projects such as properties, mortgage loans, and construction loans. REITs pool the capital of many investors to manage property and/or purchase mortgage loans. As with other trusts, they issue shares to investors representing their interest in the trust. REITs may be listed on an exchange or can trade over-the-counter (OTC) (see Chapter 14 for more info on markets). They also provide real-estate diversification and liquidity for investors.

REITs are distributed in the primary market at the IPO price. Unlike mutual funds, which are redeemed with the issuer, REITs are traded (bought and sold) in the secondary market to other investors. In addition, REITs have a finite number of shares outstanding, like closed-end funds. Because REITs are traded in the secondary market, their price may be at a discount or premium to the NAV, depending on investor sentiment.

Equity REITs take equity positions in real-estate properties; the income is derived from rent collected or profits made when the properties are sold. *Mortgage REITs* purchase construction loans and mortgages. The trust receives the interest paid on the loans and in turn passes it on to the owners of the trust (the investors). *Hybrid REITs* are a combination of equity and mortgage REITs. Hybrid REITs generate income derived from rent and capital gains (like an equity REIT) and interest (like a mortgage REIT).

REITs can *avoid* being taxed like a corporation if

- At least 75 percent of the income comes from real-estate-related activities
- At least 75 percent of the REIT's assets are in real estate, government securities, and/or cash
- At least 90 percent of the net income received is distributed to shareholders (who pay taxes on the income)

Don't get REITs confused with real-estate limited partnerships (which I cover in Chapter 11). Limited partnerships pass on (the industry term is *pass through*) income and write-offs to investors to claim on their own personal tax return; REITs pass income only through to investors.

Don't kill yourself worrying too much about REITs (not that you would); you won't get more than one or two questions on the Series 7 exam relating to REITs.

Adding Annuities to a Portfolio

Annuities are similar to mutual funds, except annuities are designed to provide supplemental retirement income for investors. Life insurance companies issue annuities, and these investments provide guaranteed payments for the life of the holder. The Series 7 exam tests you on the two basic types of annuities: fixed and variable. Because variable annuities are considered securities and fixed annuities are not (because of the guaranteed payout by the insurance company), most of the annuity questions on the Series 7 exam are about variable annuities.

Gather very specific information about your client before making recommendations. Annuities have been under the watchful eye of state insurance commissions and the SEC due to inappropriate recommendations from some brokers. Annuities typically aren't recommended for younger clients (most annuity purchasers are over the age of 50), for clients older than 75, or for a client's entire investment portfolio. For information on portfolio and securities analysis, see Chapter 13.

Looking at fixed annuities

The main thing for you to remember about *fixed annuities* is that they have fixed rates of return that the issuer guarantees. Investors pay money into fixed annuities, and the money is deposited into the insurance company's general account. After the investor starts receiving payments from the fixed annuity (usually monthly), the payments remain the same for the remainder of the investor's life. Because of the guaranteed payout, fixed annuities are *not* considered securities and therefore are exempt from SEC registration requirements.

Because the payouts associated with a fixed annuity remain the same, they're subject to *purchasing power risk* (the risk that the investment won't keep up with inflation). An investor who received payments of $1,000 per month in the 1970s may have been able to survive; however, that amount today is not even likely to pay your monthly grocery bill.

Checking out variable annuities

Insurance companies introduced variable annuities as a way to keep pace with (or hopefully exceed) inflation. In a fixed annuity, the insurance company bears the inflation risk; however, in a variable annuity, the investment risk is borne by the investor. Because the investors assume the investment risk, variable annuities are considered securities and must be registered with the SEC. All variable annuities have to be sold with a prospectus, and only individuals who hold appropriate securities and insurance licenses can sell them.

The money that investors deposit is held in a *separate account* (separate from the insurance company's other business) because the money is invested differently. The separate account is invested in securities such as common stock, bonds, mutual funds, and so on, with the hope that the investments will keep pace with or exceed the inflation rate.

The *assumed interest rate* (AIR) is a projection of the performance of the securities in the separate account over the life of the variable annuity contract. If the assumed interest rate is 4 percent and the performance of the securities in the separate account is equal to 4 percent, the investor receives the payouts that she expects. However, if the securities outperform the AIR, the investor receives higher payouts than expected. And unfortunately, if the securities held in the separate account underperform the AIR, the investor gets lower payouts than expected.

Putting money into (and receiving money from) annuities

Investors have choices when purchasing annuities and getting distributions. Investors may choose a lump-sum payment or multiple payments, depending on their needs. Investors also have a choice regarding how they want to get their distributions at retirement.

Looking at the pay-in phase

Payments into both fixed and variable annuities are made from after-tax dollars, meaning that the investor can't write the payments off on her taxes. However, payments into both fixed and variable annuities grow on a tax-deferred basis (they aren't taxed until the money is withdrawn). If an investor has contributed $80,000 into a variable annuity that's now worth $120,000, the investor is taxed only on the $40,000 difference because she has already paid taxes on the contribution. If an annuitant dies during the pay-in phase, most annuity contracts require a *death benefit* to be paid to the annuitant's beneficiary. The death benefit is typically the greater of all the money in the account or some guaranteed minimum.

Note: During the pay-in phase, an investor of a variable annuity purchases *accumulation units.* These units are similar to shares of a mutual fund.

Investors have a few payment options to select when purchasing fixed or variable annuities. Here's the rundown of options:

- **Single payment deferred annuity:** An investor purchases the annuity with a lump sum payment, and the payouts are delayed until some predetermined date.
- **Periodic payment deferred annuity:** An investor makes periodic payments (usually monthly) into the annuity, and the payouts are delayed until some predetermined date; this is the most common type of annuity.
- **Immediate annuity:** An investor purchases the annuity with a large sum, and the payouts begin within a couple months.

Most annuities in which investors are making scheduled deposits provide a waiver of premium during the pay-in phase if the annuitant becomes disabled or is confined to long-term care.

Getting the payout

Investors of both fixed and variable annuities have several payout options. These options may cover just the *annuitant* (investor) or the annuitant and a survivor. No matter what type of payout option the investor chooses, she will be taxed on the amount above the contribution. The earnings grow on a tax-deferred basis, and the investor is not taxed on the earnings until withdrawal at retirement.

Note: During the payout phase of a variable annuity, accumulation units are converted into a fixed number of *annuity units.* Investors receive a fixed number of annuity units periodically (usually monthly) with a variable value, depending on the performance of the securities in the separate account.

When an investor purchases an annuity, she has to decide which of the following payout options works best for her:

- **Life annuity:** This type of payment option provides income for the life of the *annuitant* (the individual covered by the annuity); however, after the annuitant dies, the insurance company stops making payments. This type of annuity is riskiest for the investor because if the annuitant dies earlier than expected, the insurance company gets to keep the leftover annuity money. Because it's the riskiest type of annuity for the annuitant, it has the highest payouts of all the options.
- **Life annuity with period certain:** This payout option guarantees payment to the annuitant for a minimum number of years (10, 20, and so on). For example, if the annuitant were to purchase an annuity with a 20-year guarantee and die after 7 years, a named beneficiary would receive the payments for the remaining 13 years.
- **Joint life with last survivor annuity:** This option guarantees payments over the lives of two individuals. As you can imagine, this type of annuity is typically set up for a husband and wife. If the wife dies first, the husband receives payments until his death. If the husband dies first, his wife receives payments until her death. Because this type of annuity covers the lifespans of two individuals, it has the lowest payouts.

All annuities have a *mortality guarantee.* This guarantee means that the investor receives payments as long as she lives, even if it's beyond her life expectancy.

Early withdrawal penalty

As with most other retirement plans, annuity investors are hit with a 10-percent early withdrawal penalty if they withdraw the money prior to age 59½. Yes, that's correct — the 10-percent penalty is added to the investor's tax bracket. Typically, retirement plans include a waiver of the 10-percent penalty in cases such as the purchase of a first home, age 55 and separated from work, death, or disability.

For Further Review

Although I cover the main topics related to packaged securities in this chapter — and hopefully give you a leg up on your competition — you also need to have a good understanding of the items in the following list:

- Functions of the board of directors
- Functions of the custodian bank, transfer agent, and underwriters
- The investment adviser's fees
- Trust indenture
- Advertising and sales literature including 12b-1 fees
- Tax treatment of mutual funds, REITs, UITs, and so forth
- Shareholders' rights
- Automatic reinvestments

- Redemption fee (contingent deferred sales charges)
- Payout or withdrawal plans
- Redemption and conversion privileges
- Regulated investment companies
- Conduit theory
- Constant dollar plan
- Forward pricing
- Contractual plans
- Margin on mutual funds
- Diversified investment companies
- Separate accounts investment policy
- Surrender value of accumulation units
- Distribution fees
- Restrictions
- Additional funds including; value funds, blend funds, structured funds, private equity funds, blind pool / blank check funds, and funds of hedge funds
- Share classes
- Rights of accumulation
- Life insurance policies including; whole life, variable life, universal life, and variable universal life
- Nondiscretionary fee-based accounts
- HOLDRs
- Exchange traded notes
- Statement of additional information
- Automatic withdrawal plans
- Continuing commissions
- Equity indexed annuities

Chapter 11

Working with Direct Participation Programs

In This Chapter

- Understanding the specifics of DPPs
- Distinguishing a limited partner from a general partner
- Getting a handle on the paperwork and taxes involved
- Looking at the different types of DPPs
- Reviewing additional topics tested

Direct participation programs (DPPs) can raise money to invest in real estate, oil and gas, equipment leasing, and so on. More commonly known as limited partnerships, these businesses are somewhat similar to corporations (stockholder-owned companies). However, limited partnerships have some specific tax advantages (and disadvantages) that a lot of other investments don't have. According to tax laws, limited partnerships are not taxed directly; the income or losses are passed directly through to the investors.

DPPs were once known as tax shelters because of the tax benefits to investors; however, tax law changes have taken away a lot of these advantages. As a result, DPPs have somewhat fallen out of favor for investors (though not entirely for the Series 7 designers).

In this chapter, I explain the differences between limited and general partners as well as the types of partnerships, their particular risks, and potential rewards. The info here can help you examine those risks and rewards and determine the suitability of DPPs for investors. I also explain two inevitable facts of life as they apply to partnerships: the filing of paperwork and the payment of taxes. You can also check out the "For Further Review" section at the end of this chapter for a list of related topics on the Series 7. As always, I give you some practice questions to go along with the rest of the questions in this book.

Searching for Identity: What DPPs Are (and Aren't)

Just as stockholders are owners of a corporation, limited (and general) partners are owners of a *direct participation program* (DPP). The key difference for people investing in DPPs is that they're required to tie up their investment dollars for a long period of time, though they receive tax advantages for doing so. Most DPPs are set up for real-estate projects, oil and gas projects, or equipment leasing.

The IRS determines whether an enterprise is a corporation or a limited partnership. For a limited partnership to actually be considered (and taxed) as a limited partnership, it has to *avoid* at least two of the following corporate characteristics (usually the last two):

- **Having a centralized management:** Corporations have management in one place. The challenges of managing a limited partnership from several locations make this corporate trait quite difficult for a partnership to avoid.
- **Providing limited liability:** Corporate shareholders have limited liability; well, so do limited partners. The liability of corporate shareholders is limited to the amount invested, and the liability of limited partners is limited to the amount invested plus a portion of any recourse loans taken out by the partnership (if any). Providing limited liability is pretty much unavoidable.
- **Having perpetual (never-ending) life:** Unlike corporations, which hope to last forever, limited partnerships are set up for a definite period of time. Limited partnerships are dissolved at a predetermined time — for example, when its goals are met or after a set number of years.
- **Having free transferability of partnership interest:** DPPs are difficult to get in and out of. Unlike shares of stock, which can be freely bought and sold by anyone, limited partners not only have to pass the scrutiny of a registered rep, but they also require approval of the general partner. DPP investors (limited partners) must show that they have enough money to invest initially, plus have liquidity in other investments in the event that the partnership needs a loan.

For Series 7 exam purposes, you need to remember that the easiest corporate characteristics for a partnership to avoid are perpetual life (continuity of life) and having free transferability of shares; the most difficult to avoid are providing limited liability and having a centralized management.

The DPP Characters: General and Limited Partners

By law, limited partnerships require at least one limited partner and one general partner. Limited partners are the investors, and general partners are the managers. When you're looking at general and limited partners, you want to focus on *who can and can't do what.*

General partners are responsible for the day-to-day decision making (overseeing operations, deciding when to buy or sell, choosing what to invest in, and so on) for the partnership. Limited partners (the investors) provide the bulk of the money for the partnership but, unlike general partners, can't make any of the partnership's investment decisions. Table 11-1 lays out the key things to remember about general and limited partners for the Series 7.

Table 11-1 Comparing General and Limited Partners

Category	*General Partners*	*Limited Partners*
Decision making	Are legally bound to make decisions in the best interest of the partnership; make all the partnership's day-to-day decisions	Have voting rights but can't make decisions for the partnership
Tasks	Buy and sell property for the partnership; manage the partnership's assets	Provide capital; vote; can keep general partners in check by reviewing books

Category	*General Partners*	*Limited Partners*
Liability and litigation	Have unlimited liability (can be sued and held personally liable for all partnership debts and losses)	Have limited liability (limited to the amount invested and a proportionate share of any recourse loans taken by the partnership); can inspect *all* the partnership books; can sue the general partner or can sue to dissolve the partnership
Financial involvement	Maintain a financial interest in the partnership	Provide money contributed to the partnership, recourse debt of the partnership, and nonrecourse debt for real-estate DPPs
Financial rewards	Receive compensation for managing the partnership	Receive their proportion of profits and losses
Conflicts of interest	Can't borrow money from the partnership; can't compete against the partnership (for example, they can't manage two buildings for two different partnerships in close proximity to each other)	None; can invest in competing partnerships

Pushing through Partnership Paperwork

For the Series 7, you need to know about certain paperwork that's specific to limited partnerships. In the following sections, I discuss the three required documents necessary for a limited partnership to exist.

Partnership agreement

The *partnership agreement* is a document that includes the rights and responsibilities of the limited and general partners. Included in the agreement are basics that you would probably guess such as the name of the partnership, the location of the partnership, the name of the general partner, and so on. In addition, the partnership agreement addresses the general partner's rights to

- Charge a management fee for making decisions for the partnership
- Enter the partnership into contracts
- Decide whether cash distributions will be made to the limited partners
- Accept or decline limited partners

Certificate of limited partnership

The *certificate of limited partnership* is the legal agreement between the general and limited partners, which is filed with the Secretary of State in the home state of the partnership. The certificate of limited partnership includes basic information such as the name of the partnership and its primary place of business, the names and addresses of the limited and general partner(s), and the following items:

- The objectives (goals) of the partnership and how long the partnership is expected to last
- The amount contributed by each partner, plus future expected investments
- How the profits are to be distributed
- The roles of the participants
- How the partnership can be dissolved
- Whether a limited partner can sell or assign his interest in the partnership

If any significant changes are made to the partnership, such as adding new limited partners, the certificate of limited partnership must be amended accordingly.

Subscription agreement

The *subscription agreement* is an application form that potential limited partners have to complete. The general partner uses this agreement to determine whether an investor is suitable to become a limited partner. The general partner has to sign the subscription agreement to officially accept an investor into the DPP.

One of your jobs as a registered rep is to prescreen the potential limited partner to make sure that the partnership is a good fit for the individual. Also, you need to review the agreement to ensure (to the best of your ability) that the information the investor provides is complete and accurate. Besides the investor's payment, the subscription agreement has to include items such as the investor's net worth and annual income, a statement explaining the risks of investing in the partnership, and a power of attorney that allows the general partner to make partnership investment decisions for the limited partner.

The following question tests your ability to answer questions about DPP paperwork:

All of the following statements are TRUE regarding the subscription agreement EXCEPT

(A) A general partner must sign the agreement to officially accept a limited partner.

(B) A registered rep must first examine the subscription agreement to make sure that the investor has provided accurate information.

(C) After the general partner has signed the subscription agreement, it gives the limited partner power of attorney to conduct business on behalf of the partnership.

(D) The subscription agreement is usually sent to the general partner with some form of payment.

The answer is C. The test designers want to know that you understand what this document is and that you have a grasp of who does what. The subscription agreement is a form that the potential limited partner fills out; then the registered rep reviews the document before sending it (with the investor's payment) to the general partner, who signs to accept the terms. Choice B shows where the registered rep (that's you!) comes in. Here, you assume that the "investor" is the potential limited partner, so choice B checks out.

Because this is an *except* question, the correct answer is C; the subscription agreement gives the *general partner,* not the limited partner, power of attorney to make decisions for the partnership. If you remember that limited partners don't really do much in the way of decision making (as I explain earlier in "The DPP Characters: General and Limited Partners"), you can spot the false answer right away.

Passive Income and Losses: Looking at Taxes on Partnerships

DPPs used to be called *tax shelters* because DPPs flow through (or pass through) not only income but also losses to investors (corporations only flow through income). Prior to 1986, investors could write off these losses against income from other investments. Then the IRS stepped in because they felt that this write-off was too much of an advantage for investors (or the IRS wasn't making enough money) and decided to give DPPs their own tax category. Now, because investors are not actively involved in earning the income, taxes on DPPs are classified as *passive income* and *passive losses.* (See Chapter 15 for more info on taxes and types of income.)

The key thing to remember for Series 7 purposes is that investors can write off passive losses only against passive income from other DPP investments.

Evaluating Direct Participation Programs

Direct participation programs can be offered publicly or privately. Public offerings of DPPs must be registered with the Securities and Exchange Commission (SEC) whereas private offerings (offerings to mostly wealthy investors) are not. Typically, publicly offered DPPs have a lower unit (buy-in) cost than that of privately offered DPPs.

Certainly direct participation programs do provide some advantages, but they also have additional risks that investors don't face with other types of investments, such as having to loan additional money to the partnership if needed. Therefore, when evaluating whether an investment in a DPP may be right for one of your clients, not only do you need to determine whether investing in a partnership is wise for that client, but you also need to consider the following items:

- The economic soundness of the program
- The expertise of the general partner
- The basic objectives of the program
- The start-up costs involved

Checking Out Types of Partnerships

Certainly partnerships can be formed to run any sort of business that you can imagine, but the Series 7 exam focuses on the big three: real estate, equipment leasing, and oil and gas. You need to be able to identify the risks and potential rewards for each of the following types of partnerships.

Because of the risks associated with some of the different types of DPPs, investors should have the ability to tie up their money for a long period of time and be able to recover from a loss of all the money invested in case the partnership never becomes profitable.

Building on real-estate partnership info

Real-estate partnerships include programs that invest in raw land, new construction, existing properties, or government-assisted housing. You need to know the differences among the types of programs, along with their risks and potential rewards. Here are the types of real-estate DPPs, from safest to riskiest:

- **Public housing (government-assisted housing programs):** This type of real-estate DPP develops low-income and retirement housing. The focus of this type of DPP is to earn consistent income and receive tax credits. The U.S. government (through U.S. government subsidies), via the department of Housing and Urban Development (HUD), makes up any deficient rent payments. Appreciation potential is low and maintenance costs can be high, but the DPP does benefit from a little government security. Public housing DPPs are backed by the U.S. government and, therefore, are considered the safest real-estate DPP.
- **Existing properties:** This type of DPP purchases existing properties, and the intent is to generate a regular stream of rental income. Because the properties already exist, this DPP generates immediate cash flow. The risk with this type of DPP is that the maintenance or repair expenses will eat into the profit or that tenants won't renew their leases. The properties already exist and are producing income, so the risk for this type of DPP is relatively low.
- **New construction:** This type of DPP purchases property for the purpose of building. After completing the construction, the partnership's goal is to sell the property and structure at a profit after all expenses. Building costs may be more than expected, and the partnership doesn't receive income until the property is sold, but the DPP can benefit from appreciation on both the land and the structure. Although this investment is speculative, it's not as risky as a raw land DPP.
- **Raw land:** This type of DPP invests in undeveloped land in anticipation of long-term capital appreciation; raw land DPPs don't build on or rent out the property. The partnership hopes the property purchased will appreciate in value so that the DPP can sell the property for more than the purchase price plus all expenses.

Raw land DPPs are considered the riskiest real-estate DPP because the partnership doesn't have any cash flow (no rental or sales income), and the value of the land may not increase — it may actually decrease.

The following question tests your understanding of real-estate DPPs.

Which of the following types of real-estate DPPs has the fewest write-offs?

(A) Raw land

(B) New construction

(C) Existing properties

(D) Public housing

The correct answer is Choice (A). DPPs that invest in raw land are buying property and sitting on it with the hope that it'll be worth more in the future. Because the DPP isn't spending money on improving the property and land can't be depreciated, raw land DPPs have the fewest write-offs.

Gearing up with equipment leasing

Although you may be tested on equipment leasing programs on the Series 7 exam, it's the least-tested type of DPP. Equipment leasing programs purchase equipment (trucks, heavy machinery, computers . . . you name it) and lease it out to other businesses. The objective is to obtain a steady cash flow and depreciation write-offs. The two types of leasing arrangements you need to be aware of are the operating lease and the full payout lease:

- **Operating lease:** This type of equipment leasing program purchases equipment and leases it out for a short period of time. The DPP doesn't receive the full value of the equipment during the first lease. This type of arrangement allows the DPP to lease out the equipment several times during the life of the machinery.
- **Full payout lease:** This type of equipment leasing program purchases the equipment and leases it out for a long period of time. The DPP receives enough income from the first lease to cover the cost of the equipment and any financing costs. Usually, the initial lease lasts for the useful life of the equipment.

The main thing to remember about equipment leasing is that the operating lease is riskier because the equipment becomes less valuable or outdated over time and, therefore, less rentable.

Strengthening your grasp on oil and gas

Oil and gas partnerships include programs that produce income, are speculative in nature, or are a combination of the two. You need to know how the types of programs differ, along with their risks and potential rewards. Oil and gas partnerships also have certain tax advantages that are unique:

- **Intangible drilling costs (IDCs):** IDCs are write-offs for drilling expenses. The word *intangible* is your clue that you're not talking about actual equipment. These costs include wages for employees, fuel, repairs, hauling of equipment, insurance, and so on. IDCs are usually completely deductible in the tax year in which the intangible costs occur. IDC deductions are only for the drilling and preparing of a well for the production of oil and gas. Therefore, when a well is producing, IDC write-offs are not allowed.
- **Tangible drilling costs (TDCs):** TDCs are write-offs on items purchased that have salvage value (items that can be resold). All oil and gas DPPs have TDCs, which include costs for purchasing items such as storage tanks, well equipment, and so on. These costs are not immediately written off but are *depreciated* (deducted) over seven years. Depreciation may be claimed on either a straight-line basis (writing off an equal amount each year) or an accelerated basis (writing off more in the early years and less in the later years).

  IDCs are fully deductible in the current year; TDCs are depreciated (deductible) over several years.
- **Depletion:** Depletion is a tax deduction that allows partnerships that deal with natural resources (such as oil and gas) to take a deduction for the decreasing supply of the resource. Partnerships can claim depletion deductions only on the amount of natural resources sold (not extracted and put in storage for future sale).

  Depletion deductions are only for DPPs that deal with natural resources. On the Series 7 exam, the only DPP with depletion deductions that you need to be concerned with is oil and gas.

When investing in oil, partnerships can pioneer new territory, drill near existing wells, buy producing wells, or try a combination of those methods. For Series 7 exam purposes, exploratory programs are the riskiest oil and gas DPPs because oil may never be found, and income programs are the safest oil and gas DPPs. To make your life easier (hopefully), I've composed a DPP comparison chart (see Table 11-2) to help you focus in on the main points of each type of oil and gas DPP.

Table 11-2 Advantages and Risks of Various Oil and Gas DPPs

Type	*Objective*	*Advantages*	*Risks*
Exploratory (wildcatting)	To locate and drill for oil in unproven, undiscovered areas	Long-term capital appreciation potential; high returns for discovery of new oil or gas reserves	Riskiest oil and gas DPP because new oil reserves may never be found; high IDCs because the DPP isn't working with producing wells
Developmental	To drill near producing wells with the hope of finding new reserves	Long-term capital appreciation potential with less risk than exploratory programs; oil will likely be found	The property's expensive; the drilling costs may be higher than expected; the risk of dry holes (non-producing wells) is still somewhat high; medium level of IDCs
Income	To provide immediate income by purchasing producing wells	The partnership generates immediate cash flow; the least risky of the oil and gas DPPs; no IDCs	High initial costs; the well could dry up; gas prices could go down
Combination	To provide income to help pay for the cost of finding new oil reserves	The ability to offset the costs of drilling new wells by using income generated by existing wells	Carries the risks of all the programs combined

The following question concerns different DPP investments.

Mr. Smith has money invested in a limited partnership that's expecting to have a significant amount of income over the next one to two years. Which of the following programs would BEST help Mr. Smith shelter the MOST of that income?

(A) Oil and gas exploratory

(B) Raw land purchasing

(C) Equipment leasing

(D) Existing real-estate property

The answer you want is Choice (A). Oil and gas exploratory programs spend a lot of money attempting to find and drill for oil. These programs have high IDCs (intangible drilling costs), which are fully tax-deductible when the drilling occurs. Therefore, the oil and gas exploratory programs have the largest write-offs in the early years, which could help Mr. Smith offset some or all of his passive income from the other limited partnership.

For Further Review

You should have a grasp of the items in this section for the Series 7. Look over these additional DPP-related topics and make sure you know them prior to taking the real deal:

- Oil and gas sharing arrangements; functional allocation, disproportionate sharing, and reversionary working interest
- Private placement
- Public offering
- Syndicator
- Limited partner's cost basis
- Depreciation and depletion deductions
- Accelerated depreciation versus straight-line depreciation
- Crossover point
- Recourse debt and nonrecourse debt
- Recapture
- Dissolution of a partnership
- Abusive shelter
- Additional real estate limited partnerships; blind pool and historic rehabilitation
- Alternative minimum tax

Chapter 12

Options: The Right to Buy or Sell at a Fixed Price

In This Chapter

- Understanding the specifics of options
- Feeling comfortable with an options chart
- Calculating the maximum loss, maximum gain, and break-even points
- Dealing with unconventional options
- Reviewing additional topics tested

Welcome to the wonderful world of options. I'm sure you've heard stories about the difficulty of options. Put your mind at ease — I'm here to make your life easier. Maybe I'm a little warped, but options are my favorite part of the Series 7 exam! Options are one of the more heavily tested areas — you can expect around 40 questions about them on the Series 7.

A lot of the questions are simple calculations, so in this chapter, I show you how to put numbers into an options chart to make even the more difficult calculations simple. I give you plenty of example questions so you can put those math skills to good use. I also give you a general tour of the options basics — calls and puts, in- and out-of-the-money, and so on — and introduce you to the unique LEAPS and capped options. The "For Further Review" section wraps things up and suggests other topics to study.

Brushing Up on Option Basics

Options are just another investment vehicle that (hopefully) more-savvy investors can use. An owner of an *option* has the right, but not the obligation, to buy or sell an underlying security (stock, bond, and so on) at a fixed price; as derivatives, options draw their value from that underlying security. Investors may either *exercise* the option (buy or sell the security at the fixed price) or trade the option in the market.

All option strategies (whether simple or sophisticated), when broken down, are made up of simple call and/or put options. After going over how to read an option, I explain a basic call option and help you figure out how to work with that before moving on to a put option. Next, I discuss options that are in-, at-, or out-of-the-money, and the cost of options. After you've sufficiently mastered the basics, the rest (the more difficult strategies later in this chapter) becomes easier.

Reading an option

To answer Series 7 questions relating to options, you have to be able to read an option. The following example shows you how an option may appear on the Series 7:

> Buy 1 XYZ Apr 60 call at 5

Here are the seven elements of the option order ticket and how they apply to the example:

1. **Whether the investor is buying or selling the option: Buy**

   When an investor buys (or *longs, holds,* or *owns*) an option, she is in a position of power; that investor controls the option and decides whether and when to exercise the option. If an investor is selling (*shorting* or *writing*) an option, she is obligated to live up to the terms of the contract and must either purchase or sell the underlying stock if the holder exercises the option.

2. **The contract size: 1**

   You can assume that one option contract is for *100 shares* of the underlying stock. Although this idea isn't as heavily tested on the Series 7 exam, an investor may buy or sell multiple options (for example, five) if she's interested in having a position in more shares of stock. If an investor owns five option contracts, she's interested in 500 shares of stock (check out "Off the charts: Multiple option contracts" later in the chapter for more information on this topic).

3. **The name of the stock: XYZ**

   In this case, XYZ is the underlying stock that the investor has a right to purchase at a fixed price.

4. **The expiration month for the options: Apr**

   All options are owned for a fixed period of time. The initial expiration for most options is *9 months* from the issue date. In the preceding example, the option will expire in April. Options expire at 11:59 p.m. EST (10:59 p.m. CST) on the Saturday following the third Friday of the expiration month. Remembering the EST (Eastern Standard Time) is generally easier than recalling the CST (Central Standard Time) because 11:59 p.m. EST is right before midnight.

   Don't confuse the option's expiration date with the third Saturday of the expiration month; if the expiration month starts on a Saturday, the option expires on the fourth Saturday.

5. **The strike (exercise) price of the option: 60**

   When the holder (purchaser or owner) *exercises* the option, she uses the option contract to make the seller of the option buy or sell the underlying stock at the strike price (see the next step for info on determining whether the seller is obligated to buy or sell). In this case, if the holder were to exercise the option, the holder of the option would be able to purchase 100 shares of XYZ at $60 per share.

6. **The type of option: call**

   An investor can buy or sell a call option or buy or sell a put option. Calls give holders the right to buy the underlying security at a set price; puts give holders the right to sell. So in the example scenario, the holder has the right to buy the underlying security at the price stated in the preceding step.

7. **The premium: 5**

   Of course, an option investor doesn't get to have the option for nothing. An investor buys the option at the premium. In this case, the premium is 5, so a purchaser would have to pay $500 (5 × 100 shares per option).

Looking at call options: The right to buy

A *call option* gives the holder (owner) the right to buy 100 shares of a security at a fixed price and the seller the obligation to sell the stock at the fixed price. Owners of call options are bullish (picture a bull charging forward) because the investors want the price of the stock to increase. If the price of the stock increases above the strike price, holders can either exercise the option (buy the stock at a good price) or sell the option for a profit. By contrast, sellers of call options are bearish (imagine a bear hibernating for the winter) because they want the price of the stock to decrease.

For example, assume that Ms. Smith buys 1 DEF October 40 call option. Ms. Smith bought the right to purchase 100 shares of DEF at 40. If the price of DEF increases to over $40 per share, this option becomes very valuable to Ms. Smith, because she can purchase the stock at $40 per share and sell it at the market price or sell the option at a higher price.

If DEF never eclipses the 40 strike (exercise) price, then the option doesn't work out for poor Ms. Smith and she doesn't exercise the option. However, it does work out for the seller of the option, because the seller receives a premium for selling the option, and the seller gets to pocket that premium.

Checking out put options: The right to sell

You can think of a put option as being the opposite of a call option (see the preceding section). The holder of a *put option* has the right to sell 100 shares of a security at a fixed price, and the writer (seller) of a put option has the obligation to buy the stock if exercised. Owners of put options are bearish because the investors want the price of the stock to decrease (so they can buy the stock at market price and immediately sell it at the higher strike price or sell their option at a higher premium). However, sellers of put options are bullish (they want the price of the stock to increase), because that would keep the option from going in-the-money (see the next section) and allow them to keep the premiums they received.

For example, assume that Mr. Jones buys 1 ABC October 60 put option. Mr. Jones is buying the right to sell 100 shares of ABC at 60. If the price of ABC decreases to less than $60 per share, this option becomes very valuable to Mr. Jones. If you were in Mr. Jones' shoes and ABC were to drop to $50 per share, you could purchase the stock in the market and exercise (use) the option to sell the stock at $60 per share, which would make you (the new Mr. Jones) very happy.

If ABC never drops below the 60 strike (exercise) price, then the option doesn't work out for Mr. Jones and he doesn't exercise the option. However, it does work out for the seller of the option, because the seller receives a premium for selling the option that she gets to keep.

Getting your money back: Options in-, at-, or out-of-the-money

To determine whether an option is in- or out-of-the-money, you have to figure out whether the investor would be able to get at least some of their premium money back if the option were exercised.

You can figure out how much an option is in-the-money or out-of-the-money by finding the difference between the market value and the strike price. Here's how you know where-in-the-money an option is:

- When an option is *in-the-money,* exercising the option lets investors sell a security for more than its current market value or purchase it for less — a pretty good deal.

  The *intrinsic value* of an option is the amount that the option is in-the-money; if an option is out-of-the-money or at-the-money, the intrinsic value is zero.
- When an option is *out-of-the-money,* exercising the option means investors can't get the best prices; they'd have to buy the security for more than its market value or sell it for less. Obviously, holders of options that are out-of-the-money don't exercise them.
- When the strike price is the same as the market price, the option is *at-the-money;* this is true whether the option is a call or a put.

Call options — the right to buy — go in-the-money when the price of the stock is above the strike price. Suppose, for instance, that an investor buys a DEF 60 call option and that DEF is trading at 62. In this case, the option would be in-the-money by two points (the option's intrinsic value). If that same investor were to buy that DEF 60 call option when DEF was trading at 55, the option would be out-of-the-money by five points (with an intrinsic value of zero).

A put option — the right to sell — goes in-the-money when the price of the stock drops below the strike price. For example, a TUV 80 call option is in-the-money when the price of TUV drops below 80. The reverse holds as well: If a put option is in-the-money when the price of the stock is below the strike price, it must be out-of-the-money when the price of the stock is above the strike price.

Don't take the cost of the option (the premium) into consideration when determining whether an option is in-the-money or out-of-the-money. Having an option that's in-the-money is not the same as making a profit. (See the next section for info on premiums.)

Use the phrases *call up* and *put down* to recall when an option goes in-the-money. *Call up* can help you remember that a *call* option is in-the-money when the market price is *up,* or above the strike price. *Put down* can help you remember that a *put* option is in-the-money when the market price is *down,* or below the strike price.

The following question tests your knowledge of options being in- or out-of-the-money.

Which TWO of the following options are in-the-money if ABC is trading at 62 and DEF is trading at 44?

I. An ABC Oct 60 call option

II. An ABC Oct 70 call option

III. A DEF May 40 put option

IV. A DEF May 50 put option

(A) I and III

(B) I and IV

(C) II and III

(D) II and IV

The correct answer is Choice (B). Start with the strike (exercise) prices. You're *calling up* or *putting down* from the strike prices, not from the market prices. Because call options go in-the-money when the market price is above the strike price, Statement I is the only one that works for ABC. An ABC 60 call option would be in-the-money when the price of ABC is above 60. ABC is currently trading at 62, so that 60 call option is in-the-money. For the ABC 70 call option to be in-the-money, ABC would have to be trading higher than 70. Next, use *put down* for the DEF put options, because put options go in-the-money when the price of the stock goes below the strike price. Therefore, Statement IV makes sense because DEF is trading at 44, and that's below the DEF 50 put strike price but not the 40 put strike price.

Paying the premium: The cost of an option

The *premium* of an option is the amount that the purchaser pays for the option. The premium may increase or decrease depending on whether an option goes in- or out-of-the-money, gets closer to expiration, and so on. The premium is made up of many different factors, including

- Whether the option is in-the-money (see the preceding section)
- The amount of time the investor has to use the option
- The volatility of the underlying security
- Investor sentiment (for example, whether buying calls on ABC stock is the cool thing to do right now)

One of the questions you may run across on the Series 7 exam requires you to figure out the time value of an option premium. *Time value* has to do with how long you have until an option expires. There's no set standard for time value, such as every month until an option expires costs buyers an extra $100. However, you can assume that if two options have everything in common except for the expiration month, the one with the longer expiration will have a higher premium. Hopefully, the following equation can help keep you from getting a "pit" in your stomach:

$$P = I + T$$

In this formula, P is the premium or cost of the option, I is the intrinsic value of the option (the amount the option is in-the-money), and T is the time value of the option.

For example, here's how you find the time value for a BIF Oct 50 call option if the premium is 6 and BIF is trading at 52: Call options (the right to buy) go in-the-money when the price of the stock goes above the strike price (*call up* — see the preceding section). Because BIF is trading at 52 and the option is a 50 call option, it's two points in-the-money; therefore, the intrinsic value is two. Because the premium is six and the intrinsic value is two, the premium must include four as a time value:

$$P = I + T$$

$$6 = 2 + T$$

$$T = 4$$

The following question tests your knowledge of using the formula $P = I + T$.

Use the following chart to answer the next question.

Stock	Strike Price	Calls		Puts	
LMN		July	Oct	July	Oct
40.50	30	13	14.5	0.25	0.50
40.50	40	2.5	4.5	1.5	2.75
40.50	50	0.25	0.75	10.5	12

What is the time value of an LMN Oct 30 call?

(A) 2.5

(B) 4

(C) 6.25

(D) 9.5

The answer you're looking for is Choice (B). I threw you a curveball by giving you a chart similar to what you may see on the Series 7 exam. I hope you're able to find the premium that you need to answer the question. Most of the exhibits you get on the Series 7 are simple, and solving the problem is just a matter of locating the information you need.

Using the chart, the first column shows the price of the stock trading in the market, the second column shows the strike prices for the options, and the rest of the chart shows the premiums for the calls and puts and the expiration months. Scan the chart under the October calls, which is in the fourth column; then look for the 30 strike price, which is in the first row of data. The column and row intersect at a premium of 14.5.

Now you need to find the intrinsic value (how much the option is in-the-money). Remember that call options go in-the-money when the price of the stock is above the strike price (call up). This is a 30 call option and the price of the stock is 40.50, which is 10.5 above the strike price. Plug in the numbers, and you find that the premium includes a time value of 4:

$$P(\text{premium}) = I(\text{intrinsic value}) + T(\text{time value})$$

$$14.5 = 10.5 + T$$

$$T = 4$$

Incorporating Standard Option Math

I'm here to make your life easier. Prep courses use several different types of charts and formulas to figure out things such as gains or losses, break-even points, maximum gain or loss, and so on. I believe that the easiest way is to use the options chart that follows. It's a simple *Money Out, Money In* chart you can use to plug in numbers. What's great about this chart is that you don't even necessarily have to understand what the heck is going on to determine the answers to most options questions. As this chapter progresses, I show you how incredibly useful the options chart can be.

Money Out	Money In

If it looks basic, it is — and that's the idea. Any time an investor spends money, you place that value in the Money Out side of the options chart, and any time an investor receives money, you place the number in the Money In side of the chart.

Calls same: Buying or selling call options

The most basic options calculations involve buying or selling call or put options. Although using the options chart may not be totally necessary for the more basic calculations (such as the one that follows in the next section), working with the chart now can help you get used to the tool so you'll be ready when the Series 7 exam tests your sanity with more-complex calculations.

As you work with options charts, you may notice a pattern when determining maximum losses and gains. Table 12-1 gives you a quick reference concerning the maximum gain or maximum loss an investor faces when buying or selling call options. Notice that the buyer's loss is equal to the seller's gain (and vice versa).

Table 12-1 Maximum Gains and Losses for Call Options

Buying or Selling	*Maximum Loss*	*Maximum Gain*
Buying a call	Premium	Unlimited
Selling a call	Unlimited	Premium

The key phrase to remember when working with call options is *calls same,* which means that the premium and the strike price go on the same side of the options chart.

Buying call options

The following steps show you how to calculate the maximum loss and gain for holders of call options (which give the holder the right to buy). I also show you how to find the breakeven point. Here's the order ticket for the example calculations:

Buy 1 XYZ Oct 40 call at 5

1. **Find the maximum loss.**

   The holder of an option doesn't have to exercise it, so the most she can lose is the premium. The premium is five, so this investor purchased the option for $500 (5 × 100 shares per option); therefore, you enter that value in the Money Out side of the options chart (think "money out of the investor's pocket"). According to the chart, the maximum loss (the most this investor can lose) is $500.

Money Out	Money In
$500	

2. **Determine the maximum gain.**

   To calculate the maximum gain, you have to exercise the option at the strike price. The strike price is 40, so you enter $4,000 (40 strike price × 100 shares per option) under its premium (which you added to the chart when calculating maximum loss); exercising the call means buying the stock, so that's Money Out. When exercising call options, always put the multiplied strike price under its premium. (Remember *calls same:* The premium and the strike price go on the same side of the options chart.)

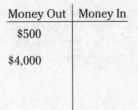

Money Out	Money In
$500	
$4,000	

Because you've already determined the maximum loss, look at the Money In portion of the options chart. The Money In is empty, so the maximum gain (the most money the investor can make) is unlimited.

When you see a question about the break-even point, the Series 7 examiners are asking, "At what point does this investor not have a gain or loss?" The simplest way to figure out this point for a call option is to use *call up* (remember that call options go in-the-money when the price of the stock goes above the strike price — see the section "Options in-, at-, or out-of-the-money"). When using *call up,* you add the strike price to the premium:

strike price + premium = 40 + 5 = 45

For this investor, the break-even point is 45. This number makes sense because the investor paid $5 for the option, so the option has to go $5 in-the-money for the investor to recoup the amount she paid. ***Note:*** The break-even point is always the same for the buyer and the seller.

Selling call options

Here, I show you how to find the maximum gain and loss, as well as the break-even point, for sellers of call options. Here's the order ticket for the example calculations:

Sell 1 ZYX Oct 60 call at 2

1. **Determine the maximum gain.**

   The seller makes money only if the holder fails to exercise the option or exercises it when the option is in-the-money by less than the premium received. This investor sold the option for $200 (2 × 100 shares per option); therefore, you enter that amount in the Money In side of the options chart. According to the chart, the maximum gain (the most that this investor can make) is the $200 premium received. ***Note:*** The exercised strike price of $6,000 (60 × 100 shares) doesn't come into play when determining the maximum gain in this example because the holder of the option would exercise the option only if it were in-the-money.

Money Out	Money In
	$200

2. **Find the maximum loss.**

   To calculate the maximum loss, you need to exercise the option at the strike price. The strike price is 60, so you enter $6,000 (60 strike price × 100 shares per option) under its premium. The $6,000 goes in the Money In side of the options chart because this investor had to sell the stock to the holder at the strike price (60 × 100 shares). When exercising call options, always enter the multiplied strike price under its premium. (Remember *calls same:* The premium and the strike price go on the same side of the options chart.)

Money Out	Money In
	$200
	$6,000

   You've already determined the maximum gain; now look at the Money Out portion of the options chart. The Money Out is empty, so the maximum loss (the most money the investor can lose) is unlimited.

When you see a question about the break-even point, the examiners are asking you, "At what point does this investor not have a gain or loss?" The simplest way to figure this out for a call option is to use *call up.* When using *call up,* you add the strike price to the premium:

$$\text{strike price} + \text{premium} = 60 + 2 = 62$$

For this investor, the break-even point is 62. This makes sense because the investor received $2 for the option, so the option has to go $2 in-the-money for this investor to lose the amount that she received for selling the option. Call options go in-the-money when the price of the stock goes above the strike price.

Puts switch: Buying or selling put options

Fortunately, when you're calculating the buying or selling of put options (which give the holder the right to sell), you use the options chart in the same way but with a slight change (see the preceding section for info on call options). Instead of using *calls same* as you do with call options, you use *puts switch* — in other words, you place the premium and the strike price on opposite sides of the options chart.

Table 12-2 serves as a quick reference regarding the maximum gain or maximum loss an investor faces when buying or selling put options.

Table 12-2 Maximum Gains and Losses for Put Options

Buying or Selling	*Maximum Loss*	*Maximum Gain*
Buying a put	Premium	(strike – premium) × 100 shares
Selling a put	(strike – premium) × 100 shares	Premium

Buying put options

This section explains how to find the maximum loss, maximum gain, and the break-even point for buyers (holders) of put options. Here's the ticket order for the calculations:

Buy 1 TUV Oct 55 put at 6

1. **Find the maximum loss.**

   Exercising an option is, well, optional for the holder, so buyers of put options can't lose more than the premium. Because this investor purchased the option for $600 (6 × 100 shares per option), you enter that value in the Money Out side of the options chart. The maximum loss (the most that this investor can lose) is the $600 premium paid.

Money Out	Money In
$600	

2. **Determine the maximum gain.**

   To find the maximum gain, you have to exercise the option at the strike price. The strike price is 55, so you enter $5,500 (55 strike price × 100 shares per option) on the opposite side of the options chart. (Remember *puts switch:* The premium and the strike price go on opposite sides of the options chart.) Exercising the option means selling the underlying stock, so that $5,500 is Money In.

Money Out	Money In
$600	$5,500

   You've already determined the maximum loss; now look at the Money In portion of the options chart. Because you find $4,900 more Money In than Money Out ($5,500 – $600), the maximum gain is $4,900.

The break-even point is the security price where the investor doesn't have a gain or loss. The simplest way to figure this point out for a put option is to use *put down* (put options go in-the-money when the price of the stock goes below the strike price). When using *put down*, you subtract the premium from the strike price:

strike price – premium = 55 – 6 = 49

For this investor, the break-even point is 49. The investor paid $6 for the option, so the option has to go $6 in-the-money in order for this investor to recoup the amount that she paid. As with call options, the break-even point is always the same for the buyer and the seller.

Selling put options

The following steps show you how to calculate the maximum gain and loss for the seller of a put option. I also demonstrate calculations for the break-even point. Here's the ticket order for the example:

Sell 1 TUV Sep 30 put at 8

1. **Determine the maximum gain.**

   The seller makes money only if the holder of the option fails to exercise it. This investor sold the option for $800 (8 × 100 shares per option); you put that number in the Money In side of the options chart. The maximum gain (the most this investor can make) is $800.

Money Out	Money In
	$800

2. **Find the maximum loss.**

   To calculate the maximum loss, you have to exercise the option at the strike price. The strike price is 30, so you place $3,000 (30 strike price × 100 shares per option) on the opposite side of the options chart. (Remember *puts switch:* The premium and strike price go on opposite sides of the options chart.)

Money Out	Money In
$3,000	$800

   You've already determined the maximum gain; now look at the Money Out portion of the options chart and compare it to the Money In. The maximum potential loss for this investor is the $2,200 difference between the Money Out and the Money In.

You calculate the break-even point for buying or selling puts the same way: You use *put down* (the strike price minus the premium) to figure out the break-even point:

strike price – premium = 30 – 8 = 22

For this investor, the break-even point is 22. Because this investor received $8 for the option, the option has to go $8 in-the-money for this investor to lose the amount she received for selling the option. Put options go in-the-money when the price of the stock goes below the strike price (put down).

Trading options: Opening and closing transactions

Although some investors hold onto their options long enough to actually exercise them, a lot of investors trade options the way that they trade other investments. On the Series 7, not only do you need to know the difference between opening and closing transactions, but you also have to be able to calculate the profit or loss for an investor trading options. This process is actually pretty easy when you break it down.

Putting things back where you found them: Doing opposite transactions

When distinguishing between opening and closing transactions, your key is to know whether this transaction is the first time or the second time the investor is buying or selling an option: The first time is an *opening*, and the second time is a *closing*.

Here are your opening transactions:

- **Opening purchase:** An opening purchase occurs when an investor first buys a call or a put.
- **Opening sale:** An opening sale is when an investor first sells a call or a put.

If an investor already has an option position, the investor has to close that position by doing the opposite — through a closing transaction. If the investor originally purchased the option, she has to sell to close it. By contrast, if she originally sold the option, she has to purchase to close. Here are the two types of closing transactions:

- **Closing purchase:** A closing purchase occurs when an investor buys herself out of a previous option position that she sold. For example, if an investor sold an XYZ Oct 40 call (opening sale), she would have to buy an XYZ Oct 40 call to close out the position. The second transaction is a closing purchase.
- **Closing sale:** A closing sale occurs when an investor sells herself out of a previous option position that she purchased. For example, if an investor bought an ABC Sep 60 put (opening purchase), she would have to sell an ABC Sep 60 put to close out the position. The second transaction is a closing sale.

When determining opening or closing transactions, whether the transactions are both calls or both puts doesn't matter.

The following question tests your knowledge of opening and closing transactions.

Mr. Dimpledell previously bought 1 XYZ Oct 65 call at 8 when the market price of XYZ was 64. XYZ is currently trading at 69, and Mr. Dimpledell decides that now would be a good time to sell the option that he previously purchased. The second option order ticket would be marked

(A) opening sale

(B) opening purchase

(C) closing sale

(D) closing purchase

The right answer is Choice (C). This is the second time that Mr. Dimpledell does something with the option that he owns; therefore, the move has to be a closing transaction, and you can immediately eliminate Choices (A) and (B). Mr. Dimpledell has to sell himself out of the position because he owns the option. The second order ticket would have to be marked *closing sale*.

Tricks of the options trade: Calculating gains and losses

In addition to knowing how to mark the order ticket, you have to be able to figure out an investor's gain or loss when trading options. This task isn't difficult after you master the options chart. The key thing to remember is that when an investor closes, she does the opposite of what she did before.

The following question tests your mastery of options trades.

Mrs. Cleveland purchased 100 shares of DPY stock at $50 per share. Two weeks later, Mrs. Cleveland sold 1 DPY Oct 55 call at 6. Mrs. Cleveland held that position for three months before selling the DPY stock at $52 per share and closing the DPY Oct 55 call at 4. What is Mrs. Cleveland's gain or loss on the transactions?

(A) $400 gain

(B) $400 loss

(C) $600 gain

(D) no gain or loss

The correct answer is Choice (A). This question introduces stock trades as well as options transactions, but that's no problem. The options chart works for questions involving actual stocks and options or just options.

When you approach the transactions one at a time, the problem-solving process is actually pretty straightforward. Mrs. Cleveland purchased 100 shares of DPY stock at $50 per share for a total of $5,000; therefore, you enter $5,000 in the Money Out side of the options chart. Next, she sold the DPY 55 call for a premium of 6, so you need to enter $600 (6 × 100 shares per option) on the Money In side of the chart because she received money for selling that option.

Three months later, Mrs. Cleveland sold the stock for $5,200 ($52 per share × 100 shares) and received money for selling the stock. Place the $5,200 in the Money In side of the options chart. When closing the option, the customer has to do the opposite of what she did before. Originally, Mrs. Cleveland sold the option, so to close, she has to buy the option (make a closing purchase). She purchased the option for $400 (4 × 100 shares per option), so enter $400 in the Money Out side of the options chart. All that's left for you to do is total up the two sides. Mrs. Cleveland has $5,800 in and $5,400 out for a gain of $400.

Money Out	Money In
$5,000	$600
$400	$5,200
$5,400	$5,800

Mastering Complex Option Calculations

You may not be happy to hear this, but some investors out there will make your life difficult. But, hey, don't be too upset, because working with these customers is how you're going to earn your six- or seven-figures-a-year salary (not including pennies). The Series 7 exam also tests your knowledge on more-complex option strategies. Of course, you can use an options chart to make your life much easier.

Long straddles and combinations

Straddles are option positions in which the investor buys a call and a put or sells a call and a put on the same underlying security with the same strike (exercise) price and the same expiration month; if the securities are the same but the strike prices and/or expiration months are different, you have a *combination* instead. What's nice is that combinations and straddles are virtually the same and the calculations are performed the same way.

This section deals with long positions, which involve purchases. (See "Short straddles and combinations" for info on sales.)

Long straddle

A *long straddle* is buying a call and a put with the same underlying stock, the same strike price, and the same expiration month. Investors who are expecting *volatility* in the underlying security purchase long straddles. These investors aren't sure which direction the stock will go, so they're covering their bases. They own a call option in case the price of the stock increases, and they own a put option in case the price of the stock decreases. Here's an example of a long straddle:

Buy 1 DEF Oct 40 call at 6

Buy 1 DEF Oct 40 put at 3

In order to have a long straddle (or combination) you must have two buys.

Long combination

A *long combination* is buying a call and a put for the same underlying stock with a different strike price and/or expiration month. As with straddles (see the preceding "Long straddle" section), an investor of a long combination is looking for a security that's volatile. The investor isn't sure which direction the security will go, so she buys a call in case the security increases in value and a put in case it decreases in value. Here's what a long combination may look like:

Buy 1 LMN Oct 40 call at 6

Buy 1 LMN Oct 30 put at 1

To distinguish a combination from a straddle, look at the expiration months and the strike (exercise) prices. If either one is different or both are different, you're dealing with a combination.

The following example tests your skill at distinguishing a straddle from a combination.

An investor who owns 1 XYZ Oct 40 call option would like to establish a long combination. Which of the following option positions would fulfill his needs?

(A) Write 1 XYZ Jan 40 put

(B) Buy 1 XZY Oct 30 put

(C) Buy 1 XYZ Oct 40 put

(D) Buy 1 XYZ Jan 30 put

The answer you're looking for is Choice (D). You can cross off Choice (A) right away because a long combination requires two purchases; Choice (A) is a sell (write), so it can't be right. You can cross off Choice (B), too, because although it looks ever so close, it involves a different security. Choice (C) would be correct if the question had indicated that the investor was looking for a straddle. A *long combination,* however, is buying a call and a put for the same security with different expiration months and/or different strike prices. Therefore, the only answer that works is Choice (D).

Try another problem to practice using the options chart (see the earlier "Incorporating Standard Option Math" section for the basics on buying and exercising options):

An investor buys 1 ABC Mar 60 call at 6 and buys 1 ABC Mar 50 put at 3. ABC subsequently increases to 68. The investor exercises the call and immediately sells the stock in the market. After the put expires unexercised, what is the investor's gain or loss?

(A) $100 gain

(B) $100 loss

(C) $500 gain

(D) $500 loss

The correct answer is Choice (B). The investor bought the call for $600 (6 × 100 shares per option), so you have to enter $600 in the Money Out section of the options chart because that was money paid from the investor's pocket. After that, the investor purchased the put for $300 (3 × 100 shares per option), so you have to enter $300 in the Money Out section of the chart. The next sentence states that the stock increased to 68, but it doesn't tell you to do anything with that yet, so you don't.

Next, you have to exercise the call option at the call strike price (always exercise at the strike price) and place the $6,000 (60 strike price × 100 shares per option) under its premium. (Remember *calls same:* The premium and strike price go on the same side of the options chart.) This investor sold the stock in the market for $6,800 (68 × 100 shares per option), which is Money In the investor's pocket. Total up each side, and you see that this investor has a loss of $100.

Money Out	Money In
$600	
$300	
$6,000	$6,800
$6,900	$6,800

When you get an option question with several steps (like the preceding one), look for the action words to tell you what to do. Action words include

- Buys, holds, owns, longs
- Sells, writes, shorts
- Exercises

Every time you see an action word, think of it as a clue to remind you that you have to put something in the options chart.

Short straddles and combinations

Short positions involve selling a call and a put with the same underlying stock. In straddles, the calls and puts have the same strike price and expiration month; with combinations, one of these values may differ.

Short straddle

A *short straddle* is selling a call and a put with the same underlying stock, the same strike price, and the same expiration month. An investor who is short a straddle is looking for *stability.* Because these investors are looking for a stock that's not going to change too much in price, short straddles are considered a *neutral position.* If the stock doesn't move in price, these investors will be able to keep the premiums they received for selling the options. A short straddle may look like this:

Sell 1 GHI Oct 50 call at 9

Sell 1 GHI Oct 50 put at 2

In order to have a short straddle (or combination), you must have two sells.

Short combination

A *short combination* involves selling a call and a put for the same underlying stock with a different strike price and/or expiration month. Similar to a short straddle, an investor who sells a combination has a neutral position and is looking for a security with stability. The investor is hoping the securities don't go in-the-money so the options are not exercised and she gets to keep the premiums received. A short combination may look like this:

Sell 1 QRS Dec 60 call at 4

Sell 1 QRS Mar 55 put at 3

Fortunately, for both straddles and combinations, you can calculate the maximum gain and maximum loss by just placing the premiums in the options chart. No exercising is necessary. For instance, suppose an investor has the following ticket orders:

Sell 1 TUV Jul 45 call at 6

Sell 1 TUV Jul 40 put at 3

Here's how you find the maximum potential loss and gain:

1. **Find the investor's maximum potential gain.**

   This problem involves a combination because the strike prices are different. However, if it were a straddle, you'd figure out the answer the same way. Place the premiums in the options chart. The investor sold the call for $600 (6 × 100 shares per option) and the put for $300 (3 × 100 shares per option). The transactions are both *sells,* so they have to go in the Money In side of the options chart. Add the numbers, and you can see that the maximum that this investor can gain (if the options never go in-the-money) is the $900 ($600 + $300) in premiums that she received.

Money Out	Money In
	$600
	$300
	$900

2. **Determine the investor's maximum potential loss.**

   With straddles and combinations, the premiums help you determine both the maximum potential gain and the maximum potential loss. After entering the premiums in the options chart, you may notice that the Money Out side of the chart is empty, so the investor's maximum potential loss is unlimited.

Break-even points for straddles and combinations

Straddles and combinations are a combination of calls and puts; therefore, you can find two break-even points (one on the way up and one on the way down). You must first add the two premiums together, because the investor either paid money twice (bought the call and bought the put) or received money twice (sold the call and sold the put). In the case cited in the preceding section, after you add the two premiums together, the total is 9 (6 + 3). Next, you use *call up* and add the combined premiums to the call strike price to get one break-even point. To get the other break-even point, use *put down* and subtract the combined premiums from the put strike price. This investor's break-even points are 31 and 54:

Combined premium: 6 + 3 = 9

Call up: Call strike + combined premium = 45 + 9 = 54

Put down: Put strike – combined premium = 40 – 9 = 31

You always have two break-even points for straddles and combinations. Make sure you *call up* (add the combined premiums to the call strike price) and *put down* (subtract the combined premiums from the put strike price) to get the break-even points.

Spreads

Investors create a *spread* position by buying an option and selling an option on the same underlying security. The maximum gain or loss with a spread position is limited. Investors create spread positions to either limit their potential loss or to reduce the premium paid.

Call spread

An investor creates a *call spread* position when buying a call and selling a call on the same underlying security. Additionally, the strike prices and/or expiration months have to be different. Here's what a call spread may look like:

Buy 1 JKL Aug 50 call at 9

Sell 1 JKL Aug 60 call at 2

The following sections show you how to find the maximum gain, maximum loss, and break-even points for spreads. The process for finding the maximum gain, maximum loss, and break-even point is the same for both call spreads and put spreads. If you put the premiums in the options chart, you will see that the investor has more money out than money in. Therefore, this investor created a *debit (long) spread.*

Put spread

An investor creates a *put spread* position when buying a put and selling a put on the same underlying stock with different expiration month and/or strike prices. Here's an example of a put spread position:

Buy 1 MNO Sep 30 put at 1

Sell 1 MNO Sep 40 put at 8

When putting the premiums in the options chart, this investor will have more money in than money out, thereby creating a *credit (short) spread.* The options chart can make figuring out the particulars, such as the maximum gain, maximum loss, and break-even points easier. Here's how you find these numbers, using the preceding put spread numbers:

1. **Determine the maximum gain.**

   Begin by entering the premiums in the options chart. This investor bought the 30 put option for $100 (1 × 100 shares per option), so that $100 is Money Out of her pocket. Then this investor sold the 40 put for a premium of $800 (8 × 100 shares per option), which you enter in the Money In side of the chart because she received money for selling that option.

Money Out	Money In
$100	$800

   You end up with more Money In than Money Out; therefore, the investor's maximum potential gain is $700 ($800 in minus $100 out).

   To help you recognize a spread, notice that when you put the two premiums in the options chart, they are *spread apart* (one on either side).

2. **Find the maximum loss.**

   You already calculated the maximum gain, so next you need to exercise both options to get the maximum loss. When exercising put options, enter the strike prices (multiplied by 100 shares) on the opposite side of the chart from their premiums because puts switch (go on the opposite side of the chart from the premium). First, exercise the 30 put and enter $3,000 (30 × 100 shares per option) in the Money In side of the chart, which is opposite from the $100 premium. Next, exercise the 40 put and enter $4,000 (40 × 100 shares per option) in the Money Out side of the options chart, which is opposite its $800 premium. Total up the two sides, and you see that the maximum potential loss is $300 ($4,100 out minus $3,800 in).

Money Out	Money In
$100	$800
$4,000	$3,000
$4,100	$3,800

Placing just the premiums in the options chart can give you the maximum potential gain or maximum potential loss but not both. To find the other answer, you must exercise both options.

Determining the break-even point for spreads

To find the break-even point, begin by finding the difference between the two premiums because you had one buy and one sell:

adjusted premium = 8 – 1 = 7

This is a put spread; therefore, you have to subtract the 7 from the higher strike price. The higher strike price is 40, so the break-even point is 33:

$$\text{break-even point (put spread)} = \text{higher strike price} - \text{adjusted premium} = 40 - 7 = 33$$

For call spreads, you have to *add* the adjusted premium (after you've subtracted the smaller premium from the larger one) to the lower strike price. For put spreads, you *subtract* the adjusted premium from the higher strike price.

The following question tests your ability to determine the break-even point on spreads.

Miguel Hammer purchased 1 Apr 40 call at 9 and shorted 1 Apr 50 call at 3. What is Miguel's break-even point?

(A) 43

(B) 46

(C) 49

(D) 53

The right answer is Choice (B). First, focus on the buy and the sell. If the investor is buying one option and selling another, you should be able to recognize it as a spread. Therefore, you have to find the difference between the two premiums:

$$\text{adjusted premium} = 9 - 3 = 6$$

Next, because it's a call spread, you have to add the adjusted premium (after subtracting the smaller from the larger) to the call strike (exercise) price to get the break-even point:

$$\text{break-even point (call spread)} = 40 + 6 = 46$$

The following question tests your ability to answer a spread story question.

Mrs. Peabody purchased 1 DEF Mar 60 put at 5 and wrote 1 DEF Mar 65 put at 9 when DEF was trading at 68. Six months later, with DEF trading at 61, Mrs. Peabody's DEF Mar 65 put was exercised. Mrs. Peabody held the shares of DEF for another two months before selling them in the market for $62 per share. Mrs. Peabody's Mar 60 put expired without ever going in-the-money. What is Mrs. Peabody's gain or loss?

(A) $100 loss

(B) $100 gain

(C) $700 loss

(D) $700 gain

The answer you're looking for is Choice (B). I like to call such problems *story* questions because they take you on a journey, and this one is a tricky one. If you got this right, you're a master of spreads.

Begin by placing the transactions in the correct side of the options chart. Because Mrs. Peabody purchased the DEF Mar 60 put at 5, you have to enter $500 (5 × 100 shares per option) on the Money Out side of the options chart because she spent that much to purchase the option. After that, she sold a DEF Mar 65 put for 9 and received $900 (9 × 100 shares per option) Money In for selling that option. The fact that DEF was trading at 61 when the option was exercised means nothing in this question, so feel free to ignore it.

Next, you have to exercise the 65 put that Mrs. Peabody sold. Because *puts switch,* you enter the strike price (multiplied by 100 shares) in the opposite side of the options chart from its premium. After you place the $6,500 in the Money Out section of the options chart, you have to sell the stock that Mrs. Peabody purchased when her option was exercised. She sold the stock in the market for $6,200 ($62 market price × 100 shares) and received cash for that transaction, so enter $6,200 in the Money In section of the chart. Total up the two sides, and you can see that good old Mrs. Peabody has a gain of $100.

Money Out	Money In
$500	$900
$6,500	$6,200
$7,000	$7,100

Just like other option story questions (with several things happening), enter only items in the options chart when you see action words. Remember, every time you see an action word, such as *purchased, wrote, exercised, sold,* and so on, you know that you have to enter something in the options chart.

Got it covered: Stock/option contracts

When an investor purchases or sells option contracts on securities she owns, that investor is choosing an excellent way to protect against loss or to bring additional funds into her account. The most common form is when an investor sells covered call options.

If an investor is selling a call option against a security that she owns, the investor is considered to be *covered.* She's covered because if the option is exercised, the investor has the stock to deliver.

Take the following position as an example:

Buy 100 shares of QRS at $47 per share

Sell 1 QRS Dec 55 call at 4

1. **Find this investor's maximum potential loss.**

   Place the purchases and sales in the options chart. This investor purchased 100 shares of QRS stock at $47 per share for a total of $4,700. That's money spent, so enter $4,700 in the Money Out side of the options chart. Next, this investor sold 1 QRS Dec 55 call for a total premium of $400 (4 × 100 shares per option) and received money for selling that option, so you enter $400 in the Money In section of the options chart.

Money Out	Money In
$4,700	$400

   This investor has more Money Out than Money In, so the investor's maximum potential loss is $4,300 ($4,700 minus $400).

2. **Determine the investor's maximum potential gain.**

   Placing the two transactions (in this case the stock purchase and the option sale) in the options chart helps you calculate the maximum gain as well as the maximum loss. To find the maximum gain, you need to exercise the option. You always exercise at the strike price, which in this case is 55. Take the $5,500 (55 × 100 shares per option) and place it under its premium. (Remember *calls same:* The exercised strike price and the premium go on the same side of the chart.) Total the two sides and you find that the Money In is $1,200 more than the Money Out, so that's the investor's maximum potential gain.

Money Out	Money In
$4,700	$400
	$5,500
$4,700	$5,900

When the investor is covered, finding the break-even point is nice and easy for stock and options. Although you can use the options chart, you really don't need to in this example case. First, look at how much the investor paid for the stock; then look at how much more she paid or received for the option. Find the difference, and you have your break-even point:

$47 stock price – $4 option premium = $43 break-even point

Because this investor paid $47 per share for the stock and received back $4 per share for selling the option, this investor would need to receive another $43 per share to break even.

Here's how to find the break-even point for stock and options:

- **If the investor purchased twice** (bought the stock and bought a protective put option), add the stock price and the premium.
- **If the investor sold twice** (sold short the stock and sold an option), add the stock price and the premium.
- **If the investor had one buy and one sell** (for example, bought the stock and sold the option or sold short the stock and bought the option), subtract the premium from the stock price.

The following example tests your knowledge on stock and option problems.

Mr. Bullwork sold short 100 shares of DIM common stock at $25 per share and bought 1 DIM Aug 30 call at 3 to hedge his position. What is Mr. Bullwork's maximum potential loss from this strategy?

(A) $300

(B) $800

(C) $2,200

(D) $2,700

The answer you're looking for is Choice (B). As always, you need to enter the initial purchase and sale into the options chart and see what you have. Your friend and client, Mr. Bullwork, sold short 100 shares of DIM common stock at $25 per share for a total of $2,500. Because Mr. Bullwork received the $2,500 for selling short, you have to put $2,500 in the Money In side of the options chart. Next, Mr. Bullwork purchased a DIM Aug 30 call to hedge (protect) his position in case the stock started increasing in value. You have to enter the $300 (3 × 100 shares per option) in the Money Out side of the options chart, because he paid money to purchase the option. Stop and take a look to see whether that calculation answers the question.

Money Out	Money In
$300	$2,500

You see more Money In at this point than Money Out, so you have a maximum gain, not a maximum loss; therefore, you have to exercise the option to get the answer you need. Make sure you exercise the option at the strike price. The strike price is 30, so enter $3,000 under its premium. (Remember *calls same:* The premium and multiplied strike price go on the same side of the chart.) Total up the two sides, and you see that the maximum potential loss for Mr. Bullwork is $800 ($3,300 – $2,500).

Money Out	Money In
$300	$2,500
$3,000	
$3,300	$2,500

Off the charts: Multiple option contracts

Now before you start freaking out, know that working with multiple option contracts isn't that much more difficult than working with single contracts. This change is simply a matter of an investor buying two, three, four, or more of the same option contract at one time. I guide you through the steps in this section.

When you work with multiple option contracts, approach the problem as though you were dealing with only one contract. You can easily do so by taking the multiple (the number of contracts) and placing it to the side of the options chart so you don't forget it. Calculate the maximum potential loss or gain for a single contract, and then multiply that answer by the number of contracts.

The following sample calculations use this ticket order:

Buy 6 ABC Oct 40 calls at 7

Sell 6 ABC Oct 55 calls at 2

1. **Find the investor's maximum potential loss.**

   Take the number of contracts (in this case it's six) and place it to the side of the options chart. Now this problem is as simple as the other options I mention in the earlier sections. In this case, you can look at the problem as though the investor is buying a call for $700 (7 × 100 shares per option), which is Money Out of the investor's pocket. Next, the investor sells (writes) the ABC Oct 55 call for $200 (2 × 100 shares per option). Because this transaction is a sale, you enter it in the Money In side of the options chart. The investor has $700 out and $200 in; therefore, the maximum loss per option is $500. Now, take a look at the multiple. Take the maximum loss and multiply it by six (six options on each side), and you end up with a maximum loss of $3,000 for this investor.

(x6) Money Out	Money In
$700	$200

Maximum loss = $500 per option x 6 = $3,000

Note: Some option strategies include having a different number of options on each side. However, you're unlikely to be tested on these strategies on the Series 7. These strategies are covered more in the Series 4 exam (the Registered Options Principal Qualification Exam).

2. **Determine the investor's maximum potential gain.**

   When dealing with spreads, the premiums give you the maximum gain or the maximum loss but not both. Because you've already so expertly determined the investor's maximum potential loss, you need to exercise both options to get the maximum potential gain. Approach the question as if you were dealing with only one option on each side. Multiply the strike price of 40 by 100 shares per option to get $4,000. Enter $4,000 under its premium of $700. (Remember *calls same:* The premium and the strike price go on the same side of the chart.) After that, you can exercise the 55 call to get $5,500 (55 strike price × 100 shares per option). Enter $5,500 under its premium of $200 (again, following the *calls same* rule). Total up the two sides, and you have $1,000 more Money In than Money Out ($5,700 – $4,700). That value is the maximum gain for one option on each side. Because this investor has six options on each side, multiply the $1,000 by six to get $6,000 for this investor's maximum potential gain.

(x6) Money Out	Money In
$700	$200
$4,000	$5,500
$4,700	$5,700

Maximum gain = $1,000 per option x 6 = $6,000

What's nice about finding the break-even point is that it works out the same whether the investor has 1, 10, 30, or more options on either side of the market. In this case, the investor bought one option and sold the other, so you need to find the difference between the two premiums. After subtracting the two premiums, you end up with an answer of 5:

$$\text{adjusted premium} = 7 - 2 = 5$$

This is a call spread (buying a call and selling a call — see the earlier "Spreads" section), so you need to add the adjusted premium (5) to the lower strike price (40) to get the break-even point. In this case, the break-even point is 45:

$$\text{break-even point}(\text{call spread}) = 40 + 5 = 45$$

Follow the same strategy for all option transactions (spreads, straddles, combinations, and so on) when dealing with multiple options: Always take the contract size and move it to the outside of the options chart when calculating the maximum gain or loss. Then multiply the gain or loss by the number of contracts.

You have to worry (and I use that term loosely) about not only multiple option contracts but also multiple options and multiples of 100 shares of stock purchases or sales. This process is a piece of cake if you follow the rules that I give you. Check out the example, which uses the following position:

Buy 400 shares of ABC common stock at $36

Buy 4 ABC Oct 30 puts at 4

1. **Determine the investor's maximum potential gain.**

   This investor purchased 400 shares of stock and four options, which gives you a multiple of four. Take the multiple and move it to the outside of the options chart. You can then look at the problem as though the investor has only 100 shares of stock and 1 option, because you'll deal with the contract size later. First, enter the $3,600 that the investor paid for the stock ($36 × 100 shares) in the Money Out side of the options chart, because the investor spent money to purchase the stock. Next, enter the $400 that the investor paid for the option (4 × 100 shares per option) in the Money Out side of the options chart because the investor purchased the option. Because the Money In side of the chart is empty, the investor's maximum potential gain is unlimited.

(x4)	Money Out	Money In
	$3,600	
	$400	

2. **Find the investor's maximum potential loss.**

   You've already determined the maximum potential gain; therefore, you need to exercise the option to get the maximum potential loss. The investor purchased a put option, so you have to enter the $3,000 (30 strike price × 100 shares per option) in the Money In side of the options chart. (Remember *puts switch:* The premium and the strike price go on opposite sides of the options chart.) Total up the two sides, and you see that you have $1,000 more Money Out than Money In, so the investor's maximum potential loss is $1,000 per option. Because this investor has four options and 400 shares, you need to multiply the $1,000 by four to get the maximum loss of $4,000.

(x4)	Money Out	Money In
	$3,600	
	$400	$3,000
	$4,000	$3,000

Maximum loss = $1,000 x 4 = $4,000

Here's how you find the investor's break-even point: In this case, the investor purchased the stock for $36 per share and the option for $4 per share. Therefore, this investor needs the price of the stock to go to $40 ($36 + $4) in order to break even:

$$\text{break-even point}(\text{call spread}) = 36 + 4 = 40$$

Dividends and splits, more or less

This section addresses how an option contract is adjusted for corporate actions such as a company declaring a dividend or splitting its stock (see Chapter 6 for more info on splits and dividends). I begin with the basics and move forward from there.

Stock dividends

When a company declares a stock dividend, here's what happens to option contracts:

- The number of option contracts remains the same.
- The strike price decreases.
- The number of shares per option contract increases.

Please peruse the following example to see how this works out. Here, the investor's initial position is

4 ABC Sep 65 call options (100 shares per option)

If ABC declares a 5-percent stock dividend, you can find the investor's position on the *ex-dividend date* (the first day the stock trades without the dividend).

Because ABC is giving a 5-percent stock dividend, the result will be 105 shares per option instead of 100 (5 percent more shares). To find the new strike price, multiply the original 65 call options by 100 shares per option to get 6,500. Next, divide the 6,500 by the 105 shares per option to get a new strike price of 61.90 (rounded to the nearest cent). The new position is

4 ABC Sep 61.90 call options (105 shares per option)

Cash dividends *do not* affect listed options. For example, suppose that an investor owns 1 ABC Oct 40 call option and ABC declares a $0.50 cash dividend. Although the price of the stock decreases by $0.50, the option still reads 1 ABC Oct 40 call.

Regular forward splits

Dealing with a regular forward split is relatively easy. In this case, you're dealing with a 2-for-1, 3-for-1, 4-for-1, and so on. I cover your approach to tackling uneven splits in the next section. In an anything-for-1 split, here's what happens:

- The number of option contracts increases.
- The strike price decreases.
- The number of shares per option remains the same (normally 100).

Check out the following example, where the investor has an initial position of

2 DEF Jul 60 calls (100 shares per option)

If DEF Corporation announces a 3-for-1 split, the investor's position on the ex-dividend date is

6 DEF Jul 20 calls (100 shares per option)

In this case, the investor has three options for every one that she had before, and the strike price is ⅓ of what it was before:

$$2 \times \frac{3}{1} = \frac{6}{1} = 6 \text{ option contracts}$$

$$60 \times \frac{1}{3} = \frac{60}{3} = 20 \text{ strike price}$$

Notice how you multiply the contracts by 3⁄1 and the strike price by the reciprocal (⅓).

A good way to double-check your work for all dividends and splits is to multiply the number of option contracts by the strike price and then by the number of shares per option. Do the same thing after you adjust the numbers for the dividend or split. Compare the answers. You should get the same number. If you don't, you did something wrong.

Uneven and reverse splits

Uneven splits are similar to dividends in that the number of option contracts remains the same but the strike price and the number of shares per option change. Uneven splits are splits that are not *x*-for-1 (for example, 3-for-2, 4-for-3, 5-for-2, and so on). Look at the following example, where the investor has an initial position of

3 GHI Jun 50 calls (100 shares per option)

If GHI announces a 5-for-2 split, the investor's position on the ex-dividend date is

3 GHI Jun 20 calls (250 shares per option)

First, because the investor has 5 shares for every 2 that she had before, you have to multiply the shares per option by 5⁄2:

$$100 \text{ shares} \times \frac{5}{2} = \frac{500 \text{ shares}}{2} = 250 \text{ shares per option}$$

Next, you have to multiply the strike price by ⅖:

$$50 \text{ strike price} \times \frac{2}{5} = \frac{100}{5} = 20 \text{ new strike price}$$

To work out a reverse split (for example, 3-for-5, 2-for-3, and so forth), use the same process. Be aware that for reverse splits, the strike price increases and the shares per option decrease.

Nonconforming Options

Certain options fit somewhat outside the realm of standard option terms. This section covers two qualifiers that change an option.

Spending time on LEAPS: Long-term options

LEAPS is short for Long-term Equity AnticiPation Securities. The initial expiration for most options is nine months. LEAPS, however, can have expirations dates of up to three years. Investors can purchase LEAPS on a large variety of stocks, the Dow, the S&P 100, and the

S&P 500. Although most options have to be paid for in full, a unique characteristic of LEAPS options is that, unlike standard options, they can be purchased on margin by an investor who comes up with 75 percent of the premium.

Setting limits with capped options

You can spot a capped index option because it has the word "CAPS" next to it. Capped index options are traded on the S&P 100 and the S&P 500. *Capped options* have a limited maximum gain or loss because the option will be capped at 30 points in-the-money. You can assume that the cap interval for a capped option is 30 points in-the-money unless the question gives you a different cap interval (which it most likely won't). Look at the example, which finds the maximum loss and maximum gain for an investor with the following order ticket:

Buy 1 OEX CAPS 450 call at 7

Holders of options don't have to exercise them, so the investor can lose no more than the premium. The maximum loss is $700 (7 × 100 shares per option).

The maximum gain is $2,300. If the investor had paid nothing for the option, the maximum this investor could make would be $3,000 (30 points in-the-money × 100 shares per option). However, this investor paid $700 for the option, so the most she can make is $2,300.

Gaining Additional Option Info

To help you get a deeper understanding of options, you need to know a few additional things that you will most certainly see on the real-deal Series 7 exam. Some of these items include who issues the options, where you can get options quotations, what an ROP is, what a risk disclosure document is, and when options expire.

Clearing through the OCC

The Options Clearing Corporation (OCC) is the issuer and guarantor of all listed options. The OCC decides which options will trade and their strike prices. In addition, when an investor decides to exercise her option, it's the OCC that randomly decides which firm on the other end will be responsible for fulfilling the terms of the option.

OPRA . . . not Oprah

The Options Price Reporting Authority (OPRA) provides last sale information and current options quotations provided by participating exchanges. OPRA collects trading information from certain exchanges such as Amex, the Boston Stock Exchange, the Chicago Board Options Exchange, the International Securities Exchange, and the Philadelphia Stock Exchange. OPRA disseminates the info it collects to investors and professionals.

Getting the go-ahead: Registered options principal

Because of the extra risk of investing in options, all option order tickets must be signed by a registered options principal (ROP), which is a manager with a Series 4 license. The registered options principal determines the amount of risk that each investor can take. Certainly, sophisticated investors with a lot of money are able to handle more risk than new option investors with a limited supply of funds.

That's ODD: Options risk disclosure document

Because options have a risk that is greater than almost any other investment, all investors must receive an options risk disclosure document (ODD) prior to their first options transaction. This ODD explains to investors the risk involved in investing in options, such as the chance of losing all money invested or, if selling call options, facing an unlimited maximum loss potential.

Last trade, last exercise, and expiration of an option

Unlike stock certificates, options do expire after a certain period of time. In addition, investors are limited as to when they can trade and exercise an option. Here's the timeline to keep in mind:

- **Last trade:** The last time an investor can trade an option is 3:02 p.m. CST on the business day prior to expiration.
- **Last exercise:** The last time an investor can exercise an option is 4:30 p.m. CST on the business day prior to expiration. If an option is in-the-money by at least 1 point at expiration, it will be automatically exercised.
- **Option expiration:** Options expire at 10:59 p.m. CST on the Saturday after the third Friday of the expiration month.

For Further Review

Although this chapter works through the more difficult and more commonly tested areas of the Series 7 exam relating to options, you also need to have a good handle on the following topics:

- The compliance registered options principal (CROP)
- The senior registered options principal (SROP)
- The Chicago Board Options Exchange (CBOE)
- The order book official (OBO)
- The order support system (OSS)
- World currency options
- Yield-based, debt, and index options
- American-style versus European-style options
- Opening and closing rotations
- Bull or bear spreads
- The tax treatment of options

- Options of the same type, series, or class
- Vertical, horizontal, and diagonal spreads
- Married put
- Hedging
- Covered options versus uncovered (naked) options
- The routing of an option order
- Volume, open interest, position, and exercise limits
- Listed options markets, including trading participants
- Options advertisements and sales literature
- The minimum and maintenance margin requirements (portfolio margin) for options

Part IV

Playing Nicely: Serving Your Customers and Following the Rules

"Our goal is to maximize your upside and minimize your downside while we protect our own backside."

In this part . . .

For the Series 7 exam (and in your real-life career as a stockbroker), you're required to know the market conditions that affect your customers' portfolios and the rules that regulate your responsibilities when you're opening, closing, transferring, and handling your customers' accounts. Then, for the times when your customers' portfolios skyrocket in value (thanks to your expertise and brilliant recommendations, of course), the Series 7 tests you on your understanding of the tax breaks available so your customers can keep more of the money you helped them earn instead of giving it away to Uncle Sam.

In this part, I detail the tools you have at your disposal — not just to scrutinize customers' accounts but also to monitor market conditions that can affect their investments. I also familiarize you with the markets where securities trade. And in addition to giving you an overview of income tax breaks and helping you distinguish long-term from short-term capital gains and losses for income tax purposes, I discuss the effect of retirement plans and contribution limits on your customers' income taxes. Finally, I review the essential rules for care and protection of your customers' accounts, and I talk a bit about the agencies that make sure you play by the rules.

Chapter 13

Doing a Little Market Research: Portfolio and Securities Analysis

In This Chapter

- Analyzing a customer's needs
- Comparing fundamental analysis to technical analysis
- Looking at the money supply
- Reviewing additional topics tested

In terms of choosing securities, throwing darts at a list of stocks seems to have fallen out of favor. So has drawing company names out of a hat. But hey, no problem. Your psychic powers may not be the most reliable, but you still have tons of tools that can help you get a good idea of where the market's heading and how certain securities may perform.

One of your main jobs as a registered representative is to figure out the best investments for your customers. To help lead people down the path of riches, you have to analyze your customer's portfolio and the market and try to find a good fit. In many cases firms hire analyists to provide registered reps with investment information, which helps you determine the best recommendations for each customer.

In this chapter, I cover topics relating to portfolio analysis, securities analysis, and money supply. The majority of this chapter is about analyzing a customer's financial conditions and seeing what happens with the money supply. Don't worry, though — I don't leave out technical and fundamental analysis; I just focus on the information that can help you get the best score on the Series 7.

Knowing Your Customer: Portfolio Analysis

Not all investors are able to take the same amount of risk, so what constitutes an excellent recommendation for one customer may be disastrous for another. When opening an account with a new customer, creating a portfolio analysis of the client's current holdings and needs (due diligence) is important so you can help more effectively. When you open such an account, you fill out a new account form with your customer's help (for details on the info that appears here, see Chapter 16). One important element on the form is the customer's investment objectives, which tell you how much risk the customer is willing to take. Of course, a customer's investment objectives aren't written in stone — they can change during his lifetime, so you also need to keep up with the customer's life changes.

The Series 7 exam takes your ability to evaluate a customer's needs into consideration — so naturally, you get tested on it. The following sections explain investment objectives, what factors impact these goals, and how you can allocate assets and appropriately manage portfolios so the investments are right in line with the customer's needs.

Understanding investment objectives

Investments aren't exactly one-size-fits-all, so asking a client about his investment objectives can be a real help. As a financial expert, you'll likely have to help clients pin down what their goals should be. I help you find out how in the next section, but for now, here are some possible investment objectives:

- **Preservation of capital:** Investing in safe securities, such as U.S. government bonds, municipal bonds, high-rated corporate bonds, and so on
- **Current income:** Investing in securities (such as bonds, preferred stock, income funds, and so on) that'll provide interest or cash dividends
- **Capital growth:** Investing in the stock of relatively new companies or ones that have a high growth potential
- **Total return:** Investing in a combination of stocks and bonds, looking for both growth and income
- **Tax advantages:** Investing in securities (such as municipal bonds, direct participation programs, retirement plans, and so on) that give tax breaks
- **Liquidity:** Looking to purchase securities that can be bought and sold easily
- **Diversification:** Investing in securities from several different companies, municipalities, and/or the U.S. government to offset the risk associated with only owning one security
- **Speculation:** Investing in securities with higher risk in an attempt to maximize profits if the securities move in the right direction
- **Trading profits:** Looking to buy and sell securities on a constant basis
- **Long-term or short-term:** Looking to tie up money for either a long time or a short time

When recommending securities to your customers, you need to make recommendations that fit their investment objectives. Some customers may fit into more than one category (for example, looking for diversification and liquidity). All customers should have a diversified portfolio (own several different securities and/or types of securities). If a customer can't afford to diversify, you want to recommend mutual funds (for info on mutual funds and other packaged securities, check out Chapter 10).

The following question tests your ability to answer a question about investment objectives.

Mr. Johnson is a 60-year-old investor who is heavily invested in the market. Mr. Johnson is looking to invest in more securities with a high degree of liquidity. Which of the following investments are you LEAST likely to recommend?

(A) DPPs

(B) Blue-chip stocks

(C) T-bills

(D) Mutual funds

The correct answer is Choice (A). Because Mr. Johnson is looking for securities with a high degree of liquidity, you're least likely to recommend DPPs (direct participation programs), or limited partnerships, because they're the most difficult investments to get in and out of. Not only do you need to prequalify the investor, but the investor also has to be accepted by the general partner (see Chapter 11 for details). However, blue-chip stocks, T-bills, and mutual funds can all be bought and sold fairly easily.

Looking at factors that influence your customer's investment profile

If an investor is clueless about how much risk he should be taking, your job is to help your client figure it out. Think of yourself as the Sherlock Holmes of the investing world and use the information you have available, such as your client's age, whether he has a family, how much money he has, and so on. Additionally, feel your client out to try to get an idea of how much risk he's comfortable taking.

Money, money, money: Checking out financial information

Obviously, financial factors influence future investments. To get an idea of your client's needs, you can start by looking at your customer's financial profile, which includes

- **Your client's net worth:** The investor's current assets and liabilities, the amount of marketable securities the client owns, and whether he has any deferred assets, such as a retirement plan
- **Money available for investing:** The client's current income and expenses, and the amount of money he has available for investments
- **Additional background items:** Whether the investor owns a home, whether he has life and/or disability insurance, his tax bracket, and his credit score

Money isn't everything: Considering nonfinancial influences

In addition to the customer's financial profile (see the preceding section), you need to be aware of nonfinancial considerations so you can choose appropriate investments. These considerations may include whether this customer is responsible for his family, the customer's age, the employment of other family members (for example, whether they work for a bank, broker-dealer, or insurance company), educational plans the customer has for himself or his children, and so on. Here's how such factors can affect an investor's objectives:

- **Age:** Older investors usually can't handle as much risk as younger investors.
- **Changes in marital status:** Recently married couples may be looking for securities that provide a certain degree of safety; for instance, they may be looking to buy a house. New divorcees may face more or fewer financial responsibilities in addition to changes in income, affecting their willingness to take risk.
- **Family responsibilities:** Investors who have a family with several dependents normally aren't as comfortable investing in more speculative securities.
- **Education:** Parents who need to save for their kids' college may need to invest in securities that are not only safer but also allow for a smaller investment now with a bigger return in the future, such as zero-coupon bonds or T-STRIPS.
- **Investment experience:** As a customer gets more used to investing, he may be willing to take more risk.

Stay updated with regard to your customers' lives. Not only does this effort make it seem like you care (which, of course, I hope you do), but it also helps you keep abreast of changing investment objectives and keep investments in line with those objectives.

Splitting up with asset allocation

Asset allocation is the process of dividing an investor's portfolio among different asset classes, such as bonds, stock, and cash. The main purpose of asset allocation is to reduce risk by diversifying the investor's portfolio. Asset allocation differs from investor to investor depending on the investor's risk tolerance.

Strategic asset allocation

Strategic asset allocation refers to the types of investments that should make up a long-term investment portfolio. Typically, the normal strategic asset allocation model suggests that you subtract the investor's age from 100 to determine the percentage of the portfolio that should be invested in stocks. For example, a 40-year-old investor should have 60 percent invested in stocks and 40 percent invested in bonds and cash or cash equivalents (such as a money market fund). A 70-year-old investor should have 30 percent invested in stocks and 70 percent invested in bonds and cash or cash equivalents.

Strategic asset allocation gives you a good starting point. If you have an aggressive investor, put a higher percentage into stocks than the model suggests; if you have a conservative investor, put a lower percentage into stocks.

Tactical asset allocation

Tactical asset allocation refers to rebalancing a customer's portfolio due to market conditions. For example, if the stock market is expected to do well in the short-term, you put a higher percentage into stocks. If the stock market is expected to do poorly over the short-term, you lower the percentage of stocks and purchase more fixed-income securities (bonds). Later sections in this chapter give you more info on how to analyze securities and markets.

Strategizing with portfolio management policies

In addition to all the other investment choices, investors may have a defensive investment strategy, an aggressive investment strategy, or some combination of the two. An investor who adopts a *defensive investment strategy* has safety of principal and interest as a top priority. A defensive investment strategy includes investments such as

- Blue-chip stocks with low volatility (stocks of well-established, financially stable companies — see Chapter 6)
- AAA rated bonds (Chapter 7)
- U.S. government bonds (Chapter 7)

An investor who adopts an *aggressive investment strategy* is attempting to maximize gains by investing in securities with higher risk. An aggressive portfolio strategy includes

- Investing in securities such as highly volatile stocks (Chapter 6)
- Investing in put and/or call options (Chapter 12)
- Buying securities on margin (Chapter 9)

Although defensive and aggressive strategies are clearly defined, most investors have a *balanced portfolio* (aggressive/defensive), which includes securities included in both an aggressive and defensive portfolio.

Knowing Your Securities and Markets: Securities Analysis

Although many brokerage firms have their own analysts, you do need to know some of the basics of securities analysis to pass the Series 7. In this section, I cover investment risks that your customers face and show you the differences between technical and fundamental analysis.

Regarding risk

Investors face many risks (and hopefully many rewards) when investing in the market. You need to understand the risks because not only can this knowledge make you sound like a genius, but it can also help you score higher on the Series 7:

- **Market (systematic) risk:** The risk of a security declining due to negative market conditions. All securities have market risk.
- **Business (nonsystematic) risk:** The risk of a corporation failing to perform up to expectations.
- **Credit risk:** The risk that the principal and interest aren't paid on time. Moody's, Standard & Poor's, and Fitch are the main bond-rating companies.
- **Liquidity (marketability) risk:** The risk that the security is not easily traded. Long-term bonds and limited partnerships have more liquidity risk.
- **Interest (money rate) risk:** The risk of bond prices declining with increasing interest rates. (Use the idea behind the seesaw from Chapter 7: When interest rates increase, outstanding bond prices decrease.) All bonds (even zero-coupon bonds) are subject to interest risk.
- **Reinvestment risk:** The risk that interest and dividends received will have to be reinvested at a lower rate of return. Zero coupon bonds, T-bills, T-STRIPS, and so on have no reinvestment risk because they don't receive interest payments.
- **Purchasing power (inflation) risk:** The risk that the return on the investment is less than the inflation rate. Long-term bonds and fixed annuities have high inflation risk. To avoid inflation risk, investors should buy stocks and variable annuities.
- **Capital risk:** The risk of losing all money invested (for options [Chapter 12] and warrants [Chapter 6]). Because options and warrants have expiration dates, purchasers may lose all money invested at expiration. To reduce capital risk, investors should buy investment-grade bonds.
- **Regulatory (legislative) risk:** The risk that law changes will affect the market.
- **Currency risk:** The risk that an investment's value will be affected by a change in currency exchange rates. Investors who have international investments are the ones most affected by currency risk.
- **Nonsystematic risk:** A risk that is unique to a certain company or a certain industry. To avoid nonsystematic risk, investors should have a diversified portfolio.
- **Political (legislative) risk:** The risk that the value of a security could suffer due to instability or political changes in a country (for example, the nationalization of corporations).
- **Prepayment risk:** The type of risk mostly associated with real-estate investments such as CMOs (Chapter 7). CMOs have an average expected life, but if mortgage interest rates decrease, more investors will refinance and the bonds will be called earlier than expected.
- **Timing risk:** The risk of an investor buying or selling a security at the wrong time thus failing to maximize profits.

On the Series 7 exam, to determine the best investment for a customer, pay close attention to the risk(s) mentioned. If the question isn't specific about the type of risk, use strategic asset allocation to determine the best answer (see the earlier "Splitting up with asset allocation" section for more information).

Deciding what to buy: Fundamental analysis

Although most analysts use some combination of fundamental analysis and technical analysis to make their securities recommendations, for Series 7 exam purposes, you need to be able to differentiate between the two types. This section discusses fundamental analysis; I cover technical analysis later in the section "Deciding when to buy: Technical analysis."

Fundamental analysts perform an in-depth analysis of companies. They look at the management of a company and its financial condition (balance sheets, income statements, the industry, management, earnings, and so on) and compare it to other companies in the same industry. In addition, fundamental analysts even look at the overall economy and industry conditions to determine whether an investment is good to buy.

In simplest terms, fundamental analysts decide *what to buy.*

A fundamental analyst's goal is to determine the value of a particular security and decide whether it's underpriced or overpriced. If the security is underpriced, a fundamental analyst recommends buying the security; if the security is overpriced, he recommends selling or selling the security short.

The following sections explain some of the fundamental analyst's tools of the trade and how to use them.

Balance sheet components

The *balance sheet* provides an image of a company's financial position at a given point in time. The Series 7 exam tests your ability to understand the components (see Figure 13-1) and how financial moves that the company makes (buying equipment, issuing stock, issuing bonds, paying off bonds, and so on) affect the balance sheet. In general, understanding how a balance sheet works is more important than being able to name all the components.

Assets	***Liabilities***
Current assets	Current liabilities
Fixed assets	Long-term liabilities
Intangible assets	
	Stockholder's equity (net worth)
	Par value (common)
	Par value (preferred)
	Paid-in capital
	Treasury stock
	Retained earnings

Figure 13-1: Components of a balance sheet.

People call this statement a balance sheet because the assets must always balance out the liabilities plus the stockholders' equity.

Assets are items that a company owns. They include

- **Current assets:** Owned items that are easily converted into cash within the next 12 months; included in current assets are cash, securities, accounts receivable, inventory, and any prepaid expenses (like rent or advertising).

  Note: Fundamental analysts also look at methods of inventory valuation, such as *LIFO* (last in first out) or *FIFO* (first in first out). In addition, they look at the methods of depreciation, which are either *straight line* (depreciating an equal amount each year) or *accelerated* (depreciating more in earlier years and less in later years).

- **Fixed assets:** Owned items that aren't easily converted into cash; included are property, plant(s), and equipment. Because fixed assets wear down over time, they can be depreciated.
- **Intangible assets:** Owned items that don't have any physical properties; included are items such as trademarks, patents, formulas, goodwill (a value based on the reputation of a company — for example, the name McDonald's is probably worth more than Fred's Sloppy Burgers), and so on.

Liabilities are what a company owes. They may be current or long-term:

- **Current liabilities:** Debt obligations that are due to be paid within the next 12 months; included in current liabilities are *accounts payable* (what a company owes in bills), wages, debt securities due to mature, *notes payable* (the balance due on money borrowed), declared cash dividends, and taxes.
- **Long-term liabilities:** Debt obligation due to be paid after 12 months; included in long-term liabilities are mortgages and outstanding corporate bonds.

Stockholders' equity (net worth) is the difference between the assets and the liabilities (basically, what the company is worth). This value includes

- **Par value of the common stock:** The arbitrary amount that the company uses for bookkeeping purposes. If a company issues 1 million shares of common stock with a par value of $1, the par value on the stockholders' equity portion of the balance sheet is $1 million.
- **Par value of the preferred stock:** The value that the company uses for bookkeeping purposes (usually $100 per share). If the company issues 10,000 shares of preferred stock, the par value on the stockholders' equity portion of the balance sheet is $1 million.
- **Paid in capital:** The amount over par value that the company receives for issuing stock. For example, if the par value of the common stock is $1 but the company receives $7 per share, the paid in capital is $6 per share. The same theory holds true for the preferred stock.
- **Treasury stock:** Stock that was outstanding in the market but was repurchased by the company.
- **Retained earnings:** The percentage of net earnings the company holds after paying out dividends (if any) to its shareholders.

Balance sheet calculations

If I were to give you all the calculations that fundamental analysts derive from the balance sheet, you'd likely be cursing under your breath (or possibly out loud). The good news is that the likelihood of your having to perform these calculations on the Series 7 is remote. The most important thing for you to know is what happens to components of the balance sheet when the company makes certain transactions (sells stock or bonds, redeems bonds, and so on).

Here are some formulas that you do need to know for the Series 7 exam:

$$\text{working capital} = \text{current assets} - \text{current liabilities}$$

$$\text{assets} = \text{liabilities} + \text{stockholder's equity}$$

$$\text{net worth} = \text{assets} - \text{liabilities}$$

Note: The last two equations say the same thing in two different ways. The reason that I list both of them is for ease of use. Depending on the question you get, one will be easier to use than the other.

If, for instance, ABC Corp. issues 10,000 bonds at par value, you can use these formulas to figure out what'll happen to the net worth and working capital. You may not even have to plug in numbers. As far as the net worth goes, you can see that it remains unchanged. The company brings in $10 million by issuing 10,000 bonds at $1,000 par. However, because ABC has to pay off the $10 million at maturity, the liabilities go up by the same amount:

$$\text{net worth} = \text{assets}\uparrow - \text{liabilities}\uparrow$$

Working capital is the amount of money a company has to work with right now. The company brings in cash by issuing the bonds, which is a current asset, but doesn't have to pay off the bonds for several years, so the current liabilities remain the same. If the current assets increase and the current liabilities remain the same, the working capital increases:

$$\text{working capital}\uparrow = \text{current assets}\uparrow - \text{current liabilities}$$

When a company issues bonds, assume that they're a long-term liability, not short-term, unless the question specifically states that the company is issuing short-term bonds.

The following question tests your ability to answer a balance-sheet-equation question.

DEF Corp. is in the process of buying a new $50,000 computer system. If it is paying for the computer system with available cash, what is the effect on the balance sheet?

(A) The net worth decreases and the working capital remains the same.

(B) The net worth remains the same and the working capital remains the same.

(C) The net worth decreases and the working capital decreases.

(D) The net worth remains the same and the working capital decreases.

The right answer is Choice (D). The company is exchanging one asset for another, and the overall liabilities remain the same, so the net worth of the company doesn't change. However, the company is using a current asset (cash) to purchase a fixed asset (the computer system), so the working capital (the amount of money that the company has to work with) decreases:

$$\text{net worth} = \text{assets} - \text{liabilities}$$

$$\text{working capital}\downarrow = \text{current assets}\downarrow - \text{current liabilities}$$

Take a look at the following scenarios and see whether you can determine how the balance sheet is affected. Here's what happens when a company

- **Declares a cash dividend:** When a company declares a cash dividend, that cost becomes a current liability to the company. Because current liabilities are part of the overall liabilities owed in the net worth equation, both the net worth and the working capital decrease.
- **Pays a cash dividend:** When the company initially declares the cash dividend, the current liabilities increase, but when the company pays that dividend, the current liabilities fall. However, the current assets also decrease because the company has to use cash to pay the dividend. If the current assets (and overall assets) decrease and the current liabilities (and overall liabilities) decrease by the same amount, the working capital and net worth both remain the same.
- **Issues stock:** When a company issues stock, it receives cash, which is a current asset (and part of the overall assets). The company doesn't owe anything to investors, so the overall liabilities (and current liabilities) remain the same. Therefore, the net worth and working capital both increase.

When you're dealing with balance sheet equations on the Series 7 exam, write down the equations and think about the questions logically. If something is increasing, use an up arrow, and if something is decreasing, use a down arrow. Hopefully, this notation can help you solve a majority of the balance sheet problems.

Income statement components

An income statement tells you how profitable a company is right now. *Income statements* list a corporation's expenses and revenues for a specific period of time (quarterly, year-to-date, or yearly). When comparing revenues to expenses, you should be able to see the efficiency of the company and how profitable it is. I don't think you need to actually see a detailed balance sheet from a company, but knowing the components of an income statement is important. Take a look at Figure 13-2 to see the way an income statement is laid out. Most of the items are self-explanatory.

Net sales
- Cost of goods sold (earnings before interest, taxes, depreciation, and amortization) (EBITDA)
- Operating expenses (including depreciation)

Operating profit (earnings before interest and taxes) (EBIT)
- Interest expenses

Taxable income (earnings before taxes) (EBT)
- Taxes

Net income (earnings after taxes) (EAT)
- Preferred dividends

Earnings available to common stockholders
- Common dividends

Retained earnings

Figure 13-2: Components of an income statement.

Income statement calculations

Here are calculations you need to know for the Series 7 that you can derive from the income statement:

$$\text{earnings per share (EPS)} = \frac{\text{net income} - \text{preferred dividends}}{\text{no. of common shares outstanding}}$$

$$\text{price/earnings (P/E) ratio} = \frac{\text{market price}}{\text{EPS}}$$

$$\text{current yield} = \frac{\text{annual dividends per common share}}{\text{market price}}$$

$$\text{dividend payout ratio} = \frac{\text{annual dividends per common share}}{\text{EPS}}$$

The following question tests your ability to answer a question on earnings per share.

Zazzoo Corp. has 1 million common shares outstanding. If Zazzoo's net income is $14 million, what are the earnings per share?

(A) $0.07

(B) $0.70

(C) $14.00

(D) Cannot be determined without knowing the preferred dividends

The answer you want is Choice (C). "Cannot be determined" is almost never the answer on the Series 7. Remember that a corporation doesn't need to issue preferred stock, only common stock. Because the question doesn't mention anything about Zazzoo's having preferred stock, you can't assume that they do; the preferred dividends are equal to zero. Therefore, solving this problem is as easy as dividing the net income by the number of common shares outstanding:

$$\text{EPS} = \frac{\text{net income} - \text{preferred dividends}}{\text{no. of common shares outstanding}} = \frac{\$14{,}000{,}000 - 0}{1{,}000{,}000} = \$14.00$$

You could *possibly* get a bunch of formulas relating to income statements and balance sheets on the Series 7 exam. However, the most you'll *probably* get is two. Understanding how income statements and balance sheets work is more important than remembering a bunch of formulas. For you die-hard math fans, I mention the formulas that you may want to know in the "For Further Review" section at the end of the chapter. If you feel that you have a handle on everything else that you need for the Series 7 exam and want to get the extra ⁴⁄₁₀ or ⁵⁄₁₀ of a point by memorizing all the formulas, go for it.

Deciding when to buy: Technical analysis

Technical analysts look at the market to determine whether the market is bullish or bearish. They look at trendlines, trading volume, market sentiment, market indices (in other words, the S&P 500), options volatility, market momentum, available funds, index futures, new highs and lows, the advance-decline ratio, odd lot volume, short interest, put-to-call ratio (options trading), and so on. These analysts believe that history tends to repeat itself and that past performance of securities and the market indicate its future performance.

Fundamental analysts decide *what to buy,* and technical analysts decide *when to buy* (timing).

Not only do technical analysts chart the market, but they also chart individual securities. Technical analysts try to identify market patterns and patterns of particular stocks in an attempt to determine the best time to purchase or sell. Even though a stock's price may vary a lot from one day to another, when plotting out stock prices over a long period of time, the prices tend to head in a particular direction (up, down, or sideways) and create a *trendline.*

Consolidation is occurring when a stock stays within a narrow trading range or *trading channel.* When plotted out on a graph, the trendline is moving horizontally (neither up nor down). If a stock stays within a narrow trading range for a long period of time (months or even years), it creates a *support* (bottom of the trading range) and *resistance level* (top of the trading range). For example, say that XYZ common stock has been trading between $40 and $42 per share for several months; the lower number ($40) is the support, and the higher number ($42) is the resistance.

When a stock declines below its support level or increases above its resistance level, a *breakout* is occurring. When a stock has been trading horizontally (sideways) for a long period of time, a breakout is considered significant. Breakouts are usually a sign that the stock is beginning a new downward or upward trend.

If a stock price is gradually moving down over a period of time, the stock's in a *downtrend.* Conversely, if the stock price is gradually moving upward over a period of time, you're looking at an *uptrend.* Here are a couple patterns technical analysts recognize as reversals of such trends:

- **Saucer and inverted saucer:** In a saucer pattern, when the stock prices are plotted for a period of time, they make a saucer shape (gradually decreasing and then gradually increasing). A saucer pattern is a bullish sign or, to be more precise, the reversal of a bearish trend. Conversely, an inverted saucer is exactly the opposite; it's a bearish sign because it's the reversal of a bullish trend.

- **Head and shoulders and inverted head and shoulders:** A head and shoulders pattern is formed when the price of a stock has been increasing, hits a high, and then starts decreasing. It involves three peaks, with the center peak as the highest. The two bumps in the road (one on the way up and one on the way down) are the shoulders, and the high point is the head. A head and shoulders top formation is a bearish sign because it's the reversal of a bullish trend. I also illustrate an inverted head and shoulders (also known as a head and shoulders bottom formation), which is a bullish sign because it's the reversal of a bearish trend.

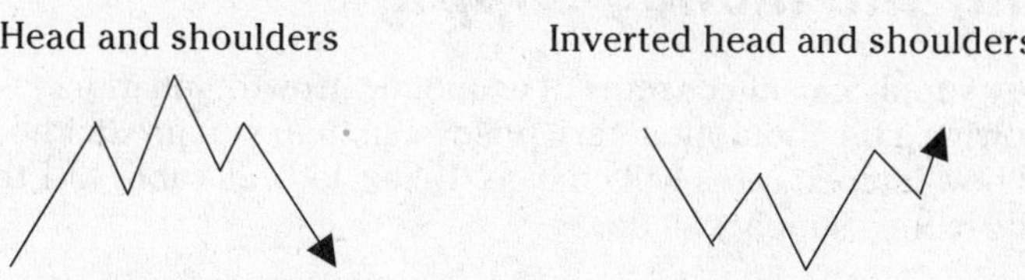

The key thing to remember about these patterns is that the saucer pattern and the inverted head and shoulders pattern are bullish signs, whereas the head and shoulders and inverted saucer patterns are bearish signs.

The market is said to be *oversold* if a market index such as the DJIA or the S&P 500 is declining but fewer stocks are declining than advancing. If the market is oversold, it's likely a good time to buy. On the other hand, the market's *overbought* if a market index such as the DJIA or the S&P 500 is increasing but fewer stocks are advancing than declining. If the market is overbought, it's likely a good time to sell or sell short (borrow securities to sell on margin).

Showing the work: Research reports

Typically, brokerage firms send out research reports to their customers (and potential customers) with certain recommendations. Research reports are documents prepared by an analyst who is part of a brokerage or investment banking firm. As with pretty much everything on the Series 7, research reports are subject to several rules:

- **Quiet periods:** Member firms are restricted from publishing or distributing research reports on a particular investment until at least 10 days after the initial public offering (IPO).
- **Information barriers:** All firms must establish information barriers (firewalls) to protect analysts from any pressure they may feel from investment bankers or any other persons who may be biased in their judgment.
- **Third-party disclosures:** Depending on the size of your firm, you may or may not have access to your own research analyst to prepare reports. A third-party research report is one in which the third party has no affiliation or contractual relationship with the distributing firm. All third-party research reports must include a disclosure unless the member firm makes nonaffiliated research available to its customers either upon request or through a website maintained by the member firm.

Following the Green: Money Supply

The money supply heavily affects the market. If the money supply is higher than average, interest rates go down, people borrow more money, and people spend more money. That all sounds great, but the situation can lead to some negatives, such as higher inflation and the weakening of U.S. currency in relation to foreign currency. The Federal Reserve Board (FRB) has to do a balancing act to help the economy grow at a slow and steady rate. This section deals with how the money supply affects the market and the tools that the Fed uses to control the money supply.

Influencing the money supply

Changes in money supply can affect rates of economic growth, inflation, and foreign exchange, so knowing a bit about monetary policy can help you predict how certain securities will fare and how interest rates will change. Take a look at Table 13-1 to see what easing and tightening the money supply can do.

Table 13-1 Effects of Easing and Tightening the Money Supply

Category	*Easing the Money Supply*	*Tightening the Money Supply*
Economy	Easy money helps the U.S. avoid or get out of a recession. Consumers can borrow money at lower interest rates.	The economy slows down because people aren't spending as much money; the rate of small business failure increases.
Market	As a result of lower interest rates, investors have more money to invest and can purchase more goods. Additionally, businesses don't have to pay as much interest to borrow money, which increases their profits. Both elements can lead to a bullish market.	High interest rates hurt the market because investors don't have extra money to spend. Additionally, corporations have to pay higher interest on loans and, therefore, report lower earnings. The market becomes bearish.
Inflation	Lower interest rates lead to higher inflation. If companies see that customers are spending money freely, they raise their prices.	A tighter money supply helps curb high inflation.
Strength of the U.S. dollar	The U.S. dollar weakens. U.S. exports increase because foreign currency strengthens (people can trade fewer units of foreign currency for more dollars); therefore, buying U.S. products is cheaper for foreign consumers. However, the U.S. dollar loses value when purchasing foreign goods, so foreign imports decrease.	The value of the U.S. dollar rises in relation to foreign currency. The U.S. dollar is subject to supply and demand, so if our money supply is tight, the value of our currency increases. Because the U.S. dollar is strong, importing foreign goods is cheaper for U.S. companies. However, U.S. exports decline because buying U.S. goods becomes more expensive for foreign companies.

When the money supply is eased (resulting in *easy money*), interest rates in general decrease. The Fed can ease the money supply by

- Buying U.S. government securities in the open market
- Lowering the discount rate, reserve requirements, and/or Regulation T (although changing Reg T isn't likely)

Occasionally, the Fed has to tighten the money supply. (Remember, the Fed wants the U.S. economy to grow at a slow, steady pace.) When the money supply is tightened (resulting in *tight money*), interest rates across the board increase. The Fed can tighten the money supply by

- Selling U.S. government securities (pulling money out of the banking system)
- Increasing the discount rate, reserve requirements, and/or Regulation T

The following section tells you more about these tools.

Opening the Federal Reserve Board's toolbox

The Federal Reserve Board, or the Fed, has the authority on behalf of the U.S. government to lend money to banks; it determines the interest rate charged to banks for these loans. You probably remember the chairman of the Fed (formerly Alan Greenspan, now Ben Bernanke) coming on TV to announce an increase or decrease in the *discount rate* (the rate the Fed charges banks for loans) and what a big deal it was. The rate the Fed charges impacts the rates banks charge each other and their public customers. Because banks charge customers higher rates than the Fed charges banks, the Fed policy affects consumers as well (through credit card fees, mortgage loans, auto loans, and so on):

Fed $ → banks $ → customers $

The Fed has a few tools in its arsenal to help control the money supply (the preceding section explains the effects of tightening and easing the supply). Here's what you need to understand about these tools for the Series 7:

- **Open market operations:** The tool the Fed uses most often, open market operations are the buying or selling of U.S. government bonds or U.S. government agency securities to control the money supply. Open market operations are performed by the Federal Open Market Committee (FOMC). If the Fed sells securities, it pulls money out of the banking system; if the Fed purchases securities in the open market, it puts money into the banking system.
- **The discount rate:** This value is the rate that the 12 Federal Reserve Banks charge member banks for loans. If the discount rate increases, the money supply tightens; by contrast, if the discount rate decreases, the money supply eases.
- **Reserve requirement:** The reserve requirement is the percentage of customers' money that banks are required to keep on deposit in the form of cash. In line with the theory of supply and demand, if the Fed increases the reserve requirement, banks have less money to lend to customers, so interest rates increase.
- **Regulation T:** Reg T is the percentage that investors must pay when purchasing securities on margin (see Chapter 9 for details). Regulation T is currently set at 50 percent, and it doesn't change very often. If the Fed raises the rate, investors have less cash, which tightens up the money supply.

Spotting interest rate indicators

The Series 7 designers expect you to recognize some signs that interest rates have increased or decreased. If the following values are high, the money supply will tighten up. The money supply is subject to supply and demand the same way securities are, so if interest rates increase due to the tightening of the money supply, you can assume that those increases will occur across the board. For example, if the Fed raises the reserve requirements, you can expect interest rates on savings accounts to increase, credit card rates to increase, bond yields to increase, mortgage rates to increase, and so on. Conversely, if interest rates decrease, you can assume that those decreases will occur across the board. Here are some key interest rate indicators:

- **Reserve requirements:** This value, controlled by the Fed, is the percentage of bank deposits that may not be loaned to customers.
- **Discount rate:** The discount rate is the interest rate that the Fed charges to member banks for loans. The discount rate is the lowest rate for all loans.
- **Fed Funds rate:** The Fed Funds rate is the interest rate that banks, broker-dealers, and financial institutions charge each other for loans. If one bank doesn't have enough money to meet the reserve requirements, the bank can borrow money from another bank that has excess reserves. In most cases, a Fed Funds loan is a loan between banks, usually overnight. It's the most volatile of all interest rates (meaning it changes the most often).
- **Call loan rate (broker loan rate):** This value is the interest rate that banks charge brokerage firms for customers' margin accounts. When customers borrow money from a broker-dealer to purchase securities on margin, the broker-dealer in turn borrows money from a bank to cover the loan that it made to the customer.
- **Prime rate:** This value is the interest rate that banks charge their best customers (usually corporations) for loans.

Looking at easy money and tight money yield curves

Yield curves are graphic representations of bond yields as compared to the amount of time until maturity. Although you aren't likely to have an exhibit relating to yield curves on the Series 7 exam, visualizing the different yield curves can really help you answer multiple choice questions about yield curves:

- **Normal (easy money) yield curve:** This figure is the type of yield curve that you'd expect; the yields on long-term debt securities are higher than the yields on short-term debt securities. If you're going to tie your money up for a year, you may be happy with a 6 percent yield, but if you're tying your money up for 30 years, you may want a yield of at least 8 percent.

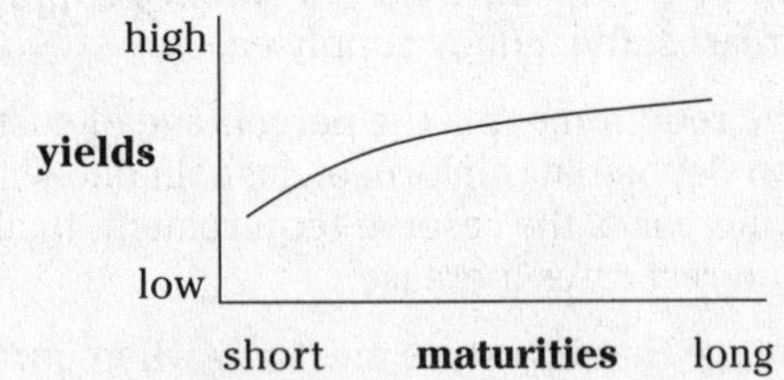

- **Inverted (tight money) yield curve:** This curve is the opposite of what you'd expect. In a tight money yield curve, short-term debt securities are actually paying higher yields than long-term debt securities. Not cool.

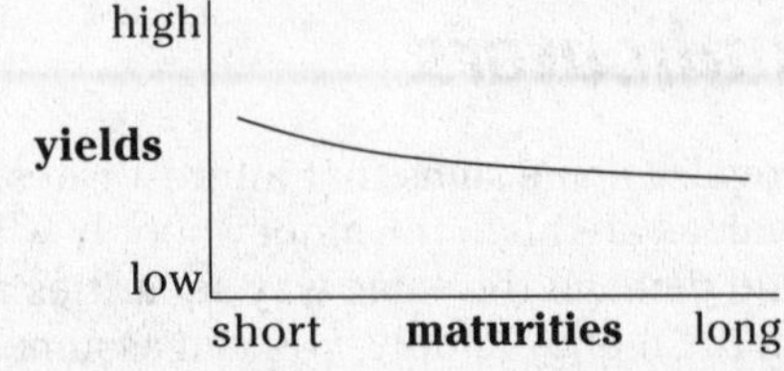

- **Flat yield curve:** When you plot this situation out on a graph, the yields on long-term and short-term debt securities are pretty much the same.

Taking a look at the Fed setup

Here's a quick lesson in government: Congress established the Federal Reserve System in 1913 to stabilize the country's chaotic financial system. The Fed controls our money supply and, therefore, our economy.

The nation is divided into 12 Federal Reserve Districts, each with its own bank. Each bank prints currency to meet the business needs of its district, and each district is distinguished by a letter printed on the face of the bill.

The Federal Reserve Board in Washington is the parent organization that oversees and controls each of the 12 Federal Reserve District Banks. The members of the board including the Chairman are nominated by the President of the United States, subject to confirmation by the Senate.

The following question tests your yield curve knowledge.

During a period of tight money, when the yield curve is inverted, which of the following securities is likely to have the highest yield?

(A) T-bills

(B) Commercial paper

(C) T-notes

(D) AA-rated corporate bonds

The correct answer is Choice (B). Because you're dealing with an inverted yield curve and tight money, short-term debt securities have higher yields than long-term debt securities. The two short-term debt securities listed are T-bills and commercial paper, so if you pick T-bills, you're on the right track. However, because T-bills are issued by the U.S. government and are considered very safe, they'd have lower yields than commercial paper (corporate debt securities with maturities of 270 days or less).

For Further Review

For you to be as prepared as possible to take the Series 7 exam, you should also have a grasp of the items in this section. Look over these additional analysis-related topics and make sure you know them prior to braving the Series 7:

- Economic indicators (leading, coincident, lagging)
- Sources of information
- U.S. balance of payments, exchange rates, and domestic versus foreign interest rates
- M1 money supply, M2 money supply, and M3 money supply
- Business cycle: expansion, peak, contraction, and trough
- Terms: gross domestic product (GDP), consumer price index (CPI), inflation, and deflation
- Principal economic theories: Keynesian (consumption function, savings, investment, the multiplier effect, marginal propensity to consume, liquidity preference), supply side, and monetarist economics
- Types of issues: blue-chip, cyclical, countercyclical, defensive, and growth company
- Risk related to purchasing growth stock, cyclical stock, speculative stock, defensive stock, utilities, and so on

- Alpha coefficient and beta coefficient
- Capital asset pricing model (CAPM)
- Aggressive versus defensive portfolio management
- Liquidity of a company: current ratio, quick assets, and acid test ratio
- A company's risk of bankruptcy: debt-to-equity ratio and bond ratio
- How a company uses its assets: inventory turnover ratio and cash flow
- How profitable a company is: margin-of-profit ratio and net profit ratio
- Earnings per share: fully diluted earnings per share, price-earnings ratio, current yield, and dividend payout ratio
- Asset coverage: net asset value per bond, bond interest coverage, and book value per share
- Return on common equity
- Accumulation/distribution
- Moving averages
- Stabilization
- Circuit breakers
- Special situation company
- Indexes, averages, and composites
- Disinflation and stagflation
- Business cycle characteristics (depression, recession, and inflation)
- Inflation/deflation and their effect on securities and the market
- The currency (interbank) market
- Financial statements

Chapter 14

Going to Market: Orders and Trades

In This Chapter

- Understanding the differences between the primary and secondary markets
- Comparing stock exchanges to the over-the-counter market
- Looking at order qualifiers
- Meeting a designated market maker and looking over the books
- Reviewing additional topics tested

Part of your function as a registered rep will be to understand and explain to customers (and potential customers) how the stock market works. I designed this chapter with that in mind (along with the fact that you need to know this stuff for the Series 7, of course).

In this chapter, I cover the basics of exchanges and the over-the-counter market, along with some of the active participants who help the market run smoothly (at least most of the time). Pay particular attention to the "Talking about order types" and "Factoring in order features" sections, because you'll definitely use that information every day after you pass the Series 7 exam. As always, practice questions and a "For Further Review" section await.

Shopping at Primary and Secondary Markets

Depending on whether the securities are new or outstanding, they trade in either the primary or secondary market. This section deals with the differences between the two.

Buying new in the primary market

The primary market (new issue market) is broken down into two categories, depending on whether the company has ever issued securities before. A security that has never been offered or sold to the public is considered a *new issue.* When securities are sold in the primary market, a bulk of the sales proceeds go to the issuer, and the balance goes to the underwriter (who buys the securities from the issuer and sells them to the public). Here are the two types of offerings on the primary market:

- **Initial public offering (IPO):** An IPO is the first time a company ever sells stock to the public to raise money. When a company is in the process of issuing securities for the first time, it's said to be *going public.*
- **Primary offering:** When a company initially offers securities, it usually holds some back for future use; it later pulls those securities out of storage and sells them in a primary offering. For example, a company may be authorized to sell 2 million shares of common stock, but in its initial public offering, it may sell only 800,000. At this point, 1,200,000 new shares remain that have never been offered to the public. One year later, when the company needs to raise additional capital to build a new warehouse, it can sell some of the remaining 1,200,000 shares in a primary offering.

Buying used in the secondary market

When the securities are already trading in the market, the sales proceeds go to another investor instead of to the issuer. The secondary market, also called the *aftermarket,* consists of four categories (see the following section for info on trading on exchanges versus over-the-counter markets):

- **First market (auction market):** The first market is the trading of listed securities on the exchange floor, such as the New York Stock Exchange (NYSE).
- **Second market (over-the-counter market):** This market is the trading of unlisted securities over-the-counter (by phone or computer).
- **Third market:** The third market is comprised of exchange-listed securities trading over-the-counter (OTC) — traders are calling in their orders or ordering online. All NYSE Amex Equities and NYSE securities and most of the securities listed on other exchanges can be traded OTC.
- **Fourth market:** The fourth market is the trading of securities between institutions without the use of a brokerage firm. Fourth-market trades are reported on Institutional Networks, or Instinet, a computerized system for institutional traders.

You're more likely to get a question on the third or fourth market than the first or second.

Making the Trade

After securities are issued publicly, they may trade on an exchange or on the over-the-counter (OTC) market.

Auctioning securities at securities exchanges

Exchanges are auction markets, where bidders and sellers get together to execute trades. I'm sure you've seen movies or TV shows featuring the New York Stock Exchange. It definitely looks very chaotic (and like it's a good place to have a heart attack or develop an ulcer). However, some sort of order is definitely there: All exchanges have a trading floor where all trades are executed. Each security listed on an exchange has its own *trading post* (location) on the floor where the auction takes place. Brokers looking to purchase shout out and/or make hand signals to indicate the price they're willing to spend to buy a particular security. Sellers, in turn, shout out the price they're willing to sell a security for. If buyers and sellers can come to an agreement, a trade is made.

The main exchange that the Series 7 tests you on is the New York Stock Exchange (NYSE), but you should be aware of others, such as NYSE Amex Equities (formerly the American Stock Exchange [AMEX]), NASDAQ OMX PHLX (an electronic exchange market for over 3,000 equity, index, and currency options), NYSE Euronext (a combination of NYSE, NYSE Arca, and Euronext), the Philadelphia stock exchange, the Chicago Board Options Exchange, and the Pacific stock exchange. *Listed securities* are ones that satisfy minimum requirements and are traded on a regional or national exchange like the NYSE. Listed securities may trade on the exchange or in the OTC market.

Although thousands of people may seem to be on the floor of the exchange, you don't need to be aware of too many titles. Most of the people on the floor of the exchange fall into one of three categories:

- **Floor brokers:** These individuals act as agents in executing buy or sell orders on behalf of their firm's customers. A floor broker may also facilitate buying and selling for her firm. Floor brokers receive buy or sell orders from their firms and either transfer the orders to a specialist or trade with another floor broker.
- **Two-dollar brokers (independent brokers):** These people assist floor brokers in getting their orders executed on busy days. (By the way, they're called two-dollar brokers because many, many years ago, they used to receive $2 per trade. Commissions may have gone up a bit since then.)
- **Designated market makers (specialists):** These market professionals manage the auction market trading for a particular security (or for a few securities, if not actively traded). For more information about a specialist, visit "Taking a Look inside the Designated Market Maker's Book," toward the end of this chapter.

Negotiating trades over-the-counter

Unlike exchanges, the OTC market is a negotiated market. Instead of yelling out bid and ask prices, traders buy and sell securities by way of telephone or computer transactions. There's no central location for trading OTC securities. Thousands of securities — both listed and unlisted — are traded this way. In fact, *unlisted securities,* which aren't listed on an exchange, can only trade OTC.

The OTC equities market is divided into NASDAQ issues (issues that meet the NASDAQ listing requirements) and non-NASDAQ issues.

U.S. government and municipal bonds trade only over-the-counter.

The NASD Automated Quotation service (NASDAQ) is an electronic quotation system that displays bid and ask prices of the most actively traded OTC stocks. Additionally, NASDAQ also includes quotes of preferred stock, convertible bonds, and warrants. The NASDAQ market is divided into two components:

- **NASDAQ Global Market (NGM):** This market includes the largest and most actively traded stocks trading OTC. The NASDAQ Global Market provides a market for over 3,900 companies, including giants such as Microsoft and Intel. To be listed on the NASDAQ Global Market, a company has to have a minimum number of shares outstanding, at least 400 round lot (100-share) shareholders, and shares with a minimum bid price of at least $5. A majority of NASDAQ stocks are NGM issues, which are *marginable* (can be purchased on margin — see Chapter 9 for info on margin accounts).
- **NASDAQ Capital Market stocks:** These securities were formerly called NASDAQ *small cap stocks.* These stocks trade OTC but don't meet the listing requirements of NGM stocks.

To make trades, people need accurate, current info on bid and ask prices. Not everyone can get the same amount of information, though. Here are the access levels of NASDAQ (the computer displays with NASDAQ information):

- **Level I:** The most basic level of NASDAQ, this quotation screen displays up-to-the-minute inside bid and ask prices for several hundred OTC stocks. Level I is the computer screen that you'll most likely have on your desk when you're working as a registered rep. Level I is the most basic level of NASDAQ and includes quotes that are subject to change (*subject quotes*).

- **Level II:** The second level of NASDAQ provides up-to-the-minute firm bid and ask prices (*firm quotes*) of each market maker (dealers or principals) for a security. Most brokerage firm traders use this level.
- **Level III:** The most complete level of NASDAQ, this level not only shows the bid and ask prices of all market makers and their firm quotes but also allows a market maker to enter and change quotes.

Understanding the Role of a Broker-Dealer

In order for a firm to be considered a broker-dealer, it must buy and sell securities from its own account and act as middlemen (or middlewomen) for securities not in inventory. Here are the differences between brokers and dealers:

- **Broker:** A firm is acting as a broker when it doesn't use its own inventory to execute a trade. A broker charges a *commission* (sales charge) for acting as a middleman between a buyer and a seller.

  For Series 7 exam purposes, the term *broker* and *agent* may be used interchangeably. A registered representative is sometimes called an agent or stockbroker because she acts as an intermediary between buyers and sellers.
- **Dealer:** A firm is acting as a dealer when it uses its own inventory to execute a trade. When a dealer sells securities to a customer using its own inventory, it charges a *markup* (sales charge). When a dealer buys securities from a customer for its own inventory, it charges a *markdown* (reducing the price a customer receives by charging a sales charge). A firm becomes a dealer in the hopes that the securities it has in its own inventory will increase in price so that the dealer can benefit from the appreciation.

  The terms *dealer, principal,* and *market maker* may be used interchangeably on the Series 7 exam.

Capacity refers to whether a firm is acting as a broker or dealer, and it must always be disclosed on the *confirmation* (receipt of trade). If a firm is acting as a broker, the commission always needs to be disclosed on the confirmation. However, if a firm is acting as a dealer, the markup or markdown doesn't always have to be disclosed.

A firm can't act as a broker and a dealer for the same trade. In other words, charging a markup (or markdown) and a commission on the same trade is a violation. (For info on rules and regulations, see Chapter 16.)

To help you remember the differences between a broker and a dealer, think of a real-estate broker. A real-estate broker (or agent) acts as an intermediary between sellers and buyers and charges a commission, just like a stockbroker does. Conversely, a dealer like a used car dealer, sells from his own inventory, charges a markup, and buys in the hopes of making a profit on that inventory.

Receiving Orders from Customers

Here's where the rubber meets the road. You can receive several types of orders from customers along with numerous order qualifiers. This section explains the types of orders and how to execute them.

Talking about order types

You can definitely expect a few questions on the Series 7 exam relating to orders. The following sections explore the order types.

Market order

A market order is for immediate execution at the best price available. A majority of the orders that you'll receive will be market orders. Here are the varieties they come in:

- **Buy order:** When an investor places a market order to buy, she's not price-specific; the investor purchases the security at the lowest ask price (the lowest price at which someone's willing to sell the security). An investor who's purchasing a security wants the price to increase (after the sale, of course) and is establishing a bullish position.
- **Sell order:** When an investor places a market order to sell, she's not price-specific; she sells the security at the highest bid price (the highest price someone's willing to pay for the security).
- **Selling short:** Selling short occurs when an investor sells securities she doesn't own. The investor is actually borrowing securities from a lender to sell. Here's how it works: Say an investor borrows 100 shares of ABC stock and sells them short at $40 per share, thus receiving $4,000. The borrower doesn't owe the lender $4,000; she owes the lender 100 shares of ABC stock. After a month or two, when ABC is trading at $20 per share, the borrower can purchase the 100 shares for $2,000 and return them to the lender, making a nice $2,000 profit (excluding commission costs). A short seller is bearish (wants the price of the security to decrease). If the price increases instead, the short seller has to buy the stock in the market at a higher price, thus losing money. All short sales must be executed in margin accounts. Short sales are subject to short-sale regulations under Regulation SHO (see the nearby sidebar).

  Note: Investors may sell short for *speculation* (believing the price of the security will decrease), *hedging* (protecting a security or several securities in the event of a market decline, or *arbitrage* (taking advantage of a price disparity on the security in different markets).

When you purchase a security, the most you can lose is the amount you invest. When you're short a security, your maximum loss potential is unlimited because the price of the stock could keep climbing, in which case you'd have to spend more money to cover your short position. Additionally, because of the additional risk, all short sales must be executed in a margin account. Chapter 9 tells you more about margin accounts.

Regulation SHO and short sales

According to *Regulation SHO,* all order tickets must be marked as *short sale* rather than long sale, which is when a customer is selling securities she owns. Additionally, all brokerage firms must establish rules to locate, borrow, and deliver securities that are to be sold short. Brokerage firms must be sure that the security can be located and delivered on the date the delivery is due before executing the short sale.

Selling short against the box

Selling short or *shorting against the box* is when an investor sells short a security that she already owns. This type of sale typically happens when an investor wants to sell a security at the current price but can't get possession of her securities right away because she's traveling or whatever. By selling short against the box, the investor is locking in the price of the security because no matter which way it goes, she will be offsetting a gain or loss on the securities owned with a loss or gain on the securities sold short.

Stop order

A stop order is used for protection; it tries to limit how much an investor can lose. Depending on whether an investor has a long or short stock position, she may enter a buy stop order or a sell stop order:

- **Buy stop orders:** These orders protect a short position (when an investor sells borrowed securities). A buy stop tells you to buy a security if the market price touches a particular price or higher. Investors who are short the stock make money when the price of the stock decreases; however, if the price increases, they lose money. For example, an investor who's short ABC stock currently trading at $25 could enter a buy stop order on ABC at $30. If ABC reaches $30 or more, the order is triggered and the order becomes a market order for immediate execution at the next price.
- **Sell stop orders:** These orders protect a long position (when an investor purchases stock); they tell you to sell a security if the market price touches a particular price or lower. Investors who are long stock make money when the price of the stock increases; if the price decreases, they lose money. For example, say an investor who is long DEF stock currently trading at $50 enters a sell stop order on ABC at $45. If DEF reaches $45 or below, the order is triggered and the order becomes a market order for immediate execution at the next price, whether higher or lower than $45.

Limit order

A customer who's specific about the price she wants to spend or receive for a security places a limit order; this order says the customer doesn't want to pay more than a certain amount or sell for less. Depending on whether an investor is interested in buying or selling, she can enter a buy limit or a sell limit order:

- **Buy limit orders:** Investors who want to purchase a security place these orders. A buy limit order is a directive to buy a particular security at the limit price or lower. For example, suppose DEF stock is trading at $35 per share but one of your customers doesn't want to pay more than $30 per share. You could place a buy limit order at $30. If the price of DEF ever reaches 30 or less, chances are good that your customer will end up with the stock.
- **Sell limit orders:** Investors who want to sell a security place sell limit orders. A sell limit order is a directive to sell a particular security at the limit price or higher. For example, suppose one of your customers owns LMN stock, which is currently trading at $62 per share, but he wants to receive at least $70 per share if he's going to sell it. This customer could place a sell limit on LMN at $70 per share. If LMN touches or goes above $70 per share, chances are good that the stock will be sold.

Stop limit order

A *stop limit order* is a combination of a stop and limit order (see the preceding sections); it's a buy stop or sell stop order that becomes a limit order after the stop price is reached. For example, an order that reads "sell 1,000 HIJ at 41 stop, 40.75 limit" means that the sell stop order will be triggered as soon as HIJ reaches 41 or below (the stop price). If this were just a stop order, the stock would be sold on the next trade (no matter what the price). But because this is a stop limit order, after the order is triggered, it becomes a limit order to buy at 40.75 or above (the limit price). In other words, this customer is interested in selling her stock if it drops to 41 but wants to receive at least 40.75 per share.

Handling limit and stop orders

Because stop and limit orders are price-specific, they may or may not be executed. Additionally, even if limit orders do reach or surpass the limit price, the order may not be executed if more orders were placed ahead of the investor's.

One of the exhibits that you may see on the Series 7 exam is a ticker tape. You may have to determine the price at which a limit order is executed or a stop order is triggered. When you're dealing with stop limit orders, remember that the order is first a stop order; after the stop order is triggered, it becomes a limit order. Using the BLiSS and SLoBS acronyms can help you out tremendously when you're trying to keep the prices straight:

- **BLiSS (buy limit or sell stop):** The BL stands for *buy limit,* and the SS stands for *sell stop.* All BLiSS orders are entered *at or below* the market price of the security. Another thing to remember about BLiSS orders is that they get reduced on the *ex-dividend date* (the first day a stock trades without a dividend).

  The *BL* in BLiSS helps you remember that the orders are placed BeLow the market price.

- **SLoBS (sell limit or buy stop):** The SL stands for *sell limit,* and the BS stands for *buy stop.* All SLoBS orders are entered *at or above* the market price of the security. Unlike BLiSS orders, SLoBS orders remain the same on the ex-dividend date.

  A good way for you to remember that SLoBS orders remain unchanged on the ex-dividend date is to remember the phrase "once a slob, always a slob."

The following question tests your understanding of trigger and execution prices.

An investor enters an order to sell MNO at 34 stop. The ticker following entry of the order is as follows:

34.75, 34.60, 34.45, 34.20, 34.10, 33.95, 34.25, 34.30, 34, 33.80

At which prices was the order triggered and executed?

(A) Triggered at 33.95 and executed at 33.80

(B) Triggered at 34.10 and executed at 33.95

(C) Triggered at 33.95 and executed at 34.25

(D) Triggered at 34.25 and executed at 33.80

The correct answer is Choice (C). The investor wants to limit losses, so she enters an order to sell if the price dips too low. The order was triggered at 33.95 and executed at 34.25. This is a sell stop order, which is a BLiSS order. BLiSS orders are triggered at or below the order price. In this case, the first transaction that was at or below 34 was 33.95, which is the trigger price. Because this is a stop order, it became a market order for immediate execution and was completed on the next trade (34.25).

The following question tests your ability to answer a stop limit question.

Julia Jingleham purchased 1,000 shares of XYZ Corp. at $45 per share. To limit her losses, a couple of weeks later, Julia places an order to sell 1,000 shares of XYZ at 43 stop 42.90 limit. The ticker following entry of the order is as follows:

43.64, 43.27, 43.30, 43.09, 42.95, 42.87, 42.85, 42.90, 42.94, 43

The order was triggered at

(A) 42.95 and executed at 42.87

(B) 42.95 and executed at 42.90

(C) 42.87 and executed at 42.94

(D) 42.87 and executed at 42.85

The right answer is Choice (B). Julia Jingleham placed this sell stop limit order to sell the stock if it drops to 43 but not sell it at less than 42.90 per share. Take care of the stop portion first, so look for where the sell stop order is triggered. Sell stop orders are BLiSS orders that are triggered at or below the stop price. The first trade that's at or below 43 is 42.95. Now that the order is triggered, it becomes a sell limit order at 42.90. Sell limit orders are SLoBS orders that are executed at or above the market price. When you move ahead from the point where it was triggered, the first trade that's at or above 42.90 is 42.90.

Factoring in order features

Besides knowing the basic types of orders (market, stop, and limit — see "Talking about order types"), you should have a handle on some additional features that may be added to the order to make your customers happy. A lot of them exist, but for the most part, the name of the order feature pretty much explains what it is:

- **Day:** If a day order hasn't been filled by the end of the trading day, it's canceled. All price-specific orders (stop and limit) are assumed to be day orders unless marked to the contrary.
- **Good-till-canceled (GTC):** Good-till-canceled orders are also called *open orders* because the order is kept open until executed or canceled. For example, say that an investor wants to purchase ABC stock at $30. While the price of ABC is at $35, she enters an open buy limit order for ABC at $30. If the price of ABC ever hits $30 or below, the order will likely be executed; however, if the price of ABC never hits $30 or below, the order stays open until canceled. Regardless of when an open order is placed, a designated market maker clears it out of his book at the end of April or October, and the order has to be reentered.

  Note: An investor may specify that she wants the order canceled next week, next month, in two months, and so on. However, the designated market maker only enters the orders as GTC, so it is up to the broker-dealer who accepted the order to cancel the order with the designated market maker on the correct date if not already executed.
- **Not held (NH):** This order gives the broker discretion about when to execute the trade. Typically, investors use not held orders when the broker believes she can get the customer a better price later in the day.

  Not held orders deal only with timing. For registered reps to choose the security, number of shares, and/or whether to buy or sell, the customer needs to open a discretionary account, which requires a written power of attorney. See Chapter 16 for details.

- **Fill or kill (FOK):** This order instructs a floor broker either to immediately execute an entire order at the limit price or better, or to cancel it.
- **Immediate or cancel (IOC):** These limit orders are similar to FOK orders except that the order may be partially filled. Any portion of the order that's not completed is canceled.
- **All or none (AON):** These limit orders have to be executed either in their entirety or not at all. AON orders don't have to be filled immediately (several attempts to fill the order completely are allowed) and may be day orders or good-till-canceled orders.

As of 2005, the NYSE does not accept AON orders.

- **At the open:** These orders are to be executed at the security's opening price. At the open orders can be market or limit orders, but if they aren't executed at the opening price, they're canceled. These orders allow for partial execution.
- **At the close (market on close):** This order is to be executed at the closing price (or as near as possible). If this order isn't completed, it's canceled.
- **Do not reduce (DNR):** This order says not to reduce the price of a stop or limit order in response to a dividend. For example, say that QRS stock is currently trading at $50 on the day prior to the ex-dividend date. If QRS previously announced a $0.50 dividend, the next day's opening price would be $49.50. If a customer had placed a DNR limit order to buy 1,000 shares of QRS at $45, the order wouldn't be reduced by the $0.50 dividend.
- **Alternative:** The alternative order is also known as a *one cancels the other order* or an *either/or order.* This type of order instructs the broker to execute one of two orders and then cancel the other. For example, say Mr. Smith owns stock at $60 per share. He enters a sell stop order at $55 for protection and a sell limit order at $70 in the event that the stock price increases. If one of the orders is executed, the other order is canceled immediately.
- **Bid wanted:** This order is an indication or notice that an investor or broker-dealer wants to sell a security at a specific price. Bid wanted is used most often when no current buyers of a security are available.
- **Offer wanted:** This order is an indication or notice that an investor or a broker-dealer wants to buy a particular security at a specific price. Offer wanted is used particularly when no current sellers of a security are available.

Reading the Ticker Tape

The ticker tape is also known as the *consolidated tape.* For subscribers, the tape delivers real-time (within 90 seconds) reports of securities transactions as they occur on different exchanges. The consolidated tape is broken down into Network A and Network B. Network A reports transactions in New York Stock Exchange (NYSE Euronext) listed securities, and Network B reports transactions of NASDAQ OMX PHLX listed securities, as well as securities listed on regional exchanges. Take a look at an example of a quote shown on a typical ticker tape:

$MSFT_{2K} = 29.76$ ▲ 0.16

Here are the five parts of a basic ticker-tape quote and how they fit with the example:

1. **The ticker symbol: MSFT**

   Each symbol represents a particular company.

2. **The number of shares traded: 2K**

   In this case, 2,000 shares were traded. If fewer than 1,000 shares are traded, the full volume is shown. For example, 400 shares would appear as 400, without any letter next to it. The abbreviations for kilos (K), millions (M), and billions (B) equate to the following amounts: K = 1,000, M = 1,000,000, and B = 1,000,000,000.

3. **The price for the last trade: 29.76**

   Here, the last trade took place at $29.76

4. **The change in direction from the previous day's closing price — ▲**

   In this case, the triangle is pointing up, so the price is higher. If the triangle points down, the price of the stock is lower than the previous day's closing price.

5. **The difference in price from the previous day's closing price: 0.16**

   In this case, the stock is trading 16 cents higher than the previous day's closing price.

It used to be easy to tell where a security traded by looking at its symbol. NYSE listed securities used to be three letters or less and AMEX listed securities used to be four letters. Today, the waters have become somewhat muddied, for example, companies that move from one market to another are able to keep the same symbols, and markets have combined (for example, NYSE Euronext and NASDAQ OMX PHLX), and you can no longer tell where a security is listed strictly by the number of letters in its symbol.

Although you're not likely to see extra letters tacked on to the standard stock symbols on the Series 7 exam, you should be aware of some of them. A ticker symbol may be followed by a period and then an extra letter to provide the following info:

Symbol	*Meaning*
.X	Mutual funds
.W	Warrants
.R	Rights
.P	Preferred stock

You may run across a bunch of other symbols (like the ones listed in the sidebar "Alphabet soup: Other ticker symbols and meanings"), but these four are all you need for the Series 7. After you pass, you can look into the other ones.

Alphabet soup: Other ticker symbols and meanings

For your personal knowledge, I've compiled a list of additional symbols that may be placed after the symbol of a security. Although you aren't likely to see these on the Series 7 exam, you'll be dealing with them after you begin your journey as a registered rep:

A = Class A shares

B = Class B shares

C = Continuance (NASDAQ exception)

D = New issue

E = Delinquent with SEC filings

F = Foreign

G = First convertible bond

H = Second convertible bond

I = Third convertible bond

J = Voting share (special)

K = Nonvoting common stock

L = Miscellaneous

M = 4th-class preferred stock

N = 3rd-class preferred stock

O = 2nd-class preferred stock

Q = In bankruptcy

S = Shares of a beneficial interest

T = With warrants or rights

U = Units

V = Pending issue and distribution

Y = American Depositary Receipt

Z = Miscellaneous situation

Taking a Look inside the Designated Market Maker's Book

A *designated market maker* (also known as a specialist or DMM*)* is a member of a stock exchange who's responsible for maintaining a fair and orderly market on a particular security. A DMM not only maintains an inventory of stock but also posts bid and ask prices and executes trades for other broker-dealers. A DMM acts as both a broker (executing trades for others) and a dealer (buying and selling securities for her own inventory) and tries to keep trading as active as possible.

A designated market maker executes orders by priority, parity, and precedence:

- **Priority:** The highest bid and lowest ask prices are executed first.
- **Parity:** If more than one order is at the highest bid and/or lowest ask price, the order(s) that came in first is/are executed first.
- **Precedence:** If the priority and parity are equal, larger orders are executed first.

Because DMMs are market makers in a particular security, they may guarantee a price for a floor broker on a trade of securities for a particular period of time. This guarantee allows the floor broker to go to the trading floor to see whether she can get a better price for her customer. In the event that she can't, she can go back to the designated market maker and do the trade for the guaranteed price. Stopping stock can only be done for public orders.

A designated market maker's main function is to maintain a fair and orderly market for a particular security. A DMM can't compete with a public order; she can only narrow the gap between the bid and ask prices if it gets too wide by placing a buy or sell order in between the highest bid and lowest ask prices. DMMs use books to keep track of these orders.

Designated market makers' books aren't written documents like they used to be; now they've gone electronic, but they're still called *specialists' books, order books, market makers' books, display books,* or just *books.* The book receives and displays orders to DMMs and allows them to execute and then publish orders to the consolidated (ticker) tape.

Take a good look at the designated market maker's book in Table 14-1 to see how it works, because the Series 7 exam may include it as an exhibit.

Table 14-1 DMM's Book (ABC Stock)

BID	*39*	*ASK (OFFER)*
8 Golden Sec. GTC	.00	7 Livingston Broker-Dealer STOP
7 Pride Broker-Dealer GTC	.01	
4 Vizzion Klempt 14 Orlando Securities	.02	
	.03	
	.04	
6 Martin Bros. STOP GTC	.05	12 High Profit Securities GTC
	.06	6 Brown and White

When you're looking at the book, the left-hand side (under "BID") indicates bid prices that investors (potential buyers) are willing to pay for a security. The right-hand side (under "ASK") indicates the prices investors (potential sellers) are willing to accept for selling the security.

On each side of the chart are names of broker-dealers looking to buy and sell the security. The numbers to the left of the names represent how many *hundreds* of shares the investors are looking to buy or sell. For example, the "8" next to Golden Securities on the bid side represents the fact that Golden Securities is looking to buy 800 shares of ABC stock at $39 good till canceled (GTC).

A designated market maker's book keeps track of stop and limit orders. Market orders aren't kept in a book because they're for immediate execution at the best price available. Any order with the word "STOP" next to it is obviously a stop order, and all the rest are limit orders. Stop orders are *not active* when placed in a specialist's book. Stop orders are triggered (activated) at the price placed in the book but then become market orders for immediate execution at the next price, whatever that may be. All orders in the specialist's book are day orders unless marked GTC. See "Receiving Orders from Customers" for more info on order types.

A customer entering a market order would either buy at the best ask price or sell at the best bid price.

As you can imagine, the Series 7 can ask numerous questions about a DMM's book. No matter what the question, you need to ignore the stop orders (pretend they aren't there) because you can't be sure what price the order will be executed at, if at all. The following points are examples of information that the Series 7 may ask for. For the data, please refer back to Table 14-1:

- **Inside market:** After ignoring the stop orders, the *inside market* is the highest bid price and the lowest ask price.

  In this case, the highest bid is 39.02 (Vizzion Klempt and Orlando Securities) and the lowest ask is 39.05 (High Profit Securities).

- **Size of the market:** The size of the market is the number of shares (or round lots) that are available at the best prices (highest bid and lowest ask) after you ignore the stop orders. You represent it as

  shares at the highest bid price × shares at the lowest ask price

  Ignoring the Martin Bros. stop, Vizzion Klempt and Orlando Securities offer the highest bid at 39.02. Vizzion Klempt wants 400 shares and Orlando wants 1,400, for a total of 1,800 shares. Ignoring the Livingston Broker-Dealer stop, High Profit Securities offers the lowest ask price at 39.05; High Profit wants to sell 1,200 shares. The size of the market is therefore 1,800 × 1,200, or 18 × 12 if given in round lots (units of 100 shares).

- **Spread:** The *spread* is the difference between the highest bid and lowest ask (ignoring the stop orders).

  In this case, the spread is $39.05 – 39.02, or $.03.

  The narrower the spread, the more actively traded the security. Because investors are buying at the lowest ask price and selling at the highest bid, there's a built-in loss, which is the difference between those two numbers (the spread). If you have a $2 spread between the highest bid and lowest ask, the price of the stock would have to increase by $2 in order for investors to break even (excluding commissions). As you can imagine, a security like that wouldn't garner much demand.

- **Where a designated market maker (specialist) can enter a bid for her own inventory:** Remember that a specialist can't compete with a public order. A specialist's duty is to keep trading as active as possible, so a specialist can enter a bid (or ask) in between the highest bid and lowest ask.

  Using this exhibit, acceptable bids from a specialist would be 39.03 or 39.04.

For Further Review

Please take a look at the following items one at a time and make sure you have a strong grasp on each of them as well as the related info in this chapter:

- Non-NASDAQ issues (OTC Pink Market and OTC Bulletin Board)
- TRACE
- Automated order execution system
- Consolidated Quotation Service (CQS)
- SuperDot (Designated Order Turnaround System)
- SuperMontage
- Automated confirmation transaction system (ACT)
- Order audit trail system (OATS)
- Trades reported out of sequence
- Odd lot and mixed lot trades
- Quotes: Workout and fast market
- Workable indication
- Handling limit orders
- Manning rule
- Rules 101-105
- Single book
- Firm with recall option
- Electronic communications networks (ECNs)
- Listing requirements
- SEC order handling rules
- Transaction reporting
- Arbitrage and risk arbitrage
- Trading halts
- Dark pools of liquidity
- Securities lending (easy to borrow, hard to borrow, failure to deliver)

Chapter 15

Making Sure the IRS Gets Its Share

In This Chapter

- Outlining the breakdown of taxes and income
- Seeing how the IRS taxes securities
- Checking taxes on gifts and inheritances
- Comparing the different types of retirement plans
- Reviewing additional topics tested

Yes, it's true what they say: The only sure things in life are death and taxes. Although taxes are an annoying necessity, investors do get tax breaks if they invest in securities for a long period of time, and you need a good understanding of the tax discounts investors receive. Additionally, the Series 7 exam tests your ability to recognize the different types of retirement plans, the specifics about each one, and the tax advantages.

In this chapter, I cover tax categories and rules, from distinguishing between types of taxes to calculating capital gains for securities received as gifts. And although enjoying retirement isn't quite as certain as pushing up daisies, I explain Uncle Sam's claim on the cash investors put into IRAs, Keoghs, and other retirement plans. As always, you can also count on some example questions and suggestions for further review.

Everything in Its Place: Checking Out Tax and Income Categories

The many lines you see on tax forms clue you in to the fact that the IRS likes to break things down into categories. The following sections explain progressive and regressive taxes, as well as types of personal income.

Touring the tax categories

The supreme tax collector (the IRS) has broken down taxes into a couple categories according to the percentage individuals pay. Your mission is to understand the different tax categories and how they affect investors:

- **Progressive taxes:** These taxes affect high-income individuals more than they affect low-income individuals; the more taxable money individuals have, the higher their income tax bracket. Progressive taxes include taxes on personal income (see the next section), gift taxes, and estate taxes (see the section "Presenting Gift and Inheritance Tax Rules"). The Series 7 contains more questions on progressive taxes than on regressive taxes.

- **Regressive taxes:** These taxes affect individuals earning a lower income more than they affect people earning a higher income; everyone pays the same rate, so individuals who earn a lower income are affected more because that rate represents a higher percentage of their income. Examples of regressive taxes are payroll, sales, property, excise, gasoline, and so on.

Looking at types of income

The three main categories of income are earned, passive, and portfolio. (If you're especially interested in the details of how investments are taxed, you can find more information at `www.irs.gov`.) You need to distinguish among the different categories because the IRS treats them differently:

- **Earned (active) income:** People generate this type of income from activities that they're actively involved in. Earned income includes money received from salary, bonuses, tips, commissions, and so on. Earned income is taxed at the individual's tax bracket.
- **Passive income:** This type of income comes from enterprises in which an individual isn't actively involved. Passive income includes income from limited partnerships (see Chapter 11) and rental property. When you see the words *passive income* on the Series 7 exam, immediately start thinking that the income comes from a limited partnership (DPP). Passive income is in a category of its own and can only be written off against passive losses.
- **Portfolio income:** This type of income includes interest, dividends, and capital gains derived from the sale of securities. The following section tells you more about taxes on portfolio income. Portfolio income may be taxed at the investor's tax bracket or at a lower rate, depending on the holding period.

Note: Gifts and inheritances are not considered income. For more on these sources of money, see "Presenting Gift and Estate Tax Rules" later in this chapter.

Noting Taxes on Investments

You need to understand how dividends, interest, capital gains, and capital losses affect investors. To make your life more interesting, the IRS has given tax advantages to people who hold onto investments for a long period of time, so familiarize yourself with the types of taxes that apply to investments and how investors are taxed.

Interest income

Interest income that bondholders receive may or may not be taxable, depending on the type of security or securities held:

- **Corporate bond interest:** Interest received from corporate bonds is taxable on all levels (federal, state, and, local, where local taxes exist).
- **Municipal bond interest:** Interest received from municipal bonds is federally tax free; however, investors may be taxed on the state and local levels, depending on the issuer of the bonds (see Chapter 8).

- **U.S. government securities interest:** Interest received from U.S. government securities, such as T-bills, T-notes, T-STRIPS, and T-bonds, is taxable on the federal level but is exempt from state and local taxes.

Even though T-bills, T-STRIPS, and any other zero-coupon bonds don't generate interest payments (because the securities are issued at a discount and mature at par), the difference between the purchase price and the amount received at maturity is considered interest and is subject to taxation.

Dividends

Dividends may be in the form of cash, stock, or product. However, cash dividends are the only ones that are taxable in the year that they're received. The following sections discuss dividends in cash, in stock, and from mutual funds.

Cash dividends

Since 2003, qualified cash dividends received from stocks are taxed at a maximum rate of 15 percent, provided the customer has held onto the stock for at least 61 days. The 61-day holding period starts 60 days prior to the *ex-dividend date* (the first day the stock trades without dividends). If the investor has held the stock for less than the 61-day holding period, he is taxed at the rate determined by his regular tax bracket.

Stock dividends

Stock dividends don't change the overall value of an investment, so the additional shares received are not taxed (for details, see Chapter 6). However, stock dividends do lower the cost basis per share for tax purposes. The cost basis is used to calculate capital gains or losses.

Dividends from mutual funds

Dividends and interest generated from securities that are held in a mutual fund portfolio are passed through to investors and are taxed as either *qualified* (up to 15 percent) or *nonqualified* (at the rate determined by the investor's tax bracket). The type(s) of securities in the portfolio and the length of time the fund held the securities dictate how the investor is taxed. Here's how mutual fund dividends are taxed:

Federally Tax Free	*15 Percent*	*Ordinary Income*
Municipal bond funds	Stock funds	Corporate bond funds
	Long-term capital gains	Short-term capital gains

One of the great things about owning mutual funds is that they're nice enough to let you know what taxes you're going to be subject to. At the beginning of each year you will receive a statement from the mutual fund that lets you know how much you received the previous year in dividends, in short-term capital gains, and in long-term capital gains. The mutual fund also sends a copy of the statement to the IRS.

The mutual fund determines the long-term or short-term gains by its holding period, not the investors'. Also, remember that you'd be subject to capital gains tax and taxes on dividends even if the money were reinvested back into the fund.

At the sale: Capital gains and losses

Capital gains are profits made when selling a security, and *capital losses* are losses incurred when selling a security. To determine whether an investor has a capital gain or capital loss, you have to start with the investor's cost basis. The *cost basis* is used for tax purposes and includes the purchase price plus any commission (although on the Series 7 exam, the test designers usually don't throw commission into the equation). The cost basis remains the same unless it's adjusted for accretion or amortization (see "Cost basis adjustments on bonds: Accretion and amortization," later in the chapter).

Incurring taxes with capital gains

An investor realizes capital gains when he sells a security at a price higher than his cost basis. Capital gains on any security (even municipal and U.S. government bonds) are fully taxed on the federal, state, and local level.

A capital gain isn't realized until a security is *sold.* If the value of an investment increases (appreciates) and the investor doesn't sell, the investor doesn't incur capital gains taxes.

Capital gains are broken down into two categories, depending on the holding period of the securities:

- **Short-term capital gains:** These gains are realized when a security is held for *one year or less.* Short-term capital gains are taxed according to the *investor's tax bracket.*
- **Long-term capital gains:** These gains are realized when a security is held for *more than one year.* To encourage investors to buy and hold securities, long-term capital gains are currently taxed at a maximum rate of 15 percent (for more information on capital gains and losses, visit the Internal Revenue Service web site at `www.irs.gov/taxtopics/tc409.html`).

Offsetting gains with capital losses

An investor realizes a capital loss when selling a security at a value lower than the cost basis. Investors can use capital losses to offset capital gains and reduce the tax burden. As with capital gains, capital losses are also broken down into short-term and long-term:

- **Short-term capital losses:** An investor incurs these losses when he has held the security for *one year or less.* Investors can use short-term capital losses to offset short-term capital gains.
- **Long-term capital losses:** An investor incurs these losses when he has held the security for *more than one year.* Long-term capital losses can offset long-term capital gains.

When an investor has a net capital loss, he can write off $3,000 per year against his earned income and carry the balance forward the next year

The following question involves capital-loss write-offs.

In a particular year, Mrs. Jones realizes $30,000 in long-term capital gains and $50,000 in long-term capital losses. How much of the capital losses would be carried forward to the following year?

(A) $3,000

(B) $17,000

(C) $20,000

(D) $30,000

The correct answer is Choice (B). Mrs. Jones has a net capital loss of $20,000 (a $50,000 loss minus the $30,000 gain). Mrs. Jones writes off $3,000 of that capital loss against her earned income and carries the additional loss of $17,000 forward to write off against any capital gains she may have the following year. In the event that Mrs. Jones doesn't have any capital gains the following year, she can still write off $3,000 of the $17,000 against any earned income and carry the remaining $14,000 forward which can be used to offset any capital gains the following year.

The wash sale rule: Adjusting the cost basis when you can't claim a loss

To keep investors from claiming a loss on securities (which an investor could use to offset gains on another investment — see the preceding section) while repurchasing substantially (or exactly) the same security, the IRS has come up with the *wash sale rule;* according to this rule, if an investor sells a security at a capital loss, the investor can't repurchase the same security or anything convertible into the same security for 30 days prior to or after the sale and be able to claim the loss. An investor doesn't end up in handcuffs for violating the wash sale rule; he simply can't claim the loss on his taxes.

However, the loss doesn't go away if investors buy the security within that window of time — investors get to adjust the cost basis of the security. For instance, if an investor were to sell 100 shares of ABC at a $2-per-share loss and purchase 100 shares of ABC within 30 days for $50 per share, the investor's new cost basis (excluding commissions) would be $52 per share (the $50 purchase price plus the $2 loss on the shares sold), thus lowering the amount of capital gains he would face on the new purchase.

The following question tests your understanding of the wash sale rule.

If Melissa sells DEF common stock at a loss on June 2, for 30 days she can't buy

I. DEF common stock

II. DEF warrants

III. DEF call options

IV. DEF preferred stock

(A) I only

(B) I and IV only

(C) I, II, and III only

(D) I, II, III, and IV

The answer you want is Choice (C). You need to remember that Melissa sold DEF at a loss; therefore, she can't buy back the same security (as in Statement I) or anything convertible into the same security (as in Statements II and III) within 30 days to avoid the wash sale rule. Warrants give an investor the right to buy stock at a fixed price (see Chapter 6), and call options give investors the right to buy securities at a fixed price (Chapter 12). However, Statement IV is okay because DEF preferred stock is a different security and is not convertible into DEF common stock (unless it's convertible preferred, which it isn't; if it were convertible, the question would have told you so). For Melissa to avoid the wash sale rule, she can't buy DEF common stock, DEF convertible preferred stock, DEF convertible bonds, DEF call options, DEF warrants, or DEF rights for 30 days. However, she can buy DEF preferred stock, DEF bonds, or DEF put options (the right to sell DEF).

Cost basis adjustments on bonds: Accretion and amortization

You use accretion and amortization when figuring out taxes on bonds; you simply adjust the cost of the bond toward par in the time that the bond matures. For more info on amortization and accretion, check out Chapter 7 and read on.

Accretion

When investors purchase bonds at a discount, the discount must be accreted over the life of the bond. *Accretion,* which involves adjusting the cost basis (price paid) of the bond toward par each year that the bond is held, increases both the cost basis of the bond and the reported interest income.

To determine the annual accretion, find the difference between the cost of the bond and par value; divide the result by the original number of years to maturity.

The following question tests your understanding of accretion.

Mr. Dancer purchases a 5-percent corporate bond with 10 years to maturity at 80. What would Mr. Dancer's annual reported income on this bond be?

(A) $20

(B) $30

(C) $50

(D) $70

The right answer is Choice (D). Mr. Dancer purchased the bond at 80 ($800), and you can assume that it matures at $1,000 (par) in 10 years (you can always assume $1,000 par unless otherwise stated — see Chapter 7). You need to take the $200 difference and divide it by 10 years to get $20. Mr. Dancer's reported income would be $70 ($50 interest plus $20 accretion).

Be prepared to answer questions about the annual accretion and yearly reported income and to calculate the capital gain or loss the investor would incur if selling the bond before maturity.

The following question tests your ability to figure out the capital gain or loss on a bond purchased at a discount.

Ms. Jones purchased a 7-percent DEF corporate bond at 80 with ten years to maturity. Six years later, Ms. Jones sold the bond at 85. What is the gain or loss?

(A) $50 gain

(B) $70 loss

(C) $150 loss

(D) None of the above

The answer you're looking for is Choice (B). First, adjust the cost basis of the bond in the time the bond matures:

$$\$800 \xrightarrow{\text{10 years}} \$1{,}000$$

The bond was purchased at $800 (80 percent of $1,000 par) and matures at $1,000 par in ten years. Next, take that $200 difference and divide it by the ten years to maturity:

$$\text{annual accretion} = \frac{\$200}{10\text{ years}} = \$20$$

Then take the $20 per year accretion and multiply it by the number of years that the investor held the bond:

$$\$20\text{ per year} \times 6\text{ years} = \$120\text{ total accretion}$$

Next, add the total accretion to the purchase price of the bond to determine the investor's adjusted cost basis:

$$\$800\text{ original cost} + \$120\text{ total accretion} = \$920(\text{adjusted cost basis})$$

After that, compare the adjusted cost basis to the selling price to determine the gain or loss:

$$\$920\text{ adjusted cost basis} - \$850\text{ selling price} = \$70\text{ capital loss}$$

Ms. Jones incurred a $70 capital loss on her sale of the DEF bond, which she can use to offset capital gains on other investments (see the earlier section "Offsetting gains with capital losses").

All discount bonds, except municipal bonds purchased in the secondary market (outstanding bonds), are accreted. If a municipal bond is purchased as an original issue discount (OID), the accretion is treated as part of the tax-free interest. If an investor purchases a municipal bond in the secondary market at a discount, the bond is not accreted, but the difference between the purchase price and the selling price (or redemption price) is treated as a capital gain.

Amortization

When bonds are purchased at a premium, the premium can be amortized over the life of the bond. You amortize the bond by adjusting the cost basis of the bond towards par each year that the bond is held; amortization decreases the cost basis of the bond and decreases the reported interest income.

To find the yearly amortization, divide the difference between the purchase price and par value by the original number of years to maturity.

The following question involves annual amortization:

Mrs. Sheppard purchases a 7-percent corporate bond with 20 years to maturity at 110. If Mrs. Sheppard decides to amortize the bond, what is the annual reported income?

(A) $5

(B) $65

(C) $70

(D) $75

The correct answer is Choice (B). Because Mrs. Sheppard purchased the bond at 110 ($1,100) and you can assume that it matures at $1,000 (par) in 20 years, you need to take the $100 difference and divide it by 20 years to get $5. Mrs. Sheppard's reported income would be $65 ($70 interest minus $5 amortization).

Corporate bondholders can elect to amortize their premium bonds or not; however, all municipal bondholders must amortize their premium bonds, whether they were purchased as a new issue or in the secondary market (used).

You can use the same basic formula that you use for accretion to determine the gain or loss on an amortization problem (see the preceding section). Only the first couple steps change. You still take the difference between the purchase price and par value and divide it by the number of years until maturity, which gives you the annual amortization. Then you multiply the annual amortization by the number of years the investor held the bond. At this point, you need to subtract that amount from the purchase price instead of adding it to the purchase price to get the adjusted cost basis. Then, as you do with accretion problems, you compare the adjusted cost basis to the selling price to determine the gain or loss.

Presenting Gift and Estate Tax Rules

Fortunately, you need to know only limited information on gift and estate tax rules for the Series 7. Although some of your clients may receive a gift or inheritance of money, paintings, a car, a little red wagon, or whatever, you only need to be concerned with a gift or inheritance of securities. Both gift taxes and estate taxes are progressive taxes (the higher the tax bracket, the higher the percentage of tax paid). Additionally, the recipient is never responsible for the taxes on the gift or inheritance. The main thing that you need to focus on is the recipient's cost basis for the securities.

Gift taxes

A gift tax is a progressive tax imposed on the transfer of certain goods. In the event that a gift tax is due, it's always paid by the donor, not the recipient. For example, if someone makes a gift to a minor in a Uniform Gift to Minors Act (UGMA) account (see Chapter 16), the donor of the gift, not the minor, is responsible for any taxes due.

The IRS does allow some gift-tax loopholes. Anyone can give a gift of up to $13,000 per person per year that's free from the gift tax and up to $5 million over the course of the gift-giver's lifetime. (See `www.irs.gov/businesses/small/article/0,,id=108139,00.html` for more information on Gift and Taxes.) Gifts between spouses aren't subject to gift taxes.

To help determine capital gains or losses (see "At the sale: Capital gains and losses"), when a gift of securities is made, the recipient assumes the donor's cost basis (purchase price of the security) as long as the securities have increased in value. If the securities decrease in value after the original purchase, the recipient assumes the cost basis of the securities on the date of the gift.

The following question tests your understanding of how the cost basis carries over with gifts of securities.

Mary Johnson purchases 100 shares of LLL common stock at a price of $60 per share. She gives the securities to her son Zed when the market price is $75 per share. What is Zed's cost basis per share?

(A) $60 per share

(B) $67.50 per share

(C) $75 per share

(D) It depends on the holding period

The correct answer is Choice (A). Because LLL increased in value after the original purchase, Zed assumes his mother's cost basis.

This next question concerns the cost basis of a gift when the market price of the stock falls.

John Johnson purchased 1,000 shares of DIM Corp. common stock at $40 per share. DIM subsequently decreased in price to $30 per share, and John gave the securities to his father-in-law, Mike. Two years later, Mike sold the stock for $37 per share. What is Mike's tax situation regarding the sale of the DIM stock?

(A) $30,000

(B) $35,000

(C) $37,000

(D) $40,000

The right answer is Choice (A). Because DIM decreased from the original purchase price, Mike assumes the cost basis of the DIM stock on the date of the gift, which was $30,000 (1,000 shares × $30).

You're more likely to get a Series 7 question about a security that increases in value before it's given as a gift.

Estate taxes

Estate tax is a tax on property that is passed along to someone's estate when the person dies. Inheriting securities is a little more straightforward than receiving gifts of securities. When an individual receives securities as a result of an inheritance, he *always* assumes the cost basis of the securities on the date of the owner's death. Additionally, securities received by inheritance are always taxed as long-term.

When a person dies, estate taxes are normally paid before assets are transferred to beneficiaries. Because the estate pays the taxes on the securities, the tax liabilities aren't passed along to the beneficiaries. As of 2010, the filing of an estate tax return is required only for estates that involve the transfer of $5 million or more. For the most current estate tax information, visit `www.irs.gov/businesses/small/article/0,,id=164871,00.html`.

Note: Presently there is a *unification of gift and estate taxes* rule that says a giver cannot give more than $5 million in gifts over his lifetime, including assets to beneficiaries upon death, without his estate being subject to additional taxes.

Exploring Retirement Plan Tax Advantages

I place retirement plans in with taxes because retirement plans give investors tax advantages. When you're reviewing this section, zone in on the differences and similarities among the different types of plans. The contribution limits are important but not as important as understanding the plan specifics and who's be qualified to open which type of plan.

Qualified versus nonqualified plans

The IRS may dub employee retirement plans as qualified or nonqualified. The distinction concerns whether they meet IRS and Employee Retirement Income Security Act (ERISA) standards for favorable tax treatment.

Tax-qualified plans

A *tax-qualified plan* meets IRS standards to receive a favorable tax treatment. When you're investing in a tax-qualified plan, the contributions into the plan are made from pretax dollars and are deductible against your taxable income. Not only are contributions into the plan tax-deductible, but the account also grows on a tax-deferred basis, so you aren't taxed until you withdraw money from the account at retirement. The two types of tax-qualified retirement plans are defined contribution and defined benefit plans. These include 401(k)s, profit-sharing plans, and money-purchase plans. Most corporate pension plans are tax-qualified plans.

Because investors don't pay tax on the money initially deposited or on the earnings, the entire withdrawal from a tax-qualified plan is taxed at a rate determined by the investor's tax bracket, which is normally lower at retirement. Additionally, distributions taken before age 59½ are subject to a 10-percent tax penalty (10 percent is added to the investor's tax bracket).

Nonqualified plans

Obviously, a nonqualified plan is the opposite of a qualified plan. *Nonqualified plans,* such as deferred compensation plans, payroll deduction plans, and 457 plans do not meet IRS and ERISA standards for favorable tax treatment. If you're investing in a nonqualified retirement plan, deposits are not tax-deductible (they're made from after-tax dollars); however, because you're dealing with a retirement plan, earnings in the plan do build up on a tax-deferred basis. People may choose to invest in nonqualified plans because either their employer doesn't have a qualified plan set up or the investment guidelines are not as strict (investors may be able to contribute more and invest in a wider choice of securities).

Because investors have already paid tax on the money initially deposited but not on the earnings, withdrawals from nonqualified plans are only partially taxed at the rate determined by the investor's tax bracket. The investor is taxed only on the amount that exceeds the amount of the contributions made.

IRA types and contribution limits

You'll likely be tested on a few different types of retirement plans and possibly the contribution limits. When you're looking at this section, understand the specifics of the types of plans and view the contribution limits as secondary. The contribution limits change pretty much yearly, and the Series 7 questions may not change that often. If you have a rough idea of the contribution limits, you should be okay. For updates and additional information, you can go to `www.irs.gov/publications/p590/ch01.html#en_us_publink1000230345`.

Traditional IRAs (individual retirement accounts)

IRAs are tax-qualified retirement plans, so deposits into the account are made from pretax dollars (they're tax-deductible). IRAs are completely funded by contributions that the *holder of the account* makes. Regardless of whether individuals are covered by a pension plan, they can still deposit money into an IRA. Here's a list of some of the key points of IRAs:

- IRAs may be set up as *single life* (when the owner is the beneficiary of the account), *joint and last survivor* (when the sole beneficiary of the account is his or her spouse and the spouse is more than ten years younger than the owner), or *uniform lifetime* (when the spouse is not the sole beneficiary or the spouse is not more than ten years younger than the owner).

- Permissible investments for IRAs include stocks, bonds, mutual funds, U.S. gold and silver coins, and real estate.
- The maximum contribution per person is $5,000 per year, with an additional catch-up contribution of $1,000 per person allowed for investors age 50 or older. Excess contributions are taxed at a rate of 6 percent until withdrawn.
- A husband and wife can have separate accounts with a maximum contribution of $5,000 per year each, whether both are working or one is working.
- Contributions into the IRA are fully deductible for individuals not covered by employer pension plans.

  If investors are covered by an employer pension plan, deposits into an IRA may or may not be tax-deductible. Although I think that the chances of your being tested on the values are slim, if an individual is covered by an employer pension plan and earns up to $56,000 per year ($90,000 jointly), deposits made into an IRA are fully deductible. The deductions are gradually phased out and disappear when an individual earns more than $66,000 per year ($110,000 jointly).
- When an investor starts to withdraw funds from an IRA, the investor is taxed on the entire withdrawal (the amount deposited, which was not taxed, and the appreciation in value). The withdrawal is taxed as ordinary income.
- Withdrawals can't begin before age 59½, or investors have to pay an early withdrawal penalty of 10 percent added to the investor's rate according to his tax bracket. An investor isn't subject to the 10-percent tax penalty in cases of death, disability, first-time homebuyers, and a few other exceptions based on Rule 72(t) (`http://www.irs.gov/retirement/participant/article/0,,id=211440,00.html`). Obviously, dead retirees won't be making withdrawals, but their beneficiaries will be. In this case, the beneficiaries aren't hit with the 10-percent penalty.
- Withdrawals must begin by April 1 of the year after the investor reaches age 70½ (the required beginning date, or RBD). Investors who don't take their required minimum distribution (RMD) by that time are subject to a 50-percent tax penalty on the amount they should have withdrawn. The IRS provides minimum distribution worksheets to help you determine the amount that needs to be taken in order to avoid the penalty (you can find them at `www.irs.gov/retirement/participant/article/0,,id=188023,00.html`).
- Deposits into IRAs are allowed up to April 15 (tax day) to qualify as a deduction for the previous year's taxes.

Roth IRAs

Anyone who doesn't make too much money can open a Roth IRA. The key difference between a traditional IRA and a Roth IRA is that withdrawals from a Roth IRA are tax-free. However, deposits made into the Roth IRA are not tax-deductible (made from after-tax dollars). Provided that the investor has held onto the Roth IRA for over five years and has reached age 59½, he can withdraw money from the Roth IRA without incurring any taxable income on the amount deposited or on the appreciation in the account.

The maximum that an individual may contribute to a traditional IRA and Roth IRA is $5,000 per year combined (or $6,000 if over age 50). As of 2008, the contribution limit increased from $4,000 to $5,000, with a catch-up contribution of $1,000 allowed for individuals age 50 and older.

Investors who earn more than $122,000 per year ($179,000 jointly) can't contribute to a Roth IRA.

Simplified employee pensions (SEP-IRAs)

An SEP-IRA is a retirement vehicle designed for small business owners, self-employed individuals, and their employees. SEP-IRAs allow participants to invest money for retirement on a tax-deferred basis. Employers can make tax-deductible contributions directly to their employees' SEP-IRAs. As of 2011, the maximum employer contribution to each employee's SEP-IRA is 25 percent of the employee's compensation (salary, bonuses, and overtime) or $49,000 (subject to cost-of-living increases in the following years), whichever is less. Employees who are part of the plan may still make annual contributions to a traditional or Roth IRA.

For Further Review

For you to be as prepared as possible to take the Series 7 exam, you should also have a grasp of the items in this section. Look over these additional tax- and retirement-plan-related topics and make sure you know them prior to taking the test:

- Foreign security taxes
- Tax (bond) swap
- LIFO, FIFO, or identified shares
- Taxes on securities owned by a corporation
- Keogh plans
- Educational (Coverdell) Savings Accounts (ESAs)
- 529 plans (qualified tuition plans – QTP)
- Rollovers
- The Employee Retirement Income Security Act (ERISA)
- Defined contribution plans such as: 401k, profit sharing plans, money purchase plans, and employee stock ownership plans
- Defined benefit plans
- Savings incentive match plans for employees (SIMPLEs)
- Corporate Taxes
- 457 plans
- 403(b) (tax-sheltered annuities)
- Profit-sharing plans, money-purchase plans, stock options, and deferred compensation programs
- Health savings accounts
- Section 529 plans
- Vesting
- Early withdrawal penalties
- Taxes when selling short
- Securities acquired through conversion

Chapter 16

No Fooling Around: Rules and Regulations

In This Chapter

- Meeting the self-regulatory organizations
- Opening and handling customer accounts
- Playing by the rules
- Reviewing additional topics tested

First off, I'd like to apologize for having to include this chapter. Unfortunately, rules are a part of life and part of the Series 7. When you're reading this, please remember that I didn't make the rules — but I do my best to make them as easy to digest as possible. Rules have become increasingly important on the Series 7 exam, especially since the Patriot Act came into the picture.

In this chapter, I cover topics related to rules and regulations. First, I help you understand who the guardians of the market are and their roles in protecting customers and enforcing rules. I also place considerable emphasis on opening, closing, transferring, and handling customers' accounts. And of course, I provide practice questions and the "For Further Review" section to guide you on your way.

The Market Watchdogs: Securities Regulatory Organizations

To keep the market running smoothly and to make sure investors aren't abused (at least too much), regulatory organizations stay on the lookout. Although you don't need to know all the minute details about each of them, you do have to know the basics.

The Securities and Exchange Commission

The Securities and Exchange Commission, or SEC, is the major watchdog of the securities industry. Congress created the SEC to regulate the market and to protect investors from fraudulent and manipulative practices. All broker-dealers who transact business with investors and other broker-dealers must register with the SEC. And that registration means something: All broker-dealers have to comply with SEC rules or face censure (an official reprimand), limits on activity, suspension or suspension of one or more associated persons (such as a registered rep or principal), a fine, and/or having their registration revoked.

SEC investigations may lead to a civil (financial) complaint being filed in a federal court. The SEC may seek disgorgement (taking away) of ill-gotten gains, civil money penalties, and injunctive relief (a cease-and-desist order from the court). If the matter is criminal in nature, the investigation is conducted by the U.S. Attorney's Office and the grand jury.

Among its other numerous functions, you need to be aware that the SEC also enforces the following acts:

- **The Securities Act of 1933:** The Act of 1933 requires the full and fair disclosure of all material information about a new issue.
- **The Securities Exchange Act of 1934:** The Act of 1934, which established the SEC, was enacted to protect investors by regulating the over-the-counter (OTC) market and exchanges (such as the NYSE). Chapter 14 tells you more about markets. In addition, the Act of 1934 regulates
  - The extension of credit in margin accounts (see Chapter 9)
  - Transactions by insiders
  - Customer accounts
  - Trading activities
- **The Trust Indenture Act of 1939:** This act prohibits bond issues valued at over $5 million from being offered to investors without an indenture. The trust *indenture* is a written agreement that protects investors by disclosing the particulars of the issue (the coupon rate, the maturity date, any collateral backing the bond, and so on). As part of the Trust Indenture Act of 1939, all companies must hire a trustee who's responsible for protecting the rights of bondholders.
- **The Investment Company Act of 1940:** This act regulates the registration requirements and the activities of investment companies.
- **The Investment Advisers Act of 1940:** This act requires the registration of certain investment advisers with the SEC. An *investment adviser* is a person who receives a fee for giving investment advice. Any investment adviser with at least $25 million of assets under management or anyone who advises an investment company must register with the SEC. All other investment advisers have to register on the state level. The Investment Advisers Act of 1940 regulates
  - Record-keeping responsibilities
  - Advisory contracts
  - Advertising rules
  - Custody of customers' assets and funds

Self-regulatory organizations

As you can imagine, due to the unscrupulous nature of some investors and registered representatives, the SEC's job is overwhelming. Fortunately, a few self-regulatory organizations (SROs) are there to take some of the burden off of the SEC's shoulders. Although membership isn't mandatory, most broker-dealers are members of one or more SROs. SRO rules are usually stricter than those of the SEC.

The four types of SROs you need to know for the Series 7 are the FINRA, MSRB, NYSE, and CBOE:

- **The FINRA (Financial Industry Regulatory Authority):** The FINRA is a self-regulatory organization that's responsible for the operation and regulation of the NASDAQ stock market, NYSE Amex Equities (formerly the American Stock Exchange), the International Securities Exchange, and the OTC (over-the-counter) market. The FINRA was created in 2007 and is a consolidation of the NASD (National Association of Securities Dealers) and the regulation and enforcement portions of the NYSE (New York Stock Exchange). FINRA is responsible for making sure that its members not only follow FINRA rules but also the rules set forth by the SEC. Additionally, the FINRA is responsible for the handling of complaints against member firms and may take disciplinary action, if necessary. The FINRA is also responsible for administering securities exams such as the Series 7 (now you know who to blame).
- **The Municipal Securities Rulemaking Board:** The MSRB was established to develop rules that banks and securities firms have to follow when underwriting, selling, buying, and recommending municipal securities (check out Chapter 8 for info on municipal bonds). The MSRB is subject to SEC oversight but does not enforce SEC rules.

  The MSRB makes rules for firms (and representatives) who sell municipal bonds but doesn't enforce them – it leaves that up to FINRA.
- **The New York Stock Exchange:** The NYSE is the oldest and largest stock exchange in the United States. The NYSE is responsible for listing securities, setting exchange policies, and supervising the exchange and member firms. As with the NASD, the NYSE has the power to take disciplinary action against member firms.
- **The Chicago Board Options Exchange:** The CBOE is an exchange that makes and enforces option exchange rules.

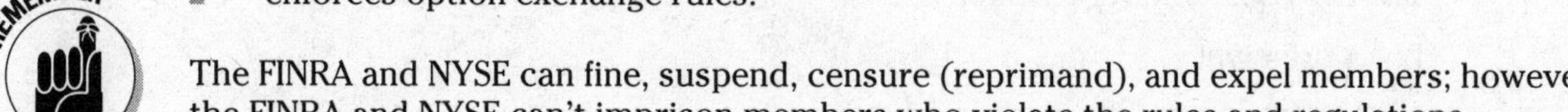

The FINRA and NYSE can fine, suspend, censure (reprimand), and expel members; however, the FINRA and NYSE can't imprison members who violate the rules and regulations.

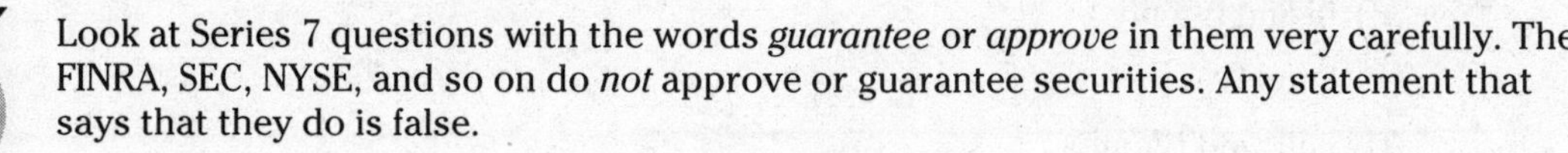

Look at Series 7 questions with the words *guarantee* or *approve* in them very carefully. The FINRA, SEC, NYSE, and so on do *not* approve or guarantee securities. Any statement that says that they do is false.

Following Protocol when Opening Accounts

The Series 7 examiners seem to be focusing more and more on the handling of customer accounts. You need to know what to do to open accounts, how to take customer orders, the rules for sending out confirmations, and so on.

Filing the facts on the new account form

When you're opening any new account for a customer, the new account form needs some basic information. Broker-dealers may, in accordance with the Patriot Act (covered later in this chapter), require a customer to provide proof of identification. Getting this information is your responsibility (or the responsibility of the broker-dealer). Here's a list of the items that need to be on the new account form:

- The name(s) and address(es) of the individual(s) who'll have access to the account
- The customer's date of birth (the customer must be of legal age to open an account)

- The type of account the customer is opening (cash, margin, retirement, day trading, prime brokerage, DVP/RVP, advisory or fee-based, discretionary, options, and so on)
- The customer's Social Security number (if the customer is an individual) or tax ID number (if the customer is a business)
- The customer's occupation, employer, and type of business (certain limitations are placed on customers who work for banks, broker-dealers, insurance companies, SROs, and so on)
- Domestic or foreign residency and/or citizenship
- Bank references and the customer's net worth and annual income
- Whether the customer is an insider of a company
- Investment objectives (see Chapter 13)
- The signatures of the registered representative and a principal

You need this information to open an account. If anything changes (for example, a customer's address), the account records need to be updated. Additionally, only individuals who are legally competent may open accounts.

The following question tests your ability to answer a question about opening a new account.

Which of the following people must sign a new account form?

I. The customer

II. The customer's spouse

III. The registered representative

IV. A principal

(A) I and II only

(B) III and IV only

(C) I and IV only

(D) I, III, and IV only

The correct answer is Choice (B). When you're opening a new account for a customer, the new account form requires only your signature and a principal's (manager's) signature. Make sure you don't assume extenuating circumstances. You need the customer's signature on a new account form only if the customer is opening a margin account. Additionally, you need the spouse's signature only if you're opening a joint account. Because the question doesn't say that the account is a margin or joint account, you can't assume that it is.

Word on the street: Numbered accounts

A *street name* or *numbered account* is an account registered in the name of the broker-dealer with an ID number. Street name accounts give the investor a certain degree of privacy and help facilitate the trading of securities (because the brokerage firm, not the customer, signs the certificates). You need to know a few rules about street name accounts for the Series 7:

- You need a written statement from the customer attesting to the ownership of the account.
- With the exception of margin accounts, a street name account may be changed by the customer into a regular account at any time.
- All margin accounts must be in street name.

The Patriot Act

The Patriot Act was enacted in 2001 to help identify and catch terrorists. As part of the Patriot Act, broker-dealers are required to

- Keep records of the information used to identify the customer (via customer identification programs, or CIPs). The CIP is a program used by financial institutions to verify the identity of customers who wish to conduct financial transactions.
- Verify that a customer doesn't appear on any list of known terrorists or terrorist organizations (the U.S. Treasury keeps this list)

Selecting the appropriate type of account

Investors can open many different types of accounts through a broker-dealer. Besides knowing a customer's investment profile (see Chapter 13), you need a basic understanding of the types of accounts for the Series 7 exam. Fortunately, most of them are pretty straightforward.

Single and joint accounts

Some investors prefer to share; others like to go it alone. Whatever their preference, adults can open up accounts that fit their needs:

- **Single (individual) accounts:** Naturally, this account is in the name of one person. The key thing for you to remember is that individuals may not open accounts in other people's names without written permission (power of attorney).
- **Joint accounts:** This account is in the name of more than one person. All individuals named on the account have equal trading authority for the account. For Series 7 exam purposes, you need to be familiar with two types of joint accounts:
  - **Joint tenants with rights of survivorship (JTWROS):** With this type of joint account, when a joint tenant named on the account dies, his or her portion of the account passes on to the surviving joint tenant. These accounts are usually set up almost exclusively for husbands and wives. In states where *community property laws* exist (currently Arizona, California, Idaho, Louisiana, Nevada, New Mexico, Texas, Washington, and Wisconsin), investments acquired during the marriage are automatically presumed to be jointly owned by the husband and wife.
  - **Joint with tenants in common (JTIC):** With this type of account, when one tenant of the account dies, his or her portion of the account becomes part of his or her estate. JTICs are usually set up for individuals who aren't related.

The following question tests your knowledge of account types.

All of the following people may open a joint account EXCEPT

(A) Two friends

(B) A husband and wife

(C) A parent and minor son

(D) Three strangers

The right choice here is (C). A joint account is an account in the name of more than one adult. Choices (A), (B), and (D) are all possible for joint accounts; however, an account opened for a minor must be a custodial account, which I discuss in the next section.

Trust accounts

Trust accounts are ones that are managed by one party for the benefit of another party. A specific type of trust account that you're most likely to see on the Series 7 exam is a custodial account. A *custodial account* is set up for a child who's too young to have his own account. A custodian (adult) makes the investment decisions for the account. Any adult can open a custodial account for a minor, so the people named on the account don't have to be related.

Custodial accounts are trust accounts and may be referred to on the Series 7 exam as UGMA or UTMA accounts because they fall under the Uniform Gifts to Minors Act or Uniform Transfer to Minors Act. A *UTMA account* is an extension of the UGMA account that allows gifts in addition to cash and securities to be transferred to the minor. The additional gifts allowed are art, real estate, patents, and royalties.

Additionally, because the minor is too young to make investment decisions for himself, some rules are specific to custodian accounts:

- There can only be one custodian and one minor per account.
- The minor is responsible for the taxes (the minor's Social Security number is registered for the account).
- The account is registered in the name of the custodian for the benefit of the minor (the custodian is responsible for endorsing all certificates).
- The account can't be held in street name (in the name of the broker-dealer with an ID number — see the earlier section "Word on the street: Numbered accounts").
- Securities can't be traded on margin or sold short (Chapter 9 covers margin accounts).
- Anyone may give a gift of cash or securities to the minor. The gift is irrevocable (can't be refused by the custodian).
- If an account receives rights, the custodian can't let the rights expire. (See Chapter 6 for info on rights.) Because rights have value, a custodian can exercise or sell the rights.

Custodial accounts are for minors, so as soon as a minor reaches the age of majority, which is determined by the minor's state of residence, the custodial account is terminated and the account is transferred to a single account in the name of the (former) minor.

Discretionary accounts

Decision making can be stressful, and some investors don't want to deal with it. With a *discretionary account,* an investor can give you (the registered rep) the right to make trading decisions for the account. All discretionary accounts need a *written power of attorney* signed by the investor, which gives trading authorization to the registered rep.

If a customer places an order but doesn't specify the security, the number of shares or units, and/or whether the customer wants to buy or sell, you need a written power of attorney. If you don't have a written power of attorney, you can't do anything but decide when to place the order (timing). For example, suppose one of your customers calls you and says that he wants to sell 100 shares of ABC common stock and you believe you can get a better price later in the day. The customer can give you verbal permission to place the order at your discretion. This type of order is called a *market not held order* and is usually good only for the rest of the day.

Here are some specific rules for discretionary orders that you're likely to see on the Series 7 exam:

- Each discretionary order must be marked as *discretionary* on the order ticket.
- As with other orders, principals must sign each order ticket.
- A principal needs to review discretionary accounts regularly to make sure reps don't trade excessively to generate commissions, which is called *churning*.

A *fiduciary* is anyone who can legally make decisions for another investor. Examples of fiduciaries are custodians (UGMA accounts), a registered rep having power of attorney, an executor of an estate, a trustee, and so on. Fiduciaries are subject to the *Prudent Man* or *Prudent Investor Rule*, which means that they must invest the fund's money in securities designated by their state's *legal list*. If their state does not have a legal list, fiduciaries should invest in securities that only a prudent person who's seeking reasonable income and preservation of capital would invest in.

Corporate accounts

Only incorporated businesses can open corporate accounts. If you're opening a corporate account, you need to obtain the tax ID number of the corporation, which is similar to an individual's Social Security number. Additionally, you need to obtain a copy of the *corporate resolution*, which lets you know who you should be taking trading instructions from (so you don't get a call like, "Hi, I'm Joe Blow, the janitor for XYZ Corporation, and I'd like to purchase 1,000 shares of ABC for our company").

If a corporation wants to open a margin account (accounts where they're borrowing some money from the broker-dealer to purchase securities — see Chapter 9), you also need a copy of the corporate charter (bylaws). The corporate charter has to allow the corporation to purchase securities on margin.

Unincorporated associations

An unincorporated association is sometimes called a voluntary organization. An unincorporated association is a group of two or more individuals who form an organization for a specific purpose (in this case, investing). If an unincorporated association has too many characteristics of a corporation, such as having a board of directors, limited liability, and so on, it may be treated and taxed at a higher rate, as if it were a corporation.

Institutional accounts

Accounts set by institutions such as banks, mutual funds, insurance companies, pension funds, hedge funds, and investment advisers are considered institutional accounts. Their role is to act as specialized investors on behalf of others.

Partnership accounts

Two or more individual owners of a business that's not set up as a corporation may set up a partnership account. All partnerships must complete a partnership agreement, which the broker-dealer has to keep on file. The *partnership agreement*, like a corporate resolution, states who has trading authorization for the account so you know who you're supposed to be taking orders from.

No matter which type of account you open, portfolio diversification is key.

Trading by the Book When the Account Is Open

After you've opened a new account, you have to follow additional rules and regulations to keep working in the business. You need to know how to receive trade instructions and how to fill out an order ticket, as well as settlement and payment dates for different securities.

Filling out an order ticket

When you're working as a registered rep, completing documents such as order tickets will become second nature because you'll have them in front of you. When you're taking the Series 7, you don't have that luxury, but you still need to know the particulars about what to fill out.

Getting the particulars on paper (or in binary form)

When your customer places an order, you have to fill out an order ticket. Order tickets may be on paper or entered electronically. Regardless of how you enter the order, it needs to contain the following information:

- The registered rep's identification number
- The customer's account number
- The description of the security (stocks, bonds, symbol, and so on)
- The number of shares or bonds that are being purchased or sold
- Whether the registered rep has discretionary authority over the account
- Whether the customer is buying, selling long (selling securities that are owned), or selling short (selling borrowed securities — see Chapter 9)
- For option tickets, whether the customer is buying or writing (selling), is covered or uncovered, and is opening or closing (see Chapter 12 for info on options)
- Whether it's a market order, good-till-canceled (GTC) order, day order, and so on
- Whether the trade is executed in a cash or margin account
- Whether the trade was solicited or unsolicited
- The time of the order
- The execution price

Figure 16-1 shows you what standard paper order tickets may look like.

Designating unsolicited trades

Normally, you'll be recommending securities in line with a customer's investment objectives. If, however, the customer requests a trade that you think is unsuitable, it's your duty to inform him about it. You don't have to reject the order (it's the customer's money, and you're in the business to generate commission). If the customer still wants to execute the trade, simply mark the order as *unsolicited,* which takes the responsibility off your shoulders.

BUY

B	EXCHANGE	BRANCH	ACCOUNT No.	TYPE	R.R. No.	DAY OPEN
QUANTITY	SECURITY			PRICE LIMIT	EXECUTION PRICE	

CUSTOMER NAME AND ADDRESS	SOLICITED _ UNSOLICITED _ DISCRET'Y A/C _	CANCEL
FUNDS, LOCATION	AMOUNT INTEREST COM. NET	
BOUGHT FROM		
NEW	BROKERAGE	**SOARING SECURITIES**	CHECKED BY

SELL

S	EXCHANGE	BRANCH	ACCOUNT No.	TYPE	R.R. No.	LONG SHORT	DAY OPEN
QUANTITY	SECURITY			PRICE LIMIT	EXECUTION PRICE		

CUSTOMER NAME AND ADDRESS	SOLICITED _ UNSOLICITED _ DISCRET'Y A/C _	CANCEL
SECURITY LOCATION	AMOUNT INTEREST OR ST. TAX SEC. COM. NET	
SOLD TO		
EXEC. BRKR.	BROKERAGE	**SOARING SECURITIES**	CHECKED BY

Figure 16-1: Buy and sell order tickets have spaces for the info you need to make a trade.

A trip to the principal's office: Securing a signature

Principals are managers of a firm. All brokerage firms, no matter how small, must have at least one principal. When you open or trade an account, you have to bring the new account form or order ticket to a principal to sign. Principals need to approve all new accounts, all trades in accounts, and all advertisements and sales literature; they also handle all complaints (lucky break for you!). A principal doesn't have to approve a prospectus or your recommendations to your customers.

Although you'll generally bring an order ticket to a principal right after taking an order, the principal can sign the order ticket later in the day. If you're questioned about this on the Series 7 exam, you want to answer that the principal needs to approve the trade on the same day, not before or immediately after the trade.

Checking your calendar: Payment and settlement dates

Securities that investors purchase have different payment and settlement dates. Here's what you need to know:

- **Trade date:** The day the trade is executed. An investor who buys a security owns the security as soon as the trade is executed, whether or not he has paid for the trade.
- **Settlement date:** The day the issuer updates its records and the certificates are delivered to the buyer's brokerage firm.
- **Payment date:** The day the buyer of the securities must pay for the trade.

Unless the question specifically asks you to follow FINRA or NYSE rules (which I doubt it will), assume the Fed regular way settlement and payment dates as they appear in Table 16-1. The FINRA and NYSE rules both require payment for securities to be made no later than the settlement date, but the Federal Reserve Board states that the payment date for corporate securities is five business days after the trade date.

Table 16-1 Regular Way Settlement and Payment Dates

Type of Security	*Settlement Date (in Business Days after the Trade Date)*	*Payment Date (in Business Days after the Trade Date)*
Stocks and corporate bonds	3	5
Municipal bonds	3	3
U.S. government bonds	1	1
Options	1	5

Cash trades (which are same-day settlements) require payment for the securities and delivery of the securities on the same day as the trade date.

In certain cases, securities may not be able to be delivered as in the preceding chart. In these cases, the seller may specify that there's going to be a *delayed delivery*. There can also be a *mutually agreed upon* date in which the buyer and seller agree on a delayed delivery date prior to or at the time of the transaction.

The *when, as, and if issued (when-issued transaction)* method of delivery is used for a securities issue that has been authorized and sold to investors before the certificates are ready for delivery. This method is typically used for stock splits, new issues of municipal bonds, and Treasury securities (U.S. government securities). The settlement date for when-issued securities can be any of the following:

- A date to be assigned
- Three business days after the securities are ready for delivery
- On the date determined by the FINRA

Confirming a trade

A *trade confirmation* (receipt of trade) is the document you send to a customer after a trade has taken place. You have to send out trade confirmations after each trade, at or before the completion of the transaction (the settlement date). Here's a list of information included in the confirmation:

- The customer's account number
- The registered rep's ID number
- The trade date
- Whether the customer bought (BOT) or sold (SLD)
- The number of shares of stock or the par value of bonds purchased or sold
- The yield (if bonds)
- The Committee on Uniform Security Identification Procedures (CUSIP) number, a security ID number
- The price of the security
- The total amount paid or received, not including commission
- The commission, which is added on purchases and subtracted on sales (if the broker-dealer purchased for or sold from its own inventory, the markdown or markup doesn't have to be disclosed)
- The *net amount,* or the amount the customer paid or received after adding or subtracting the commission (if the investor purchased or sold bonds, the accrued interest is added or subtracted during this calculation)

Meeting the requirements for good delivery

In the securities industry, good delivery doesn't mean "in 30 minutes or it's free" (even the pizza delivery places don't promise that anymore). To constitute good delivery of certificates, the securities have to be in a certain form. The transfer agent is responsible for good delivery. Here are the general requirements:

- They must be in good physical condition (not mutilated).
- They must be endorsed.
- The exact number of shares or bonds must be delivered.
- The correct denomination of the certificates must be delivered.

And here are the requirements for good delivery of specific securities:

- **Bearer (coupon) bonds:** These unregistered bonds must be in $1,000 or $5,000 denominations only.

  For a bearer bond to be in good delivery form, it must be delivered with all unpaid coupons (representing interest payments) attached. See Chapter 7 for more info on bonds.
- **Registered bonds:** These bonds must be in multiples of $1,000 par value with a maximum par value of $100,000.

- **Stock:** Because the most easily traded unit of stock is 100 shares (a round lot), stock certificates must be in denominations of one of the following:
  - Multiples of 100 shares — 100, 200, 300, 400, and so on
  - Divisors of 100 shares — 1, 2, 4, 5, 10, 20, 25, 50, or 100
  - Units that add up to 100 shares — 40 shares + 60 shares, 91 + 9, 80 + 15 + 5, and so on

Odd lot trades (trades of less than 100 shares) or odd lot portions of orders are exempt from the good delivery rule.

The following question tests your ability to answer a good delivery question.

All of the following are considered good delivery for a 560-share order EXCEPT

(A) two 200-share certificates, one 100-share certificate, and one 60-share certificate

(B) 56 10-share certificates

(C) six 60-share certificates, five 30-share certificates, and five 10-share certificates

(D) one 400-share certificate and two 80-share certificates

The correct answer is Choice (D). Choice (A) is good because the 200-share certificates and 100-share certificates are multiples of 100 shares, and the 60-share trade (odd lot portion) is exempt. Choice (B) is good because 10 is a divisor of 100 (it goes into 100 evenly). Choice (C) is good because 60 + 30 + 10 adds up to 100, and the extra 60-share certificate is exempt because it's an odd-lot portion. However, Choice (D) is bad delivery because even though the 400-share certificate is okay, the two 80-share certificates aren't good because they don't add up to 100.

Always look at the shares first to determine whether you have good delivery. I see a lot of students look at the number of certificates before they check the number of shares per certificate. The Series 7 designers want to know more about your understanding of concepts than your multiplication and addition skills, so you probably won't have to figure out the total number of shares in each answer choice — they should all add up to the number of shares in the order (in the preceding example, 560).

Following up with account statements

An *account statement* gives the customer information about his holdings in the account along with the market value at the time the statement was issued. Customers are supposed to receive account statements on a regular basis. The timing for issuing account statements should be pretty easy for you to remember. Here's how often you have to send out statements, from most to least often (remember the acronym *AIM*):

- **Active accounts:** If any trading was executed within the month, the customer must receive an account statement for that month.
- **Inactive accounts:** If the customer is not actively trading his account and is just holding a position, an account statement must be sent out at least quarterly (every three months).
- **Mutual funds:** No matter how much (or little) trading was done, a customer needs to receive an account statement semiannually (every six months).

Keeping your dividend dates straight

When customers are purchasing securities of a company that's in the process of declaring or paying a dividend, you need to be able to tell those customers whether they're entitled to receive the dividend. Because stock transactions settle in three business days, the customers are entitled to the dividend if they purchase the securities at least three days prior to the *record date.* Here's a list of the four need-to-know dates for the Series 7 exam:

- **Declaration date:** The day that the corporation officially announces that a dividend will be paid to shareholders.
- **Ex-dividend date:** The first day that the stock trades without dividends. An investor purchasing the stock on the ex-dividend date isn't entitled to receive the dividend; because stock transactions take three business days to settle, the ex-dividend date is automatically two business days before the record date.

  The ex-dividend date is the day that the price of the stock is reduced by the dividend amount. (Chapter 6 tells you more about dividends and related calculations.) When a stock is purchased ex-dividend (on or after the ex-dividend date), the seller is entitled to the dividend, not the buyer. Because the dividend may not be paid for up to a month, the buyer is required to sign a *due bill* indicating that the dividend belongs to the seller. In the case of a cash dividend, the due bill is in the form of a *due bill check,* which is payable on the date the dividend is paid by the issuer. In addition, if an investor buys a stock on time to receive a dividend but for some reason will not receive the certificates on time (by the record date), the seller must send a *due bill* to the buyer. A due bill states that the buyer is entitled to the rights of ownership even though he's not yet receiving the certificates.
- **Record date:** The day the corporation inspects its records to see who gets the dividend. To receive the dividend, the investor must be listed as a stockholder in company records.
- **Payment (payable) date:** The day that the corporation pays the dividend.

As you can see from the diagram, the buyer receives the dividend if he purchases the stock before the ex-dividend date. If the stock is purchased on or after the ex-dividend date, the seller receives the dividend.

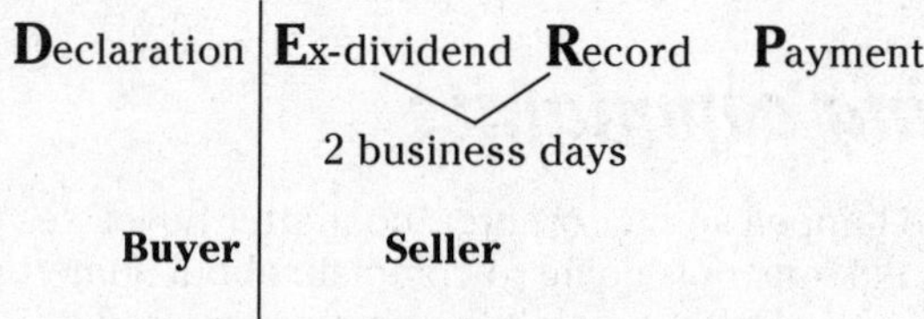

To help you remember the sequence of dates, use the phrase *Don't Eat Rubber Pickles.* I know it sounds ridiculous, but the more ridiculous, the easier it is to remember.

The board of directors must announce three dates: the declaration date, the record date, and the payment date. The ex-dividend date doesn't need to be announced because it's automatically two business days before the record date. However, mutual funds have to announce all four dates because they may set their ex-dividend date at any time (even on the record date).

The following question tests your ability to answer a dividend question.

Wedgie Corp. has just announced a $0.50 cash dividend. If the record date is Wednesday, March 10, when is the last day an investor can purchase the stock and receive the dividend?

(A) March 4

(B) March 5

(C) March 7

(D) March 8

The answer you're looking for is Choice (B). In order for an investor to purchase the stock and receive a previously declared dividend, he must purchase the stock at least one business day before the ex-dividend date. This question is a little more difficult because you have a weekend to take into consideration.

The ex-dividend date is March 8, which is two business days prior to the record date. This investor has to buy the stock before the ex-dividend date in order to receive the dividend, so he has to buy it March 5 or before (because the 6th and 7th are Saturday and Sunday). The last day an investor can purchase the stock and receive the dividend is March 5.

March 5th	March 8th	March 10th	
Declaration	**E**x-dividend	**R**ecord	**P**ayment
	2 business days		
Buyer	**Seller**		

If a stock is sold short (if the investor is selling a borrowed security), the lender of the stock sold short is entitled to receive the dividend. (See Chapter 9 for details on margin accounts.) Also, the trades in the example problems are regular way settlement (three business days after the trade date); remember that cash transactions settle on the same day as the trade date. In the case of dividends, if an investor purchases stock for cash, he receives the dividend if he purchases the stock anytime up to and including the record date.

Handling complaints

It's bound to happen sooner or later, no matter how awesome you are as a registered rep: One of your customers is going to complain about something (like unauthorized trades, guarantees, and so on). Complaints aren't considered official unless they're in writing. The FINRA wants you to follow the proper procedure for handling complaints. The following sections cover formal and informal proceedings.

Code of procedure (litigation)

The *code of procedure* is the FINRA's formal procedure for handling securities-related complaints between public customers and members of the securities industry (broker-dealers, registered reps, clearing corporations, and so on). The public customer has the choice of resolving the complaint via the formal code of procedure or the informal code of arbitration (see the next section).

In the code of procedure, the District Business Conduct Committee (DBCC) has the first jurisdiction over complaints. If the customer or member isn't satisfied with the results, he can appeal the decision to the FINRA Board of Governors. Decisions are appealable all the way to the Supreme Court.

Code of arbitration

The *code of arbitration* is an informal hearing (heard by two or three arbiters) that's primarily conducted for disputes between members of the FINRA. Members include not only broker-dealers but also individuals working for member firms.

For example, if you (a registered rep) have a dispute with the broker-dealer that you're working for, you can take the broker-dealer to arbitration. If a customer has a complaint against a broker-dealer or registered rep, the customer has the choice of going through code of procedure (see the preceding section) or code of arbitration, unless the customer has given prior written consent (usually by way of the new account form) stating that he will settle disputes only through arbitration.

The decisions in arbitration are binding and nonappealable, so they're less costly than court action.

Mediation

If an investor and/or broker-dealer are looking for a more informal way to handle disputes, they may voluntarily decide to go to mediation. Disputes settled through mediation are heard by an independent third party. Unlike arbitration, mediation is nonbinding.

Transferring accounts

If a customer wants to transfer an account from one broker-dealer to another, the customer has to fill out an account transfer form with the new broker-dealer listing the securities held at the old broker-dealer. Transfer instructions are then sent from the new broker-dealer to the old one. Account transfers are often executed through the ACAT (Automated Customer Account Transfer) Service. For members to use the ACAT service, they have to be members of the National Securities Clearing Corporation (NSCC).

The old broker-dealer has *three business days* to either validate or take exception (for an invalid account number, wrong Social Security number, and so on) to the transfer instructions sent from the new broker-dealer. After the old broker-dealer validates the account, that dealer has *three business days* to transfer the account to the new broker-dealer.

Committing Other Important Rules to Memory

Brokers and investors must follow numerous rules in order to keep themselves from facing fines or worse. In this section, I list a few of the more important rules.

Obeying the Telephone Act of 1991

To make sure that certain standards are used when calling potential customers (such as not calling them at midnight), the Telephone Act of 1991 was created. When you're dealing with *potential customers* on the phone, you need to know these rules:

- You can't make calls before 8 a.m. or after 9 p.m. local time of the potential customer.
- You have to give your name, company name, company address, and phone number.
- If you get a potential customer who's tired of being called, you should place that person on a *do not call list.* Each firm must maintain its own do not call list and have the U.S. Government's National Do Not Call List available.
- You may not send unsolicited ads by fax machine.

The Telephone Act of 1991 does not apply to existing customers (customers who have executed a trade or had a security in the firm's account in the previous 18 months) or calls from nonprofit organizations. Existing customers who want to be placed on the "do not call" list after opening an account cannot be solicited but can be updated on the status of their account.

Sticking to the 5-percent markup policy

The 5-percent policy (FINRA 5 Percent Markup Policy) is more of a guideline than a rule. The policy was enacted to make sure that investors receive fair treatment and aren't charged excessively for broker-dealer services in the over-the-counter (OTC) market. The guideline says that brokerage firms shouldn't charge commissions, markups, or markdowns of more than 5 percent for standard trades.

The following trades are subject to the 5-percent markup policy:

- **Principal (dealer) transactions:** A firm buys securities for or sells securities from its own inventory and charges a markdown or markup.
- **Agency (broker) transactions;** A firm acts as a middleman (broker) and charges a commission.
- **Riskless (simultaneous) transactions:** A firm buys a security for its own inventory for immediate resale to the customer (riskless to the firm).
- **Proceeds transactions:** A firm sells a security and uses the money to immediately buy another security. You must treat this transaction as one trade (you can't charge on the way out and on the way in).

The 5-percent markup policy covers *over-the-counter trades of outstanding, nonexempt securities with public customers.* If securities are exempt from SEC registration, they're exempt from the 5-percent policy. Additionally, if a dealer pays $20 per share to have a security in inventory (dealer cost) and the market price is $8 per share, the dealer can't charge customers $20 per share so that it doesn't take a loss.

Under extenuating circumstances, the brokerage firm may charge more. Justifiable reasons for charging more (or less) than 5 percent include

- Experiencing difficulty buying or selling the security because the market price is too low or too high
- Handling a small trade — for example, if a customer was to place an order for $100 worth of securities, you'd lose your shirt if you were to charge only 5 percent ($5); in this case, you wouldn't be out of line if you were to charge 100 percent (by the same token, if a customer was to purchase $1 million worth of securities, 5 percent [$50,000] would be considered excessive)
- Encountering difficulty locating and purchasing a specific security

- Incurring additional expenses involved in executing the trade
- Dealing with odd lot trades (for details, see "Meeting the requirements for good delivery," earlier in this chapter)
- Trading nonliquid securities
- Executing transactions on foreign markets

Avoiding violations

You need to be aware of some violations not only for the Series 7 exam but also so you stay out of trouble. Some of the violations are more connected with broker-dealers, some with registered reps, and some with investment advisers:

- **Commingling of funds:** Combining a customer's fully paid and margined securities or combining a firm's securities with customer securities.
- **Interpositioning:** Having two securities dealers act as agents for the same exact trade so that two commissions are earned on one trade.
- **Giving (or receiving) gifts:** Giving or receiving a gift of more than $100 per customer per year. Business expenses (lunch, dinner, hotel rooms, and so on) are exempt from this MSRB rule (see "Self-Regulatory Organizations," earlier in this chapter).
- **Making political contributions (paying to play):** Under the Investment Advisers Act of 1940, investment advisers are prohibited from providing investment advisory services for a fee to a government client for two years after a contribution is made. This rule applies not only to the adviser, executives, and employees making contributions to certain elected officials but also to candidates who may later be elected. In addition, investment advisers are prohibited from soliciting contributions for elected officials or candidates if the investment adviser is seeking or providing government business.
- **Freeriding:** Allowing a customer to buy or sell securities without paying for the purchase.
- **Backing away:** Failure on the part of a securities dealer to honor a firm quote.
- **Churning:** A violation whereby a registered rep excessively trades a customer's account for the sole purpose of generating commission.
- **Matching orders:** Illegally manipulating the price of a security. to make the trading volume appear larger than it really is such as two brokerage firms working in concert by trading the same security back and forth.
- **Painting the tape:** Creating the illusion of trading activity due to misleading reports on the consolidated tape — for example, reporting a trade of 10,000 shares of stock as two separate trades for 5,000 shares each.
- **Frontrunning:** A violation in which a registered rep executes a trade for himself, his firm, or a discretionary account based on knowledge of a block trade (10,000 shares or more) before the trade is reported on the ticker tape.
- **Prearranging trades:** A prearranged trade is an illegal agreement between a registered rep and a customer to buy back a security at a fixed price.
- **Marking the close/marking the open:** Executing a series of trades within minutes of the open or close of the market to manipulate the price of a security.
- **Paying the media:** A violation in which brokerage firms or affiliated persons pay an employee of the media to affect the price of a security; for example, paying a TV stock expert to recommend a security that the firm has in its inventory.

- **Spreading market rumors:** Members are prohibited from spreading false market rumors that may prompt others to either buy or sell a security.
- **Paying for referrals:** Members or persons associated with a member (for example, registered reps) are prohibited from paying cash or noncash compensation to any person except those registered with the member firm or other FINRA members. A violation occurs in the event that compensation is paid to a nonmember for locating, introducing, or referring a client.

Following the money: Anti-money-laundering rules

The *Bank Secrecy Act* establishes the U.S. Treasury Department as the regulator for anti-money laundering programs. All broker-dealers are required to develop programs to detect possible money-laundering abuses. In addition, all broker-dealers must review the Office of Foreign Asset Control's (OFAC) Specially Designated National's (SDN) list to make sure that they're not doing business with individuals or organizations that are on the list. Anti-money-laundering programs are designed to help prevent dirty money that has been cleaned (made to look like it came from a legitimate source) from being used to fund terrorist activities, illegal arms sales, drug trafficking, and so on. Here are three stages of money laundering that you must be aware of for the Series 7 exam (please, don't try this at home):

1. **Placement**

   In this initial stage of money laundering, the funds, derived from criminal activity, are transferred into the financial system (typically via banks and broker-dealers).

2. **Layering**

   Layering is the money launderers' attempt to disguise the source of the funds, usually by moving the funds from one place to another through a series of transactions.

3. **Integration**

   Integration is the final stage of money laundering, when illegal funds are mixed *(commingled)* with legitimate funds. Launderers usually accomplish this step through businesses that operate using cash, importing and exporting companies, and so on.

Broker-dealers and other financial institutions must report any *cash or cash equivalent* deposits, withdrawals, or transfers of *$10,000* or more through a Currency Transaction Report (CTR) to FinCEN (the U.S. Treasury Financial Crimes Network). An institution must report suspicious activity of *$5,000 or more of any type of transaction* to FinCEN by filing a Suspicious Activity Report (SAR).

Here are some indications of money laundering at the opening of the account:

- Concern with U.S. government reporting requirements
- Reluctance to reveal information about business activities
- Suspect ID such as a license or passport that looks like it was made in someone's basement
- Irrational transactions that are inconsistent with objectives
- A fiduciary (the person who can legally make decisions for another investor) who's reluctant to provide information about the customer
- An individual's lack of general knowledge of his industry

And here are some shady signals to look out for after the account is open:

- Deposits of large amounts of cash or money orders
- *Structuring* — the making of cash or cash-equivalent deposits (such as money orders) of just under $10,000 to avoid having them be reported to the U.S. government
- Wire transfers to noncooperative countries
- Sudden and unexplained wire activity
- Making a deposit and transferring it to another party without any business purpose
- Buying a long-term investment and liquidating it in the short-term
- Transfers between multiple accounts for no apparent reason
- Depositing bearer bonds and requesting the money immediately
- A total lack of concern about risks and commissions

The signs of money laundering tend to make sense, so when answering a Series 7 exam question about money laundering, think to yourself, "If it looks like a duck and quacks like a duck, it's probably a duck" — or in financial terms, "If it looks and seems like money laundering, it's probably money laundering."

The Investor's Bankruptcy Shield: FDIC and SIPC

The Federal Deposit Insurance Corporation (FDIC) provides deposit insurance, which guarantees a certain level of safety to people who have money on deposit at a bank. FDIC protects accounts from bank failure (bankruptcy). At the present time, each depositor is protected up to $250,000.

The Securities Investor Protection Corporation (SIPC) protects the customer against broker-dealer bankruptcy. Although it's not a government agency, this private, nonprofit organization was created by the government in 1970. The SIPC protects each separate customer's assets (securities and cash) up to $500,000 total, of which no more than $250,000 can be cash.

Although brokerage firms are required to follow *net capital rules* — specifically SEC Rule 15c3-1 — that are designed to minimize the chances of broker-dealer failure and protect customer assets, broker-dealers occasionally (too often) declare bankruptcy.

The following question concerns SIPC coverage.

John Fredericks has a cash account with $150,000 in securities and $300,000 cash and a margin account with $50,000 in equity. Additionally, John has a joint cash account with his wife Mary with 250,000 in securities and $300,000 cash. If John's broker-dealer goes bankrupt, what is his coverage under SIPC?

(A) $450,000

(B) $500,000

(C) $850,000

(D) $950,000

The right choice is (D). If one of your customers has a cash and margin account titled under one name, as John does, it's treated as though it belongs to one customer. Therefore, John's cash and margin account is covered up to $500,000, of which no more than $250,000 can be cash. He's covered for the $200,000 in securities ($150,000 in securities plus the $50,000 equity) and $250,000 of the $300,000 cash for a total of $450,000. Next, the joint account with his wife is treated as though from a separate customer. Therefore, that account is covered for the $250,000 in securities and $250,000 in cash. Add the two together, and you see that John is covered for a total of $950,000 ($450,000 plus $500,000).

If an investor is not fully covered under SIPC, the investor is still owed money by the bankrupt broker-dealer; therefore, the investor becomes a *general creditor* of the firm for the balance owed.

For Further Review

Although I cover the main topics relating to rules and regulations, you need to know plenty more to be properly prepared to take the Series 7. You should have a good grasp on the following:

- Regulation S-P
- Opening accounts for the employees of other brokerage firms
- Multiple accounts
- Back office procedure (wire room, purchasing and sales, margin, and cashier)
- Limited power of attorney and full power of attorney
- Death of an account holder
- Simplified arbitration and simplified industry arbitration
- Penny stock rules
- Seller's option
- Delivery versus payment (DVP)
- Payment and delivery instructions
- Extension of payment dates
- Stock or bond power and power of substitution
- Frozen accounts
- Erroneous reports, errors, cancels, and rebills
- Rejection and reclamation
- Transfer on death (TOD)
- Ominibus account
- FINRA Rule 5130 and FINRA Rule 5121
- Rules for brokers: moonlighting, private securities transactions, and bankruptcy
- Rules for insiders including penalties
- Rules for penny stocks

- Rules of fair practice and the uniform practice code
- Office of Supervisory Jurisdiction (OSJ)
- Corporate bankruptcy
- Fidelity bonds
- Regulatory reporting requirements
- Business continuity and disaster recovery plans
- Handling of complaints
- Best execution obligations
- Rule of financial disclosure
- Proxies
- NYSE listing requirements
- Advertisements and sales literature
- FINRA Rule 2211
- U-4 and U-5 forms
- Securities licenses
- Continuing education
- Prime brokerage accounts
- Record-keeping
- Form 13D and Form 13G
- Regulation FD (Full Disclosure)
- Sell out and buy in
- Delivery versus payment, cash on delivery, and receives versus payment
- Holding customers' mail
- Exam requirements for registered reps
- Don't know (DK) notice
- Rules for sending, receiving, and safeguarding cash, checks, and securities
- Soft dollar arrangements
- T+1
- Annual reports
- Protecting the customer's personal information, safeguarding laptops, and encrypting e-mails
- Sources of market and investment information (such as news outlets, the Internet, research reports, product-specific periodicals, the Trade Reporting Facility, and so forth)

Part V
Putting Your Knowledge to Good Use: A Practice Exam

In this part . . .

Okay. This is your time to shine. Grab your sharpened pencils, your stopwatch, and some paper. Here's where the rubber meets the road and you find out whether you're an old Model T or a Maserati. If you've followed my advice, completed your Series 7 prep course to get a handle on the subject matter, and used this book as a substantive review, you can expect to do well on this exam. After finishing, make sure you check out the answer explanations that follow. You can consider yourself ready for the real deal if you score 80 or better the first time you take the practice test. Your goal of becoming a stockbroker awaits you at the finish line, and you're almost there! Get ready, get set, go!

Chapter 17

Bring It On: Practice Exam Part I

This chapter is where you get your chance to shine like a star.

This part of the practice exam has 125 questions in random order, just as they are in the actual Series 7 exam. Please read carefully — many test-takers make careless mistakes because they miss key words or read too quickly. Focus on the information you do need to know and ignore the information that you don't need. Read the last sentence twice to make sure you know what the question is asking.

Mark your answers on the answer sheet provided or on a separate piece of paper. You may use a basic calculator and scrap paper for notes and figuring. As you're taking the exam, be sure to circle the questions you find difficult. This step can help you determine what you really need to review.

To simulate the real exam, try to finish Part I in three hours or less. Please resist the urge to look at the answers and explanations as you work through the exam; save the grading for later. After you finish Part I, you can either check your answers (you can find the answers and detailed explanations in Chapter 18, along with an answer key at the end of that chapter), or take a break and then proceed directly to Part II in Chapter 19, where you find the final 125 questions (the break during the actual test is 30 to 60 minutes long, so you can probably squeeze a snack in there).

Good luck!

Practice Exam Part 1 Answer Sheet

1 Ⓐ Ⓑ Ⓒ Ⓓ	33 Ⓐ Ⓑ Ⓒ Ⓓ	65 Ⓐ Ⓑ Ⓒ Ⓓ	97 Ⓐ Ⓑ Ⓒ Ⓓ
2 Ⓐ Ⓑ Ⓒ Ⓓ	34 Ⓐ Ⓑ Ⓒ Ⓓ	66 Ⓐ Ⓑ Ⓒ Ⓓ	98 Ⓐ Ⓑ Ⓒ Ⓓ
3 Ⓐ Ⓑ Ⓒ Ⓓ	35 Ⓐ Ⓑ Ⓒ Ⓓ	67 Ⓐ Ⓑ Ⓒ Ⓓ	99 Ⓐ Ⓑ Ⓒ Ⓓ
4 Ⓐ Ⓑ Ⓒ Ⓓ	36 Ⓐ Ⓑ Ⓒ Ⓓ	68 Ⓐ Ⓑ Ⓒ Ⓓ	100 Ⓐ Ⓑ Ⓒ Ⓓ
5 Ⓐ Ⓑ Ⓒ Ⓓ	37 Ⓐ Ⓑ Ⓒ Ⓓ	69 Ⓐ Ⓑ Ⓒ Ⓓ	101 Ⓐ Ⓑ Ⓒ Ⓓ
6 Ⓐ Ⓑ Ⓒ Ⓓ	38 Ⓐ Ⓑ Ⓒ Ⓓ	70 Ⓐ Ⓑ Ⓒ Ⓓ	102 Ⓐ Ⓑ Ⓒ Ⓓ
7 Ⓐ Ⓑ Ⓒ Ⓓ	39 Ⓐ Ⓑ Ⓒ Ⓓ	71 Ⓐ Ⓑ Ⓒ Ⓓ	103 Ⓐ Ⓑ Ⓒ Ⓓ
8 Ⓐ Ⓑ Ⓒ Ⓓ	40 Ⓐ Ⓑ Ⓒ Ⓓ	72 Ⓐ Ⓑ Ⓒ Ⓓ	104 Ⓐ Ⓑ Ⓒ Ⓓ
9 Ⓐ Ⓑ Ⓒ Ⓓ	41 Ⓐ Ⓑ Ⓒ Ⓓ	73 Ⓐ Ⓑ Ⓒ Ⓓ	105 Ⓐ Ⓑ Ⓒ Ⓓ
10 Ⓐ Ⓑ Ⓒ Ⓓ	42 Ⓐ Ⓑ Ⓒ Ⓓ	74 Ⓐ Ⓑ Ⓒ Ⓓ	106 Ⓐ Ⓑ Ⓒ Ⓓ
11 Ⓐ Ⓑ Ⓒ Ⓓ	43 Ⓐ Ⓑ Ⓒ Ⓓ	75 Ⓐ Ⓑ Ⓒ Ⓓ	107 Ⓐ Ⓑ Ⓒ Ⓓ
12 Ⓐ Ⓑ Ⓒ Ⓓ	44 Ⓐ Ⓑ Ⓒ Ⓓ	76 Ⓐ Ⓑ Ⓒ Ⓓ	108 Ⓐ Ⓑ Ⓒ Ⓓ
13 Ⓐ Ⓑ Ⓒ Ⓓ	45 Ⓐ Ⓑ Ⓒ Ⓓ	77 Ⓐ Ⓑ Ⓒ Ⓓ	109 Ⓐ Ⓑ Ⓒ Ⓓ
14 Ⓐ Ⓑ Ⓒ Ⓓ	46 Ⓐ Ⓑ Ⓒ Ⓓ	78 Ⓐ Ⓑ Ⓒ Ⓓ	110 Ⓐ Ⓑ Ⓒ Ⓓ
15 Ⓐ Ⓑ Ⓒ Ⓓ	47 Ⓐ Ⓑ Ⓒ Ⓓ	79 Ⓐ Ⓑ Ⓒ Ⓓ	111 Ⓐ Ⓑ Ⓒ Ⓓ
16 Ⓐ Ⓑ Ⓒ Ⓓ	48 Ⓐ Ⓑ Ⓒ Ⓓ	80 Ⓐ Ⓑ Ⓒ Ⓓ	112 Ⓐ Ⓑ Ⓒ Ⓓ
17 Ⓐ Ⓑ Ⓒ Ⓓ	49 Ⓐ Ⓑ Ⓒ Ⓓ	81 Ⓐ Ⓑ Ⓒ Ⓓ	113 Ⓐ Ⓑ Ⓒ Ⓓ
18 Ⓐ Ⓑ Ⓒ Ⓓ	50 Ⓐ Ⓑ Ⓒ Ⓓ	82 Ⓐ Ⓑ Ⓒ Ⓓ	114 Ⓐ Ⓑ Ⓒ Ⓓ
19 Ⓐ Ⓑ Ⓒ Ⓓ	51 Ⓐ Ⓑ Ⓒ Ⓓ	83 Ⓐ Ⓑ Ⓒ Ⓓ	115 Ⓐ Ⓑ Ⓒ Ⓓ
20 Ⓐ Ⓑ Ⓒ Ⓓ	52 Ⓐ Ⓑ Ⓒ Ⓓ	84 Ⓐ Ⓑ Ⓒ Ⓓ	116 Ⓐ Ⓑ Ⓒ Ⓓ
21 Ⓐ Ⓑ Ⓒ Ⓓ	53 Ⓐ Ⓑ Ⓒ Ⓓ	85 Ⓐ Ⓑ Ⓒ Ⓓ	117 Ⓐ Ⓑ Ⓒ Ⓓ
22 Ⓐ Ⓑ Ⓒ Ⓓ	54 Ⓐ Ⓑ Ⓒ Ⓓ	86 Ⓐ Ⓑ Ⓒ Ⓓ	118 Ⓐ Ⓑ Ⓒ Ⓓ
23 Ⓐ Ⓑ Ⓒ Ⓓ	55 Ⓐ Ⓑ Ⓒ Ⓓ	87 Ⓐ Ⓑ Ⓒ Ⓓ	119 Ⓐ Ⓑ Ⓒ Ⓓ
24 Ⓐ Ⓑ Ⓒ Ⓓ	56 Ⓐ Ⓑ Ⓒ Ⓓ	88 Ⓐ Ⓑ Ⓒ Ⓓ	120 Ⓐ Ⓑ Ⓒ Ⓓ
25 Ⓐ Ⓑ Ⓒ Ⓓ	57 Ⓐ Ⓑ Ⓒ Ⓓ	89 Ⓐ Ⓑ Ⓒ Ⓓ	121 Ⓐ Ⓑ Ⓒ Ⓓ
26 Ⓐ Ⓑ Ⓒ Ⓓ	58 Ⓐ Ⓑ Ⓒ Ⓓ	90 Ⓐ Ⓑ Ⓒ Ⓓ	122 Ⓐ Ⓑ Ⓒ Ⓓ
27 Ⓐ Ⓑ Ⓒ Ⓓ	59 Ⓐ Ⓑ Ⓒ Ⓓ	91 Ⓐ Ⓑ Ⓒ Ⓓ	123 Ⓐ Ⓑ Ⓒ Ⓓ
28 Ⓐ Ⓑ Ⓒ Ⓓ	60 Ⓐ Ⓑ Ⓒ Ⓓ	92 Ⓐ Ⓑ Ⓒ Ⓓ	124 Ⓐ Ⓑ Ⓒ Ⓓ
29 Ⓐ Ⓑ Ⓒ Ⓓ	61 Ⓐ Ⓑ Ⓒ Ⓓ	93 Ⓐ Ⓑ Ⓒ Ⓓ	125 Ⓐ Ⓑ Ⓒ Ⓓ
30 Ⓐ Ⓑ Ⓒ Ⓓ	62 Ⓐ Ⓑ Ⓒ Ⓓ	94 Ⓐ Ⓑ Ⓒ Ⓓ	
31 Ⓐ Ⓑ Ⓒ Ⓓ	63 Ⓐ Ⓑ Ⓒ Ⓓ	95 Ⓐ Ⓑ Ⓒ Ⓓ	
32 Ⓐ Ⓑ Ⓒ Ⓓ	64 Ⓐ Ⓑ Ⓒ Ⓓ	96 Ⓐ Ⓑ Ⓒ Ⓓ	

Time: 3 hours for 125 questions

Directions: Choose the correct answer to each question. Then fill in the circle on your answer sheet that corresponds to the question number and the letter indicating your choice.

1. If a bond's YTM is 6 percent, which of the following would MOST likely be refunded by the issuer?

   I. Coupon 6½ percent, maturing in 2025, callable in 2015 at 104

   II. Coupon 5½ percent, maturing in 2025, callable in 2014 at 104

   III. Coupon 5½ percent, maturing in 2025, callable in 2014 at 100

   IV. Coupon 6½ percent, maturing in 2025, callable in 2015 at 100

   (A) I and II

   (B) II and IV

   (C) II only

   (D) IV only

2. Which of the following have ownership positions in a corporation?

   I. Convertible bondholders

   II. Convertible preferred stockholders

   III. Common stockholders

   IV. Mortgage bondholders

   (A) II and III

   (B) I, II, III, and IV

   (C) II and IV

   (D) II only

3. Common stockholders of PXPX Corporation have which of the following rights and privileges?

   (A) The right to receive an audited financial report weekly

   (B) The right to vote for cash dividends to be paid

   (C) A residual claim to assets at dissolution

   (D) The right to vote for stock dividends to be paid

4. Which of the following types of preferred stock allows the investor to reduce inflation risk?

   (A) Cumulative

   (B) Noncumulative

   (C) Convertible

   (D) Participating

5. CSA common stock presently has an earnings per share of $3 and pays a $0.30 quarterly dividend. If CSA's market price is $48, what is the current yield?

   (A) 0.67 percent

   (B) 2.5 percent

   (C) 5.0 percent

   (D) 5.25 percent

6. Mike Moneybags purchased ten 6-percent Treasury notes at 101-12. What was the total dollar amount of the purchase?

   (A) $1,011.20

   (B) $10,112.00

   (C) $1,013.75

   (D) $10,137.50

7. On Wednesday, March 16th, one of your customers purchases ten 6-percent Treasury bonds maturing in 2020. If the bonds pay interest on January 1 and July 1, how many days of accrued interest are added to the purchaser's price?

   (A) 75

   (B) 76

   (C) 79

   (D) 80

Go on to next page

8. Jake Hanson lives in New York and is considering purchasing a bond. He has settled on either a 5-percent municipal bond offered by New York or a 7-percent corporate bond offered by The Greenhorn Corporation, which has headquarters in New York. Jake needs some guidance and would like you to help him determine which bond will provide him with the greatest return. Which of the following information do you need to obtain before you can make the appropriate recommendation?

(A) The business of his employer

(B) His current tax bracket

(C) How long he has lived in New York

(D) His other holdings

9. An investor who is long a call option will realize a profit if exercising the option when the underlying stock price is

(A) below the strike price minus the premium paid

(B) above the strike price

(C) above the strike price plus the premium paid

(D) below the strike price

10. One of your clients is new to investing and has limited resources. Which of the following investments would you least likely recommend to this investor?

(A) Growth funds

(B) T-bills

(C) Blue-chip stock

(D) Collateralized debt obligations

11. Which of the following is required on the registration statement for a new issue?

I. The capitalization of the issuer

II. Complete financial statements

III. What the money raised will be used for

IV. The names and addresses of all of the issuer's control persons.

(A) I, II, and III

(B) I, III, and IV

(C) I, II, and IV

(D) I, II, III, and IV

12. Under the Securities Act of 1933, which of the following securities must be registered with the SEC?

(A) Closed-end funds

(B) Variable annuities

(C) Open-end funds

(D) All of the above

13. Which of the following trades occur in the secondary market?

I. A syndicate selling new issues of municipal bonds to the public

II. A DMM on the New York Stock Exchange purchasing stock for his own account

III. A trade between a bank and an insurance company without using the services of a broker-dealer

IV. A corporation selling new shares of its common stock to the public using the services of a broker-dealer

(A) I and IV

(B) II and III

(C) I, II, and III

(D) II, III, and IV

14. A customer's confirmation must include

I. the markdown, if the member acted as a principal in a NASDAQ security

II. the amount of any commission, if the member acted as an agent

III. whether the member acted as an agent or a principal

IV. the markup if the member acted as a principal in a NASDAQ security

(A) I and III

(B) II and IV

(C) I, III, and IV

(D) I, II, III, and IV

15. Which of the following would qualify as management companies?

(A) Face-amount certificate companies

(B) Unit investment trusts

(C) Closed-end funds

(D) None of the above

Go on to next page

16. Which of the following is TRUE regarding qualified retirement plans?

(A) Contributions are made with 100-percent pretax dollars.

(B) Contributions are made with 100-percent after-tax dollars.

(C) Distributions are taxable only prior to age 59½.

(D) Distributions are subject to a 10-percent penalty.

17. Variable annuities must be registered with the

I. Department of State

II. State Banking Commission

III. State Insurance Commission

IV. Securities and Exchange Commission

(A) I and II

(B) I and III

(C) I and IV

(D) III and IV

18. All of the following items must be included on a trade confirmation EXCEPT

(A) the customer's account number

(B) the customer's signature

(C) the price of the security

(D) the commission, if the trade took place on an agency basis

19. Which of the following is true of the Telephone Act of 1991?

I. You cannot make calls before 8 a.m. or after 9 p.m. in the local time zone of the customer.

II. You are required to provide your name, company name, company address, and phone number.

III. Individuals who ask not to be called need to be placed on the company's do-not-call list.

IV. You may not send unsolicited ads by fax machine.

(A) I and III

(B) II and IV

(C) I, II, and III

(D) I, II, III, and IV

20. An agent's recommendations to a customer

I. must be approved in advance by a manager

II. must be in line with the customer's risk tolerance and investment objectives

III. must be reviewed by a principal if they result in a trade

IV. must be in accordance with Federal Reserve Board rules

(A) I and IV

(B) II and III

(C) II, III, and IV

(D) I and II

21. If one of your clients wants to order municipal securities that you believe to be unsuitable for her investment objectives, what should you do?

(A) Execute the order as long as you mark the order ticket as "unsolicited."

(B) You must refuse the order unless the client changes her investment objectives.

(C) You must obtain the permission of the firm's compliance officer before executing the order.

(D) You may only execute the order with prior permission of a principal of the firm.

22. Mr. T. Jefferson bought ten municipal bonds at 105 with ten years to maturity. Three years later, he sold the bonds for 102. His tax consequence is a

(A) $150 gain

(B) $150 loss

(C) $300 gain

(D) $300 loss

Go on to next page

23. Which of the following are types of progressive taxes?

I. Gift taxes

II. Estate taxes

III. Sales taxes

IV. Property taxes

(A) I and II

(B) II, III, and IV

(C) III and IV

(D) I, II, III, and IV

24. All broker-dealers need to maintain customer identification programs and should check the names of all new clients against

(A) a list maintained by the SEC

(B) a do-not-call list maintained by the firm

(C) a list compiled by FINRA

(D) a list of specially designated nationals (SDNs) maintained by OFAC

25. Which of the following statements is NOT true of life-cycle funds?

(A) As life-cycle funds get nearer to their target date, the portfolio holdings will be adjusted to purchase more equity securities and less fixed-income securities.

(B) These funds are usually set up as funds of funds.

(C) The asset allocation of the fund will be rebalanced on a regular basis to make sure that the risk/reward balance is correct given the target date of the fund.

(D) The objective of the fund assumes that most investors cannot tolerate as much risk as they get older.

26. The ex-date is

(A) the date on which the corporation ceases paying a dividend

(B) the date on and after the date the seller is entitled to the dividend

(C) the third business day before the record date

(D) the day the stock price is increased by the amount of the dividend

27. Investors who have international investments are subject to

I. political risk

II. currency risk

III. regulatory risk

(A) I and II

(B) II and III

(C) I and III

(D) I, II, and III

28. Sigmund Handskin, an investor, wants to purchase Series EE savings bonds. Which of the following statements is TRUE?

I. The bonds are purchased at a discount from their face value.

II. EE bonds are sold in multiples of $1,000 only.

III. Default risk is extremely small.

IV. The accrued interest is exempt from federal income taxes.

(A) I and II

(B) I and III

(C) III and IV

(D) I, II, III, and IV

29. One of the functions of a broker's broker in the municipal bond business is to do which of the following?

(A) Protect government interests

(B) Act as a syndicate member in the sale of new municipal bonds

(C) Help sell municipal bonds that syndicates have had difficulty selling

(D) Release the name of the firm on behalf of which the broker's broker is acting

30. An investor with no other position in XYZ writes 1 XYZ Aug 30 put at 2.75. If the put option is exercised when XYZ is trading at 27.50 and the investor immediately sells the stock in the market, what is his gain or loss?

(A) $25 gain

(B) $25 loss

(C) $250 gain

(D) $250 loss

Go on to next page

31. Mrs. Smith purchases 100 shares of ABC at 35 and writes a 40 call at 5.50. If ABC stock increases to 60 and the call is exercised, Mrs. Smith has a

(A) $2,500 gain

(B) $3,050 loss

(C) $2,000 loss

(D) $1,050 gain

32. Which of the following are factors that affect the marketability of municipal GO bonds?

I. The quality

II. Call features

III. The issuer's name

IV. Credit enhancements

(A) I and II

(B) II and III

(C) I, II, and III

(D) I, II, III, and IV

33. If a customer wants to open a new account but refuses to provide some of the financial information requested by the member firm, which of the following statements is TRUE?

(A) The firm may open the account for the customer and make recommendations freely.

(B) The firm may open the account if it can determine from other sources that the customer has the financial means to handle the account.

(C) The firm may open the account and take unsolicited trades only.

(D) The firm may not accept any trades for the account until the information is received from the customer.

34. Mr. Mayvis has a margin account with a current market value of $20,250 and a debit balance of $3,000 with Regulation T at 50 percent. How much excess equity does the investor have in the account?

(A) $20,250

(B) $3,000

(C) $17,250

(D) $7,125

35. Which of the following is included in a preliminary prospectus?

I. The purpose for the funds being raised

II. Financial statements

III. A written statement in red citing that the prospectus may be amended and a final prospectus issued

IV. The final offering price

(A) I and II

(B) I, II, and III

(C) II and IV

(D) I, II, III, and IV

36. Which of the following is true of accredited investors?

(A) They have had an annual income in excess of $200,000 for at least the last three years.

(B) They have had an annual income in excess of $100,000 for at least the last two years.

(C) They have a net worth of at least $1,000,000, excluding any equity they have in their primary residence.

(D) They have a net worth in excess of $200,000.

37. All of the following orders could be placed on the DMM's order display book EXCEPT

I. market orders

II. stop orders

III. limit orders

IV. GTC orders

(A) I only

(B) II and III

(C) II and IV

(D) I, II, and III

38. Which of the following provides last sale information and current options quotations provided by participating exchanges?

(A) EMMA

(B) OPRA

(C) SOES

(D) TRACE

Go on to next page

39. The SEC and FINRA require customer statements to be sent out for inactive accounts at least

(A) monthly

(B) quarterly

(C) semiannually

(D) annually

40. Which of the following securities is traded on an exchange and is an entity that makes mortgage loans to developers and has a portfolio of properties?

(A) DPPs

(B) ETNs

(C) Hybrid REITs

(D) Mutual funds

41. Which of the following are needed to open a margin account for a corporation?

I. Corporate charter and resolution

II. New account form

III. Hypothecation agreement

IV. Credit agreement

(A) I and II

(B) I and IV

(C) III and IV

(D) I, II, III, and IV

42. The Municipal Bond Index is

(A) the average yield on 25 revenue bonds with 30-year maturities

(B) the average yield on 20 selected municipal bonds with 20-year maturities

(C) the average dollar price of 40 highly-traded GO and revenue bonds

(D) the average yield on 11 selected municipal bonds with 20-year maturities

43. Which of the following partnership documents needs to be filed with the secretary of state in the home state of the partnership?

I. The certificate of limited partnership

II. The partnership agreement

III. The subscription agreement

(A) I only

(B) II and III

(C) I and III

(D) I, II, and III

44. Martina Martin is new to investing but has determined that her primary objective is making sure that she is prepared for retirement. Which of the following is the MOST important factor for you to consider when helping her set up her investment portfolio?

(A) Age

(B) Net worth

(C) Education level

(D) Previous investment history

45. An investor buys 100 shares of common stock of T-Prompters, Inc. at $15 per share. Six months later, T-Prompter Inc. is trading at 12.40–12.65, and the registered representative offers to purchase the 100 shares back from the investor for his own account at $14.25 per share. This procedure is

(A) permitted by FINRA rules

(B) permitted with the written permission of a manager of the firm

(C) prohibited because it violates the Code of Procedure

(D) prohibited because it is a guarantee against a loss

46. Which of the following is rated by most securities rating services?

(A) Market risk

(B) Investment risk

(C) Quantity

(D) Quality

Go on to next page

47. Under federal law, stock CANNOT be tendered from which of the following accounts?

(A) Short margin accounts

(B) Margin accounts with no excess equity

(C) Cash accounts

(D) Long margin accounts

48. Which of the following items are required on an order ticket?

I. The time of the order

II. A description of the security (stocks, bonds, symbol, and so on)

III. Whether the registered rep has discretionary authority over the account

IV. The registered rep's identification number

(A) I, III, and IV

(B) I and III only

(C) I, II, and IV

(D) I, II, III, and IV

49. All of the following are important factors when determining the markup or commission on a municipal bond trade EXCEPT

(A) the fact that you and the firm you work for are entitled to make a profit

(B) the difficulty of the trade

(C) the 5-percent markup policy

(D) the market value of the securities at the time of the trade

50. When compared to statutory voting, cumulative voting provides an advantage to

I. larger shareholders

II. mortgage bondholders

III. smaller shareholders

IV. convertible bondholders

(A) I only

(B) II and IV

(C) III only

(D) II and III

51. Which of the following is NOT a benefit of investing in ADRs?

(A) The dividends are received in U.S. currency.

(B) The transactions are done in U.S. currency.

(C) ADRs are subject to antifraud rules.

(D) Currency risk is minimized.

52. CMOs are typically rated

(A) AAA

(B) AA

(C) BBB

(D) SP1

53. Which of the following best describes a syndicate member's financial liability if a syndicate is established on an Eastern account basis?

(A) Divided liability to purchase securities from the issuer and divided responsibility for securities that remain unsold by the syndicate

(B) Divided liability to purchase securities from the issuer and undivided responsibility for securities that remain unsold by the syndicate

(C) Undivided liability to purchase securities from the issuer and divided responsibility for securities that remain unsold by the syndicate

(D) Undivided liability to purchase securities from the issuer and undivided responsibility for securities that remain unsold by the syndicate

54. Keith Coalburner has written a letter of complaint regarding his recent purchase of municipal bonds to his broker-dealer. Upon receipt of the complaint, the broker-dealer must first

(A) immediately repurchase the securities at a price at or slightly above Keith's purchase price

(B) guarantee to make the customer whole

(C) return any markup or commission charged

(D) accept the complaint and write down any action taken

Go on to next page

55. An online site that provides detailed information to nonprofessional investors relating to municipal securities, including up-to-the-minute prices, is called

(A) The Blue List

(B) OPRA

(C) EMMA

(D) NASDAQ

56. Under which of the following circumstances would an investor face an unlimited maximum loss potential?

I. Short 2 DIM Nov 40 puts

II. Short 400 shares of DIM common stock

III. Short 6 DIM Nov 50 uncovered calls

IV. Short 3 DIM Nov 50 covered calls

(A) I and II

(B) I and III

(C) II and III

(D) II and IV

57. A registered representative executes the following trades for a speculative investor:

Buy 1 GHI May 30 call at 8

Sell 1 GHI May 35 call at 3

Are these trades suitable for this investor?

(A) It is impossible to tell with the information given

(B) Probably not, because the risk is not high enough for a speculative investor

(C) Yes, buying and selling options are always appropriate for speculative investors

(D) No, because it is impossible to make a profit with these positions

58. Fred Freedom has held 100 shares of UPP stock for six months and decides to purchase a nine-month call on UPP. If the UPP call option expires and Fred decides to sell the UPP stock four months after the expiration of the call, what is Fred's tax position?

(A) Short-term capital gain or long-term capital loss

(B) Long-term capital gain or short-term capital loss

(C) Long-term capital gain or long-term capital loss

(D) Short-term capital gain or short-term capital loss

59. John Dow and Jane Dough, who are engaged but unmarried, want to open a new account registered as joint tenants with rights of survivorship. Which of the following should occur?

(A) A principal of the firm should be notified immediately about the account registration so that a report can be filed with FINRA.

(B) The agent must refuse to open the account.

(C) The agent must notify a principal of the firm and a report must first be filed with the SEC.

(D) The agent may open the account, but should first discuss the rules of a JTWROS account with the unmarried couple.

60. Which of the following occurs under the provisions of the Uniform Gifts to Minors Act (UGMA) when a minor reaches the age of majority?

(A) The account must be transferred to the donor.

(B) The account is automatically changed to a UTMA account.

(C) The account is closed, and the new adult receives a check in the amount equal to the market value of the account less any commission.

(D) The account must be transferred to the donee after she reaches adulthood.

Go on to next page

61. If a client has a margin account with $18,000 in securities and a debit balance of $7,000, and Regulation T is 50 percent, which of the following statements is FALSE?

(A) The account has a buying power of $4,000.

(B) If the client withdraws any excess equity, the debit balance decreases by the amount of the withdrawal.

(C) The account has excess equity of $2,000.

(D) The securities held in the account most likely increased in value.

62. Which type of margin account requires a minimum equity of $25,000?

(A) A portfolio margin account

(B) A short account

(C) A day-trading account

(D) A corporate account

63. Prior to buying or selling options, a customer must first receive a(n)

(A) ODD

(B) OCC

(C) margin agreement

(D) OPRA

64. Priority, precedence, and parity rules of bids and offers dictate trading activity on the

(A) OTC pink market

(B) fourth market

(C) New York Stock Exchange

(D) OTC market

65. Who maintains a fair and orderly market on the New York Stock Exchange trading floor?

(A) Floor brokers

(B) Two-dollar brokers

(C) Designated market makers

(D) Order book officials

66. The 5-percent markup policy applies to

(A) riskless or simultaneous transactions

(B) markdowns on stock sold from inventory

(C) commissions charged when executing trades for a customer

(D) all of the above

67. All of the following would be considered good delivery between brokers for 570 shares of stock EXCEPT

(A) 5 certificates for 30 shares each and 6 certificates for 70 shares each

(B) 10 certificates for 50 shares each and 1 certificate for 70 shares

(C) 1 certificate for 200 shares, 1 certificate for 300 shares, and 35 certificates for 2 shares each

(D) 10 certificates for 30 shares each, 4 certificates for 50 shares each, and 1 certificate for 70 shares

68. Skippy Barrier III has 1,000 shares of DIM common stock in his portfolio. Skippy would like to protect himself in the event that the market price of DIM drops. Which of the following orders would best meet Skippy's needs?

(A) A buy stop order

(B) A sell stop order

(C) A buy limit order

(D) A sell limit order

69. Which of the following is NOT an advantage for a customer adding REITs to her portfolio?

(A) Having a professionally managed portfolio of real estate assets

(B) Preferential dividend treatment

(C) Being able to use a REIT as a potential hedge against a negative price movement in other equity securities

(D) Liquidity

Go on to next page

70. All of the following items would be found on the official statement of a municipal bond issue EXCEPT

(A) the markup

(B) a description of the issuer

(C) the coupon rate

(D) a legal opinion

71. Which of the following are true about the annuitization of a variable annuity?

I. The value of the annuity units is fixed.

II. The number of annuity units is fixed.

III. The value of the annuity units varies.

IV. The number of annuity units varies.

(A) I and II

(B) II and III

(C) II and IV

(D) None of the above

72. Which of the following investments requires a registered representative to obtain written verification of an investor's net worth?

(A) Hedge funds

(B) Variable annuities

(C) Direct participation programs

(D) Triple-tax-free municipal bonds

73. The Federal Reserve Board is responsible for which of the following?

(A) Easing the money supply

(B) Setting Regulation T

(C) Printing currency

(D) All of the above

74. A head and shoulders bottom formation indicates

(A) the reversal of a bullish trend

(B) the reversal of a bearish trend

(C) that the stock is moving sideways

(D) that it might be a good time to sell short

75. Michael Moneybags purchased 1,000 shares of WOW common stock at $26 per share. Six months later, WOW is trading at $60 and Michael expects a slight decline in the market price for a short period of time. However, Michael has a lot of confidence that WOW is a great company and he remains bullish on WOW's common stock overall. Providing Michael is correct in his assessment, which of the following positions would provide Michael a level of protection while still being able to generate additional income?

(A) Sell 1,000 WOW short and purchase 10 WOW Dec 65 calls for $300 each

(B) Buy 10 WOW straddles at 60

(C) Sell 10 WOW Dec 65 calls for $300 each and place a 1,000-share sell-stop order for WOW at 57

(D) Buy 10 WOW Oct 60 puts for $500 each

76. One of your customers purchases 100 shares of ARGH at 44.10 and 1 OEX Sep 360 put at 4.50. A few months later, ARGH is trading at 42.55 and the OEX index is trading at 349. If your customer closes the stock position and exercises his OEX put, what is his gain?

(A) $155

(B) $495

(C) $1,100

(D) $35,395

77. Which of the following levels of NASDAQ includes subject quotes?

(A) Level I

(B) Level II

(C) Level III

(D) Level IV

78. A registered representative may open all of the following customer accounts EXCEPT

(A) an account in the name of Mr. Wegner for Mrs. Wegner

(B) a minor's account by a custodian

(C) a corporate account by a designated officer

(D) a partnership account by a designated partner

Go on to next page

79. All of the following increase SMA in a long account EXCEPT

I. selling securities from the account

II. the purchase of additional securities in the account

III. receipt of a cash dividend

IV. a decrease in the market value of securities held in the account

(A) I and III

(B) II and IV

(C) I, III, and IV

(D) II, III, and IV

80. DEF Corporation issued stock to the public at $9 per share. If the manager's fee was $0.15 per share, the takedown was $0.50 per share, and the concession was $0.30 per share, what was the spread?

(A) $0.45

(B) $0.65

(C) $0.80

(D) $0.95

81. Exchange-listed securities trading over-the-counter takes place in the

(A) first market

(B) second market

(C) third market

(D) fourth market

82. Which of the following statements is true regarding NASDAQ Level I, II, or III?

(A) Level II is where market makers enter their quotes.

(B) Level I is the level used by registered representatives.

(C) Level III is used by traders.

(D) Level II only displays the highest bid and lowest ask prices.

83. Mutual funds must send financial statements to shareholders at least

(A) monthly

(B) bimonthly

(C) quarterly

(D) semiannually

84. Which of the following best defines selling dividends?

(A) Providing customers with a clear plan on how to invest dividends they receive

(B) Enticing customers to buy mutual fund shares just before the ex-dividend date so that they can receive a dividend

(C) Encouraging customers to sell stock just before a dividend is paid so that the stock will be easier to sell

(D) Encouraging customers to withdraw dividends from mutual funds and to invest in other securities so that you, as a registered rep, will receive additional commission

85. Which of the following establishes the U.S. Treasury Department as the regulator for anti-money- laundering programs?

(A) The Bank Secrecy Act

(B) OFAC

(C) SDN

(D) None of the above

86. Investing in a real-estate DPP program includes which of the following advantages?

I. Depreciation

II. Appreciation

III. Depletion

IV. Cash flow

(A) I and II

(B) III and IV

(C) I, II, and IV

(D) I, II, III, and IV

87. The Fed would be inclined to increase the money supply in which of the following conditions?

(A) Declining yields on bonds

(B) Declining gross domestic product (GDP)

(C) Declining interest rates

(D) Rising housing prices

Go on to next page

88. All of the following terms are related to research reports sent out by brokerage firms EXCEPT

(A) quiet periods

(B) information barriers

(C) open market

(D) third-party disclosures

89. FDIC covers each

(A) depositor for up to $250,000

(B) investor for up to $250,000

(C) depositor for up to $500,000

(D) investor for up to $500,000

90. An investor owns the following investments:

50 New York 5-percent general obligation bonds maturing in 2020 and rated AA

50 Florida University 6.25-percent revenue bonds maturing in 2021 and rated AA

50 Nevada Turnpike 5.75-percent revenue bonds maturing in 2020 and rated AA

What type of diversification does this represent?

(A) Maturity

(B) Quality

(C) Quantity

(D) Geographical

91. A customer buys 1 DUD Jun 55 put at 4.50 when DUD is trading at 53.40. Just prior to expiration, the option is trading at 4.55 bid-4.65 asked. If the customer closes his position with a market order, what is the gain or loss?

(A) $5 gain

(B) $5 loss

(C) $160 gain

(D) $160 loss

92. An investor has shorted XYZ common stock at 55. XYZ common stock has recently dropped to 30 and the investor expects that the price will continue to decrease over the long term. If the investor would like to hedge against a possible increase in the price, the investor should

(A) buy an XYZ call

(B) sell an XYZ call

(C) buy an XYZ put

(D) buy an XYZ combination

93. Grant Goldbarr purchased 1 ABC 60 put at 3.50 and purchased 100 shares of ABC at 62. Six months later, with ABC trading at 64, Grant closes his put for 0.75 and sells his stock at the market price. What is Grant's gain or loss as a result of these transactions?

(A) $75 loss

(B) $75 gain

(C) $275 loss

(D) $275 gain

94. If an investor buys a three-year LEAPS contract on issuance, which expires unexercised, what is the investor's tax consequence at expiration?

(A) Short-term capital loss

(B) Long-term capital gain

(C) Long-term capital loss

(D) Short-term capital gain

95. A customer, without giving written authorization, may permit a registered representative to exercise his judgment as to

(A) whether to buy or sell

(B) the security

(C) the price and timing to enter the order

(D) the number of shares

Go on to next page

96. Which of the following are nonexempt securities?

I. Municipal unit investment trust shares

II. U.S. government bond fund shares

III. Variable annuity accumulation units

IV. Fixed annuities

(A) I and II

(B) III only

(C) III and IV

(D) I, II, and III

97. If Buddy Seagull has a limited amount of funds and wants to invest in the pharmaceutical industry but does not want to limit his investments to only one or two companies, which type of fund would be MOST suitable?

(A) A hedge fund

(B) A sector fund

(C) A balanced fund

(D) A money-market fund

98. What is the principal tax benefit for investing as a limited partner in an exploratory oil and gas drilling program?

(A) Tax credits

(B) Depreciation expenses

(C) Recourse loans

(D) Intangible drilling costs

99. If the U.S. dollar has fallen in comparison with foreign currencies, which of the following statements is TRUE?

(A) U.S. exports are likely to fall.

(B) Foreign currencies buy fewer U.S. dollars.

(C) U.S. products cost more for foreign consumers.

(D) U.S exports increase.

100. Ginny Goldbarr purchased 2 LMN 50 calls and paid a premium of 3 for each option. Ginny also purchased 2 LMN 50 puts and paid a premium of 2 for each option. At the time of purchase, LMN was trading at $50.25. Just prior to expiration, LMN was trading at $44.50, and Ginny decided to close her options for their intrinsic value. Excluding commission, Ginny had a

(A) $50 profit

(B) $50 loss

(C) $100 profit

(D) $100 loss

101. You have a new client who is in a high tax bracket and is looking for investments with a tax advantage. Which of the following securities would you LEAST likely recommend?

(A) Municipal bonds

(B) Collateralized mortgage obligations

(C) Retirement plans

(D) Direct participation programs

102. An investor wants to generate some income on a stock that she believes will remain at relatively the same price for the next year or so. Which of the following option positions would meet her goal?

(A) Buying a combination

(B) Writing a straddle

(C) Buying a call

(D) Buying a put

103. Adjustable-rate preferred stock has a dividend that adjusts according to

(A) prevailing interest rates

(B) the amount of dividend given to common stockholders

(C) the coupon rate on the issuer's bonds

(D) the rate on CMOs

104. Regulation SHO covers the

(A) resale of restricted securities

(B) short sale of securities

(C) resale of ETFs

(D) margin requirement for listed options

Go on to next page

105. Which of the following items are found on an indenture of a bond?

I. The maturity date

II. Callable or convertible features

III. The coupon rate

IV. The name of the trustee

(A) II, III, and IV

(B) I, II, and III

(C) II and III

(D) I, II, III, and IV

106. The Legal List is for

(A) fiduciaries

(B) investment advisers

(C) municipal finance professionals

(D) corporate accounts

107. Which of the following are important to investors evaluating direct participation programs?

I. The economic soundness of the program

II. The expertise of the general partner

III. The basic objectives of the program

IV. The start-up costs

(A) I, II, and III

(B) I, II, and IV

(C) II, III, and IV

(D) I, II, III, and IV

108. What is the required beginning date (RBD) for traditional IRAs?

(A) The year after the investor reaches the age of 59½

(B) The year the investor turns the age of 70½

(C) April 1st of the year after the investor reaches the age of 70½

(D) April 15th of the year after the investor reaches the age of 70½

109. A repurchase agreement usually takes place between which two parties?

(A) The FINRA and the Fed

(B) The Fed and the NYSE

(C) Commercial banks and the Fed

(D) The NYSE and the FINRA

110. One of your clients is expecting to receive a lot of money over the next three years. Your client would like to shelter some of that money by investing in a DPP. Which of the following types of DPPs will help your client shelter the most money?

(A) Oil and gas income

(B) Oil and gas developmental

(C) Oil and gas combination

(D) Oil and gas wildcatting

111. Which of the following governmental bodies receives no revenue from ad-valorem taxes?

(A) County governments

(B) State governments

(C) School districts

(D) Local municipalities

112. According to MSRB rules, a customer confirmation must include

(A) the markup or markdown

(B) the location of the indenture

(C) the maturity date

(D) whether the trade was done on an agency or dealer basis

113. John believes that the market is about to become bearish and would like to be able to profit in the event that he is correct. Which of the following investments would meet John's needs?

I. Inverse ETFs

II. Selling SPX calls

III. High-yield bond funds

IV. Selling OEX puts

(A) I and II

(B) II and IV

(C) I, II, and III

(D) I, II, and IV

Go on to next page

114. Ferret Enterprises pays a quarterly dividend of $0.25 per share and has an EPS of $2.50. What is the dividend payout ratio?

(A) 10 percent

(B) 40 percent

(C) 57 percent

(D) 100 percent

115. Gerry Goldbar purchases a new OID municipal zero-coupon for 80. If Gerry holds the bond to maturity, what is his tax consequence?

(A) $0

(B) $200 ordinary income over the time the bond is held to maturity

(C) $200 capital gain

(D) None of the above

116. Which of the following securities are exempt from the Trust Indenture Act of 1939?

I. Treasury bonds

II. General obligation bonds

III. Mortgage bonds

IV. Revenue bonds

(A) I, II, and III

(B) I, II, and IV

(C) I and III

(D) II and IV

117. Which of the following disputes must be resolved using the Code of Arbitration?

I. A dispute between a member of FINRA and a registered rep

II. A dispute between a member of FINRA and a customer

III. A dispute between two members of FINRA

IV. A dispute between a bank and a member of FINRA

(A) IV only

(B) II and IV

(C) I and III

(D) I, III, and IV

118. Duke Wallwalker purchased an LTSBR Corporation convertible bond at 95 on January 20, 2009. The bond is convertible at $40, and the investor converts his bond into stock on January 21, 2012. If the bond is trading at 104 and the common stock is trading at $42, for tax purposes, these transactions will result in

(A) a $10 gain

(B) a $10 loss

(C) a $90 gain

(D) neither a gain nor a loss

119. XYZ is currently trading at 24.10–24.25. A designated market maker in XYZ could enter a bid at which of the following prices?

(A) 24.10

(B) 24.12

(C) 24.25

(D) 24.27

120. RANs, BANs, TANs, and CLNs are issued by municipalities seeking

(A) to insure their municipal securities

(B) the approval of the SEC

(C) long-term financing

(D) short-term financing

121. If an official statement has a dated date of May 1st, but the first coupon payment is set at December 1st, it means that the first payment is a

(A) long coupon

(B) mistake printed on the official statement

(C) short coupon

(D) normal payment for a seven-month bond

122. Which of the following statements regarding municipal revenue bonds is NOT true?

(A) Revenue bonds are not subject to a debt ceiling.

(B) Revenue bonds may be issued by interstate authorities.

(C) The maturity date of the issue will usually exceed the useful life of the facility backing the bonds.

(D) Debt service is paid from revenue received from the facility backing the bonds.

Go on to next page

123. Which of the following statements regarding the Code of Arbitration are NOT true?

I. Claims of $25,000 or less can use simplified arbitration.

II. The deadline for providing a complaining customer requesting a copy of the signed predispute arbitration agreement is seven business days.

III. It deals with settling disputes between members.

IV. It deals with violations of the Conduct Rules.

(A) I and III

(B) II and IV

(C) II and III

(D) None of the above

124. All of the following may be sources of revenue for a revenue bond EXCEPT

(A) property taxes

(B) user fees

(C) tolls

(D) airports

125. A municipal revenue bond was issued under a net revenue pledge. The following numbers are reported for the current year:

$38,000,000 of gross revenues

$20,000,000 in operating and maintenance expenses

$5,000,000 of interest expenses

$1,000,000 of principle repayment

What is the debt service coverage ratio?

(A) 2:1

(B) 3:1

(C) 4:1

(D) 5:1

STOP DO NOT TURN THE PAGE UNTIL TOLD TO DO SO.
DO NOT RETURN TO A PREVIOUS TEST.

Chapter 18

Answers and Explanations to Practice Exam Part I

Congratulations — if you've reached this point, you've completed Part I of the practice exam in Chapter 17. (If you haven't, flip back and take the test. You don't want to spoil all the surprises, do you?) You can either stop here and review your answers, or, if you're really, really brave, you can go to Part II of the practice test in Chapter 19. If you're going to Part II, take a 30- to 60-minute break before proceeding (like in the real exam).

Review, review, review. And if I haven't mentioned this yet, reviewing is definitely a good idea. Look at the questions you had problems with, retake all the questions you got wrong, and make sure you get them right the second (or third) time around. If you're short on time but just can't wait to see how you fared, you can check out the abbreviated answer key (without the explanations) at the end of this chapter. I explain how the Series 7 is scored in the section "Making the Grade," just before the answer key. But I strongly suggest you come back later and — you guessed it — review.

Wait at least a week or two before taking the same test again. Retaking the test won't help your cause if you're just memorizing the answers.

1. **D.** (Chapter 7) You have to remember to look at this question from a corporation's point of view. As a practical matter, the issuer will most likely refund the issue that will cost it the most money over the life of the issue. The first thing that an issuer would look at is the coupon rate (highest coupon first), next would be the call premium (lowest call premium first), after that, the call date (earliest call date first), and last, the maturity (longest maturity first). Following this formula leads you to Choice (D).
2. **A.** (Chapter 6) Common stockholders have equity (ownership) positions, as do preferred stockholders. However, bondholders are creditors, not owners.
3. **C.** (Chapter 6) Common stockholders of PXPX Corporation — or, for that matter, any publicly traded corporation — have a residual claim to the assets of the corporation at dissolution. PXPX Corp. common stockholders are entitled to receive a report containing audited financial statements on a yearly, *not* weekly, basis. Finally, PXPX Corp. stockholders never get to vote on dividends to be paid (whether stock or cash); dividends are decided by the board of directors.
4. **C.** (Chapter 13) Preferred stockholders and bondholders are subject to inflation risk. Inflation risk is the risk that the fixed interest or dividend payments will become worth less over time in terms of purchasing power. By purchasing convertible preferred stock, investors may convert their preferred stock into common stock of the same corporation at any time. Common stock has a greater chance of keeping pace with inflation, which reduces the inflation risk.
5. **B.** (Chapter 13) The quarterly dividend is \$0.30, which makes the annual dividend \$1.20 (\$0.30 × 4 quarters).

$$\text{current yield} = \frac{\text{annual dividends}}{\text{market price}} = \frac{\$1.20}{\$48.00} = 2.5\%$$

6. **D.** (Chapter 7) Government notes and bonds are quoted in 32nds. Therefore, a quote of 101-12 means 101 12/32, which translates to 101.375 (12 divided by 32 on your calculator equals 0.375). Next, you have to move the decimal point over one position to the right because bonds are quoted as a percentage of $1,000 par. So, the price of each bond is $1,013.75, and because the investor purchased ten bonds, the overall cost is $10,137.50.

7. **A.** (Chapter 7) You have to remember that accrued interest on U.S. government bonds is calculated in actual days instead of 30-day months like corporate and municipal bonds. U.S. government bonds settle in one business day from the trade date, so the settlement date is March 17th (3/17). Next, you need to subtract the previous coupon date, which is January 1st (1/1), from the settlement date.

3/17	January +1
1/1	February –2
2 months 16 days	–1
× 30	
60 + 16 = 76 – 1 = 75 days	

Next, multiply the 2 months by 30 days to get a total of 60 days. Then add the 16 days you get after subtracting 1 day from 17 days and you have a total of 76 days (60 + 16). Because U.S. government bonds are calculated in actual days, you need to add an extra day for January (31 days in January) and subtract 2 days for February (28 days in February). After subtracting the 1 from 76, you get an answer of 75 days. ***Note:*** Don't add or subtract days for the settlement month (in this case March) because you didn't go through the end of the month.

8. **B.** (Chapter 8) In order to determine the best investment for Jake, you must do a tax-equivalent yield (TEY) calculation. To accomplish this, you need to know Jake's tax bracket. Remember, the interest received from municipal bond investments is tax-free, and investors in higher tax brackets save more money by investing in municipal bonds when compared to other investments. The Series 7 examiners are testing you to make sure you know that the other items listed here are not relevant to the question.

9. **C.** (Chapter 12) For an investor to profit when holding a long call, the investor has to exercise the option when the market price is above the strike (exercise) price plus the premium paid.

10. **D.** (Chapter 7) Collateralized debt obligations (CDOs) are asset-backed securities backed by a pool of bonds, loans, or other debt instruments. CDOs are broken down into *tranches* (slices) of differing amounts of risks and/or maturities. Because of the complexity of these investments, they're not suitable for new or smaller investors; they're more suitable for institutional or sophisticated investors.

11. **D.** (Chapter 5) When a company decides to go public, it must file a registration statement with the SEC. The registration statement must include

    - The issuer's name and a description of its business
    - The names and addresses of all of the issuer's control persons (in other words, officers, directors, and investors owning 10 percent or more of the issuer's securities)
    - What the money raised will be used for
    - The capitalization of the issuer
    - Complete financial statements
    - Whether there are any legal proceedings against the issuer

12. **D.** (Chapter 5) The securities listed in this question are all nonexempt, meaning that they all have to register with the SEC. The Securities Act of 1933 requires all new nonexempt issues of securities sold to the public to be registered. In general, exempt issues include municipal securities, U.S. government securities, bank issues, private placements, intrastate offerings, and securities issued by nonprofit organizations.

13. **B.** (Chapter 5) Remember, new issues are always sold in the primary market regardless of whether they're municipal bonds or common stock. By contrast, sales of outstanding securities always take place in the secondary market.

14. **D.** (Chapter 16) A confirmation sent to a customer must disclose the amount of markup or markdown charged for a principal transaction in a NASDAQ security, whether the member acted in an agency or a principal capacity, and, if the member acted as an agent, the amount of commission.

15. **C.** (Chapter 10) Open-end and closed-end funds are considered management companies because they have actively managed portfolios and are defined as such according to the Investment Company Act of 1940. Because face amount certificate companies and unit trusts do not have actively managed portfolios, they're not considered management companies and have their own classification.

16. **A.** (Chapter 15) Qualified plans under IRS laws allow investors to invest money for retirement with *pre-tax dollars* (you can write qualified plan contributions off on your taxes). In addition, earnings accumulate on a *tax-deferred* basis (the investor isn't taxed until withdrawal). However, distributions (tax-deferred earnings and contributions) for which the participant receives a tax deduction are 100-percent taxable.

17. **D.** (Chapter 10) Tricky, tricky . . . the Series 7 examiners want to make sure you know that a variable annuity is derived from two separate products: an insurance contract and securities held in a separate account. Consequently, a variable annuity must be registered with the State Insurance Commission (for the insurance contract) and the Securities and Exchange Commission (for the securities held in the separate account).

18. **B.** (Chapter 16) The customer's signature is not required on a trade confirmation. However, the customer's account number, the registered rep's ID number, the trade date, whether the customer bought or sold, the number of shares or par value of bonds, the yield (if bonds), the CUSIP number, the price of the security, the total amount paid, the commission (if on an agency basis), and the net amount are all required on the confirmation.

19. **D.** (Chapter 16) The Telephone Act of 1991 is designed to set standards for individuals soliciting business. All of the choices listed are included in the act.

20. **B.** (Chapter 16) Recommendations made to a customer must fit that customer's objectives and risk tolerance. A review by a principal is necessary if the recommendations result in a trade. For the Series 7 exam purposes, individual recommendations are governed by FINRA, not the FRB (Federal Reserve Board).

21. **A.** (Chapter 16) If a registered representative believes that a customer is making an unsuitable trade, the representative may enter the order but must mark the order ticket "unsolicited." In this question, the client is making a trade that you believe is unsuitable for her, but you can still execute the trade as long as you mark the order ticket as "unsolicited," which will protect you and make your client happy.

22. **B.** (Chapter 15) I recommend that you set up the equation as if you're dealing with one bond and then multiply the answer by 10 at the end. Mr. Jefferson purchased the bonds at $1,050 (105 percent of 1,000 par) and the bonds are maturing at $1,000 par. So as far as the IRS is concerned, Mr. Jefferson is losing $5 per year ($50 loss divided by 10 years) on the value of a bond. Because he sold the bonds in three years, the total amount of amortization per bond would be $15. After subtracting the $15 from the $1,050 purchase price, you

see that the new cost basis is $1,035. After three years, Mr. Jefferson should sell the bonds for $1,035 each to break even. Because the bonds were sold for $1,020 (102 percent of 1,000 par), he had a loss of $15 per bond. Because Mr. Jefferson had 10 bonds, he had a capital loss of $150.

$$\$1{,}050 \xrightarrow{\text{10 years}} \$1{,}000$$

$$\$50 = \$5 \text{ per year amortization}$$

$$\$5 \times 3 \text{ years} = \$15 \text{ total amortization}$$

$$\$1{,}050 - \$15 \text{ amortization} = \$1{,}035(\text{new cost basis})$$

$$\$1{,}035(\text{new cost basis}) - \$1{,}020(\text{selling price}) = \$15 \text{ loss per bond} \times 10 \text{ bonds} = \$150 \text{ loss}$$

23. **A.** (Chapter 15) Progressive taxes are ones in which high-income individuals are taxed at a higher rate than low-income individuals. Examples of progressive taxes are personal income, gift, and estate taxes. Regressive taxes are ones in which all individuals are taxed at the same rate. Regressive taxes include payroll, sales, property, excise, gasoline, and so on.

24. **D.** (Chapter 16) The Bank Secrecy Act establishes the U.S. Treasury Department as the regulator of anti-money-laundering programs. As such, all broker-dealers are required to have programs set up to help detect the possibility of money laundering. Broker-dealers must also review the OFAC's (Office of Foreign Asset Control's) SDN (Specially Designated Nationals) list to determine that they're not doing business with organizations or individuals that are on the list.

25. **A.** (Chapter 10) Life-cycle funds are actually funds of funds, which are based on an investor's age. Investors buy a life-cycle fund designed for people their age. Life-cycle funds adjust their holdings every so often so that investors are taking less risk as they get older. Because younger investors can afford to take more risk, a larger percentage of their portfolio is in equities and less is in fixed-income securities. As investors get older, they should have an increasing number of fixed-income securities and less equity securities. Life-cycle funds automatically take care of that for investors.

26. **B.** (Chapter 16) The *ex-date* or *ex-dividend date* is two business days before the record date and is the date that the buyer would be purchasing the stock without a dividend. On the ex-date, the stock is *reduced* by the amount of the dividend. The corporation is still responsible for paying the dividend, and because the buyer isn't entitled to it, the seller is.

27. **D.** (Chapter 13) Investors in foreign securities face all the risks listed along with a few others, depending on the type of securities held. Political (legislative) risk is the risk that the value of a security may suffer due to instability or political changes in a country. Currency risk is the risk that the value of an investment may be affected due to a change in exchange rates. Regulatory risk is the risk that legislative changes may affect the market.

28. **B.** (Chapter 7) EE bonds are U.S. government savings bonds like the ones your grandparents used to give you when all you really wanted was the GI Joe doll with the kung-fu grip. EE bonds are purchased at a discount from the face value and mature at their face value several years later. Because they're U.S. government bonds, the default risk is extremely small. Accrued interest is exempt from state and local taxes but not federal taxes, and the EE bonds may be purchased in denominations as small as $25 when purchased electronically or $50 for an actual paper certificate.

29. **C.** (Chapter 8) No, the Series 7 examiners did not make a typo by using the word "broker" twice. A broker's broker helps sell any bonds a syndicate has left and doesn't disclose the identity of the firm on whose behalf it is acting. Brokers' brokers act solely as agents for the firm on whose behalf the broker's broker is acting; they do not prepare bids or serve as wholesalers.

30. **A.** (Chapter 12) The easiest way for you to see what's going on is to set up an options chart. This investor wrote (sold) the XYZ put for a premium of 2.75, so you have to put $275 (2.75 × 100 shares per option) in the "Money In" side of the chart because the investor received the money for selling the option. Next, the option was exercised, so you have to put $3,000 (the 30 strike price × 100 shares per option) in the "Money Out" side of the chart because "puts switch," meaning that the exercised option has to go on the opposite side of the chart from the premium. After that, the investor sold the 100 shares of stock in the market for $27.50 per share for a total of $2,750, which goes in the "Money In" side of the chart because the investor received money for selling the stock. Total up the two sides and you see that the investor received $3,025 and spent $3,000 for a whopping profit of $25.

Money Out	Money In
$3,000	$275
	$2,750
$3,000	$3,025

$3,025(money in) – $3,000(money out) = $25 gain

31. **D.** (Chapter 12) The easiest way for you to see what's going on is to set up an options chart. Mrs. Smith purchased 100 shares of ABC at 35, so you have to put $3,500 (35 × 100 shares) in the "Money Out" side of the chart. Next, Mrs. Smith wrote (sold) an ABC call for 5.50, so you have to put $550 (5.50 × 100 shares per option) in the "Money In" side of the chart. After the stock increased, the call was exercised, so you have to put the exercised strike price of $4,000 (40 strike price × 100 shares per option) under its premium of $550 because "calls same," meaning that for call options, the premium and the exercised strike price go on the same side of the chart. Total up the two sides and you see that Mrs. Smith had a gain of $1,050.

Money Out	Money In
$3,500	$550
	$4,000
$3,500	$4,550

$4,550(money in) – $3,500(money out) = $1,050 gain

32. **D.** (Chapter 8) Factors that affect the marketability (how easy it is to buy and sell) of municipal GO (general obligation) bonds are the quality, maturity date, call features, coupon rate, block size, dollar price, issuer's name, sinking fund, and credit enhancements (in other words, insurance).

33. **B.** (Chapter 16) You will find that this is not an unusual situation. When you're opening an account for a new customer, the customer may not feel comfortable sharing all her financial information with you. However, you can still do trading in the account and make recommendations if you can determine financial information from other sources, such as D&B cards. Say, for example, that the D&B card says that the customer is the CEO of a corporation that made $5 billion last year. You can assume the customer has a lot of money. The recommendations you make to a customer should be suitable to her investment objectives and financial situation. If you can't determine the information from other sources, you can still make trades and recommendations that would be suitable for all investors, such as mutual funds or U.S. government securities.

34. **D.** (Chapter 9) Because this margin account has a debit balance, it's a long account; short accounts have a credit balance. The easiest way to deal with margin questions of this type is to set up a long margin account formula:

LMV – DR = EQ

LMV = Long Market Value (the current market value of the stocks held in the account)

DR = The Debit Record or Debit Balance (the amount borrowed from the broker-dealer plus any interest)

EQ = Equity (the owner's portion of the account)

LMV – DR = EQ

\$20,250 – \$3,000 = \$17,250

Reg. T × LMV = \$10,125

\$7,125 excess equity

Because the LMV equals \$20,250 and the DR equals \$3,000, the EQ has to be \$17,250. From there, you have to compare what the investor should have in equity to be at 50 percent (Regulation T) of the LMV with what is actually in equity. With Regulation T at 50 percent, which is standard, the investor should have \$10,125 in EQ to be at 50 percent. However, the investor actually has \$7,125 more than that, so that is the investor's excess equity.

35. **B.** (Chapter 5) A preliminary prospectus includes the purpose for the funds and financial statements. Because a preliminary prospectus (red herring) is printed before the final price is established, it may include a projected price range that is subject to change.

36. **C.** (Chapter 5) Certain purchases, such as a Regulation D private placement, may require investors to be accredited (although they have a 35 unaccredited investor exclusion). Accredited investors are ones with a net worth of at least \$1 million excluding any equity they may have in their primary residence, or ones with an annual income of at least \$200,000 (or \$300,000 for joint accounts) for the last two (not three) years that's expected to stay at least the same for the current year.

37. **A.** (Chapter 14) Here's another of those annoying EXCEPT questions that require a false answer. DMMs (Designated Market Makers) place orders in their book that are away from the current market price. Market orders are for immediate execution at the best price available, so there's no reason to place them in a book.

38. **B.** (Chapter 12) OPRA (Options Price Reporting Authority) provides last sale information and current options quotations provided by participating exchanges. OPRA collects the information from NYSE Amex Equities, formerly the American Stock Exchange (Amex), the Boston Stock Exchange (BSE), the Chicago Board Options Exchange (CBOE), the International Securities Exchange (ISE), and the Philadelphia Stock Exchange (PHLX). After the information is collected from all the exchanges, OPRA consolidates and disseminates the information.

39. **B.** (Chapter 16) The SEC and FINRA require member firms to send customer account statements at least quarterly (once every 3 months) for inactive accounts. To help you remember how often account statements should be sent out, think "AIM":

    A = Active account (monthly)

    I = Inactive account (quarterly)

    M = Mutual fund (semi-annually)

40. **C.** (Chapter 10) Hybrid REITs (Real Estate Investment Trusts) trade on an exchange, provide mortgage loans to developers, and hold a portfolio of securities. Hybrid REITs are a combination of equity (ownership) and mortgage REITs.

41. **D.** (Chapter 9) When a corporation opens a margin account, the corporation has to provide a corporate charter, which needs to say that the corporation can buy securities on margin, and a corporate resolution, which says who has the trading authority for the account. A new account form is always needed for any type of account. The corporation

also needs a hypothecation agreement, which allows the broker-dealer to hold the securities in street name so that they can be used as collateral for a loan. In addition, the corporation needs a credit agreement, which sets the terms for the loan.

42. **C.** (Chapter 8) The Municipal Bond Index is the average dollar price of 40 highly-traded GO and revenue bonds with an average maturity of 20 years and a rating of "A" or better.

43. **A.** (Chapter 11) The certificate of limited partnership is the legal agreement between the general and limited partners and is the only partnership paperwork that needs to be filed with the secretary of state. The certificate of limited partnership includes the primary place of business, the names and addresses of the limited and general partner(s), the objectives of the partnership, the amount contributed by each partner, the roles of the partners, and so on.

44. **A.** (Chapter 13) Certainly, any information you can get about your client will help you set up a portfolio that fits the client's needs. However, because Martina's primary investment objective is making sure that she's prepared for retirement, you need to begin by looking at her age. Someone who is younger can take more risk than someone who is older.

45. **D.** (Chapter 16) Pursuant to Conduct Rules (not the SEC), registered representatives may never guarantee a customer against losses; therefore, this action is never permitted. If the investor wanted to sell the shares, he would have to sell them at the bid price of $12.40, not $14.25.

46. **D.** (Chapter 7) The expression "quality over quantity" applies here. Rating services are concerned with quality, defined as the issuer's (or guarantor's) default risk or ability to pay interest and principal on time. The two biggest rating services are Moody's and Standard & Poor's. The highest ratings for these rating services are Aaa and AAA, respectively.

47. **A.** (Chapter 9) Remember, you can't tender stock that is borrowed, and stock in a short account is borrowed stock.

48. **D.** (Chapter 16) All order tickets need to include the items listed in the question plus the customer's account number; the number of shares or bonds being purchased or sold; whether the customer is buying, selling, or selling short; whether the customer is covered or uncovered (option orders); whether it's a market order, good-till-canceled, and so on.

49. **C.** (Chapter 8) Because municipal securities are exempt from SEC registration, they're not subject to the FINRA 5-percent markup policy.

50. **C.** (Chapter 6) Cumulative voting allows shareholders to aggregate (combine) their votes and vote for whomever they please. For argument's sake, if an investor owned 1,000 common shares and there were four members of the board of directors open for vote, the investor could use all of the 4,000 votes (1,000 shares × 4 members) for a single candidate, if desired. Cumulative voting can be used to make it easier for smaller shareholders to gain representation on the board of directors.

51. **D.** (Chapter 6) The purpose of ADRs (American Depositary Receipts) is to facilitate the trading of foreign securities in U.S. markets. ADRs carry currency risk because distributions on ADRs must be converted from foreign currency to U.S. dollars on the date of distribution. The trading price of the ADR is actually quite affected by currency fluctuation, which can devalue any dividends and/or the value of the stock.

52. **A.** (Chapter 7) CMOs are backed by home mortgages, which are considered to be very safe (although not as safe as in previous years), and therefore are generally rated AAA.

53. **D.** (Chapter 5) An Eastern account has undivided responsibility and undivided liability for any bonds that remain unsold by other syndicate members, meaning that a syndicate member is responsible for a percentage of bonds left unsold.

54. **D.** (Chapter 16) After receiving Keith's written complaint, the municipal securities broker-dealer must accept the complaint and write down any action taken to resolve the complaint. All broker-dealers should keep a complaint file for each customer and keep accurate records of any communications or actions taken regarding a complaint.

55. **C.** (Chapter 8) EMMA (Electronic Municipal Market Access) is a centralized online site that nonprofessional, retail investors can use to locate key information about municipal securities. Available on this site are official statements for most new municipal bond offerings and up-to-the-minute access to prices for outstanding municipal bonds.

56. **C.** (Chapter 12) You have to remember that sellers (shorters or writers) of options always face more risk than buyers; the buyer's risk is limited to the amount invested. However, sellers of put options do not face a maximum loss potential that's unlimited because put options go in-the-money when the price of the stock goes down below the strike price, and it can only go down to 0. Sellers of uncovered calls face a maximum loss potential that is unlimited because call options go in-the-money when the price of the stock goes above the strike price, and the seller has to purchase the stock at a price that could go higher and higher. Additionally, investors who short stock as in Statement II face a maximum loss potential that's unlimited because the investors have taken a bearish position and lose money when the price of the security increases, and there's nothing stopping the stock from increasing in value. Investors who have sold covered calls don't face an unlimited maximum loss potential because they have the stock to deliver if exercised.

57. **D.** (Chapter 12) These trades aren't suitable for any investor because it's impossible for the investor to make a profit. I've set up an options chart to demonstrate to you how this is so. First, put the premiums for the options in the chart. Because the investor bought the May 30 call option at 8, you have to put $800 (8 premium × 100 shares per option) in the "Money Out" side of the chart. Next, put $300 (3 premium × 100 shares per option) in the "Money In" side of the chart because the investor sold that option. Because the investor has $800 out and $300 in, you know that the investor's maximum loss potential is $500 ($800 – $300). To get the maximum gain, you have to exercise both options. Because "calls same," you have to put the exercised strike prices below their respective premiums in the chart. Place $3,000 (30 strike price × 100 shares per option) under its premium of $800 and place $3,500 (35 strike price × 100 shares per option) under its premium of $300. After that, you have to total the sides to see that because the "Money In" side and the "Money Out" side of the chart each equal $3,800, there's no way the investor can make a profit.

Money Out	Money In
$800	$300
$3,000	$3,500
$3,800	$3,800

58. **C.** (Chapter 15) Remember that short-term gains or losses are ones that take place in one year or less. The fact that Fred purchased a call option does not affect his holding period on the stock that he purchased. Because Fred has held the stock for 19 months (1 year and 7 months), the sale of the stock would be treated as a long-term capital gain or long-term capital loss.

59. **D.** (Chapter 16) No rules prohibit opening an account registered as joint tenants with rights of survivorship (JTWROS) for two unmarried persons. The registered representative should, however, take all steps to be sure that the unmarried individuals understand the resulting consequences should one party to the account die. For example, in an account registered JTWROS, if one of the engaged parties to the account (for example, John Dow) dies, the deceased party's ownership interest in the account passes to the surviving tenant (Jane Dough) rather than to the deceased party's (John Dow's) estate.

60. **D.** (Chapter 16) Under the terms of the Uniform Gifts to Minors Act, the account must be handed over to the new adult when a minor reaches the age of majority. You don't need to know the age of majority because it varies from state to state, but it's usually between the ages of 18 and 21.

61. **B.** (Chapter 9) Because this margin account has a debit balance, it's a long account; short accounts have a credit balance. The easiest way to deal with margin questions of this type is to set up a long margin account formula:

LMV – DR = EQ

LMV = Long Market Value (the current market value of the stocks held in the account)

DR = The Debit Balance or Debit Record (the amount borrowed from the broker-dealer plus any interest)

EQ = Equity (the owner's portion of the account)

LMV – DR = EQ

$18,000 – $7,000 = $11,000

Reg. T × LMV = <u>$9,000</u>

$2,000 excess equity

Because the LMV equals $18,000 and the DR equals $7,000, the EQ has to be $11,000. From there, you have to compare what the investor should have in equity to be at 50 percent (Regulation T) of the LMV with what is actually in equity. With Regulation T at 50 percent, which is standard, the investor should have $9,000 in EQ to be at 50 percent. However, because the investor has $11,000 in equity, the excess equity is $2,000.

Because the account has excess equity (SMA), it has buying power. Remember, it is SMA/RT to use your buying power, which tells you that you need to divide the SMA by Regulation T to determine the buying power:

SMA/RT = SMA / Regulation T = $2,000 / 50% = $4,000

Long accounts like this one generate excess equity by the securities held in the account increasing in value.

If the investor withdraws the excess equity, she's essentially borrowing more money from the account and the debit balance increases, not decreases.

62. **C.** (Chapter 9) A day-trading account requires an initial margin of $25,000, and the investor must keep $25,000 minimum equity in the account to keep trading. A portfolio margin account is relatively new and looks at the risk of the portfolio as a whole to determine the margin requirement. Only certain investors are able to take advantage of portfolio margin because it requires a certain degree of sophistication and a minimum equity of around $150,000.

63. **A.** (Chapter 12) Because of the additional risk involved when investing in options, such as the ability to lose all money invested or facing unlimited maximum loss, all investors must receive an ODD (Options risk Disclosure Document) prior to the first transaction. The ODD is not an advertisement; it contains the pitfalls of investing in options. After the customer receives the ODD, the ROP (Registered Options Principal) has to approve the account. Next, you can do the trade, and after that, the customer has to sign and return an OAA (Options Account Agreement).

64. **C.** (Chapter 14) When several bids or offers are made at the same price at a given time on the NYSE floor, the auction rules of priority (highest bid and lowest ask first), precedence (if orders are at the same price, the one that came in first is executed first), and parity (if all else is equal, the larger order is done first) allow for the efficient execution of orders.

65. **C.** (Chapter 14) The Designated Market Maker (DMM or Specialist) is responsible for maintaining a fair and orderly market on the NYSE floor.

66. **D.** (Chapter 16) The 5-percent markup policy is a guideline for broker-dealers to use when executing trades of outstanding securities for public customers. In most cases, for a standard-sized trade of nonexempt securities, broker-dealers should not charge a commission, markup, or markdown that is in excess of 5 percent. The 5-percent policy applies to both commission charges on agency transactions and to markups and markdowns on principal transactions, including riskless and simultaneous transactions.

67. **D.** (Chapter 16) This is an EXCEPT question, and you must find the false answer. Good delivery between brokers requires delivery of certificates to be in multiples of 100 shares (100, 200, 300, and so on), divisors of 100 shares (1, 2, 4, 5, 10, 20, 25, 50), or shares that add up to 100 (for example, 60 + 40, 70 + 30, or 75 + 25). The odd-lot portion of the trade (the 70 shares) is exempt from the rule; in other words, you could have one certificate for 70 shares. Choices (A), (B), and (C) are all considered good delivery; however, Choice (D) is not because the 10 certificates for 30 shares don't match up with any other tickets that can get it to equal 100.

68. **B.** (Chapter 14) Remember that stop orders are used for protection. Because Skippy owns the stock, he would have to enter a sell stop order below the market price of the security. In the event that the price of the stock hits or drops below the stop price, the order would be triggered and the stock would be sold on the next transaction.

69. **B.** (Chapter 10) As with most other investment company products, REITs have a professionally managed portfolio. Many investors use REITs as a potential hedge against a downturn in the market because often there is an inverse relationship between the real estate market and stock prices. In addition, REITs typically have a high degree of liquidity. However, there is no preferential dividend treatment for REITs.

70. **A.** (Chapter 8) The official statement for a municipal bond issue is similar to a prospectus for a corporate issue. The items that you find on an official statement include the offering terms, the underwriting spread, a description of the bonds, a description of the issuer, the offering price, the coupon rate, the feasibility statement, and the legal opinion.

71. **B.** (Chapter 10) When an investor of a variable annuity starts withdrawing money from the annuity, the accumulation units are converted into a fixed number of annuity units. However, the value of the annuity units varies based on the performance of the securities held in the separate account.

72. **C.** (Chapter 11) Because direct participation programs (limited partnerships) may require limited partners to come up with additional cash beyond their initial investment, investors must provide a written verification of net worth. After the general partner signs the subscription agreement, the investor is accepted as a limited partner.

73. **D.** (Chapter 13) The Federal Reserve Board was established in 1913 to stabilize the country's chaotic financial system. It performs all the services listed in Choices (A), (B), and (C), in addition to other duties it performs; therefore, Choice (D) is correct.

74. **B.** (Chapter 13) A head and shoulders bottom formation (inverted head and shoulders formation) is a bullish sign because it means that the stock hit a bottom and is starting to reverse. In other words, a head and shoulders bottom formation is a bullish sign because it's the reversal of a bearish trend.

75. **C.** (Chapter 12) Because Michael owns 1,000 shares of WOW stock and wants to generate additional income, he could sell covered calls against the WOW that he owns. Additionally, by placing a sell-stop order for WOW slightly below the market price, Michael is protected against a major loss if WOW drops significantly.

76. **B.** (Chapter 12) The easiest way for you to see what's going on is to set up an options chart. Your customer purchased 100 shares of ARGH at 44.10, so you have to put $4,410 (44.10 × 100 shares) in the "Money Out" side of the chart. Next, your customer purchased an OEX put for 4.50, so you have to put $450 (4.50 × 100 shares per option) in the "Money Out" side of the chart. If your customer closes the stock position (to close means to do the opposite . . . if he originally bought, to close, he has to sell) for 42.55, you have to put

$4,255 (42.55 stock price × 100 shares) in the "Money In" side of the chart. Then, because you're dealing with an option that settles in cash instead of delivery of the underlying security, you need to put the profit of $1,100 in the "Money In" side of the chart. To get the $1,100, you have to remember that put options go in-the-money when the price of the stock goes below the strike price, which it is by 11 (360 – 349), and options are for 100 shares. Total up the two sides, and you see that your customer has a profit of $495.

Money Out	Money In
$4,410	$4,255
$450	$1,100
$4,860	$5,355

$\$5{,}355(\text{money in}) - \$4{,}860(\text{money out}) = \$495 \text{ gain}$

77. **A.** (Chapter 14) If you chose "Level IV," you need to be aware that there is no Level IV. Level I is the most basic level of NASDAQ and the one that you're most likely to have on the computer on your desk (or at least near you). Level I includes up-to-the-minute inside bid and ask prices for several hundred OTC stocks. Level I shows subject quotes because they're subject to change as trades take place.
78. **A.** (Chapter 16) Here's that EXCEPT question type again! You're looking for a false answer here. Although a custodian may open an account with an agent for a minor, a designated officer may open a corporate account with an agent, and a designated partner may open a partnership account with an agent, an agent is not permitted to open an individual account in the name of a third person. This means that Choice (A) is the correct false answer that you're looking for.
79. **B.** (Chapter 9) This question is a tough one because of the way that it's worded. I suggest that you write "increases SMA," "decreases SMA," or "doesn't change SMA" next to each possible answer before answering the question.

    I. Selling securities in a margin account increases the SMA by half the amount of the sale and decreases the debit balance by half the amount of the sale (increases SMA)

    II. The purchase of additional securities in a long margin account has no affect on the SMA unless using the buying power, which you can't assume (doesn't change SMA)

    III. Money being deposited into the margin account by way of cash dividend or cash payment increases the SMA by the amount of the deposit (increases SMA)

    IV. A decrease in the market value of the securities doesn't change the SMA. Remember, you don't lose SMA until you use it (doesn't change SMA)

    Now that you have this part down, look at the question again to see what it's asking. Because this is an EXCEPT question, you're looking for the statements that do not increase the SMA, which are Statements II and IV.
80. **B.** (Chapter 5) The spread is the sum of the manager's fee ($0.15) and the takedown ($0.50): $0.15 + $0.50 = $0.65. The selling concession is paid out of the takedown and is not added to the spread equation.
81. **C.** (Chapter 14) First market is listed securities trading on an exchange. Second market is unlisted securities trading OTC (over-the-counter). Third market is listed securities trading OTC. Fourth market is institutional trading without using a broker-dealer.
82. **B.** (Chapter 14) Level III is where market makers enter their firm quotes and is the most complete access level of NASDAQ. Level II and Level III display all market makers and their firm quotes, and viewing is not limited to the highest bid and lowest ask. Level II is used by traders. Level I is the level used by registered representatives and displays the highest bid and lowest ask prices.

83. **D.** (Chapter 16) Under the Investment Company Act of 1940, mutual funds must provide semiannual reports to shareholders. To help you remember how often account statements should be sent out, think "AIM":

    A = Active account (monthly)

    I = Inactive account (quarterly)

    M = Mutual fund (semiannually)

84. **B.** (Chapter 16) Selling dividends is a violation in which a registered representative entices an investor to purchase a security in time to receive a previously declared dividend. Remember, there is no advantage to purchasing a security prior to the ex-dividend date (the first day the security trades without a dividend) because the price of the stock is reduced by the amount of the dividend on the ex-dividend date. Therefore, even though a customer might receive a $0.50 dividend, the price of the stock is reduced by $0.50, so there's no advantage.

85. **A.** (Chapter 16) The Bank Secrecy Act establishes the U.S. Treasury Department as the regulator for anti-money-laundering programs. All broker-dealers are required to develop programs to detect possible money-laundering abuses.

86. **C.** (Chapter 11) Real estate DPPs (direct participation programs — limited partnerships) provide advantages for investors such as depreciation deductions, appreciation potential, and cash flow, but not depletion. Depletion only applies to partnerships that deal in natural resources that can be depleted (used up), such as oil or gas.

87. **B.** (Chapter 13) In this question, if the GDP (Gross Domestic Product) is declining, business is slowing down and possibly heading towards a recession, and the Fed would want to stimulate the economy by making more money available. Increasing the money supply through lower interest rates usually increases business activity. However, when there are declining yields and interest rates, and rising house prices, there is a danger of increased inflation if the Fed increases (eases) the money supply.

88. **C.** (Chapter 13) Research reports are documents prepared and sent out by research analysts. During the "quiet period," firms are restricted from publishing or distributing research reports until at least 10 days after the IPO (initial public offering). Information barriers are designed to protect research analysts from outside influence. Third-party disclosures are required if a brokerage firm hires an outside analyst to do research. Open market operations are when the federal reserve board buys and sells U.S. government securities; therefore, Choice (C) is the correct answer.

89. **A.** (Chapter 13) The FDIC (Federal Deposit Insurance Corporation) provides depositors insurance against failed (bankrupt) banks for up to $250,000. SIPC protects investors from broker-dealer failure up to $500,000, of which no more than $250,000 can be cash.

90. **D.** (Chapter 8) Because the investor bought 50 of each bond, they were all rated AA, and they mature around the same time, you can rule out maturity, quality, and quantity as your answers. The investor's funds are an example of geographic diversification because the bonds are from a variety of issuers around the United States.

91. **A.** (Chapter 12) Although you may not need an options chart to figure out the answer to this one, creating a chart is good practice, and I think it lessens your chances of making mistakes. First, because the customer purchased the option for 4.50, you need to place $450 (4.50 × 100 shares per option) in the "Money Out" portion of the chart. Next, you have to close the option for 4.55 because you buy at the ask price and sell at the bid price. To close the option, the customer has to do the opposite of what he did originally; if he originally bought the option, as he did here, to close, he has to sell. So you need to put $455 in the "Money In" side of the chart. Now you can see that the customer had a $5 gain because he received $455 for selling the option and paid $450 for buying the option.

Money Out	Money In
$450	$455

92. **A.** (Chapter 12) To hedge means to protect. If the investor would like to hedge his position, he should buy a call on XYZ. Remember that the investor is short the stock and must buy XYZ back at some point to close his short position. Buying an XYZ call gives the investor the right to buy back XYZ at a fixed price, which would allow the investor to protect the position and not face an unlimited maximum loss potential.

93. **A.** (Chapter 12) The easiest way for you to see what's going on is to set up an options chart. Because Grant bought the put for 350 (3.50 × 100 shares per option) and the stock for 6,200 (62 × 100 shares), you need to put "350" and "6,200" in the "Money Out" side of the chart. Next, Grant sold the stock for $6,400 (64 × 100 shares) and closed (do the opposite — if originally you bought, to close you have to sell) the option for $75 (0.75 × 100 shares per option). So you have to put "$6,400" and "$75" in the "Money In" side of the chart. Total up the two sides and you see that he had a $75 loss.

Money Out	Money In
$350	$6,400
$6,200	$75
$6,550	$6,475

$\$6{,}550(\text{money out}) - \$6{,}475(\text{money in}) = \$75 \text{ loss}$

94. **C.** (Chapter 15) Options are always taxed as capital gains or capital losses. This investor purchased an option that expired worthless, and, therefore, he lost money. Because the investor held the leap for over one year, it's taxed as a long-term capital loss.

95. **C.** (Chapter 16) Without having discretionary authority, registered representatives may not decide on whether to buy or sell, the security to purchase or sell, or the amount of shares or dollar amount to purchase for the customer. Registered representatives may, however, without written power of attorney, choose the price or timing of an order.

96. **D.** (Chapter 5) You must distinguish a nonexempt security from an exempt security. A non-exempt security is one that is not exempt from SEC registration; in other words, it must be registered with the SEC. Variable annuities, which carry investment risk, are nonexempt securities under the Securities Act of 1933 and must be registered before public sale. Similarly, unit trusts and mutual funds are nonexempt even though the underlying securities may be exempt, such as municipals and U.S. government securities. However, a fixed annuity is an insurance product exempt from registration with the SEC. It's not considered a security because of the guaranteed payout.

97. **B.** (Chapter 10) A specialized or sector fund invests a minimum of 25 percent of its assets in a particular region or industry and would be the most suitable for Buddy.

98. **D.** (Chapter 11) Intangible drilling costs (IDCs), the costs involved in actually getting to the oil, provide a tax benefit to investors of an oil and gas exploratory (wildcatting) program. IDCs are items such as labor and surveys. IDCs are deductible expenses in the year in which they occur.

99. **D.** (Chapter 13) If you look at the answer choices carefully, you'll see that Choices (A) and (D) are opposite, which tells you that one of them has to be true. When the U.S. dollar loses value compared to a foreign currency, U.S exports increase because foreign currency strengthens in comparison and now buys more dollars. As a result, U.S. goods are cheaper than normal for foreign consumers.

100. **C.** (Chapter 12) The easiest way for you to see what's going on is to set up an options chart. Ginny purchased 2 calls and 2 puts, so the first thing you should do is put the multiplier of "× 2" on the outside of the chart; this way, it's as if you're dealing with single options. Because she bought the calls for 300 each (3 × 100 shares per option) and the puts for 200 each (2 × 100 shares per option), you need to put "300" and "200" in the "Money Out" side of the chart. Next, Ginny closed her options for their intrinsic value (the in-the-money amount). Because put options go in-the-money when the price of the stock

goes below the strike price, just the put option is in-the-money, not the call option. With the strike price at $44.50 and the strike price at 50, the put is 5.50 in-the-money ($50.00 – $44.50). So you need to put $550 in the "Money In" side of the chart because Ginny closed the option (to close means to do the opposite — if you originally bought, you have to sell to close). Total up the two sides and you see that Ginny had a profit of $50 per option. Because Ginny bought 2 options, she had a profit of $100.

(x2) Money Out	Money In
$300	$550
$200	
$500	$550

$$\$550(\text{money in}) - \$500(\text{money out}) = \$50 \text{ gain per option} \times 2 = \$100 \text{ gain}$$

101. **B.** (Chapter 13) CMOs (collateralized mortgage obligations) offer no tax advantages to buyers. However, the interest received on municipal bonds is federally tax-free and sometimes state-tax-free. In addition, retirement plans allow investors to deposit money tax-free (in most cases) and the money grows on a tax-deferred basis. DPPs (direct participation programs) allow for additional write-offs, such as depreciation and depletion, which provide for a cash flow that's greater than the net income.

102. **B.** (Chapter 12) She is trying to generate income, so she has to sell something. The only answer that has her selling something is Choice (B). Writing (selling) a straddle would allow her to generate income on a stock that's remaining stable, because she would receive the premiums for selling the straddle and be able to profit if neither the call option nor the put option that are part of the straddle go too much in-the-money.

103. **A.** (Chapter 6) Adjustable (floating rate) preferred stock receives a dividend that adjusts according to prevailing interest rates.

104. **B.** (Chapter 14) Regulation SHO covers the short sale of securities. According to Regulation SHO, all order tickets must be marked as short sale (as compared to long sale). In addition, brokerage firms must establish rules to locate, borrow, and deliver securities that are to be sold short.

105. **D.** (Chapter 7) The bond indenture (deed of trust) is the legal agreement between the issuer and investors. The bond indenture includes the maturity date, the par value, the coupon rate, any collateral securing the bond, any callable or convertible features, and the name of the trustee.

106. **A.** (Chapter 16) The Legal List is for fiduciaries (a *fiduciary* is someone who can legally make decisions for another investor). Fiduciaries are subject to the "Prudent Investor Rule," which means that they must invest in securities on the state's legal list or, if there isn't one, invest in securities that only a prudent investor would purchase.

107. **D.** (Chapter 11) All the choices listed are important to evaluate for investors of direct participation programs.

108. **C.** (Chapter 15) Withdrawals must begin by April 1st of the year after the investor turns age 70½. At that point, the investor has to take a required minimum distribution (RMD), which can be determined by looking at the IRS's required minimum distribution worksheet.

109. **C.** (Chapter 7) Repurchase agreements (REPOs) are usually initiated by commercial banks. Repurchase agreements enable banks to borrow money from the Fed (Federal Reserve Board) to help meet reserve requirements. This feat is accomplished with the sale of securities (typically overnight), which includes an agreement to buy the securities back at a higher price.

110. **D.** (Chapter 11) An oil and gas wildcatting (exploratory) program would best suit your client's needs. Oil and gas wildcatting programs drill in unproven areas and create quite a lot of write-offs in the early years. However, if oil is hit, a wildcatting program will bring in a lot of money.

111. **B.** (Chapter 8) Remember that state governments do not collect ad-valorem (property) taxes. Ad-valorem taxes are assessed by local governments (for example, towns and counties). Generally, state governments receive the most income from income taxes and sales taxes.

112. **D.** (Chapter 16) The Series 7 examiners may try to trip you up by throwing in an irrelevant answer choice (like the date of maturity) to find out whether you know your MSRB (municipal securities rulemaking board) rules. MSRB rules require that confirmations include whether the trade was executed on a principal (dealer) or agency basis. The amount of the dealer's markup or markdown on a principal trade does not have to be disclosed, but the commission on an agency trade does need to be disclosed.

113. **A.** (Chapter 10) If John wants to profit from a possible decline in the market, he has to employ bearish strategies. Inverse ETFs (exchange-traded funds) are funds that trade on an exchange and use derivative products, such as options, to attempt to profit from a decline in the underlying securities, such as the S&P 500. Selling SPX (S&P 500) calls is a bearish strategy in which the seller profits if the underlying securities stay the same or decline in value. High-yielding bond funds (junk bond funds) are more likely to be damaged if the market declines in value, and selling OEX (S&P 100) puts is a bullish, not bearish, strategy.

114. **B.** (Chapter 13) When you're determining the dividend payout ratio, you have to remember that the formula is as follows:

$$\text{dividend payout ratio} = \frac{\text{annual dividends per common share}}{\text{EPS(earnings per share)}}$$

Because this question gives you the quarterly dividend, you need to multiply by 4 to get the annual dividend of \$1.00 (\$0.25 × 4).

$$\text{dividend payout ratio} = \frac{\$1.00}{\$2.50} = 40\%$$

115. **A.** (Chapter 15) Municipal original issue discount bonds must be accreted; the discount is treated as part of the investor's tax-free interest. Because these municipal discount bonds must be accreted, the cost basis is equal to the par value, and, as a tax consequence, Gerry will have no losses or gains if he holds the bond to maturity.

116. **B.** (Chapter 16) The Trust Indenture Act of 1939 regulates all corporate bond issues exceeding \$5 million. Treasury bonds and municipal bonds, such as general obligation bonds and revenue bonds, are exempt.

117. **C.** (Chapter 16) As you can see, the one common denominator is that all the answer choices have the word "FINRA" in them, which tells you that being a FINRA member must be pretty important. The Code of Arbitration is mandatory in member-against-member disputes including a member firm and one of its registered reps. However, FINRA has no jurisdiction over banks or over disputes between nonmembers such as customers or issuers; in cases such as these, the nonmember decides whether to use arbitration or a Code of Procedure hearing to settle a dispute.

118. **D.** (Chapter 15) There are no tax consequences to Duke for converting a bond into shares of common stock. In order for Duke to have a taxable gain or loss, the shares Duke received as a result of his conversion to common stock must be sold.

119. **B.** (Chapter 14) A designated market maker cannot compete with public orders, so Choices (A) and (C) are no good. The responsibility of a designated market maker is to keep trading as active as possible by narrowing the spread if necessary. Therefore, the only answer that works is Choice (B) because that answer is in-between the bid and ask prices.

120. **D.** (Chapter 8) Municipal short-term notes such as RANs (revenue anticipation notes), BANs (bond anticipation notes), TANs (tax anticipation notes), and CLNs (construction loan notes) are used to provide short-term (interim) financing until a permanent, long-term bond issue is floated, until tax receipts increase, or until revenue flows in.

121. **A.** (Chapter 7) You can assume that bonds normally make interest payments semiannually (once every 6 months). However, because the first payment for this bond doesn't take place until 7 months after the dated date, the first payment is a long coupon. After the first payment, all additional coupon payments will be made every 6 months.

122. **C.** (Chapter 8) You need to be careful in this case because the Series 7 examiners are asking you for a false statement. The maturity of revenue bonds may be 25 to 30 years, but the facility being built by the income received from the revenue bond issue is usually expected to last a lifetime. Revenue bonds may be issued by interstate authorities, such as tolls, and the debt service (interest and principal) on the bonds is paid from revenue received from the facility backing the bonds. In addition, revenue bonds are not subject to a debt ceiling; general obligation bonds are.

123. **B.** (Chapter 16) This question asks which statement is NOT true, so you're looking for any false answer choice. The deadline for providing a customer who wants to file a complaint and demands a copy of the signed predispute arbitration agreement is ten days, not seven. Arbitration does not deal with conduct issues; a Code of Procedure hearing would have jurisdiction. Choice (B) is therefore the correct answer. As for the incorrect answers, simplified arbitration is available for claims of $25,000 or less, which is true and, therefore, incorrect. Arbitration is the required method of resolving disputes between members, which is also true and, therefore, incorrect.

124. **A.** (Chapter 8) The Series 7 examiners want to make sure you can distinguish funds raised for municipal revenue bonds from those raised for general obligation bonds. Tolls, fees, airports, power plants, water, wastewater, and so forth may all be fund generators that subsidize revenue bonds. Property taxes (ad valorem taxes) support general obligation bonds.

125. **B.** (Chapter 8) Because these bonds were issued under a net revenue pledge (which almost all are), bondholders are paid from net revenues after operation and maintenance are paid. To calculate the answer to this question, remember that net revenue equals gross revenue minus operating and maintenance expenses. Here, net revenue is $18 million ($38 million – $20 million). You also need to calculate debt service, which is the combination of interest and principal repayment. Here, debt service is $6 million ($5 million + $1 million). Finally, to compute the debt service ratio, you must divide net revenue by debt service.

$$\text{debt service coverage ratio} = \frac{\text{net revenues}}{\text{debt service}} = \frac{\$18{,}000{,}000}{\$6{,}000{,}000} = 3 \text{ to } 1$$

Making the Grade

Here's how the Series 7 exam is scored:

- You get one point for each correct answer.
- You get zero points for each incorrect answer.

A passing score is 72 percent. To calculate your grade for this half of the exam, multiply the number of correct answers by 0.8 or divide it by 125. Whatever grade you get, make sure you round down, not up. For example, a grade of 71.6 is a 71 percent, not a 72. If you got 90 or more questions right, you're getting a passing score so far.

Of course, you simply need 180 correct answers on the whole test. So you could get only 55 questions correct here and still pass if you get a perfect score on the next part (I don't recommend this strategy, though).

The actual test contains ten additional experimental questions (five in each part) that don't count toward your actual score. You can't tell these questions apart from the questions that do count, so you may have to answer a few more questions right to get your 70 percent. Don't sweat it. Simply come prepared, stay focused, and do your best.

Answer Key for Part 1 of the Practice Exam

1. **D**	13. **B**	25. **A**	37. **A**	49. **C**
2. **A**	14. **D**	26. **B**	38. **B**	50. **C**
3. **C**	15. **C**	27. **D**	39. **B**	51. **D**
4. **C**	16. **A**	28. **B**	40. **C**	52. **A**
5. **B**	17. **D**	29. **C**	41. **D**	53. **D**
6. **D**	18. **B**	30. **A**	42. **C**	54. **D**
7. **A**	19. **D**	31. **D**	43. **A**	55. **C**
8. **B**	20. **B**	32. **D**	44. **A**	56. **C**
9. **C**	21. **A**	33. **B**	45. **D**	57. **D**
10. **D**	22. **B**	34. **D**	46. **D**	58. **C**
11. **D**	23. **A**	35. **B**	47. **A**	59. **D**
12. **D**	24. **D**	36. **C**	48. **D**	60. **D**

61. **B**
62. **C**
63. **A**
64. **C**
65. **C**
66. **D**
67. **D**
68. **B**
69. **B**
70. **A**
71. **B**
72. **C**
73. **D**
74. **B**
75. **C**
76. **B**
77. **A**
78. **A**
79. **B**
80. **B**
81. **C**
82. **B**
83. **D**
84. **B**
85. **A**
86. **C**
87. **B**
88. **C**
89. **A**
90. **D**
91. **A**
92. **A**
93. **A**
94. **C**
95. **C**
96. **D**
97. **B**
98. **D**
99. **D**
100. **C**
101. **B**
102. **B**
103. **A**
104. **B**
105. **D**
106. **A**
107. **D**
108. **C**
109. **C**
110. **D**
111. **B**
112. **D**
113. **A**
114. **B**
115. **A**
116. **B**
117. **C**
118. **D**
119. **B**
120. **D**
121. **A**
122. **C**
123. **B**
124. **A**
125. **B**

Chapter 19

Nothing but Net: Practice Exam Part II

If you've just finished Part I and are continuing to Part II, please make sure that you give your brain a rest for at least half an hour before starting this half of the exam. Just like Part I, this part of the practice exam has 125 questions. For those of you who couldn't wait to take Part II and bypassed Part I, I review the test basics here.

As in the real Series 7 exam, the questions in Parts I and II are in random order. Please read carefully. You can limit your careless mistakes by focusing in on the key words. Zone in on the information you do need to know to answer the question and ignore the information that doesn't help you. I suggest reading the last sentence twice to make sure you know what the question's asking. You may use scrap paper and a basic calculator for figuring.

Mark your answers on the answer sheet provided in this chapter or on a separate piece of paper. As you're taking the exam, circle or highlight the questions that you find troublesome. After taking and grading the exam, look over the questions that you got wrong and the questions that you circled or highlighted. Review the test, retake all the questions that you circled or answered wrong, and make sure that you get them right this time. To simulate the real exam, try to finish this part in three hours or less. Please resist the urge to look at the answers and explanations until you've finished the exam. You can check your answers and get detailed explanations in Chapter 20. Good luck!

Practice Exam Part II Answer Sheet

1 Ⓐ Ⓑ Ⓒ Ⓓ	33 Ⓐ Ⓑ Ⓒ Ⓓ	65 Ⓐ Ⓑ Ⓒ Ⓓ	97 Ⓐ Ⓑ Ⓒ Ⓓ
2 Ⓐ Ⓑ Ⓒ Ⓓ	34 Ⓐ Ⓑ Ⓒ Ⓓ	66 Ⓐ Ⓑ Ⓒ Ⓓ	98 Ⓐ Ⓑ Ⓒ Ⓓ
3 Ⓐ Ⓑ Ⓒ Ⓓ	35 Ⓐ Ⓑ Ⓒ Ⓓ	67 Ⓐ Ⓑ Ⓒ Ⓓ	99 Ⓐ Ⓑ Ⓒ Ⓓ
4 Ⓐ Ⓑ Ⓒ Ⓓ	36 Ⓐ Ⓑ Ⓒ Ⓓ	68 Ⓐ Ⓑ Ⓒ Ⓓ	100 Ⓐ Ⓑ Ⓒ Ⓓ
5 Ⓐ Ⓑ Ⓒ Ⓓ	37 Ⓐ Ⓑ Ⓒ Ⓓ	69 Ⓐ Ⓑ Ⓒ Ⓓ	101 Ⓐ Ⓑ Ⓒ Ⓓ
6 Ⓐ Ⓑ Ⓒ Ⓓ	38 Ⓐ Ⓑ Ⓒ Ⓓ	70 Ⓐ Ⓑ Ⓒ Ⓓ	102 Ⓐ Ⓑ Ⓒ Ⓓ
7 Ⓐ Ⓑ Ⓒ Ⓓ	39 Ⓐ Ⓑ Ⓒ Ⓓ	71 Ⓐ Ⓑ Ⓒ Ⓓ	103 Ⓐ Ⓑ Ⓒ Ⓓ
8 Ⓐ Ⓑ Ⓒ Ⓓ	40 Ⓐ Ⓑ Ⓒ Ⓓ	72 Ⓐ Ⓑ Ⓒ Ⓓ	104 Ⓐ Ⓑ Ⓒ Ⓓ
9 Ⓐ Ⓑ Ⓒ Ⓓ	41 Ⓐ Ⓑ Ⓒ Ⓓ	73 Ⓐ Ⓑ Ⓒ Ⓓ	105 Ⓐ Ⓑ Ⓒ Ⓓ
10 Ⓐ Ⓑ Ⓒ Ⓓ	42 Ⓐ Ⓑ Ⓒ Ⓓ	74 Ⓐ Ⓑ Ⓒ Ⓓ	106 Ⓐ Ⓑ Ⓒ Ⓓ
11 Ⓐ Ⓑ Ⓒ Ⓓ	43 Ⓐ Ⓑ Ⓒ Ⓓ	75 Ⓐ Ⓑ Ⓒ Ⓓ	107 Ⓐ Ⓑ Ⓒ Ⓓ
12 Ⓐ Ⓑ Ⓒ Ⓓ	44 Ⓐ Ⓑ Ⓒ Ⓓ	76 Ⓐ Ⓑ Ⓒ Ⓓ	108 Ⓐ Ⓑ Ⓒ Ⓓ
13 Ⓐ Ⓑ Ⓒ Ⓓ	45 Ⓐ Ⓑ Ⓒ Ⓓ	77 Ⓐ Ⓑ Ⓒ Ⓓ	109 Ⓐ Ⓑ Ⓒ Ⓓ
14 Ⓐ Ⓑ Ⓒ Ⓓ	46 Ⓐ Ⓑ Ⓒ Ⓓ	78 Ⓐ Ⓑ Ⓒ Ⓓ	110 Ⓐ Ⓑ Ⓒ Ⓓ
15 Ⓐ Ⓑ Ⓒ Ⓓ	47 Ⓐ Ⓑ Ⓒ Ⓓ	79 Ⓐ Ⓑ Ⓒ Ⓓ	111 Ⓐ Ⓑ Ⓒ Ⓓ
16 Ⓐ Ⓑ Ⓒ Ⓓ	48 Ⓐ Ⓑ Ⓒ Ⓓ	80 Ⓐ Ⓑ Ⓒ Ⓓ	112 Ⓐ Ⓑ Ⓒ Ⓓ
17 Ⓐ Ⓑ Ⓒ Ⓓ	49 Ⓐ Ⓑ Ⓒ Ⓓ	81 Ⓐ Ⓑ Ⓒ Ⓓ	113 Ⓐ Ⓑ Ⓒ Ⓓ
18 Ⓐ Ⓑ Ⓒ Ⓓ	50 Ⓐ Ⓑ Ⓒ Ⓓ	82 Ⓐ Ⓑ Ⓒ Ⓓ	114 Ⓐ Ⓑ Ⓒ Ⓓ
19 Ⓐ Ⓑ Ⓒ Ⓓ	51 Ⓐ Ⓑ Ⓒ Ⓓ	83 Ⓐ Ⓑ Ⓒ Ⓓ	115 Ⓐ Ⓑ Ⓒ Ⓓ
20 Ⓐ Ⓑ Ⓒ Ⓓ	52 Ⓐ Ⓑ Ⓒ Ⓓ	84 Ⓐ Ⓑ Ⓒ Ⓓ	116 Ⓐ Ⓑ Ⓒ Ⓓ
21 Ⓐ Ⓑ Ⓒ Ⓓ	53 Ⓐ Ⓑ Ⓒ Ⓓ	85 Ⓐ Ⓑ Ⓒ Ⓓ	117 Ⓐ Ⓑ Ⓒ Ⓓ
22 Ⓐ Ⓑ Ⓒ Ⓓ	54 Ⓐ Ⓑ Ⓒ Ⓓ	86 Ⓐ Ⓑ Ⓒ Ⓓ	118 Ⓐ Ⓑ Ⓒ Ⓓ
23 Ⓐ Ⓑ Ⓒ Ⓓ	55 Ⓐ Ⓑ Ⓒ Ⓓ	87 Ⓐ Ⓑ Ⓒ Ⓓ	119 Ⓐ Ⓑ Ⓒ Ⓓ
24 Ⓐ Ⓑ Ⓒ Ⓓ	56 Ⓐ Ⓑ Ⓒ Ⓓ	88 Ⓐ Ⓑ Ⓒ Ⓓ	120 Ⓐ Ⓑ Ⓒ Ⓓ
25 Ⓐ Ⓑ Ⓒ Ⓓ	57 Ⓐ Ⓑ Ⓒ Ⓓ	89 Ⓐ Ⓑ Ⓒ Ⓓ	121 Ⓐ Ⓑ Ⓒ Ⓓ
26 Ⓐ Ⓑ Ⓒ Ⓓ	58 Ⓐ Ⓑ Ⓒ Ⓓ	90 Ⓐ Ⓑ Ⓒ Ⓓ	122 Ⓐ Ⓑ Ⓒ Ⓓ
27 Ⓐ Ⓑ Ⓒ Ⓓ	59 Ⓐ Ⓑ Ⓒ Ⓓ	91 Ⓐ Ⓑ Ⓒ Ⓓ	123 Ⓐ Ⓑ Ⓒ Ⓓ
28 Ⓐ Ⓑ Ⓒ Ⓓ	60 Ⓐ Ⓑ Ⓒ Ⓓ	92 Ⓐ Ⓑ Ⓒ Ⓓ	124 Ⓐ Ⓑ Ⓒ Ⓓ
29 Ⓐ Ⓑ Ⓒ Ⓓ	61 Ⓐ Ⓑ Ⓒ Ⓓ	93 Ⓐ Ⓑ Ⓒ Ⓓ	125 Ⓐ Ⓑ Ⓒ Ⓓ
30 Ⓐ Ⓑ Ⓒ Ⓓ	62 Ⓐ Ⓑ Ⓒ Ⓓ	94 Ⓐ Ⓑ Ⓒ Ⓓ	
31 Ⓐ Ⓑ Ⓒ Ⓓ	63 Ⓐ Ⓑ Ⓒ Ⓓ	95 Ⓐ Ⓑ Ⓒ Ⓓ	
32 Ⓐ Ⓑ Ⓒ Ⓓ	64 Ⓐ Ⓑ Ⓒ Ⓓ	96 Ⓐ Ⓑ Ⓒ Ⓓ	

Time: 3 hours for 125 questions

Directions: Choose the correct answer to each question. Then fill in the circle on your answer sheet that corresponds to the question number and the letter indicating your choice.

1. Mark Schwimmerr owns 2,500 shares of TP Corporation. Which of the following actions would dilute Mark's equity?

   I. Primary share offerings (registered)

   II. A stock split

   III. Payment of a stock offering

   IV. Secondary share offerings (registered)

   (A) I only

   (B) II only

   (C) I, II, and IV

   (D) I, II, III, and IV

2. A customer, Phillip Regis, has an established margin account with a long market value of $20,300 and a debit balance of $7,500, with Regulation T at 50 percent. What amount does the long market value have to decrease below to trigger a maintenance call?

   (A) $20,300

   (B) $7,500

   (C) $10,150

   (D) $10,000

3. Which of the following is the most likely reason for the yield curve to become inverted?

   (A) The Fed has eased short-term credit.

   (B) The Fed has tightened short-term credit.

   (C) The Fed has eased long-term credit.

   (D) The Fed has tightened long-term credit.

4. The Trade Reporting and Compliance Engine (TRACE), promotes better market transparency by allowing trade details to be released to the investing public that purchases

   (A) corporate bonds in the OTC secondary market

   (B) warrants

   (C) CMOs

   (D) new issue primary market securities

5. Mike Smith is one of your clients. Mike is 55 years old, has a wife, two young adults going to college, and two children living at home. You have helped Mike determine his investment profile and how much risk he should be willing to take. However, Mike is hot on a particularly speculative security that doesn't fit his investment profile. Mike calls you saying he wants to purchase $20,000 worth of this security. What should you do?

   (A) Accept the order and mark it as unsolicited.

   (B) Refuse the order because it doesn't fit his investment profile.

   (C) Do nothing until talking to a principal.

   (D) Limit Mike's exposure by making sure that he doesn't purchase more than $5,000 worth of this speculative security.

6. An investor enters a buy stop limit for XYZ at $40. Trades occur as follows:

   39.38, 39.75, 40.13, 40.50, 40.25

   At what price is this order executed?

   (A) 39.75

   (B) 40.13

   (C) 40.50

   (D) It is not executed

Go on to next page

7. Use the following exhibit to answer this question:

NY Close	Strike	Calls		Puts	
ABC		Sep	Dec	Sep	Dec
50.50	40	12	14.13	0.75	1.50
50.50	50	1	2.50	0.88	1.75
50.50	60	0.50	0.75	10	12

What is the breakeven point for an investor who purchases an ABC Dec 60 put?

(A) 48

(B) 50

(C) 70

(D) 72

8. All of the following are good delivery for a trade of 930 shares EXCEPT

(A) 1 certificate for 900 shares, 1 for 30 shares

(B) 2 certificates for 400 shares each, 2 for 50 shares each, 2 for 15 shares each

(C) 4 certificates for 200 shares each, 10 for 13 shares each

(D) 4 certificates for 200 shares each, 13 for 10 shares each

9. An investor has a child who will be going to college in 15 years. Which of the following is a suitable investment?

(A) T-bills

(B) T-notes

(C) Treasury receipts

(D) EE savings bonds

10. Which of the following statements is TRUE about revenue bonds?

(A) Their value is measured by the municipal project's capacity for generating revenue.

(B) They are secured by a mortgage-backed bond.

(C) They are a type of general obligation bond.

(D) They are subject to the statutory debt limitations of the issuing jurisdiction.

11. Which of the following is the balance sheet equation?

(A) assets = liabilities + shareholder's equity

(B) assets + liabilities = shareholder's equity

(C) shareholder's equity + assets = liabilities

(D) None of the above

12. Regarding the taxation of dividends from corporate securities, which TWO of the following are TRUE?

I. Qualified dividends are taxed at the investor's income tax rate.

II. Qualified dividends are taxed at a maximum rate of 15 percent.

III. Nonqualified dividends are taxed at the investor's tax rate.

IV. Nonqualified dividends are taxed at a maximum rate of 15 percent.

(A) I and III

(B) I and IV

(C) II and III

(D) II and IV

Go on to next page

13. All of the following change the conditions of an option contract EXCEPT

(A) a stock split

(B) a cash dividend

(C) a stock dividend

(D) none of the above

14. Zeppelin Marx Corporation announces a 2-for-1 stock split. What can John Dough expect if possessing 60 shares of Zeppelin Marx stock?

I. John will be sent a Zeppelin Marx stock certificate for 60 shares of stock.

II. John will be sent a Zeppelin Marx stock certificate for 120 shares of stock.

III. John must turn in his 60 shares of stock to be replaced by a certificate from Zeppelin Marx for 120 shares.

IV. John will receive official certification from Zeppelin Marx that his 60 shares of stock are now worth 120 shares.

(A) IV only

(B) I only

(C) I and IV

(D) II and III

15. Where can an investor find the most information about a new municipal issue?

(A) In a prospectus

(B) In an official statement

(C) In a tombstone ad

(D) In a registration statement

16. Which of the following statements made by a registered rep is not prohibited?

(A) "The stock will double in price."

(B) "The earnings of the company will be better than expected."

(C) "I can guarantee that you will not lose money on this stock."

(D) "A research report shows that the company's financial performance may be better than expected."

17. Which two of the following are true of Roth IRAs?

I. Contributions are made from after-tax dollars.

II. Contributions are made from pretax dollars.

III. Distributions are tax-free.

IV. Distributions are taxed on the amount above the amount of the contribution.

(A) I and III

(B) I and IV

(C) II and III

(D) II and IV

18. Which of the following are true of broker-dealer business continuity and disaster recovery plans?

I. They must be in written form.

II. Firms must have backup of data (both hard copies and electronic).

III. Firms must have some sort of alternative communication between the firm and its employees.

IV. They must be approved by a principal.

(A) I, II, and III

(B) II, III, and IV

(C) I, II, and IV

(D) I, II, III, and IV

19. One of your clients wants to start adding some diversity to her portfolio by investing in mutual funds. Which of the following is the most important consideration when choosing a mutual fund?

(A) Whether the fund is load or no-load

(B) Management fees

(C) Investment objectives

(D) 12b1 fees

Go on to next page

20. Common stockholders in a corporation can do which of the following?

(A) Elect the corporation's board of directors

(B) Make decisions about the day-to-day dealings, such as the office supply dealer used by the corporation

(C) Receive interest payments

(D) Expect to be paid par value for their stock if the corporation goes out of business

21. Which of the following investments are suitable for a 21-year-old investor who has limited resources but would like to start investing on a regular basis?

I. Growth funds

II. Collateralized debt obligations (CDOs)

III. Call options

IV. Hedge funds

(A) I only

(B) II and IV

(C) I, II, and III

(D) I, III, and IV

22. According to the Investment Advisor's Act of 1940, which of the following are considered investment advisers?

(A) Securities lawyers giving paid advice on investments

(B) Economics professors giving paid advice on investments

(C) Registered reps giving paid advice on investments

(D) All of the above

23. Which of the following statements is TRUE regarding municipal revenue bond issues?

(A) The bonds are backed by the issuer's unlimited taxing power.

(B) User fees provide revenue for bondholders.

(C) The bonds' feasibility is not dependent on the earnings potential of the facility or project.

(D) Revenue bonds are most suitable for investors with high risk tolerance.

24. Jameson and Johnson Securities sent Art a confirmation of his latest trade of Johnstone Corporation common stock. Which of the following items should be on the confirmation?

I. The trade date and the settlement date

II. Whether Jameson and Johnson acted as an agent or a principal

III. The name of the security and how many shares were traded

IV. The amount of commission paid if Jameson and Johnson acted as an agent

(A) I and III

(B) I, II, and III

(C) I, III, and IV

(D) I, II, III, and IV

25. If a customer, Jessica James, gives limited power of attorney to her registered representative, which of the following is TRUE?

(A) The registered representative still needs verbal authorization from Jessica for each trade.

(B) Jessica must sign a power-of-attorney document.

(C) The registered representative must sign a power-of-attorney document.

(D) Jessica must initial each order before it is entered.

26. Which of the following is NOT a characteristic of a real estate investment trust (REIT)?

(A) Pass-through treatment of income only

(B) Pass-through treatment of income and losses

(C) At least 75 percent of the assets must be invested in real-estate-related projects

(D) Ownership of real property without management responsibility

Go on to next page

27. A principal is responsible for approving new accounts opened for

I. individuals

II. corporations

III. banks

IV. trusts

(A) I only

(B) I and II

(C) I, II, and III

(D) I, II, III, and IV

28. When the FINRA is considering the possibility that a brokerage account is being churned, they consider all of the following EXCEPT

(A) the number of trades

(B) the amount of money in the account

(C) the objectives of the customer

(D) the amount of profit or loss

29. What effect will occur if the federal open market committee (FOMC) sells government securities in the open market?

(A) It will cause inflation.

(B) It will not affect the money supply.

(C) It will tighten the money supply.

(D) It will ease the money supply.

30. George Lincoln opens a margin account and signs a loan consent, hypothecation, and credit agreement. Which of the following statements are TRUE?

I. George's stock may not be kept in street name.

II. A portion of George's stock may be pledged for a loan.

III. George will be required to pay interest on the money borrowed.

IV. George's stock must be cosigned by the broker/dealer.

(A) I and IV

(B) II and III

(C) I and II

(D) None of the above

31. Terri Hogan is a customer who wants to invest in securities. Which of the following is most likely to provide Terri with the highest dividend rate?

(A) Straight preferred

(B) Convertible preferred

(C) Participating preferred

(D) Callable preferred

32. Time Bandit Securities agrees to underwrite 10 percent of an Eastern account issue for $100 million and sells out its allotment of $10 million. Other firms participating in the transaction aren't able to sell their bonds due to the weakness of the American market, and $25 million of the bonds remain unsold. What is Time Bandit Securities financial obligation?

(A) $0

(B) $250,000

(C) Shared responsibility for $25 million

(D) $2.5 million

33. To protect investors of variable life insurance policies who become disabled, there is a rider called a(n)

(A) disability rider

(B) waiver of premium

(C) early withdrawal rider

(D) none of the above

34. As a client's investment objectives change, a registered rep should keep track of those changes so that he can rebalance the client's portfolio and make proper recommendations. Which of the following changes may affect a customer's investment objectives?

I. Growing older

II. Getting divorced

III. Having triplets

IV. Getting a higher paying job

(A) I and III

(B) I, II, and III

(C) II, III, and IV

(D) I, II, III, and IV

Go on to next page

35. JKLM Corporation has declared a $0.40 dividend payable to shareholders of record on Thursday, September 14. What would happen to the opening price of JKLM on Tuesday, September 12th?

(A) It would be reduced by the amount of the dividend

(B) It would remain the same

(C) It would be increased by the amount of the dividend

(D) Cannot be determined

36. Larry Eagle is a resident of Michigan. Mr. Eagle purchased a Michigan municipal bond. What is the tax treatment of the interest that Larry earns on his Michigan bond?

I. It is exempt from local taxes.

II. It is exempt from state taxes.

III. It is exempt from federal taxes.

(A) III only

(B) I and III

(C) II and III

(D) I, II, and III

37. Who is responsible for paying the taxes when securities in a Uniform Gifts to Minors Act (UGMA) account are sold at a profit?

(A) The minor

(B) The donor

(C) The custodian

(D) The parent or guardian

38. An investor wants to invest in a DPP that's relatively safe. Which of the following are you LEAST likely to recommend?

(A) A real-estate partnership that invests in raw land

(B) An oil and gas developmental program

(C) An oil and gas income program

(D) An equipment leasing program

39. All of the following activities are a registrar's functions EXCEPT

(A) accounting for the number of shares outstanding

(B) auditing the transfer agent

(C) ensuring that the outstanding shares do not exceed the number of shares on the corporation's books

(D) transferring shares into the name of the new owner

40. All of the following information is required on a preliminary prospectus EXCEPT

(A) the final offering price

(B) the purpose for which the issuer is raising the funds

(C) a statement in red lettering stating that items on the preliminary prospectus are subject to change before the final prospectus is issued

(D) the issuer's history and financial status

41. Which of the following situations requires a broker-dealer to file a currency transaction report?

(A) A customer purchases $20,000 worth of stock with a check from a joint account.

(B) A customer opens an account with $14,000 cash.

(C) A customer opens an account with a wire transfer from his personal account for $25,000.

(D) A customer deposits corporate bonds with a par value of $30,000.

42. A mutual fund has an NAV of $9.30 and a POP of $10. What is the sales charge of this fund?

(A) 5 percent

(B) 6 percent

(C) 7 percent

(D) 8 percent

Go on to next page

43. Investments that move in the opposite direction of the economic cycles are known to be counter-cyclical. Historically, investments that are known to be counter-cyclical include

(A) gold stock

(B) utility stock

(C) pharmaceutical stock

(D) food company stock

44. On a competitive bid for a new municipal underwriting, the difference between the syndicate bid and the reoffering price is the

(A) discount price

(B) offering price

(C) spread

(D) bid price

45. If a customer wants to open a cash account at a brokerage firm, the signature(s) of which of the following is/are required?

I. The registered representative

II. The customer

III. The principal

IV. The guarantor

(A) IV only

(B) I and III

(C) I, II, and III

(D) I, II, III, and IV

46. Which of the following orders are NOT held in a designated market maker's book?

I. Not-held orders

II. Stop orders

III. Limit orders

IV. Market orders

(A) I and II

(B) II and III

(C) III and IV

(D) I and IV

47. A sell stop order is entered

I. below the support level of the stock

II. above the resistance level of the stock

III. to limit the loss on a long stock position

IV. to limit the loss on a short stock position

(A) I and III

(B) I and IV

(C) II and III

(D) II and IV

48. In an initial margin transaction, an investor purchases 100 shares of WXY at $24 per share. What is the margin call?

(A) $1,200

(B) $1,800

(C) $2,000

(D) $2,400

49. The indenture of a corporate bond includes all of the following EXCEPT

(A) the coupon rate

(B) the credit rating

(C) the name of the trustee

(D) the maturity date

50. Which of the following items can be found in the certificate of limited partnership?

I. The goals of the partnership and how long it's expected to last

II. The authority of the general partner to charge a fee for making management decisions for the partnership

III. How the profits are to be distributed

IV. The amount contributed by each partner, plus future expected investments

(A) I, II, and III

(B) II, III, and IV

(C) I, III, and IV

(D) I, II, III, and IV

Go on to next page

51. All of the following securities may pay a dividend EXCEPT

(A) warrants

(B) common stock

(C) American depositary receipts (ADRs)

(D) participating preferred stock

52. Marty Martinez wants to create a short combination using his existing option. If Marty is short 1 DEF Aug 60 call, which of the following option positions should Marty purchase or sell?

(A) Long 1 DEF Aug 70 put

(B) Long 1 DEF Aug 60 put

(C) Short 1 DEF Aug 50 put

(D) Short 1 DEF Aug 60 put

53. Which of the following is/are true of a REIT?

I. It must invest at least 75 percent of its assets in real-estate-related activities.

II. It must be organized as a trust.

III. It must distribute at least 90 percent of its net investment income.

IV. It must pass along losses to shareholders.

(A) I, II, III, and IV

(B) I, II, and III

(C) I only

(D) II and IV

54. An investor purchases 300 shares of DUD Corp. at $45 per share and purchases 3 DUD Oct 40 puts at 6. What is the customer's break-even point?

(A) 39

(B) 45

(C) 46

(D) 51

55. Under the Securities Act of 1933, which of the following securities are exempt from registration and disclosure provisions?

(A) Railroad equipment trust certificate

(B) Municipal bonds

(C) Commercial paper maturing in 270 days or less

(D) All of the above

56. One of your customers is interested in investing in an oil and gas limited partnership. As his registered rep, which of the following steps are you required to take?

I. Prescreen the customer.

II. Determine the economic soundness of the program.

III. Explain the risks of investing in limited partnerships.

IV. Have your customer fill out a partnership agreement.

(A) I and III

(B) I, II, and III

(C) II, III, and IV

(D) I, II, III, and IV

57. Which of the following funds changes its balance to hold more fixed-income securities and less equity securities as the years pass?

(A) A balanced fund

(B) A hedge fund

(C) A life-cycle fund

(D) A growth fund

58. For investors interested in purchasing CMOs, which of the following tranches is considered the safest?

(A) Planned amortization class

(B) Targeted amortization class

(C) Companion

(D) Z

59. The first time a company ever issues securities is called a(n)

(A) IPO

(B) first market trade

(C) rights offering

(D) None of the above

Go on to next page

60. When comparing short-term bonds with long-term bonds, which of the following is characteristic of short-term bonds?

(A) Short-term bonds respond to interest changes more than long-term bonds.

(B) Short-term bonds usually have greater yields.

(C) Short-term bonds are more likely to be called than long-term bonds.

(D) Short-term bonds usually provide greater liquidity than long-term bonds.

61. Broker-dealers may charge a

I. commission

II. markup

III. markdown

(A) I only

(B) I and II

(C) II and III

(D) I, II, and III

62. Use the following exhibit to answer this question:

TUV	*Strike*	*May*	*Aug.*	*Nov.*
60.50	50	12	14.50	16
60.50	50p	a	0.50	1.25
60.50	60	2	3.25	5
60.50	60p	1.50	2.75	4

(p – put, a – not traded)

If an investor buys a TUV Nov 60 put and writes a TUV Nov 50 put, what is the maximum gain?

(A) $275

(B) $325

(C) $675

(D) $725

63. One of your customers wants to add some diversity to his portfolio by investing in some defensive stocks. Which of the following stocks would you recommend?

I. CCCold Refrigerator Corporation common stock

II. Smoky Tobacco Inc. common stock

III. Forgetful Vodka Corp. common stock

IV. Impee Auto Corporation common stock

(A) I and IV

(B) II and III

(C) I, III, and IV

(D) II, III, and IV

64. Mr. Smith has an inactive account with stocks and bonds at a broker-dealer. How often is the firm required to send Mr. Smith an account statement?

(A) Once a month

(B) Once a week

(C) Once every three months

(D) Once every six months

65. All of the following orders are reduced on the order book for a cash dividend on the ex-date EXCEPT

(A) buy limit

(B) sell stop

(C) sell stop limit

(D) buy stop

66. All of the following impact the marketing of a municipal bond issue EXCEPT

(A) the rating

(B) the interest

(C) the date of maturity

(D) the dated date

67. IRAs may be set up in all of the following ways EXCEPT

(A) single life

(B) life with period certain

(C) joint and last survivor

(D) uniform lifetime

Go on to next page

68. An investor who purchases a variable life insurance policy faces which of the following risks?

(A) The insurance company may have to increase the premium if the securities held in the separate account underperform the market.

(B) The insurance company may decrease the premium if the securities held in the separate account outperform the market.

(C) The policy may have no cash value if the securities held in the separate account perform poorly.

(D) The death benefit may fall below the minimum in the event that the securities held in the separate account underperform.

69. All of the following are nonfinancial influences that may help determine an investor's investment profile EXCEPT

(A) the investor's age

(B) the amount of marketable securities the investor owns

(C) the number of dependents

(D) investment experience

70. Which of the following is TRUE of a durable power of attorney?

(A) It would be automatically revoked in the event that the grantor is declared incompetent.

(B) It gives power of attorney to someone else in the event that an individual becomes incompetent.

(C) It gives power of attorney to someone else in the event that an individual dies.

(D) Once in place, it may not be revoked by the grantor.

71. A 7-percent corporate bond is offered on a 7.50 basis. Which of the following statements is TRUE?

(A) The nominal yield is higher than the yield to maturity.

(B) The current yield is higher than the nominal yield.

(C) The nominal yield is equal to the yield to maturity.

(D) The current yield is lower than the nominal yield.

72. Barbara Billington has a margin account with a market value of $30,000 and a debit balance of $12,000. If Barbara wants to purchase an additional $10,000 of stock in this account, what amount must she deposit?

(A) $2,000

(B) $3,000

(C) $5,000

(D) $10,000

73. Ginny Goldtrain is a wealthy investor who is in the highest income bracket. Ginny is looking for an investment that would limit her tax liability and put her on equal footing with investors in lower income-tax brackets. Which of the following securities would you MOST likely recommend?

(A) High-yield bonds

(B) CMOs

(C) Municipal bonds

(D) Hedge funds

74. Contributions to health savings accounts

I. are made in pretax dollars

II. are made in after-tax dollars

III. grow on a tax-free basis

IV. may be invested in mutual funds

(A) I, II, and III

(B) I, III, and IV

(C) I and II

(D) II and IV

Go on to next page

75. In what order are distributions paid under a net revenue pledge?

I. Debt service

II. Operations and maintenance

III. Surplus fund

IV. Debt service reserve

(A) I, III, II, IV

(B) IV, II, I, III

(C) I, II, III, IV

(D) II, I, IV, III

76. Brett Overtrade is a registered representative who works for Missed Again Securities. Brett has just learned of the death of one of his customers. Which of the following actions should Brett take regarding his deceased customer's account?

I. Mark his customer's account as deceased.

II. Cancel all open orders.

III. Wait for the proper legal papers.

(A) I and II

(B) I and III

(C) II and III

(D) I, II, and III

77. The trading volume for some large institutional orders is concealed from the public. What is this called?

(A) Fourth market trades

(B) Dark pools of liquidity

(C) Third market trades

(D) A violation

78. Use the following exhibit of a Designated Market Maker's Book to answer this question:

XYZ Corp.

Bid	***41***	***Offer***
2 Bache	41.01	
18 Needum	41.02	
8 Flower 3 Dimm	41.03	2 Rise N Shine (stop) GTC
	41.04	
6 Sampson (stop) GTC	41.05	
	41.06	22 Salmon
	41.07	4 Dean GTC 6 Holdum

What is the inside market?

(A) 41.02 – 41.06

(B) 41.03 – 41.06

(C) 41.03 – 41.07

(D) 41.05 – 41.07

79. Which of the following bonds most likely has the highest coupon rate?

(A) DEF Corp. mortgage bonds

(B) DEF Corp. collateral trusts

(C) DEF Corp. debentures

(D) DEF Corp. equipment trusts

80. Your client, Dana Griffin, is about to retire and she wants predictable income. Which of the following would NOT be a good investment for Dana?

I. AA rated IDB

II. U.S. Treasury note

III. AA rated debenture

IV. Income bonds

(A) II only

(B) I and III

(C) II and IV

(D) IV only

Go on to next page

81. What is the maximum loss on a debit spread?

(A) The difference between the premium paid and the premium received

(B) The difference between the two strike prices multiplied by 100, less the premium paid, plus the premium received

(C) The difference between the two strike prices multiplied by 100, less the premium paid

(D) The difference between the two strike prices multiplied by 100

82. Sal Gold is new to investing and wants to purchase a security that will provide him with current income with minimal risk. Which of the following are you LEAST likely to recommend?

(A) An income fund

(B) Treasury bonds

(C) An international fund

(D) AA rated municipal bonds

83. Which of the following is the issuer and guarantor of all listed options?

(A) The OCC

(B) The OAA

(C) The ODD

(D) The CBOE

84. If your customer, William Goate, purchases shares in a municipal bond fund, which of the following statements is TRUE?

(A) Dividends are subject to alternative minimum tax.

(B) Dividends are taxable to all investors.

(C) Capital gains distributions are taxable.

(D) Capital gains distributions are not taxable.

85. All of the following are exchange markets EXCEPT

(A) NYSE Amex Equities

(B) NYSE Euronext

(C) NASDAQ Global Market

(D) NASDAQ OMX PHLX

86. These municipal notes provide interim financing for a municipality that's waiting for a grant from the U.S. government.

(A) BANs

(B) TRANs

(C) GANs

(D) CLNs

87. An investor is holding 1 ABC Oct 35 call option. Which of the following option positions, if purchased by this customer, would create a long straddle?

(A) Short 1 ABC Nov 35 call option

(B) Short 1 ABC Oct 30 call option

(C) Long 1 ABC Oct 40 call option

(D) Long 1 ABC Oct 35 put option

88. Luke Landworker holds 10 XYX May 30 calls. XYX increases to $40, and he exercises the calls. Luke tells his registered rep to sell the stock immediately after purchase. If these trades are executed in a margin account, how much does Luke have to deposit?

(A) $3,000

(B) $30,000

(C) $35,000

(D) No deposit is required

89. Regarding margin accounts, which two of the following are TRUE?

I. Minimum maintenance on a long account is 25 percent.

II. Minimum maintenance on a short account is 25 percent.

III. Minimum maintenance on a long account is 30 percent.

IV. Minimum maintenance on a short account is 30 percent.

(A) I and II

(B) I and IV

(C) II and III

(D) III and IV

Go on to next page

90. Use the following exhibit to answer this question:

Balance Sheet of ABCD Corp.

Assets		Liabilities	
Cash	$300,000	Accounts payable	$300,000
Accounts receivable	$1,500,000	Taxes payable	$250,000
Inventory	$1,200,000	Bonds maturing this year	$800,000
Goodwill	$2,000,000	Bonds maturing in 5 years	$2,000,000
Machinery	$1,500,000		
Land	$5,000,000		

What is the net worth of ABCD Corporation?

(A) $3,150,000

(B) $1,650,000

(C) $8,150,000

(D) $10,150,000

91. What is the maximum gain for an investor who purchases a capped option?

(A) Unlimited

(B) Strike price times 100, less the cost of the premium

(C) $3,000 plus the premium

(D) $3,000 minus the premium

92. One of the advantages of portfolio margin is that it allows

(A) smaller investors the opportunity to purchase securities on margin

(B) less sophisticated investors a chance to purchase securities on margin

(C) investors to avoid maintenance calls

(D) investors greater leverage

93. Which of the following statements regarding municipal bonds with call provisions is TRUE?

(A) Bonds are likely to be called when interest rates fall.

(B) Call provisions favor investors.

(C) Bonds are likely to be called when interest rates rise.

(D) Call provisions are not advantageous to issuers.

94. TUVW Corporation common stock is currently trading in the market for $22 per share. TUVW Corp. pays an annual dividend of $0.60 per share and has an earnings per share (EPS) of $4. What is the PE ratio?

(A) 4.50

(B) 5

(C) 5.50

(D) Cannot be determined

95. Which of the following is a listing for stocks of companies that do not make the listing requirements for NASDAQ?

(A) TRACE

(B) TRF

(C) Pink Market

(D) OATS

96. Sam Smith sends an e-mail to his registered rep, John Johnson, complaining about the amount of commission he was charged on his last trade. According to FINRA rules, what should John Johnson do with the complaint?

(A) Ignore it because the complaint needs to be in writing

(B) Print it out and give it to his principal

(C) Print it out and send it to FINRA

(D) Forward it to FINRA's complaint department

Go on to next page

97. An investor deposited $75,000 to become a member of an oil and gas limited partnership. In addition, he deposited $20,000 in recourse debt. For this calendar year, he reports a $10,000 cash distribution, $30,000 in depreciation, and $25,000 in depletion. What is the investor's cost basis?

(A) $10,000

(B) $30,000

(C) $50,000

(D) $70,000

98. Which of the following sequences reflects the priority of payments made when a limited partnership is liquidated?

I. Secured creditors

II. General creditors

III. Limited partners

IV. General partners

(A) I, II, III, IV

(B) IV, II, III, I

(C) IV, II, I, III

(D) I, IV, II, III

99. All of the following are types of blue-sky registration EXCEPT

(A) registration by cooperation

(B) registration by coordination

(C) registration by qualification

(D) registration by filing

100. A TUV Oct 60 call is trading for 9 when TUV is at $65. What is the time value of this option?

(A) 0

(B) 4

(C) 5

(D) 9

101. Which of the following need approval from a brokerage firm's principal?

I. New accounts

II. Recommendations

III. Handling of complaints

IV. Trades in all accounts

(A) I and II

(B) I, III, and IV

(C) II, III, and IV

(D) I, II, III, and IV

102. A quote of 5.20 bid 5.18 offered is *most* likely a quote on which of the following:

(A) A T-bond

(B) A T-bill

(C) A general obligation (GO) bond

(D) A Fannie Mae (FNMA) bond

103. Which of the following municipal bonds is backed by lease payments made by an underlying facility?

(A) IDR

(B) LTGO

(C) LRB

(D) BAB

104. If a corporation pays a cash dividend, how does it affect its balance sheet?

I. Assets decrease

II. Liabilities decrease

III. Net worth decreases

IV. Net worth remains the same

(A) I and III

(B) II and III

(C) I, II, and III

(D) I, II, and IV

105. All of the following are included on a confirmation for noncallable municipal bonds that were purchased on a yield basis EXCEPT

(A) the purchase price

(B) the par value

(C) the yield to maturity

(D) the taxable equivalent yield

Go on to next page

106. Which of the following option positions provides an investor with potential premium income while limiting the maximum loss potential?

(A) Debit spread

(B) Credit spread

(C) Long straddle or long combination

(D) Short straddle or short combination

107. A customer wants her registered representative to purchase a security that is incompatible with her investment objectives. What action should the registered representative take under FINRA rules?

(A) Enter the order and note that it was unsolicited.

(B) Enter the order only if the customer puts her request in writing.

(C) Obtain the approval of the firm's compliance officer before entering the order.

(D) The registered representative cannot enter the order.

108. All of the following calculations can be determined by finding the information on a corporation's balance sheet EXCEPT

(A) working capital

(B) net worth

(C) current yield

(D) quick assets

109. Which of the following are money market securities?

(A) Commercial paper

(B) Treasury bonds

(C) American depositary receipts (ADRs)

(D) Warrants

110. Income derived from an investment in a real-estate limited partnership is termed

(A) earned income

(B) passive income

(C) portfolio income

(D) capital gains

111. Which of the following actions can the Fed take to ease the money supply?

I. Increase reserve requirements

II. Lower reserve requirements

III. Buy T-bills

IV. Sell T-bills

(A) I and III

(B) I and IV

(C) II and III

(D) II and IV

112. An investor purchases 1 TUV Sep 30 call for a premium of 4. This option will expire

(A) on the third Saturday in September

(B) on the third Friday in September

(C) on the Saturday following the third Friday in September

(D) on a date to be assigned by the CBOE

113. All of the following are true regarding limited partners EXCEPT

(A) They have access to unlimited financial information regarding the partnership.

(B) They may participate in management decisions because limited partners have a tremendous amount of risk.

(C) They may vote to terminate a partnership.

(D) They may invest in competing partnerships.

114. What is the primary objective for an individual who invests in undeveloped land?

(A) Depletion deductions

(B) Depreciation deductions

(C) Appreciation potential

(D) Tax-deferred income

Go on to next page

115. Which two of the following are TRUE regarding the advertising relating to municipal fund securities such as 529 college savings plans?

I. Sales charges may be reflected in the performance information.

II. Sales charges may not be reflected in the performance information.

III. The ad should state the minimum sales load.

IV. The ad should state the maximum sales load.

(A) I and III

(B) I and IV

(C) II and III

(D) II and IV

116. All of the following are true of a letter of intent EXCEPT

(A) It may be backdated for up to 90 days.

(B) The investor has 13 months from the initial transaction under the letter of intent to deposit enough money to receive a breakpoint.

(C) The fund may hold shares in escrow.

(D) Investors may purchase shares of the fund on margin while under the letter of intent.

117. What is the maximum potential loss for an investor who sells a call option?

(A) The strike price × 100 shares

(B) The strike price × 100 shares, less the premium

(C) The strike price × 100 shares, plus the premium

(D) Unlimited

118. An investor purchased 1,000 shares of WXY at $40. If WXY announces a 5 for 4 split, what is the investor's position after the split?

(A) 1,250 WXY at $32

(B) 1,250 WXY at $50

(C) 800 WXY at $32

(D) 800 WXY at $50

119. The economic theory that supports controlling the money supply in order to stimulate economic growth is called

(A) the Federal Reserve Board

(B) the Keynesian theory

(C) supply-side economics

(D) the monetarist theory

120. If the value of the U.S. dollar declines in relation to foreign currencies, all of the following are true EXCEPT

(A) U.S. exports become more competitive.

(B) Foreign imports of U.S. products increase.

(C) U.S. imports of foreign goods increase.

(D) Foreign exports become less competitive.

121. Which of the following is characteristic of commercial paper?

(A) It is quoted as a percent of par.

(B) It is proof of ownership of the corporation.

(C) It is issued to raise capital for a corporation.

(D) It is junior to convertible preferred stock.

122. Which of the following is true about advertising for a municipal fund security?

I. It must be approved by a principal of the firm selling the securities.

II. It must not be fraudulent.

III. It must first be approved by the MSRB.

IV. It must be approved by the state administrator in each state in which the security is to be sold.

(A) I only

(B) I and II

(C) III and IV

(D) I, II, III, and IV

Go on to next page

123. What is the penalty for excess contributions to a traditional IRA?

(A) 6 percent

(B) 10 percent

(C) 15 percent

(D) 50 percent

124. A mutual fund that invests only in securities within a specific industry is called a

(A) Balanced fund

(B) Growth fund

(C) Hedge fund

(D) Sector fund

125. At what time must an individual begin withdrawals from a Roth IRA?

(A) At age 59½

(B) At age 70½

(C) On April 1st of the year after turning 70½

(D) None of the above

STOP DO NOT TURN THE PAGE UNTIL TOLD TO DO SO. DO NOT RETURN TO A PREVIOUS TEST.

Chapter 20

Answers and Explanations to Practice Exam Part II

Congratulations! You've just completed Part II of the practice exam (unless you're just randomly flipping through the book). After grading both Parts I and II, you should have a good idea of where you stand regarding the Series 7 exam. Kudos if you did really well on both Parts I and II.

In this part, I decided to step it up a notch and add a few questions with exhibits. Exhibit questions aren't really any harder, they're just different, and you need to make sure that seeing one doesn't throw you off your game.

As with the first part, review all the questions that you got wrong and the ones you struggled with. Test yourself again by answering all the questions you highlighted and the questions you answered incorrectly, and make sure you get them right this time! Please give yourself a week or two before taking the same test again. Memorizing answers can give you a false sense of security, and you won't get an accurate forecast of how well you'll do on the Series 7 exam (you certainly don't want your score to be as unpredictable as the weather). I encourage you to take as many Series 7 practice exams as possible.

If you're short on time but just can't wait to see how well you did, you can check out the abbreviated answer key (without the explanations) at the end of this chapter. I explain how the Series 7 is scored in the section "Knowing the Score," just before the answer key. But I strongly suggest you come back later and do a more thorough review.

1. **A.** (Chapter 5) Another primary issue of shares would dilute Mark's ownership because new shares would be coming to the market. Don't forget that when a corporation issues stock dividends, splits its stock, or makes a secondary offering, the percent of equity does not change.

2. **D.** (Chapter 9) The answer to this question is Choice (D). To calculate the long market value that would trigger a maintenance call, use the following formula (DR = debit balance):

$$\frac{4\times \text{DR}}{3}=\frac{4\times \$7{,}500}{3}=\frac{\$30{,}000}{3}=\$10{,}000$$

3. **B.** (Chapter 13) The main function of the Fed is to try to attempt to keep the economy growing at a slow, steady rate. If the Fed feels that the economy is growing too quickly, it can increase the discount rate. The discount rate is the rate that the Fed charges member banks for short-term loans. If the yield curve becomes inverted, short-term bonds have a higher yield than long-term bonds.

4. **A.** (Chapter 14) The Series 7 exam tests you on your knowledge of TRACE. The trade reporting system known as TRACE is approved by FINRA for corporate bonds trading in the OTC secondary market. Therefore, Choice (A) is the correct answer. Choices (B), (C) and (D) are incorrect because warrants are not applicable to corporate bond trading, and municipal securities and asset-backed securities are specifically excluded from the TRACE reporting requirements.

5. **A.** (Chapter 16) You can accept the trade and mark it as unsolicited. Even if a customer wants to purchase a security that doesn't fit his investment profile, you can still accept it in most cases by marking it as unsolicited. I call this the CYD (cover your derriere) rule. As long as you mark the ticket as unsolicited, you save yourself some aggravation (and maybe arbitration) if Mike loses money on the deal.

6. **D.** (Chapter 14) Since this is a buy stop limit order, you need to break it down into two parts, the buy stop portion and the buy limit portion. First, you need to take care of the buy stop portion, which is a SLoBS (Sell Limit, Buy Stop) order. SLoBS orders get triggered at or above the order price (in this case $40). In this case, the first number at or above 40 is 40.13, which is the trigger price. At this point, you have to take care of the buy limit portion. A buy limit is a BLiSS (Buy Limit, Sell Stop) order, which will be executed at or below the order price ($40). Since the order was triggered at 40.13 and never went to 40 or below after that, the order was just triggered but never executed.

7. **A.** (Chapter 12) To determine the breakeven point for a put option, you have to subtract the premium from the strike price of 60. To find the premium for the Dec 60 put, look under the last column. The last column is for December puts. Next, find the 60 strike price from the second column — it's in the bottom row. If you intersect the bottom row with the last column (the lower right-hand corner), you'll see that the premium is 12. By subtracting 12 from 60, you get a breakeven point of 48.

8. **C.** (Chapter 16) To determine good delivery, always look at the shares. The certificates must be in multiples of 100 shares (for example, 100, 200, 300, and so on), divisors of 100 shares (1, 2, 4, 5, 10, 20, 25, and 50), or shares that add up to 100 (for example, 80 + 20, 75 + 15, 60 + 30 + 10, and so on). Choice (A) is okay because 900 is a multiple of 100 and the odd lot portion (30 shares) is exempt. Choice (B) is fine because 400 is a multiple of 100, 50 is a divisor of 100, and the odd lot portion (30 shares) is exempt. Choice (D) works because 200 is a multiple of 100 and 10 is a divisor of 100. Choice (C) is the bad one (in this case, the one you're looking for) because even though 200 is a multiple of 100, 13 doesn't divide into 100 evenly.

9. **C.** (Chapter 7) T-strips or Treasury receipts are long-term zero-coupon bonds backed by the full faith and credit of the U.S. government. Zero-coupon bonds are ideal investments to plan for future events because investors don't face reinvestment risk. In addition, the purchase price for long-term zero-coupon bonds is comparatively low.

10. **A.** (Chapter 8) The Series 7 examiners want to see that you can distinguish revenue bonds from general obligation bonds. In this question, Choice (A) is the correct answer. Revenue bonds are backed by a project's earning capacity. Choices (B), (C), and (D) are incorrect because revenue bonds are not secured by a specific pledge of property, are not a type of general obligation bond, and are not subject to debt limitations the way that many general obligation bonds are.

11. **A.** (Chapter 13) When you look at a corporation's balance sheet, the left-hand side lists all the assets and the right-hand side lists all the liabilities plus the shareholders' equity. The left side and the right side balance out (equal the same amount of money).

12. **C.** (Chapter 15) Dividends are profits shared by corporations. Dividends can be taxed as either qualified (up to a maximum rate of 15 percent) or nonqualified (according to the investor's tax bracket). In order for the dividends to be qualified, the investor must have held onto the stock for at least 61 days. The 61-day holding period starts 60 days prior to the ex-dividend date.

13. **B.** (Chapter 12) This question is looking at how an option contract is adjusted for corporate actions. Cash dividends don't affect listed options because they don't change the amount of shares a company has outstanding. However, if a company splits its stock or gives a stock dividend, the terms of an option contract change (in other words, the more option contracts, the lower the strike price and/or the more shares per contract).

14. **B.** (Chapter 6) If John is in possession of the stock (even though most stock is now held in book-entry form), he will be sent another certificate for 60 shares of Zeppelin Marx stock, not just "notification" of the new 120-share value.

15. **B.** (Chapter 8) An official statement includes all relevant information about a new municipal bond. Municipal bonds don't have a prospectus, but an official statement is along the same lines. An official statement gives information about the municipal issue, such as the reason the bonds are being issued, what revenues are going to be used to pay the bonds, the issuer's payment history, and so forth. A tombstone ad is a brief advertisement that does not go into detail about the security being issued and a registration statement is used by corporations when they are filing with the SEC.

16. **D.** (Chapter 16) This question is a double negative ("not prohibited"), so it's asking which statement a registered representative *can* make. The answer is pretty much a matter of logic. Choices (A), (B), and (C) are all guarantees. A registered rep who makes guarantees may get into trouble. However, Choice (D) is not a guarantee and may be said to an investor as long as it's true.

17. **A.** (Chapter 15) The main difference between traditional IRAs and Roth IRAs is the tax implications. Contributions to traditional IRAs are made from pretax dollars (you can write them off on your taxes), whereas contributions to Roth IRAs are made from after-tax dollars (you can't write them off on your taxes). However, distributions (withdrawals) from traditional IRAs are taxed on the amount above contribution, whereas withdrawals from Roth IRAs are tax-free. When withdrawing from a Roth IRA, neither the amount invested, which was already taxed, nor the amount the account has gone up in value (appreciation) is taxed, which is a great benefit to Roth IRA holders.

18. **D.** (Chapter 16) All firms must now have business continuity and disaster recovery plans to be prepared in the event of a significant disruption in their business. These plans must be in written form, be approved by a principal, and address the following information:

    - The existence of backup data
    - A means of alternative communication between a firm and its employees, customers, and regulators
    - The creation of an alternative location for all employees
    - A means of giving customers fast access to their securities and funds

19. **C.** (Chapter 10) Certainly all the choices listed are important, but the most important one is the investment objectives of the mutual fund. In other words, you need to know whether the investor is looking for a growth fund, an income fund, a municipal bond fund, an international fund, and so on. When comparing funds with the same investment objectives, all of the other things, such as comparing management fees, whether the fund is load or no-load, and so on, come into play.

20. **A.** (Chapter 6) Common stockholders may cast votes for candidates to be members of the board of directors; therefore, Choice (A) is the correct answer. Choice (B) is incorrect because while common stockholders may vote on important issues that affect the welfare of the corporation, they do not have voting rights on the day-to-day operations of the corporation, like buying office supplies. Choice (C) is incorrect because a stockholder doesn't receive interest payments, bondholders do. Finally, Choice (D) is incorrect because a common stockholder's initial investment can be lost if a corporation fails; therefore, par value is not guaranteed.

21. **A.** (Chapter 10) The clues in this question are that the investor is 21 years old, has limited resources, and would like to start investing on a regular basis. This investor is screaming out to be put in a mutual fund. Typically, investors of mutual funds are in it for the long haul, they're not in and out like they may be with other investments. Ideally, this investor should probably be set up on a dollar cost averaging plan whereby he invests *x* amount of dollars every so often (for instance, once a month). Because this investor is young, he or she can take a little more risk, so a growth fund would be ideal. CDOs, buying call options, and hedge funds are too risky, require too much money, and/or require a certain degree of sophistication.

22. **C.** (Chapter 16) Lawyers, accountants, teachers, and engineers are not advisers unless they're offering advice outside of their job descriptions. In Choice (A), the lawyer is a securities attorney. In Choice (B), the teacher is an economics professor. A registered rep of a brokerage firm must become licensed as an adviser or adviser representative to be able to offer advice for a fee. In most cases, registered reps may only be paid for executing trades.

23. **B.** (Chapter 8) The answer is Choice (B). Choices (A), (C), and (D) are incorrect. Revenue bonds are generally considered low-risk because they're issued by municipalities. The riskiest municipal bonds are IDRs (Industrial Development Revenue bonds), which are backed by a corporation, not the municipality.

24. **D.** (Chapter 16) When a client receives a trade confirmation (receipt of trade), the confirmation must show the trade date, settlement date, the name of the security, how many shares were traded, whether the broker-dealer acted as an agent or principal, and the amount of commission if traded on an agency basis.

25. **B.** (Chapter 16) The correct answer is (B) because when Jessica grants her registered representative a limited power of attorney, she is the one who must sign the document. Although a principal must approve before the registered representative exercises his or her discretionary authority, the registered representative does not have to sign the document, and Jessica's approval of each order is not required.

26. **B.** (Chapter 10) Real Estate Investment Trusts pass through income earned by the real-estate investments, but not losses. Real-estate limited partnerships pass through income and losses to investors because DPPs aren't responsible for paying business taxes.

27. **D.** (Chapter 16) I hope this was an easy one for you. Principals must approve all new accounts and must sign all new account forms.

28. **D.** (Chapter 16) Churning is a violation that occurs when a registered rep trades an investor's account excessively for the sole purpose of generating commission. When FINRA is looking to see whether an account has been churned, they look at things like the number of trades (are there too many?), the amount of money in the account (is the registered rep only trading a small portion of the account?), the objectives of the customer (does she buy and hold or does she like to trade a lot?), and so on. However, the amount of profit or loss in the account is not considered (although if the customer had a large profit in the account, I doubt that she'd be complaining).

29. **C.** (Chapter 13) The selling of U.S. government securities in the open market pulls dollars out of the banking system that tightens the money supply (and increases short-term interest rates).

30. **B.** (Chapter 9) Because George is borrowing money through a margin account to purchase securities, he must leave the stock in the broker-dealer's safekeeping, pay interest on the loan, register the stock in street name, and agree to allow the broker-dealer to pledge the securities because he signed a loan consent agreement.

31. **D.** (Chapter 6) The Series 7 examiners want to make sure that you know the difference between the different types of securities. Both convertible preferred and participating preferred stocks tend to carry lower dividend rates because they give Terri an extra benefit, which is the right to convert to common shares at a fixed price or the right to earn more than the stated rate if the issuer has a good year and makes an extra dividend payment. Straight preferred stock has no conversion or participating features and probably carries a better rate than convertible and participating stocks. Choice (D) is the correct answer, however, because callable preferred stock allows the issuer to "call" the securities away from Terri; therefore, callable preferred stock tends to pay higher rates than any of the other answer choices to offset this call risk.

32. **D.** (Chapter 5) The Series 7 examiners are trying to see whether you know what components are superfluous in calculating liability for Eastern account issues. Choice (D) is the correct answer. Because this is an Eastern account, Time Bandit has undivided liability for 10 percent of the unsold bonds (10% × $25 million = $2.5 million).

33. **B.** (Chapter 15) Variable life insurance policies often have a rider or statement of condition that allows individuals to keep their policy in force if they become disabled. This waiver of premium forgives policyholders of paying additional premiums if they become totally disabled.

34. **D.** (Chapter 16) Certainly just about anything you can think of could change a client's investment objectives. As people get older, they usually can't take as much risk. Conversely, investors who get higher-paying jobs are likely to want to take additional risk. Someone who is getting (or has gotten) divorced is likely to have less money (due to alimony payments, one person paying for the house instead of two, child support payments, and so on). Obviously, having triplets puts a financial burden on an investor (unless she gets a reality show).

35. **A.** (Chapter 6) Remember, the ex-dividend date (the first day the stock trades without the dividend) is two business days before the record date. In this case, the record date is Thursday, September 14, which makes the ex-dividend date Tuesday, September 12. The opening price on the ex-dividend date is reduced by the amount of the dividend ($0.40 in this case).

36. **D.** (Chapter 8) When you purchase a municipal bond issued within your home state, the interest you receive is triple tax-free (exempt from federal, state, and local taxes). In addition, if you purchase a bond issued by a U.S. territory (such as Puerto Rico, U.S. Virgin Islands, Guam, Samoa, and Washington, D.C.), the interest is triple-tax free. However, if you purchase a bond issued by another state, the interest is exempt from federal taxes only.

37. **A.** (Chapter 16) The correct answer is Choice (A). All taxes on the account are the responsibility of the minor because the UGMA account was opened for the benefit of the minor and the account is registered with the minor's Social Security number.

38. **A.** (Chapter 11) Of the choices listed, a real-estate partnership that invests in raw land is the riskiest. Partnerships that invest in raw land are considered speculative, as are oil and gas wildcatting programs. The risk of investing in raw land is that even though the property is purchased at a low price, developers may not be interested in that area and the partnership may be stuck with relatively worthless property.

39. **D.** (Chapter 16) In order to answer "ownership transfer" questions correctly on the Series 7 exam, you must be able to distinguish a registrar's functions from a transfer agent's functions. If that isn't stressful enough, you have an "except" question, which means you're looking for a false answer. As for functions, a registrar accounts for the number of shares on the corporation's books to ensure that the outstanding shares don't exceed the total number of shares on the books. The registrar also audits the transfer agent. The correct answer is Choice (D) because the transfer agent — not the registrar — records the names of stockholders, cancels old shares, and transfers shares to new owners' names.

40. **A.** (Chapter 5) The final offering price would not be found on the preliminary prospectus (red herring) because the price hasn't been finalized at this point. After the issuer and the syndicate manager come up with a final offering price, they place it on the final prospectus.

41. **B.** (Chapter 16) When determining whether a broker-dealer has to file a currency transaction report (CTR), you need to look at the size of the trade first. Any cash or cash equivalent (for example, a money order) transaction of $10,000 or more requires that you file a CTR to FinCEN (the U.S. Treasury Financial Crimes Network) to determine whether it may be money laundering. In Choice (B), the investor is depositing $14,000 in cash, which is over the $10,000 threshold. In addition, an SAR (Suspicious Activity Report) must be filed for any transaction of $5,000 or more for any trade or transfer that just looks suspicious.

42. **C.** (Chapter 10) To determine the sales charge percentage of a fund, use the following equation:

$$\text{Sales charge \%} = \frac{\text{POP} - \text{NAV}}{\text{POP}} = \frac{\$10.00 - \$9.30}{\$10.00} = \frac{\$0.70}{\$10.00} = 7\%$$

The POP is the public offering price, which is the price that investors pay, including the sales charge. The NAV is the net asset value and is where the fund should be trading, excluding the sales charge.

43. **A.** (Chapter 13) The correct answer is Choice (A). Historically, precious metals, like gold, are counter-cyclical and move opposite of the economic cycles. Choices (B), (C), and (D) are incorrect because utility, pharmaceutical, and food companies are defensive or non-cyclical, and their movement isn't tied to the economic cycle.

44. **C.** (Chapter 5) On a competitive bid for a new municipal underwriting, the difference between the bid to the issuer and the dollar price at which the underwriter reoffers the bonds to the public is the *spread,* which, importantly, is also the underwriter's compensation.

45. **B.** (Chapter 16) Remember, when a customer opens a cash account, the only signatures that are required are that of the registered rep and a principal of the firm. However, if a customer were to open up a margin account, she'd have to sign a margin agreement.

46. **D.** (Chapter 14) A designated market maker's book (specialist's book) keeps track of stop and limit orders. Market orders are for immediate execution at the best price available and, therefore, are not placed in the book. Not-held orders are held by the floor broker, who has discretion concerning the time and the price at which the order will take place, so these orders aren't held in the designated market maker's book either.

47. **A.** (Chapter 14) Sell stop orders are used for protection. A sell stop order is placed below the support level of the stock and limits the loss on a long position. For argument's sake, say that a stock has a trading range of 30 to 32. An investor may enter a sell stop order at 29.50 to protect herself if the stock drops to 29.50 or below. If the price of the stock hits 29.50, the sell stop order becomes a market order for immediate execution at the next available price.

48. **C.** (Chapter 9) Because this investor is opening a margin account (initial transaction), additional rules other than the 50-percent Regulation T requirement are in play. When purchasing securities for the first time, investors must pay in full, pay Regulation T (50 percent) of the transaction, or pay $2,000. If the cost is less than $2,000, the investor pays in full. If the cost is more than $2,000 but Regulation T is less than $2,000 (as it is in this case), the investor pays $2,000. If the cost of the securities is more than $2,000 and Regulation T is greater than $2,000, the investor pays the Regulation T amount.

49. **B.** (Chapter 7) The *indenture* (trust indenture or deed of trust) of a bond is a legal contract between the issuer and the trustee representing the investors. The bond indenture includes the coupon rate (nominal yield), the maturity date, the name of the trustee, collateral that may be backing the bond, and so on. However, the credit rating isn't found on the indenture because that's something that would change if the financial condition of the issuer changes.

50. **C.** (Chapter 11) The certificate of limited partnership is the legal agreement between the limited and general partners and has to be filed with the secretary of state. The certificate of limited partnership includes the name of the partnership, the partnership's primary place of business, the names and addresses of the limited and general partners, the goals of the partnership and how long it's expected to last, the amount contributed by each partner, how the profits are to be distributed, the roles of the participants, how the partnership can be dissolved, and whether a limited partner can sell or assign his or her interest in the partnership. The authority that allows the general partner to charge a fee for making management decisions is found in the partnership agreement.

51. **A.** (Chapter 6) The correct answer is Choice (A). Because warrants are basically long-term options to buy stock at a fixed price from the issuer, they can't pay dividends.

52. **C.** (Chapter 12) To create a short combination, Marty has to sell a call and sell a put on the same stock with different expiration months and/or strike prices. Because you need to have two sells to create a short combination, you can cross off Choices (A) and (B). The difference between a straddle and a combination is in the expiration months and the strike prices. If the expiration months are the same and the strike prices are the same, you have a straddle. If the expiration months and/or the strike prices are different, you're looking at a combination.

53. **B.** (Chapter 10) Choice (B) is the correct answer because three components are true about a REIT. As indicated by its acronym, a REIT is a Real Estate Investment Trust. REITs engage in real-estate activities and are organized as trusts. In order to qualify for favorable tax treatment, a REIT must pass through at least 90 percent of its net investment income to its shareholders. Statement IV is false because, although a REIT can pass through income to investors, it can't pass through losses.

54. **D.** (Chapter 12) The easiest way to calculate the break-even point for stock/option problems is to take a look at what's happening. This investor purchased the stock for $45 per share and then purchased the options for $6 per share. The investor paid $51 ($45 + $6) per share out of pocket, so the investor needs the stock to be at $51 per share in order to break even.

55. **D.** (Chapter 5) All the securities listed are exempt from the registration and disclosure provisions under the Securities Act of 1933.

56. **B.** (Chapter 11) Investors of limited partnerships bear additional risks, such as the possibility of money being tied up for a long period of time, little or no liquidity, the making of additional loans to the partnership, and so on. As a registered rep, you need to prescreen your customers to see whether they're a good match for the partnership. You should also look at the partnership and management itself to see whether they have a good track record and whether the partnership makes sense. You need to explain the risks to your customer and have your customer fill out a subscription agreement, not a partnership agreement. The subscription agreement needs to include a check, a signature giving the general partner power of attorney, financial statements, and so on.

57. **C.** (Chapter 10) Life-cycle funds are ideal for investors of any age. The idea behind them is that investors buy into life-cycle funds that are targeted for their age. The percentage of equities held by the fund decreases over time, whereas the percentage of fixed-income securities increases, because investors should hold a higher percentage of fixed-income securities as they age. For example, say a 45-year-old investor buys into a life-cycle fund that's targeted for investors who are currently between the ages of 44–47. At this particular point, the fund may have a nearly 50-50 split between equity securities and fixed-income securities. The fund rebalances every so often so that 10 years into the future, the fund may have 40 percent invested in equity securities and 60 percent invested in fixed-income securities. Ten years after that, the fund may have a 30-70 split between equity and fixed-income securities. This fund is designed to take the guesswork out of the equation for investors.

58. **A.** (Chapter 7) *Planned amortization class* (PAC) tranches are considered the safest of all tranches because a large portion of the prepayment and extension risk is absorbed by a companion tranche. *Targeted amortization class* (TAC) tranches are considered second in terms of safety because they're subject to additional prepayment and extension risk. Companion tranches are considered risky because the average life of a companion tranche varies greatly as interest rates change. Z tranches are basically zero-coupon tranches and are the most volatile of all tranches because they receive no payments until all the CMO tranches are retired.

59. **A.** (Chapter 14) An *IPO* (initial public offering) is the first time a corporation ever sells securities to the public. A first-market trade is a trade of exchange-listed securities trading on an exchange. A rights offering is when a company offers new shares to existing shareholders at a discount.

60. **D.** (Chapter 13) The correct answer is Choice (D) because short-term bonds are more liquid (more actively traded) than long-term bonds. Choices (A), (B), and (C) are incorrect because the characteristics in those answer choices describe long-term bonds, and the question asks you for characteristics of short-term bonds.

61. **D.** (Chapter 14) Broker-dealers act as both brokers (middlemen) and dealers (selling securities out of their own inventory). When broker-dealers act as brokers, they're purchasing or selling securities for an investor through a market maker. When acting as brokers, they charge a commission. When acting as dealers, they either buy securities from investors to

add to their own inventory or sell securities to investors from their own inventory. In this case, the broker-dealer charges a markup (if the customer is buying) or a markdown (if the customer is selling). So, all answer choices given are correct depending on the capacity of the trade.

62. **D.** (Chapter 12) The best way to determine the maximum gain is to set up an options chart. The first thing you need to do is find the premiums for the two options. Looking at the exhibit, you can see that the premium for the TUV Nov 60 put is 4 and the premium for the TUV Nov 50 put is 1.25. Because the investor purchased the 60 put, you have to put 400 (4 premium × 100 shares per option) on the "Money Out" side of the chart. Next, you have to put 125 (1.25 premium × 100 shares per option) on the "Money In" side of the chart because the investor sold that option. After doing that, you can see that you have $275 more in money out than money in, so that's the investor's maximum loss. To get the maximum gain, you have to exercise both options. Because "puts switch," you have to put the exercised strike price of $6,000 on the opposite side of its premium and the exercised strike price of $5,000 on the opposite side of its premium.

Money Out	Money In
$400	$125
$5,000	$6,000
$5,400	$6,125

After totaling up the two sides, you can see that the maximum gain is $725, because there's $725 more money in than out.

63. **B.** (Chapter 13) Defensive stocks perform consistently no matter how poorly the economy's doing. Stock of corporations that sell goods such as alcohol, tobacco, pharmaceutical supplies, food, and so on issue defensive stocks. However, companies that sell appliances, automobiles, and so on aren't defensive because they sell items that don't sell well in a weak economy.

64. **C.** (Chapter 16) The broker-dealer must send out account statements at least once every three months (quarterly) for an inactive account. If there has been any activity during a particular month, the brokerage firm must send out an account statement that month. Mutual funds must send out account statements once every six months (semiannually).

65. **D.** (Chapter 14) Here's another question where you must find the false answer. Choices (A), (B), and (C) are wrong because only orders placed below the market price are reduced for cash dividends on the order book. Buy limits and sell stops (BLiSS orders) are entered below the market price. Buy stops are entered above the market price, so Choice (D) is the false — and therefore, correct — answer.

66. **D.** (Chapter 8) Because this is an "except" question, you must find the false answer. The correct answer is Choice (D). The dated date of a bond issue is the date on which the issue begins to earn interest, which has less impact on marketing than the other answer choices.

67. **B.** (Chapter 15) IRAs may be set up as single life, joint and last survivor, or uniform lifetime. *Life with period certain* is a way to set up payout for an annuity, not an IRA. *Single life* is when the owner is the beneficiary of the account. *Joint and last survivor* is when the sole beneficiary of the account is a spouse who is more than ten years younger than the owner. *Uniform lifetime* is when the spouse is not the sole beneficiary or the spouse is not more than ten years younger than the owner.

68. **C.** (Chapter 15) Similar to variable annuities, variable life insurance policies have a separate account of securities. All variable life insurance (VLI) policies have a set premium and a minimum death benefit. However, if the securities held in the separate account perform well, the policy will build up cash value, which will increase the death benefit.

69. **B.** (Chapter 13) Certainly, all the choices listed are important when determining a client's investment profile. However, this is an "except" question, which means that you're looking for an investment influence that is financial. The amount of marketable securities an investor owns is part of her financial profile as well as other things like net worth, money available for investing, current income, expenses, home ownership, and so on.

70. **B.** (Chapter 16) A durable power of attorney gives power of attorney to someone else to handle financial affairs in the event that the grantor becomes incapacitated. A durable power of attorney is unlike a regular power of attorney, which terminates once the grantor becomes incapacitated.

71. **B.** (Chapter 7) The easiest way to figure out this question is to use the seesaw. Because the bond in question is a 7-percent bond, you have to put 7 percent above the NY (Nominal Yield, or coupon rate). Next, put the 7.50 basis above the YTM (Yield To Maturity). Now you can see that because the YTM is greater than the NY, the right side of the seesaw has to go up. Once the right side goes up, you can determine that the current yield (CY) is higher than the nominal yield (coupon rate).

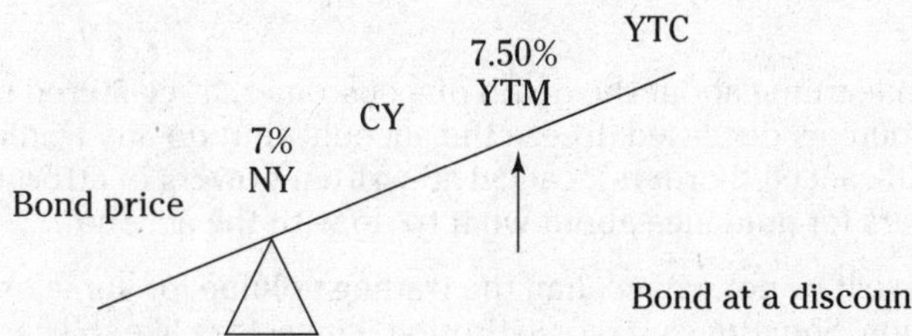

72. **A.** (Chapter 9) Normally, if Barbara were purchasing $10,000 worth of stock on margin, she'd have to deposit $5,000 to meet the margin call (you can assume Regulation T is 50 percent of the purchase). First, you have to find out whether she has any excess equity in her margin account to help offset the $5,000 payment. Use the following equation:

    LMV – DR = EQ

    After setting up the equation, enter the market value of the securities ($30,000) under the long market value (LMV). Next, enter the $12,000 under the debit record (DR), also known as the *debit balance*. When you subtract the DR from the LMV, you come up with an equity (EQ) of $18,000. Multiply Regulation T (50 percent) by the LMV to get the amount of equity the customer needs to have in the account to be at 50 percent. This investor needs only $15,000 in equity to reach 50 percent, and this investor has $18,000, $3,000 more than necessary:

    LMV – DR = EQ
    $30,000 – $12,000 = $18,000
    Reg T × LMV = <u>$15,000</u>
    $3,000 excess equity

    The $3,000 is excess equity (SMA, or special memorandum account), which she can use to help offset the margin call for the $10,000 worth of stock she wants to buy:

    $5,000 margin call – $3,000 excess equity = $2,000 to deposit

73. **C.** (Chapter 8) The interest received on municipal bonds is federally tax-free. Because Ginny is in the highest income tax bracket, she can save more tax money by investing in municipal bonds. This strategy will put her on equal footing with other investors because neither high-income nor low-income investors have to pay taxes on the interest received from municipal bonds. Therefore, municipal bonds are more advantageous to investors in high income tax brackets.

74. **B.** (Chapter 15) Health savings accounts are tax-exempt trusts or custodial accounts set up with a qualified health savings account trustee. The trustee for a health savings account can be a bank, insurance company, or anyone approved by the IRS to be a trustee for IRAs. Health savings accounts may only be set up for individuals or families that have a high-deductible health plan (HDHP). In addition, the individual may not be covered by Medicare. Contributions are made on a pretax basis and grow on a tax-free basis. In addition, many investors deposit their health savings account money in mutual funds. Withdrawals can be made tax-free as long as the funds are used for qualified medical expenses.

75. **D.** (Chapter 8) Under a net revenue pledge, operation and maintenance expenses are always paid first, and then the net revenues are used to pay the debt service. Consequently, Choice (D) is the correct answer because payments are made in this order:

    1. Maintenance and operating expenses
    2. Debt service
    3. Debt service reserve
    4. Surplus

76. **D.** (Chapter 16) Upon learning about the death of a customer, a registered representative should mark the account as deceased, freeze the account (not do any trading), cancel all open orders (good-till-canceled orders), cancel all written powers of attorney, and await the proper legal papers for guidance about what to do with the account.

77. **B.** (Chapter 14) Believe it or not, concealing the trading volume for some orders from the public is not a violation. Sometimes large institutional investors like to keep the trading volume of some of their orders hidden from other institutional investors. This practice is called "dark pools of liquidity." They usually do this so as not to provide too much information to some of their competitors.

78. **B.** (Chapter 14) When looking at the Designated Market Maker's Book (specialist's book), ignore the stop orders. After ignoring the stop orders, take the highest bid price, which is 41.03, and the lowest ask price, which is 41.06, to get the answer.

79. **C.** (Chapter 7) Mortgage bonds, collateral trusts, and equipment trusts are all forms of secured bonds. Because these bonds are secured with collateral, the collateral securing the bonds is sold to satisfy the bondholders if the issuer defaults. However, debentures are not backed with collateral and are therefore riskier. Because more risk equals more reward, debenture holders can expect a coupon rate that's higher than that of the secured bonds.

80. **D.** (Chapter 7) Of the answer choices given, Choice (D) is the least preferable and, therefore, the correct answer. AA rated bonds, U.S. treasury notes and AA rated debentures can yield predictable income. By contrast, income bonds are issued when a corporation is coming out of bankruptcy and trying to reorganize. Therefore, income bonds only pay interest if the corporation can meet the interest payment and normally trade without accrued interest. Income bonds are not suitable for Dana because she's seeking predictable income.

81. **A.** (Chapter 12) You'll find that this question is actually much easier than you may have originally thought. To get the maximum loss on a debit (long) spread, all you have to do is put the premiums in the option chart to see that you have more money out than in. The difference between those two numbers is the maximum loss.

82. **C.** (Chapter 10) Although international funds may be okay to help diversify a portfolio, they're certainly the riskiest of all the choices given. International funds invest in securities outside of the investor's home country. International funds have additional risks that many other securities don't have, such as currency risk (the risk that the currency exchange rate will be bad). Also, the investor faces political risk (the risk that political changes in a country may adversely affect the price of securities). You should definitely steer this investor away from international funds.

83. **A.** (Chapter 12) The OCC (Options Clearing Corporation) is the issuer and guarantor of all listed options. The OCC determines which options will be traded and guarantees that option holders can always exercise their options.

84. **C.** (Chapter 10) Dividends that are distributed by municipal bond funds are federally tax-free, but any capital gain distribution is taxable. Choice (C) is the right answer.

85. **C.** (Chapter 14) NYSE Amex Equities, NYSE Euronext, and NASDAQ OMX PHLX are all exchange (auction) markets, but NASDAQ Global Market (NGM) is a listing of the larger and most actively traded stocks trading OTC (over-the-counter). The OTC market is a negotiated market, not an exchange market.

86. **C.** (Chapter 8) Hopefully, the "G" in "GANs" was enough to help you get the correct answer. GANs are *grant anticipation notes,* which a municipality issues to provide temporary financing while waiting for a grant from the U.S. government.

87. **D.** (Chapter 12) "Long" means to buy, so to have a long straddle, you can't have any sells (shorts). Thus, you can cross off Choices (A) and (B). To create a long straddle, the investor needs to buy a call and buy a put with the same stock, same strike price, and same expiration date. The only answer that works is Choice (D).

88. **D.** (Chapter 9) Luke owns the calls that he's exercising. Luke exercises the options at a profit of $10 per share (less the premium) and is selling the stock immediately, so no deposit's required. It certainly wouldn't make much sense to have Luke pay $30 per share when exercising the options and then have the firm send Luke a check for $40 per share. The key here is that Luke exercised the option and sold the stock on the same day.

89. **B.** (Chapter 9) The margin requirement for both long and short margin accounts is set at 50 percent. However, the minimum maintenance for a long account is 25 percent and the minimum maintenance for a short account is 30 percent.

90. **C.** (Chapter 13) To determine the net worth of a company, use the following equation:

    net worth = assets – liabilities

    net worth = $11,500,000 – $3,350,000 = $8,150,000

91. **D.** (Chapter 12) The maximum gain or loss on a capped option is not unlimited. The maximum gain or loss on a capped option is 30 points in the money times 100 shares per option, or $3,000. However, because the investor had to purchase the option, the most that she can make is $3,000 minus whatever she paid for the premium.

92. **D.** (Chapter 9) *Portfolio margin* looks at the risk of an investor's portfolio as a whole when determining margin requirements. Portfolio margin allows investors greater leverage but is only available to more sophisticated investors, and those investors must keep a minimum equity in their account of around $150,000.

93. **A.** (Chapter 7) The correct answer is Choice (A) because issuers call bonds when interest rates are falling. Choice (B) is incorrect because after the notes are called, new bonds at the lower rate are issued to raise funds in order to call the outstanding bonds with the higher rate. Choice (D) is incorrect because municipal bond call provisions are advantageous to issuers; the call provisions reduce fixed costs by providing issuers with the ability to redeem bonds before maturity.

94. **C.** (Chapter 13) You can quickly cross off Choice (D), because this answer can be determined. To determine the price/earnings (PE) ratio, use the following formula:

    $$\text{PE ratio} = \frac{\text{market price}}{\text{EPS}} = \frac{\$22.00}{\$4.00} = 5.50$$

    The answer is 5.50, Choice (C).

95. **C.** (Chapter 14) Yes, in this case, Choice (C) is the one that stands out like a sore thumb. The OTC Pink Market is a speculative trading marketplace for stocks of companies too small to make the listing requirements of NASDAQ. TRACE (Trade Reporting and Compliance Engine) reports all trades of long-term corporate bonds and U.S. government agency bonds. FINRA/NASDAQ Trade Reporting Facility (TRF) is an electronic trade reporting and reconciliation service operated on the ACT (Automated Confirmation Transaction) system. The TRF handles broker-to-broker transactions executed over the counter. OATS (Order Audit Trail System) is an automated computer system that tracks the life of an OTC order from entry to execution or cancellation.

96. **B.** (Chapter 16) All written complaints need to be handled by a principal and kept on file. Even though the complaint was sent via e-mail, it's still considered a written complaint. The complaint does not need to be forwarded or sent to FINRA.

97. **B.** (Chapter 11) The investor's cost basis is the maximum potential loss for the investor. The investor deposited a total of $95,000 ($75,000 + $20,000 recourse loan). Cash distributions, depreciation, and depletion lower the investor's cost basis. So,

$95,000 – $10,000 – $30,000 – $25,000 = $30,000

98. **A.** (Chapter 11) This question is actually somewhat of a logic question, and I actually put the statements in order for you. Secured creditors (loans secured with collateral) are paid first, followed by general creditors (loans not secured with collateral), then limited partners (the main investors), and lastly, the general partners.

99. **A.** (Chapter 5) All securities sold in a state must be registered in that state (also known as blue-sky registration). Coordination, qualification, and notification (filing) are all types of state registration; registration by cooperation is not. If an agent wants to sell in a state, the security, the registered rep, and the broker-dealer must be registered in that state.

100. **B.** (Chapter 12) The easiest way to figure out the answer to this question is to use the equation P = I + T, where

- P = the Premium of the option
- I = the Intrinsic value of the option (how much it is in the money)
- T = the Time value of the option (how much the investor is paying for the time to use the option)

$$P = I + T$$
$$9 = 5 + T$$
$$T = 4$$

First, put the premium of 9 into the equation. Next, because the option is 5 points in the money (call options go in the money when the price of the stock goes above the strike price), insert the intrinsic value of 5 in the equation. Because the premium is 9 and the option is 5 points in the money, the time value is 4.

101. **B.** (Chapter 16) Principals of a firm must approve all new accounts, advertising used by the firm, handling of complaints, trades in all accounts, and so on. However, as far as the Series 7 exam goes, principals don't need to approve recommendations made by registered reps. In real life, I would get approval before making recommendations if I were you. You have to remember that principals must sign all order tickets, and if you don't clear a recommendation with them first, they may be reluctant to do so.

102. **B.** (Chapter 7) If you want to pass the Series 7 exam, you have to know your quotes. The correct answer is Choice (B) because it's the only discounted instrument, and discounted instruments (such as T-bills) are quoted on a discount yield basis.

103. **C.** (Chapter 8) LRBs (lease revenue bonds) are similar to IDRs (industrial development revenue bonds), but instead of the bonds being backed by corporations, they're backed by lease payments made by office buildings, universities, prisons, and so forth. LTGOs (limited tax general obligation bonds) are a type of GO (general obligation) bond that's backed by taxes that aren't used to back other bonds. BABs (build America bonds) are taxable municipal bonds in which the U.S. Treasury either reimburses the issuer or gives a tax credit to investors for up to 35 percent of the interest cost.

104. **D.** (Chapter 13) You can use logic to answer this question. When the company pays a cash dividend, it pays off some of its liabilities because the dividend was declared previously. The net worth does not change because assets (cash) and liabilities decrease by the same amount.

105. **D.** (Chapter 8) Remember that an "except" question is looking for a false answer. The correct answer is Choice (D). Taxable equivalent yields cannot be shown because every investor has a unique tax issue and bracket.

106. **B.** (Chapter 12) If the investor is looking for potential premium income, she must have sold something, so you can rule out Choice (C). Because the maximum loss potential for a short straddle or short combination is unlimited and the investor wants to limit her loss, you can cross out Choice (D). Actually, the only answer that works is a credit spread. To create a credit (short) spread, the investor sells an option that will be in the money first and purchases the option that will go in the money later. If the option never goes in the money, the investor gets to keep the premium of the option sold. To limit the loss, the investor purchases an option that will go in the money later. This position provides potential premium income and limits the maximum potential loss.

107. **A.** (Chapter 16) Under FINRA rules, the representative should execute the trade in accordance with the customer's request and note on the trade ticket that the order was unsolicited.

108. **C.** (Chapter 13) You can calculate the working capital, net worth, and quick assets by looking at a corporation's balance sheet, but you need information on the income statement to calculate the current yield.

109. **A.** (Chapter 7) Money market securities are a popular topic on the Series 7 exam. Remember that commercial paper, as well as negotiable certificates of deposit, are money market securities.

110. **B.** (Chapter 15) Any income derived from an investment in a limited partnership is termed passive. Passive gains can only be written off against passive losses. Earned income includes money made from salary, bonuses, tips, and so on. Portfolio income includes money made from interest, dividends, and capital gains made from investing in securities.

111. **C.** (Chapter 13) The Fed can lower reserve requirements to ease the money supply. The Fed can also buy T-bills from banks to increase the money supply.

112. **C.** (Chapter 12) Listed options expire at 11:59 p.m. EST (10:59 p.m. CST) on the Saturday following the third Friday of the expiration month. The last time to trade an option is 4:00 p.m. EST (3:00 p.m. CST) on the third Friday of the expiration month. The last time to exercise an option is 5:30 p.m. EST (4:30 p.m. CST) on the third Friday of the expiration month.

113. **B.** (Chapter 11) Limited partners have access to all of the financial information regarding the partnership, they may vote to terminate the partnership, and they may invest in competing partnerships. However, limited partners may not make management decisions; that right is limited to the general partner(s).

114. **C.** (Chapter 11) The primary reason for investing in undeveloped land is appreciation potential. People who invest in undeveloped land either privately or by way of a real-estate DPP are hoping that their land will be of more value sometime in the near future.

115. **B.** (Chapter 10) You can use logic to determine the answer to this one. The idea is that you can't paint an overly rosy picture to investors. Advertisements of municipal fund securities should show the maximum sales charge that an investor faces, and they should also show performance statistics, including the sales charge, which lowers the amount of return.

116. **D.** (Chapter 10) A letter of intent comes into play when a mutual fund offers a breakpoint (discount for large dollar purchases). An investor who can't deposit enough money intially to receive that breakpoint may sign a letter of intent. The letter of intent allows the investor 13 months to deposit enough money to receive the breakpoint. It may apply to purchases made up to 90 days before signing the letter of intent, and the fund may hold shares in escrow to be sold if the investor doesn't live up to the terms of the agreement. However, investors may never purchase mutual fund shares on margin because new securities can't be purchased on margin for at least 30 days, and mutual funds are always new shares.

117. **D.** (Chapter 12) I figured I'd give you an easy one towards the end of the test. When buying a call option, the maximum potential gain is unlimited, so an investor who's selling a call option faces an unlimited maximum potential loss.

118. **A.** (Chapter 6) After the split, stockholders are going to have 5 shares for every 4 that they had before. If the number of shares is going to increase, the price of the stock is going to decrease to make up for the additional shares. After the split, the investor should have the

same overall market value of securities. Use the following equation to determine the number of shares and the stock price after a split:

$$\text{shares after split} = \text{shares} \times \frac{A}{B}, \text{ so } 1{,}000 \times \frac{5}{4} = 1{,}250 \text{ shares}$$

$$\text{price after split} = \text{stock price} \times \frac{B}{A}, \text{ so } \$40 \times \frac{4}{5} = \$32$$

119. **D.** (Chapter 13) The correct answer is Choice (D) because controlling the money supply implies a hands-on approach that's referred to as the *monetarist theory*. Choice (A) is incorrect because, although the Federal Reserve Board (FRB) controls the money supply, they're not an economic theory. Choice (B) is incorrect because the *Keynesian theory* is about big (some say stifling) government intervention; it's more about raising taxes and government control over businesses. Choice (C) is incorrect because the *supply-side economic theory* calls for low taxes and low government spending to stabilize the economy.

120. **C.** (Chapter 13) This is another one of those logic questions. If the value of the U.S. dollar decreases in relationship to foreign currencies, it becomes weak and Americans buys less foreign goods while foreigners buy more U.S. goods. Because you're looking for the false answer, it has to be Choice (C).

121. **C.** (Chapter 7) Commercial paper is generally issued for the purpose of raising capital for a corporation. Choice (A) is incorrect because commercial instruments are not quoted as a percent of par. Choice (B) is incorrect because a commercial instrument is proof of a debt, not ownership. Choice (D) is incorrect because commercial instruments are a debt security; therefore, if a claim is filed against the issuing corporation, the commercial instrument holds a senior position to preferred stock.

122. **B.** (Chapter 16) Municipal fund securities include 529 college savings plans. All securities advertising must be approved by a principal of the firm and cannot be fraudulent (antifraud rules apply to everything). The MSRB and the states do not have to approve advertising.

123. **A.** (Chapter 15) In most instances, individuals may invest up to $5,000 per year in an IRA ($6,000 if they're age 50 or older). Investors who deposit more than that will be fined on their excess contributions at 6 percent until that excess contribution is removed.

124. **D.** (Chapter 10) A specialized or *sector* fund invests within a single industry or geographical area.

125. **D.** (Chapter 15) Withdrawals from a Roth IRA may begin any time after the investor reaches age 59½. However, there's no required beginning date (RBD) or required minimum distribution (RMD) for Roth IRAs like there is for other retirement plans. You need to remember that the money withdrawn from a Roth IRA is tax-free, so the IRS doesn't care when these investors take their money because it isn't getting any of it.

Knowing the Score

Here's how the Series 7 exam is scored:

- You get one point for each correct answer.
- You get zero points for each incorrect answer.

A passing grade is 72 percent. In other words, you need at least 180 correct answers on the whole test to get one step closer to your Nobel Prize in stockbrokerage (okay, economics). That's an average of about 90 correct answers per part.

To calculate your score for this part only, multiply the number of correct answers by 0.8 or divide it by 125. If you're one of the brave ones who took both Parts I and II in one sitting, you can multiply your correct answers by 0.4 or divide them by 250. Whatever grade you get, make sure you round down, not up. For example, a grade of 71.6 is a 71 percent, not a 72.

Answer Key for Part II of the Practice Exam

1. **A**
2. **D**
3. **B**
4. **A**
5. **A**
6. **D**
7. **A**
8. **C**
9. **C**
10. **A**
11. **A**
12. **C**
13. **B**
14. **B**
15. **B**
16. **D**
17. **A**
18. **D**
19. **C**
20. **A**
21. **A**
22. **C**
23. **B**
24. **D**
25. **B**
26. **B**
27. **D**
28. **D**
29. **C**
30. **B**
31. **D**
32. **D**
33. **B**
34. **D**
35. **A**
36. **D**
37. **A**
38. **A**
39. **D**
40. **A**
41. **B**
42. **C**
43. **A**
44. **C**
45. **B**
46. **D**
47. **A**
48. **C**
49. **B**
50. **C**
51. **A**
52. **C**
53. **B**
54. **D**
55. **D**
56. **B**
57. **C**
58. **A**
59. **A**
60. **D**
61. **D**
62. **D**
63. **B**
64. **C**
65. **D**
66. **D**
67. **B**
68. **C**
69. **B**
70. **B**
71. **B**
72. **A**
73. **C**
74. **B**
75. **D**
76. **D**
77. **B**
78. **B**
79. **C**
80. **D**
81. **A**
82. **C**
83. **A**
84. **C**
85. **C**
86. **C**
87. **D**
88. **D**
89. **B**
90. **C**

91. **D**
92. **D**
93. **A**
94. **C**
95. **C**
96. **B**
97. **B**
98. **A**
99. **A**
100. **B**
101. **B**
102. **B**
103. **C**
104. **D**
105. **D**
106. **B**
107. **A**
108. **C**
109. **A**
110. **B**
111. **C**
112. **C**
113. **B**
114. **C**
115. **B**
116. **D**
117. **D**
118. **A**
119. **D**
120. **C**
121. **C**
122. **B**
123. **A**
124. **D**
125. **D**

Part VI
The Part of Tens

"I'm really not that concerned about passing the Series 7 Exam. I'm undefeated in nearly 300 games of Monopoly."

In this part . . .

This part is standard in all *For Dummies* books (and top-ten lists are kind of an American institution), so here are two sets of ten tips for your reading pleasure. First, before you go to take the Series 7 exam, check out the ten exam traps to avoid. Next, you've tortured yourself for the past four to six weeks to prepare for the Series 7, so let me help you hit the ground running with ten ways to start your career as a stockbroker off right.

Chapter 21

Ten Series 7 Exam Traps to Avoid

In This Chapter

- Identifying the most common mistakes that Series 7 exam-takers make
- Uncovering the secrets for avoiding Series 7 exam traps

After all the time, effort, and sacrifice you put into studying, elevating the importance of the Series 7 exam to an unrealistically high level is easy. Step back for a moment. Keep it in perspective. This situation is not life or death. If you don't pass the test the first time, the worst thing that happens is that you have to retake it.

On the other hand, getting tripped up by some trivial exam traps after you've come this far would be a shame. This chapter lists some common mistakes and gives you some last-minute advice to help you over the last hurdles that stand between you and your first million dollars as a stockbroker.

Easing Up on the Studying

Perhaps you stop studying because you're getting good scores on practice exams and your confidence is high. If you're scoring 80s on exams that you're seeing for the first time, shoot for 85s. If you're getting 85s, shoot for 90s. The point is that you should continue to take exams until the day before your scheduled exam day. I firmly believe that every day away from studying ultimately costs you points on your exam that you can't afford to lose.

By the same token, make sure you don't wait too long before taking the exam. If you have to wait several weeks before you can take the exam, you lose your sense of urgency, and it's almost impossible to keep up the intense level of preparation needed for many months at a time. If you're taking a prep course before you schedule your Series 7, follow your instructor's advice as to when you should take the exam. If you're directing your own course of study, after you're passing practice exams consistently with 80s or better, take the test as soon as possible. The longer you wait to take the exam, the more likely you are to forget the key points and complex formulas. If your test date is too far in the future, you also risk falling into the I'll-study-later trap, where you think you can double your efforts later to make up for any wasted time. Overall, losing your sense of urgency leads to complacency and a lack of motivation, which probably aren't skills broker-dealers are looking for in their employees.

Assuming the Question's Intent

You glance at the question quickly and incorrectly anticipate what the exam question is really asking you. You pick the wrong answer because you were in such a rush, you didn't see the word *except* at the end of the question. What a shame.

You don't want to fail the exam when you really know the material. Read each question carefully and look for tricky words like *except, not,* and *unless.* Then read all the answer choices before making your selection. (For more info on test-taking strategies that apply to certain question types, see Chapter 3.)

Reading into the Question

You're thinking *but what if* before you even look at the answer choices. When reviewing questions with students, I constantly get questions like "Yeah, but what if he's an insider?" or "What if he's of retirement age?" The bottom line is that you shouldn't add anything to the question that isn't there. Don't be afraid to read the question at face value and select the right answer, even if it occasionally seems too easy. Eliminate answer choices that are too much of a stretch, and remember that when two answer choices are opposites, one of them is most likely correct.

Becoming Distracted When Others Finish

You haven't even started looking over the questions you marked for review when the woman next to you leaps from her seat, picks up her results (with a little victory dance), and makes a break for the door.

Don't let people who are taking the exam with you psych you out. If others finish ahead of you, perhaps they're members of Mensa or maybe this is the fifth time they've taken the exam — practice makes perfect. They may even be taking a totally different exam. Besides the Series 7, the testing centers also offer other securities exams with fewer questions (a 65-question Series 63 exam, a 100-question Series 66 exam, a 130-question Series 65 exam, and so on). Keep focused and centered on taking your own exam. The only time you need to be concerned with is your own — whether you're on track.

Not Dressing for Comfort

You're trying to calculate the taxable equivalent yield on Mr. Dimwitty's GO bond, but the pencil keeps slipping out of your sweaty hand. You swear the test center has the heat cranked up to 80 degrees. Hmm. Maybe wearing your warmest wool sweater wasn't the best idea.

Dress comfortably. Don't wear a tie that's so tight it cuts off the circulation to your brain. You're under enough stress just taking the exam. Dress in layers. A T-shirt, a sweatshirt, and a jacket are great insulation against the cold. Another advantage is that you can shed layers of clothing (without ending up sitting in your underwear) if the exam room is too warm.

Forgetting to Breathe

You walk into the test center brimming with confidence. All of a sudden the exam begins and some of the words look like they're in a foreign language. Your heart starts pounding, and you feel like you're going to pass out.

If stress becomes overwhelming, your breathing can become shallow and ineffective, which only adds to your stress level. Focus yourself before the exam by closing your eyes and taking a few deep breaths. This same process of closing your eyes and breathing deeply is a great way to calm yourself if you become stressed or anxious at any time during the exam.

Trying to Work Out Equations in Your Head Instead of Writing Them Down

While taking the exam, your memory starts to cloud and, somehow, the fact that two plus two equals five begins to make sense to you and the only formula you can remember is that there are 12 inches in a foot.

Memorize your equations while you're studying for your Series 7 exam so you know them cold before you arrive at the test site. If your nerves are getting the best of you and clouding your memory, jotting down the more difficult equations that you want to remember as soon as you receive permission to start the exam may be helpful (this process is known as a *brain dump*). When working out complicated math problems, you have six pieces of scrap paper to work with (and a basic calculator). Use them. For example, some formulas, such as those for determining the debt service coverage ratio or the value of a right (cum rights), require you to find sums and differences before you can divide. Even simple calculations, such as finding averages, can involve quite a few numbers. In problems with multiple parts, it's easy for you to accidentally skip steps, plug in the wrong numbers from the question, or forget values that you calculated along the way. Writing things out helps you keep things in place without cluttering your short-term memory.

Spending Too Much Time on One Question

To calculate the number of days of accrued interest on a T-bond, you decide to draw pictures of the calendar for the last four months. As you finish penciling the dates in those tiny boxes, you look at the clock and realize ten minutes have passed. Oops!

All questions have the same point value. If you spend too much time on one question, you may lose points for many questions you didn't have time to even look at because you wasted so much time on the one that gave you trouble. If you find yourself taking too long to answer a question, take your best guess, mark it for review, and return to it later.

Changing Your Answers for the Wrong Reasons

You change an answer just because you already selected that same letter for the preceding three or four questions in a row. Just a touch of paranoia, right?

You've probably been told from the time you first started primary school not to change your answers. Trust your instincts and go with your original reaction. You have only two good reasons to change your answer:

- You find that you initially forgot or didn't see the words *not* or *except* and you initially chose the wrong answer because you didn't see the tricky word.
- You find that the answer choice you originally selected is not the best answer after all.

Calculating Your Final Score Prematurely

You waste valuable time concentrating on the number of questions you think you got wrong instead of focusing on the Series 7 exam questions you still have to answer.

Just read each question carefully, scrutinize the answer choices, and select the best answer. You'll find out whether you passed right after you complete the exam; it's not like you need to figure out your possible grade in advance to avoid sleepless nights until you receive your score. If you have additional time, use it to check your answers to the questions you marked for review.

Chapter 22

Ten Ways to Start Your Career Off Right

In This Chapter

- Understanding how to survive and prosper as a stockbroker
- Socking away (or investing) money

Passing the Series 7 exam can be one of the high points in your life. You've dedicated yourself to attaining your goal, put your life (and partying) on hold while you studied, and fulfilled your commitment to long hours of studying and hard work. You're now ready to reap the rewards. As you begin your new profession, you'll encounter many new hurdles. I give you this chapter to help prepare you for what to expect and, hopefully, to maximize your chances of a long, successful career.

Win at the Numbers Game

As with any other sales job, selling securities to investors is a numbers game. Some people actually track the number of calls it takes to open a new account, but I'm not among them. There are no specific economic benchmarks; however, you may have to make 500 cold calls to get to talk to 150 people. Out of these 150 people, you may generate ten leads. Out of every ten leads, you may open up one account.

The point is that you have to pick up that phone day in and day out and make the calls. If you're making 200 to 300 phone calls per day, you're likely to open an account every few days. However, if you're making 50 phone calls a day, you'll probably open up an account every couple weeks, and unless you hook a whale (a huge investor who likes to trade), you'll have trouble paying for gas for your new car. Remember that you're participating in a numbers game and that every "no" brings you one call closer to a "yes."

Be an Apprentice

There's no better way to hit the ground running than to have a top producer as a role model. Find the person in your firm with sales techniques that are most comfortable for you and invest as much time as possible watching how this mentor conducts herself on a daily basis. Top producers earn the most income because they've found a way to stand out in a competitive market.

Maybe this person can take you under her wing and show you the ropes in return for leads you develop while under her supervision. You can even have a contract between you and your mentor that sets forth the agreed-upon terms for each of you for a fixed period of time.

Do Your Homework

Take time to find out as much as possible about the securities you're trying to sell. When you know what you're talking about, you inspire confidence from potential new customers. Spend some of your free time watching investing programs and reading the *Wall Street Journal* or any other trade magazines or newspapers you can get your hands on. The more you learn, the more comfortable you'll be on the phone, and the more sales you'll make.

Treat the Minnow like a Whale

More often than not, new customers don't disclose all their financial background to you. However, whether a customer has $10,000 or $10 million to invest, the money is important to her. Treat every customer as though she's the most valuable person in the world. Who knows? You may be speaking to someone with a lot of money to invest now or someone who will have a lot of money to invest in the future, or your customer may be a friend or family member of someone with substantial resources. Remember, a strong referral is a most influential lead.

Smile When You Dial

Be positive. You're going to have good days and bad days. You have to accept that as part of the business, but don't let it get you down. If you need to, take a five-minute break to gather your thoughts. If you aren't in a positive state of mind, you'll reflect that in the way you talk to existing or potential customers.

When a Security Falls, Don't Be a Stranger

You can't guarantee success, and that's okay. Savvy investors know that not every investment can end up a winner, no matter how good the situation looks in the beginning. If you recommend a security and it gets beaten down, call your customer. The customer is just waiting to hear from you. This call may be right up there with the most uncomfortable tasks you'll ever have to perform. Remember, however, that a savvy customer is most likely aware of what's going on, and your news won't be a surprise. Customers just want to be comforted and reassured that you'll be there with them — in good times and bad. Hopefully, the other seven or eight securities that you recommended are doing well.

Put In the Hours

Of course, you have to educate yourself about selling your products and cold-calling. In the beginning, be prepared to put in approximately ten hours each day. As you grow more experienced, you'll receive more leads and open more accounts in a shorter period of time, but in the beginning, you have to play the numbers game in order to earn money while you develop a more confident sales pitch.

Broaden Your Horizons

Consider obtaining other licenses to increase your skills and your ability to compete in the securities and financial industry. For example, the Series 65 or 66 (investment adviser exams) allows you to receive a fee for giving investment advice; Series 24 (the principal's license exam) allows you to manage other registered reps; and a Life, Accident, and Health Insurance license allows you to sell insurance policies and variable annuities to customers. If you take prep courses to obtain these licenses, you may also be exposed to a network of professionals who can become a source of future referrals.

Pay Yourself First

The stock market (and you with it) will have many peaks and valleys, but your financial security doesn't have to be quite so uneven. In the peak times, put away half your earnings when you receive your big paychecks. Tell yourself that you aren't going to make a big purchase until you have a certain amount socked away (see the upcoming section on setting goals). I've seen too many new brokers go out and buy a new car, a new boat, or whatever with their first big paycheck, expecting to make that much every month. The first time they have a bad month, they're wondering how they're going to make the payments (and possibly pay the rent). Remember, stockbrokers are supposed to be good with money. Burying yourself in debt looks kind of bad.

Keep hunger in your efforts, not your stomach

When I first began my career as a stockbroker, the sales manager at the securities firm where I worked began the staff meetings by introducing himself and stating that he'd earned $100,000 his first year in the business and spent $150,000 of it — and he considered that to be a good thing! Somehow that just doesn't make sense either mathematically or logically (no matter how much your spending stimulates the economy). Some of the other trainees at the meeting were very impressed with the sales manager's suggestion, especially when he told us that he stayed hungry by spending so much more than he earned.

I remember looking at the sales manager and the other trainees who were attending this meeting and thinking, "What an idiot!" You'll get a lot of foolish suggestions along the way. If you want to stay hungry in your efforts, work hard, sock away (or invest) half your earnings, and pretend that money isn't there. Otherwise, you may be hungry for another reason — you can't afford to buy food!

Set Some Goals: The Brass Ring

Focus on your goals. Successful people have realistic short-term and long-term goals and a plan to achieve them. Whether your short-term goal is to put $5,000 away per month or to open ten new accounts, identifying what you want to do is the first step in creating a plan for your future.

What's the first thing every broker wants to do with the first big paycheck? You guessed it — buy a new car. Although that glistening Porsche can be an awesome incentive, set yourself smaller milestones to reach prior to making a big purchase. You can break down long-term goals, such as paying for a wedding, buying a new car, or purchasing your first house, into monthly income goals after you figure out the costs involved. Take a picture of your dream car or house and put it in a frame on your desk to remind you of the reward that awaits you.

Whatever your plan is, setting your mind on what you want, defining the steps you have to take to get there, and focusing your efforts on accomplishing each goal are the essential elements of a lucrative and rewarding career. Remember, you control your destiny.

Appendix

Memorizing Important Figures and Formulas

You can't bring your notes (or this Appendix!) into the exam center, so be sure to squirrel the following info away in your brain and write it on the scrap paper provided *after* the test begins.

Adjust for stock splits (Chapter 6)

$$\text{Shares after split} = \text{Shares} \times \frac{A}{B}$$

$$\text{Price after split} = \text{Stock price} \times \frac{B}{A}$$

Determine the outstanding shares (Chapter 6)

Outstanding shares = issued shares – treasury stock

Rights formula (Chapter 6)

$$\text{value of a right}_{\text{cum rights}} = \frac{\text{M (market price)} - \text{S (subscription price)}}{\text{N (number of rights needed to purchase one share)} + 1}$$

Ex-rights formula (Chapter 6)

$$\text{value of a right}_{\text{ex-rights}} = \frac{\text{M (market price)} - \text{S (subscription price)}}{\text{N (number of rights needed to purchase one share)}}$$

Calculate the current yield of a stock or bond (Chapter 7)

$$\text{CY} = \frac{\text{annual interest}}{\text{market price}}$$

Calculate the conversion ratio of a convertible preferred stock or convertible bond (Chapter 7)

$$\text{conversion ratio} = \frac{\text{par value}}{\text{conversion price}}$$

Bond seesaw (Chapter 7)

Bond price NY CY YTM YTC Bond at par

Calculate the taxable equivalent yield of a municipal bond (Chapter 8)

$$\text{taxable equivalent yield(TEY)} = \frac{\text{municipal yield}}{100\% - \text{investor's tax bracket}}$$

Long margin account formula (Chapter 9)

Long market value (LMV) – debit record (DR) = equity (EQ)

Short margin account formula (Chapter 9)

Short market value (SMV) + equity (EQ) = credit record (CR)

Calculating the buying or shorting power (Chapter 9)

$$\text{buying or shorting power} = \frac{\text{SMA}}{\text{Reg T}}$$

Calculate the sales charge % of a mutual fund (Chapter 10)

$$\text{sales charge \%} = \frac{\text{ask} - \text{bid}}{\text{ask}} = \frac{\text{POP} - \text{NAV}}{\text{POP}}$$

Calculate the public offering price of a mutual fund (Chapter 10)

$$\text{public offering price} = \frac{\text{net asset value}}{100\% - \text{sales charge \%}}$$

Options chart (Chapter 12)

Money Out	Money In
Investor spends money	Investor receives money

Calculate the time value of an option (Chapter 12)

Premium (P) = intrinsic value (I) + time value (T)

Balance sheet formula (Chapter 13)

Assets = liabilities + stockholder's equity

Calculate working capital (Chapter 13)

Working capital = current assets – current liabilities

Calculate net worth (Chapter 13)

Net worth = assets – liabilities

Price/earnings ratio formula (Chapter 13)

$$\text{price/earnings (P/E) ratio} = \frac{\text{market price}}{\text{EPS}}$$

Index

Numerics

• A •

• B •

• D •

• G •

• H •

• I •

• J •

• K •

• L •

• N •

• S •

• T •

• U •

• V •

• W •

• Y •

• Z •

Notes

Notes

Notes

Notes

Notes

Notes

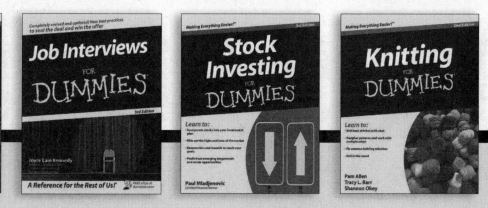

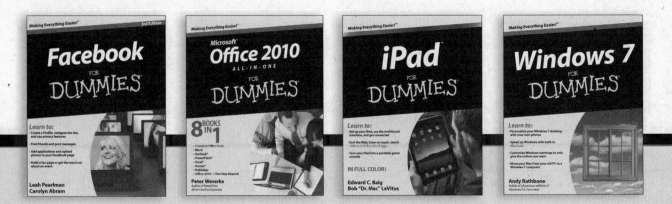

DUMMIES.COM®

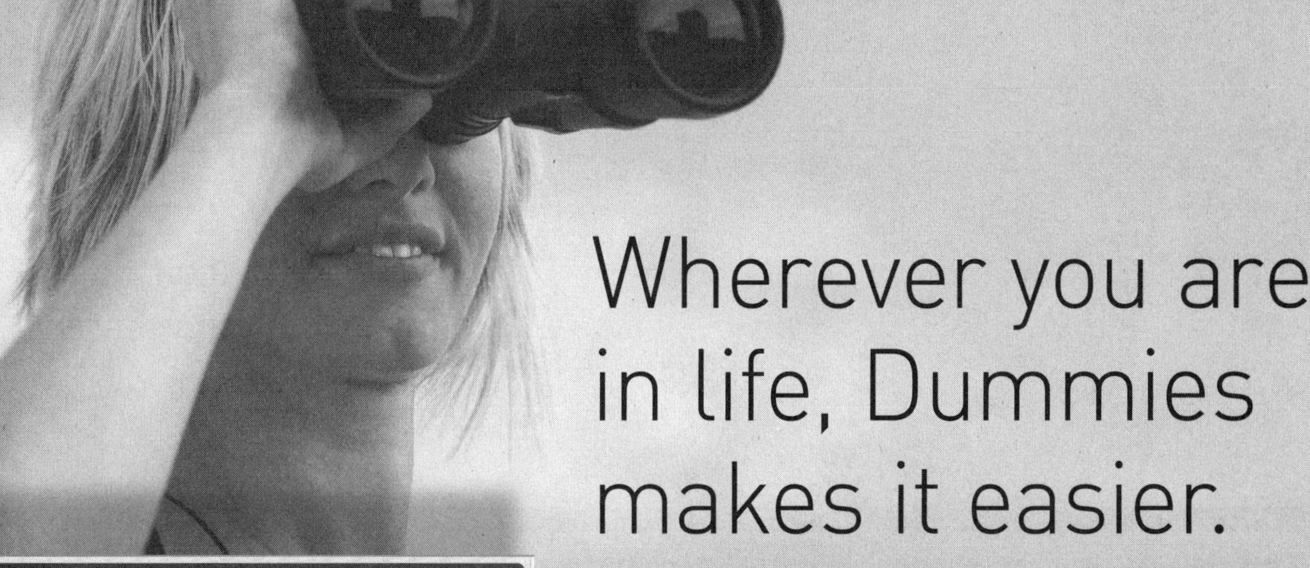

Wherever you are in life, Dummies makes it easier.

From fashion to Facebook®,
wine to Windows®, and everything in between,
Dummies makes it easier.

Visit us at Dummies.com